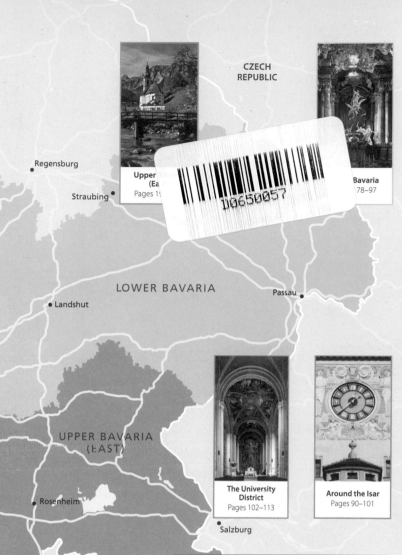

Regensburg

Straubing

CZECH
REPUBLIC

Upper
(Ea
Pages 1

Bavaria
78–97

LOWER BAVARIA

Landshut

Passau

UPPER BAVARIA
(EAST)

Rosenheim

Salzburg

**The University
District**
Pages 102–113

Around the Isar
Pages 90–101

**The Museums
District**
Pages 114–131

Old Town (South)
Pages 58–73

Munich

THE UNIVERSITY
DISTRICT

THE MUSEUMS
DISTRICT

OLD TOWN
(NORTH)

AROUND
THE ISAR

OLD TOWN
(SOUTH)

EYEWITNESS TRAVEL

MUNICH & THE BAVARIAN ALPS

EYEWITNESS TRAVEL

MUNICH & THE BAVARIAN ALPS

Main Contributors
Izabella Galicka, Katarzyna Michalska

LONDON, NEW YORK,
MELBOURNE, MUNICH AND DELHI
www.dk.com

Produced By Wydawnictwo Wiedza i Życie S.A., Warsaw

Contributors Izabella Galicka, Katarzyna Michalska

Consultant Sergiusz Michalski

Illustrators Lena Maminajszwili, Bohdan Wróblewski, Piotr Zubrzycki

Photographers Dorota And Mariusz Jarymowiczowie

Cartographers Magdalena Polak, Dariusz Romanowski, Kartographie Huber (Munich)

Jacket Design And Graphics Paweł Kamiński

Graphic Designer Paweł Pasternak

Editors Robert G. Pasieczny, Dorota Szatańska

Technical Editor Anna Kożurno-Królikowska

Designers Ewa Roguska, Piotr Kiedrowski

Dorling Kindersley Limited

Editor Lucilla Watson

Translator Mark Cole (Linguists for Business)

Dtp Designers Jason Little, Conrad Van Dyk

Production Sarah Dodd

Printed and Bound in China by L. Rex Printing Co. Ltd.

First Published in Great Britain in 2002 by Dorling Kindersley Limited

80 Strand, London, WC2R 0RL

14 15 16 17 10 9 8 7 6 5 4 3 2 1

Reprinted with revisions 2006, 2008, 2010, 2012, 2014

Copyright © 2002, 2014 Dorling Kindersley Limited, London

A Penguin Random House Company

A CIP catalogue record is available from the British Library.

ISBN 978 1 4093 2903 9

Floors are Referred to throughout in accordance with European usage; i.e. the "first floor" is the floor above ground level.

MIX
Paper from
responsible sources
FSC™ C018179
www.fsc.org

**The information in this
DK Eyewitness Travel Guide is checked regularly/annually.**
Every effort has been made to ensure that this book is as up-to-date as possible at the time of going to press. Some details, however, such as telephone numbers, opening hours, prices, gallery hanging arrangements and travel information are liable to change. The publishers cannot accept responsibility for any consequences arising from the use of this book, nor for any material on third party websites, and cannot guarantee that any website address in this book will be a suitable source of travel information. We value the views and suggestions of our readers very highly. Please write to: Publisher, DK Eyewitness Travel Guides, Dorling Kindersley, 80 Strand, London, WC2R 0RL, UK, or email: travelguides@dk.com.

Front cover main image: View from the bell tower of Peterskirche, Munich

◀ The impressive Paulskirche seen from Theresienwiese

Contents

How to Use
this Guide **6**

Gothic figure of a Dancing Moor from
the Stadtmuseum, Munich

Introducing
Munich and the
Bavarian Alps

Discovering Munich &
the Bavarian Alps **10**

Putting Munich & the
Bavarian Alps on
the Map **16**

A Portrait of
the Bavarian Alps **20**

View of Munich, with the Neues Rathaus
in the foreground

A verdant, flower-filled meadow near Schwangau, in the Allgäu

The Allgäu **226**

Northern Swabia **242**

Travellers' Needs

Where to Stay **262**

Where to Eat & Drink **270**

Shops & Markets **286**

Outdoor Activities & Specialist Holidays **290**

Pork salamis

Survival Guide

Practical Information **296**

Travel Information **306**

General Index **316**

Acknowledgments **333**

Munich & the Bavarian Alps Through the Year **34**

The History of Munich and Bavaria **38**

Munich Area by Area

Munich at a Glance **56**

The Propyläen in Munich, designed by Leo von Klenze

Old Town (South) **58**

Old Town (North) **74**

Around the Isar **90**

The University District **102**

The Museums District **114**

Further Afield **132**

Shopping in Munich **144**

Entertainment in Munich **146**

The Bavarian Alps Area by Area

The Bavarian Alps at a Glance **160**

Upper Bavaria (North) **162**

Lower Bavaria **178**

Upper Bavaria (East) **198**

Upper Bavaria (South) **210**

The Frauenkirche *(see pp64–5)*, one of Munich's most prominent landmarks

HOW TO USE THIS GUIDE

This guide will help you to get the most out of your stay in Munich and the Bavarian Alps. The first section, *Introducing Munich and the Bavarian Alps*, locates the city and the region geographically and gives an outline of its history and culture. The subsequent sections, *Munich Area by Area* and *The Bavarian Alps Area by Area*, describe the main sights and attractions. Feature spreads, with maps, illustrations and drawings, focus on important sights. Information about accommodation and restaurants is given in *Travellers' Needs*, while the *Survival Guide* provides useful tips on everything you need to know, from money to getting around.

Munich

In this guide, Munich has been divided into five central areas and a Further Afield section. Each of the five areas opens with an introduction to the part of Munich it covers, describing its history and character. This is followed by a Street-by-Street illustration of the heart of the area. The most important sights and attractions are covered in detail on two or more full pages and are also shown on the area map. Finding your way around each chapter is made simple by the numbering system used throughout.

Sights at a Glance lists the chapter's sights by category: Churches, Museums and Galleries, Historic Buildings, Streets and Piazzas.

1 Area Map For easy reference, the sights are numbered and located on a map. The sights are also shown on the *Street Finder* on pages 148–57.

A locator map shows where you are in relation to other areas of the city centre.

Numbered circles pinpoint all the listed sights on the area map.

2 Street-by-Street Map This gives a bird's-eye view of the heart of each sightseeing area.

Stars indicate the sights that no visitor should miss.

A suggested route for a walk is shown in red.

3 Detailed information All the sights in Munich are described individually. Addresses and practical information are provided. The key to the symbols used in the information block is shown on the back flap.

The Bavarian Alps

Each map in this section concentrates on a specific theme: *Museums and Galleries, Churches, Squares, Parks and Gardens, Remarkable Parisians.* The top sights are shown on the map; other sights are described on the following two pages.

1 Introduction
The landscape, history and character of each region is described here, showing how the area has developed over the centuries and what it offers to the visitor today.

Colour coding makes each area in the guidebook easy to find.

2 Regional Map This shows the main road network and gives an overview of the whole region. All entries are numbered and there are also useful tips on getting around the region by car and train.

3 Detailed information on each sight
All the important towns and other places to visit are described individually. They are listed in order, following the numbering on the regional map. Each entry contains detailed information on opening times and how to get there.

Story boxes explore specific subjects further.

For all the top sights, a Visitors' Checklist box provides the practical information you need to plan your visit.

4 Major Sights At least one page is dedicated to each major sight. Historic palaces and parks are shown in detail. Dissected views of buildings and floorplans of museums and galleries and buildings are colour-coded to show you the best ways to enjoy the exhibits.

INTRODUCING MUNICH & THE BAVARIAN ALPS

Discovering Munich &
the Bavarian Alps   10–15

Putting Munich & the
Bavarian Alps on the Map   16–19

A Portrait of
the Bavarian Alps   20–33

Munich & the Bavarian Alps
Through the Year   34–37

The History of
Munich & Bavaria   38–53

DISCOVERING MUNICH & THE BAVARIAN ALPS

The following tours have been designed to take in as many of Munich's highlights as possible and to discover the natural beauty and cultural heritage of its surrounding region. First comes a 2-day tour of the city and a 7-day tour for those who want to spend more time exploring Munich's attractions. The latter comprises seven single day trips that can be individually combined. The same is true for the 7-day tour covering Munich and Bavaria. Finally, two themed itineraries have been designed for anyone looking to tailor their trip according to a specific interest. For each of these itineraries extra suggestions are provided for those who want to extend their stay. Pick, combine and follow your favourite tours, or simply dip in and out and be inspired.

A Tour of Bavarian Baroque

- Marvel at the grand Baroque buildings of **Asamkirche**, **Theatinerkirche** and the **Schleißheim Palace** in Munich.

- Follow a "Baroque trail" to Lower Bavaria via **Scheyern**, **Metten**, **Osterhofen**, **Aldersbach** and **Passau**.

- Admire *Lüftmalerei* paintings, Baroque splendour and traditional Bavarian architecture in **Bad Tölz**, **Benediktbeuern**, **Kochel am See** and **Mittenwald**.

- Travel via picturesque **Murnau**, **Ettal** and **Oberammergau** to the UNESCO World Heritage Site, **Wieskirche**.

Key

— Bavarian Baroque tour

— Bavarian Mountains, Castles and Monasteries tour

— Week in Bavaria

Map labels: Nördlingen, Eichstätt, Harburg, Ingolsta, Donauwörth, Neuburg an der Donau, Danube, Lech, Paar, Augsburg, Friedberg, Werlach, Landsberg am Lech, Memmingen, Ottobeuren, Andechs, Felda, Wessobrunn, Starnberg See, Schongau, Hohenpeißenbe, Kempten, Steingaden, Wieskirche, Murnau, Wasserburg, Füssen, Ober-ammergau, Lindau, Bodensee, Bad Hindelang, Schwangau, Linderhof, Ettal, Garmisch-Partenkirche, Eibsee, Oberstdorf, Zugspitze, Mittenwal

Wieskirche, Upper Bavaria (South)
Constructed in 1754 at the spot where a farmer's wife had seen tears flow from the eyes of an abandoned statue of Christ, this church is regarded as a masterpiece of 18th-century southern German architecture.

◀ View of Karlplatz in Munich in 1900

Olympiapark, Munich
Built on the collected rubble from the bomb-devastated ruins of World War II, Olympiapark was the site of the 1972 Olympic Games, which ended in tragedy.

A Week in Bavaria

- Enjoy fine art, cultural events and shopping in **Munich**.

- Take a ferry across the **Königssee** and marvel at the impressive views of the **Alps**.

- See the rolling green hills and craggy peaks of the **Alps** and the vast waters of **Bodensee** in the **Allgäu**.

- Explore 2,000 years of history in **Augsburg** and enjoy the medieval charm of the **Romantische Straße**.

- Discover the beautiful towns of **Eichstätt** and **Neuburg an der Donau** together with the pretty river valley of **Altmühl**.

- Visit the picturesque cities of **Landshut** and **Straubing** and see the green countryside of Lower Bavaria.

A Tour of Bavarian Mountains, Castles & Monasteries

- Visit **Schloss Herrenchiemsee** and the **Frauenchiemsee** monastery located on the islands in **Chiemsee**.

- Follow the **Deutsche Alpenstraße** from **Berchtesgaden** to **Schloss Neuschwanstein** and **Bodensee**.

- Tour the beautiful **Romantische Straße** from **Füssen** to **Augsburg**.

- Visit **Landsberg**, the monastery **Wessobrunn**, and **Andechs** with its famous church and brewery.

- Marvel at the stunning mountain views around **Starnberger See**.

Two Days in Munich

Spend two days in Munich to get a first impression of Bavaria's vibrant capital. Explore the sights in the historical city centre and the buzzing University District.

- **Arriving** Munich Airport is located about 28 km (17 miles) northeast of the city. S-Bahn trains S1 and S8 and the Aiport–Bus take 45 minutes to the city's main railway station.

- **Transport** Munich has an excellent public transport system, visitors can take advantage of buses, trams, the U-Bahn and S-Bahn.

Day 1

Morning Start the day at Munich's landmark, **Frauenkirche** *(pp64–5)*. Admire the pretty views from the twin pepperpot towers here and see the mysterious black footprint beneath the towers, which is believed to have been left by the Devil. At **Marienplatz** *(p66)* watch the figures dance to the clock chimes of the **Neues Rathaus** (New Town Hall) *(p63)*. Next, climb the tower of **Peterskirche** *(p66)* for a stunning view of the city. Explore the city's quaint market **Viktualienmarkt** *(p68)* before heading to the Jewish centre, **Jüdisches Zentrum Jakobsplatz** *(p69)*. Don't miss the interesting **Stadtmuseum** *(p69)*, a complex of six buildings, which houses the town museum.

Afternoon After lunch, stroll through the medieval lanes around the city's former private residences, **Münzhof** *(p87)* and **Alter Hof** *(p87)*. Stop for a drink in the famous tavern **Hofbräuhaus** *(p88)* before browsing the shops in luxurious **Maximilianstraße** *(p88)* and Theatinerstraße. Marvel at the Baroque splendour of **Theatinerkirche** *(p83)* and be awed by the dazzling interiors of the two churches on Neuhauser Straße; **Bürgersaal** *(p54)* and **Michealskirche** *(p54)*. End the day by spending the evening in the vibrant district around **Gärtnerplatz** *(p68)*.

Day 2

Morning Head to the bustling Prinzregentenstraße to visit the **Bayerisches Nationalmuseum** *(pp112–13)*, which houses an eclectic collection of artworks. Continue on to the **Haus der Kunst** *(p111)*, which showcases temporary exhibitions of contemporary artists. Afterwards, enjoy a stroll in the scenic green **Englischer Garten** *(p110)*.

Evening Devote the evening to shopping in the trendy stores, stop by the cosy cafés and admire the Art Nouveau architecture in the lively district of **Schwabing** *(p109)*. Follow the elegant **Ludwigstraße** *(p106)*, pass the university, **Ludwig- Maximilians-Universität** *(p107)* and St Ludwig's church, **Ludwigskirche** *(p107)* to **Odeonsplatz** *(p109)*, where the monumental **Feldherrnhalle** *(p82)* marks the beginning of the historical city centre.

To extend your trip...

Make a day trip to **Dießen** *(p216)* to see the fine artwork in the early Rococo Marienmünster and enjoy the beautiful scenery around Ammersee.

A Week in Munich

Take time out to see the memorable sights of Bavaria's capital, including interesting museums, iconic churches and historical buildings.

- **Arriving** Arrive and depart from Munich Airport.

- **Transport** A good public transport system helps to easily get around the city. Buses, trams, the U-Bahn and S-Bahn are quick and reliable.

Days 1 and 2

See the city itinerary above.

Day 3

Explore beautiful courtyards, rich museums and the Renaissance Antiquarium in the **Residenz** *(pp78–81)*. Next, relax in the formal greenery of the **Hofgarten** *(p89)*. After a stroll along the Isar river,

Golden sculpture of St Mary with the Church of Our Lady in the background, Marienplatz

visit the fascinating **Deutsches Museum** *(pp98–101)*.

Days 4

Spend the day immersed in fine arts in the **Museums District** *(pp114–31)*, where visitors will be spoilt for choice. Choose between seeing ancient art in the **Staatliche Antikensammlungen** *(p118)* or the **Glyptothek** *(p119)*, admiring exquisite paintings of 14th to 18th century in the **Alte Pinakothek** *(pp122–5)*, 19th century masters in the **Neue Pinakothek** *(pp126–9)*, modern art and design in the **Pinakothek der Moderne** *(pp120–21)* or head to the striking **Museum Brandhorst** *(p130)*.

Day 5

Get ready to see great architecture and the wonders of modern technology in this part of Munich. Explore the superbly landscaped **Olympiapark** *(pp138–9)* and look out for the elegant sweeping roofs of the Olympic sports facilities. Take the lift up to the Olympiaturm and enjoy the lovely views of the city and the Alps. Head to the other side of the street to the **BMW Museum** *(pp138–9)*, which is a real treasure chamber full of vintage and futuristic vehicles.

Days 6

Be impressed by the beauty and ducal splendor of the stately **Schloss Nymphenburg** *(pp136–7)*. Look out for the portraits of the city's beautiful women in the Schönheitsgalerie. See the incredibly ornate carriages of the Bavarian kings in the palace's Marstallmuseum and the enchanting pavilions in the spacious park. Next, take a stroll through the adjacent **Botanischer Garten** *(p138)*. Don't miss the impressive greenhouses here.

Day 7

Start the day close to the Isar river at the monumental **Annakirche** *(p94)* in the pretty district of Lehel. Cross the river to the impressive Bavarian parliament building, **Maximilianeum** *(p95)* on the right bank. At Max-Weber-Platz board the tram for a long, but worthwhile trip to **Bavaria-Filmstadt** *(p142)*, one of Europe's major film studios, located outside the city. Also, take time out to visit the posh suburb of **Grünwald** *(p142)*. Continue via tram to medieval **Burg Grünwald** *(p142)*, which has an interesting Roman collection.

> **To extend your trip…**
> Spend a day in **Freising** *(p169)* and another exploring **Wasserburg am Inn** *(p208)* and **Dachau** *(p175)*.

A Week in Bavaria

- **Duration** 7 days – extends to a 10-day tour with the extra suggestions.
- **Airports** Arrive and depart from Munich Airport.
- **Transport** Towns and cities around Munich can be reached by trains and buses. To explore the countryside, a rental car is recommended.

Day 1 and 2: Munich
See the city itinerary on p12.

Day 3: Königssee

Head southeast from Munich in the direction of the snow-capped Alps. Arrive at crystal-clear **Königssee** *(p204)*, which has a lovely fjord-like setting between sheer mountain ridges. Take the electric-powered ferry to St. Bartholomä and listen to the famous echo along the way. Next, admire the impressive escarpment of the legendary Watzmann massif and take a pleasant walk to enchanting Obersee. Return to Munich to spend the night.

Cruising the Danube near Kelheim, Lower Bavaria

> **To extend your trip…**
> The stunning scenery and thrilling landscapes are unmissable in this part of Bavaria. Take time out to go hiking in the mountains here.

Day 4: The Allgäu

Take a day trip to the **Allgäu** *(pp226–41)* and admire the gently rolling green hills, the vast Bodensee (Lake Constance) and the lovely village of **Wasserburg** *(p237)*. Explore the historical city centre of **Lindau** *(pp238–9)*, located on an island in the lake. Marvel at the beauty of the peaks of the Alps enroute to the health resorts of **Oberstdorf** *(p236)* and **Bad Hindelang** *(p236)*. Nearby, the Breitach river gorge and Sturmannshöhle cave are major attractions. Spend the evening back in the city of Munich.

> **To extend your trip…**
> Spend a day hiking, sunbathing or sailing at **Lake Constance** *(p237)*.

Day 5: Augsburg and the Romantische Straße

Founded by the Emperor Augustus, **Augsburg** *(pp252–7)* has an impressive Mannerist town hall and fine art work in the Gothic Dom St. Maria. From the former Roman city, follow the **Romantische Straße** *(p250)* north. Along the route, look out for pretty gabled houses in **Donauwörth** *(p250)*, the fantastically preserved castle in **Harburg** *(p249)* and the romantic historic town centre of **Nördlingen** *(pp246–7)* in its unusual setting in the Ries basin, the impact crater of an enormous meteorite.

Day 6: Neuburg to Weltenburg

Take a detour and go via **Ingolstadt** *(pp170–71)* to visit **Neuburg an der Donau** *(pp172–3)*. This former ducal residence offers a strikingly beautiful historic town centre. From here, continue on to **Eichstätt** *(pp166–7)*, one of most delightful towns in Bavaria, located in the **Altmühl Valley** *(p187)*. Follow the river to Kelheim and go along the Danube to **Weltenburg** *(p186)*. Stop to explore its age-old monastery located on the river bank.

> **To extend your trip…**
> Spend the day kayaking on the rivers and go on a "fossil hunt" *(p168)* in the quarries of the Altmühl river valley.

Day 7: Lower Bavaria

Make an early start for a day trip to **Landshut** *(pp182–4)*, one of the most impressive destinations in Lower Bavaria. Don't miss the Gothic **Martinskirche** *(p184)* and the ancient castle, **Burg Trausnitz** *(p185)*. In **Straubing**, *(pp188–9)* explore the charming town centre and admire the famous Roman treasure in the **Gäubodenmuseum** *(p188)*.

Königssee and the pilgrimage church of St Bartholomä

A Tour of Bavarian Baroque

- **Duration** 7 days – extends to a 10–day tour with the extra suggestions.
- **Airports** Arrive and depart from Munich Airport.
- **Transport** It is advisable to use the public transportation system while exploring Munich and its surrounding areas. For destinations in the countryside a rental car is recommended.

Starting from Munich these tours highlight outstanding Baroque architecture in the city and its immediate hinterland as well as in different regions of Bavaria. For more on Bavaria's traditional architecture, see pp26–27.

Day 1 and 2: Munich
Devote two days to discovering superb Baroque buildings in the city. Munich's quintessential Baroque church is the **Asamkirche** (pp70–71) close to the medieval **Sendlinger Tor** (p72). The adjacent **Asam Haus** (p72) was the home of Egid Quirin Asam. A short walk through the historical lanes in the city centre leads to the **Damenstift St. Anna** (p73). In the northern part of the Old Town, don't miss the **Preysing–Palais** (p82), the **Theatinerkirche** (p83) and the **Cuvilliés–Theater** (p81) of the **Residenz** (pp78–81). Spend the next day visiting **Schleißheim Palace** (pp176–7) known for its gallery of Baroque painting. Be sure to check out its unique Baroque park.

Day 3 and 4: Baroque Trail from Munich to Lower Bavaria
Follow a "Baroque trail" from Munich to Lower Bavaria. Visit the Benedictine monastery in **Scheyern** (p169) before seeing the opulently decorated Michealskirche and library of the local Benedictine abbey in **Metten** (p186). Next, check out Osterhofen's stupendous **Asambasilika** (p197) and the church of Mariä Himmelfahrt in **Aldersbach** (p196). Spend an entire day in the Baroque city

of **Passau** (pp192–5) and listen to the daily concert in the impressive **Dom St. Stephan** (p192), which boasts one of the biggest organs in the world. Return to Munich for the night.

> **To extend your trip…**
> Explore the hilly region of the **Bavarian Forest** (p197) and the primeval forest in **Nationalpark Bayerischer Wald** (p191).

Day 5: Bad Tölz, Kochel am See and Mittenwald
Discover *trompe l'oeil* paintings, called *Lüftlmalerei* (p216), Baroque splendour and traditional Bavarian architecture, south of Munich, in **Bad Tölz** (p224). A must visit is the former Benedictine monastery and its late Baroque church in **Benediktbeuern** (p223). In **Kochel am See** (p223), see the Michaelskirche and explore the traditional alpine buildings in **Freilichtmuseum Glentleiten** (p223). Finally, head to **Mittenwald** (p222) and admire its fantastic mountain views and explore an interesting museum of violin-making here.

> **To extend your trip…**
> See the pretty architecture of the monastery at **Tegernsee** (p224) and visit its popular brewery. Relax and enjoy the wonderful mountain views from the lake.

Late Gothic town hall featuring the coat of arms in Kempten

Day 6: Murnau to Oberammergau
South of Munich is home to pretty **Murnau** (p219), which offers wonderful mountain views, Enrico Zucalli's Nikolauskirche and the small Baroque Mariahilf-Kirche. Admire the modern art of the famous **Blaue Reiter group** (p219) in the Art Nouveau Münter-Haus. Another Baroque masterpiece is the Benedictine abbey found in picturesque **Ettal** (p220). Nearby, is **Oberammergau** (p220) with its lavishly painted houses. Continue on to the UNESCO World Heritage Site, **Wieskirche** (pp218–19), a Rococo jewel and an impressive highlight of this tour.

Day 7: Kempten, Memmingen and Ottobeuren
Discover Baroque splendour and Rococo opulence in romantic **Kempten's** (pp240–41) Residenz and Lorenzkirche. **Memmingen** (pp230–31) boasts beautiful Gothic half-timbered houses, but also a great town hall with Rococo stuccowork and the Kreuzherrenkirche with Baroque interior decoration. Baroque grandeur is also the signature feature of **Ottobeuren** (p233) – the "Swabian Escorial" is one of the biggest monastic complexes in Europe.

> **To extend your trip…**
> Enjoy wellness in accordance with the principles of Sebastian Kneipp in nearby **Bad Wörishofen** (p233).

Opulent interiors of the famous Cuvilliés-Theater, Munich

For practical information on travelling around Munich and the Bavarian Alps, see pp310–15

A Tour of Bavarian Mountains, Castles & Monasteries

- **Duration** 7 days – extends to a 10–day tour with the extra suggestions.
- **Airports** Arrive and depart from Munich Airport.
- **Transport** A rental car is highly recommended.

These tours cover famous castles and beautiful alpine landscapes. For more on Bavaria's castles see pp50–51.

Day 1: Burghausen and Altötting

Head east to **Burghausen** (p202) at the Austrian border and explore Europe's longest castle – which will take up some time. In nearby, **Altötting** (p202) the Heilige Kapelle, which houses the famous Black Madonna is one of Germany's oldest Marian shrines and is worth a visit.

To extend your trip…
Follow the Inn river valley to **Wasserburg** (p208), **Rott** (p209) and **Neubeuern** (p209) and go on a scenic drive from **Aschau** (p206) via **Geigelstein to Reit im Winkel** (p205).

Day 2: Chiemsee

Head for the vast **Chiemsee** (p207) southeast of Munich. Start early in the morning to catch a boat either from Gstadt or Prien's waterfront area, Stock to Herreninsel, the largest island on the lake. **Schloss Herrenchiemsee** (p206), built by Ludwig II, is located here. The palace was never finished, but is nonetheless incredibly luxurious considering it's still incomplete. From Herreninsel, take another boat to Fraueninsel, where the Benedictine monastery Frauenchiemsee is a sight to see.

Day 3 and 4: Upper Bavaria and the Allgäu

Discover on the **Deutsche Alpenstraße** (pp224–5) some of the most beautiful parts of the Bavarian Alps. Begin in **Berchtesgaden** (p204), where be sure to visit the Salzbergwerk (salt works). Take time out to spend a day in quaint **Bayrischzell** (p225) and go on hiking in the Wendelstein mountains. In **Garmisch-Partenkirchen** (p221) take the train to **Eibsee** (p221) and then the cable car up Germany's highest peak, Zugspitze. Watch out for breathtaking views of the Alps. In **Linderhof** (p220), see another of Ludwig's fairytale castles. Next, continue on to Schwangau to see **Schloss Hohenschwangau** (p234), which is open for visitors. Don't forget to visit **Schloss Neuschwanstein** (p234), certainly Bavaria's most famous castle.

To extend your trip…
Take a wonderful drive and enjoy panoramic views of the Alps and the Allgäu enroute to **Lindau** (pp238–9), located on the Bodensee.

Day 5: The Allgäu to Northern Swabia

Enjoy the beautiful scenery along the southern part of the Romantische Straße. Start in **Füssen** (p234) at the foothills of the Alps. Its medieval castle houses a wonderful art gallery. From the village of Schwangau, it is not far to **Steingaden** (p218) and **Wieskirche** (p218). **Schongau** (p218) has its medieval city centre and its castle from the 15th century intact, when the town was the second ducal residence. Close to **Augsburg** (pp252–7), **Friedberg** (pp250–59) is still protected by centuries old defensive walls.

To extend your trip…
Follow the Romantische Straße north up to Würzburg in Franconia.

Day 6: Landsberg am Lech, Hoher Peißenberg and Andechs Monastery

Visit the historic city of **Landsberg am Lech** (pp214–15). Explore its lovely alleys and squares, see its striking architecture and walk through the famous Bayertor and along the medieval town walls. Close by is the imposing monastery at **Wessobrunn** (p216). Soak up the great views of mountains and lakes on Hoher Peißenberg east of **Hohenpeißenberg** (p218). Afterwards, make a pilgrimage to the **Andechs Monastery** (p216) known for its famous church and brewery.

Day 7: Starnberger See

Spend a relaxing day at **Starnberger See** (p217), enjoying the stunning mountain views. Next, follow the trail of Bavaria's famous King Ludwig II. Ludwig was a frequent visitor to Possenhofen's palace, where Austria's empress, Elisabeth, spent her childhood. A historic small ferry takes visitors from Feldafing to pretty Roseninsel with its romantic park and villa.

King Ludwig II's magical Neuschwanstein castle in the Allgäu

Putting Munich and the Bavarian Alps on the Map

Southern Bavaria, the southernmost part of Germany, consists of three administrative regions: Upper Bavaria (Oberbayern), Swabia (Schwaben) and Lower Bavaria (Niederbayern). The region borders the Czech Republic, Austria and, across Lake Constance, Switzerland. To the north it is bounded by the Danube, and the south by the Alps. Munich, on the River Isar, is the capital (Land), with 1.4 million inhabitants.

Key
- Motorway
- Major road
- Secondary road
- Railway
- National border
- Ferry route

0 kilometres   100

0 miles   100

For map symbols *see back flap*

Central Munich

Central Munich boasts a variety of architectural styles, and each of the five areas has its own unique atmosphere. Marienplatz, and the Old Town around it, abounds in old-world architecture, and is the main tourist area. Along the River Isar, green areas are flanked by grand 19th-century urban thoroughfares. The great thoroughfare of Ludwigstraße/Leopoldstraße sets the tone for the northern quarter, which includes the picturesque Schwabing and Englischer Garten districts. The suburb of Maxvorstadt to the northwest has a wealth of museums and art galleries.

Lenbachhaus
The home of the 19th-century portrait painter Franz von Lenbach is built in the style of an Italian villa and is fronted by a picturesque garden.

Asamkirche
Also known as the Church of St Johann Nepomuk, it is named after the Asam brothers who built it. The finest work of their careers, it is also one of the most oustanding examples of European Baroque architecture.

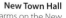

New Town Hall
The coat of arms on the New Town Hall features the monk who symbolizes Munich. The city took its name from the legendary monks (*München* meaning "monk settlement") who settled there.

Art Nouveau House at Ainmillerstraße 22
This house exemplifies the Art Nouveau, or Secessionist, style of architecture in Munich. The symmetrical division of the façade is combined with painted pseudo-classical floral ornaments.

Villa Stuck
The painter Franz von Stuck conceived the architectural design and interior decoration of his residence. The finely decorated reception rooms and studies combine Art Nouveau, Symbolist and Neo-Classical elements.

Key

Main sight

For map symbols *see back flap*

A PORTRAIT OF THE BAVARIAN ALPS

Three out of every four Germans say they would like to live in Bavaria, especially southern Bavaria. As it is one of the most picturesque and also one of the most prosperous parts of Europe, this is not so surprising. For many foreigners, Bavaria is quintessentially German; this is not, however, strictly true, as Bavaria has always nurtured its own distinct political framework and culture.

Southern Bavaria is inhabited by three main groups of people: a branch of the Swabian tribes of Württemberg, in the western region, who are the descendants of the legendary Baiuvarii; the Upper Bavarians, in the central region, and the Lower Bavarians, centred in the eastern region.

To this day, there are still distinct regional differences in the Bavarians' dialect, folklore and cuisine and, arguably, in their mentality as well. The shared characteristics that they have are a love of tradition, a certain conservatism and a strong sense of loyalty to the Free State of Bavaria (Freistaat Bayern). Bavarian culture and customs were developed as much in court circles as by the peasantry. This development on two social levels has left its mark on the character of the people and their traditions. The latter include an affinity with the soil, and a tendency to a certain stubbornness and defiance coupled with warm hospitality and friendliness. These qualities are combined with tolerance and at times a fondness for absolute rulers and politicians ranging from men such as Maximilian I, Maximilian I Josef and Franz-Josef Strauss to eccentrics and dreamers such as Ludwig II.

Summer in the old quarter of Lindau

◀ Oktoberfest celebrations in Munich

Peaceful sub-Alpine landscape

The landscape of the Bavarian Alps

When they look up at the sky, the Bavarians see the colours of their national flag – white and sky-blue. On clear days the sky takes on a Mediterranean translucence; this may be because Bavaria is the bridge between northern Europe and the Mediterranean region. Munich is in fact much closer to Venice than it is to Berlin.

Bavaria's mild climate and varied scenery combine to create an idyllic landscape. Lush green meadows populated with grey and brown Alpine cattle alternate with thick woodland, countless brooks and streams, rocky outcrops, lakes and rolling hills, against which rise majestic Alpine peaks. When the famous

Bay window of a house in Garmisch-Partenkirchen

Föhn (warm Alpine wind) blows, the Alps can be clearly seen from as far as 100 km (60 miles) away. The local architecture complements the scenery perfectly. Picture-postcard towns and villages, large monasteries, castles and palaces, and village churches with their onion domes fit together in perfect harmony. A typical feature of the region is the way in which high art is combined with kitsch. Exquisite Baroque churches and monasteries with ephemeral frescoes stand side by side with simple peasant art, while the splendid Neo-Classical architecture of the Wittelsbachs contrasts with the enchanting fairy-tale castles of Ludwig II.

Nativity scene painted on the façade a house in Hindelang

Religion, tradition and culture

Bavaria is a land of defiant, ritualised Catholicism, which once effectively blocked the march of Protestant Germany to Rome. It is no surprise then to find that Bavaria has its own conservative ruling party, the CSU, and that in place of the ubiquitous "Guten Tag", the people here greet each other with "Grüß Gott" ("Greetings to

God"). The Bavarian national anthem, which is played every day when the local television station closes for the night, begins with the words: "God be with you, land of Bavaria."

Catholic ritual is omnipresent – during the celebration of Sunday Mass, at innumerable church fairs, and during processions and pilgrimages. However, piety expresses an affirmation of life rather than prudishness. Many stereotypes are attached to the Bavarians: among the best known are green hats with feathers in them, short *Lederhosen* and knee-socks, beer-mugs joyfully held on high.

Folk traditions have survived too: perhaps nowhere else in the world is there such a proliferation of folk festivals and music groups. Almost everywhere you can see the characteristic but regionally differentiated men's *Trachten*, which includes a short jacket with bone buttons, and the women's *Dirndl*, with their wide, low-cut dresses and a narrow waistcoat. Simplified versions of these costumes are also worn as everyday clothing, even by Bavarian politicians. More refined and lavish versions are worn when attending official functions or going to the opera.

Futuristic style museum (foreground) and administrative building of the BMW works in Munich

Decoration for a maypole

Beer-drinking is another integral part of South Bavarian folk tradition. Some 620 breweries work to quench beer-lovers' thirst. Bavaria has some of the oldest breweries in the world (including the Weihenstephan brewery), and it was the first place where a ducal decree (1516) banned the use of any other ingredients than barley, hops and water in beer-making. The best way to drink beer is from a large, litre mug, known as a Maß, or "measure", preferably in a beer garden beneath a chestnut tree, in the cellars of a monastic brewery, or in a marquee to the strains of folk music, as during the famous Oktoberfest.

The Sources of Bavaria's Wealth

For centuries farming and trade have been the main source of Bavaria's wealth. It is the largest supplier of farm produce in Germany. It also has the largest hop harvest in the world. After World War II Bavaria's economy expanded enormously, with some of Germany's largest com-panies based here, such as Audi, BMW and Siemens. Bavaria has chemicals, aircraft, printing, electronics and tourism industries.

The Maß – the best way to drink beer

Landscape of the Bavarian Alps

Southern Bavaria is one of Germany's most picturesque and scenically varied regions. To the south it is bordered by the Alps, with their breathtaking limestone peaks and verdant slopes. To the north it is bounded by the Danube, with its marshy flood plains. The region's landscape consists of undulating hills and many mountain streams and lakes, which were formed by glaciers during the Ice Age. Much of the terrain takes the form of pasture and fields, or is covered in forests, while industrialization has remained unobtrusive.

Alpine meadows are covered in lush grass which produces high-quality hay and provides rich grazing for cattle.

Mountain peaks with breathtaking escarpments are a common sight.

A hop plantation in Hallertau, which is the largest hop-producing region in Bavaria. Wooden poles overgrown with hops are a characteristic sight.

Mountain streams have over millennia cut their way through the Alpine rocks, creating scenic gorges. The picturesque Wimbachklamm is accessible to hikers.

Local buildings harmonize with the surrounding landscape.

Southern Bavarian Lakes

Huge glaciers that melted centuries ago left many lakes in southern Bavaria. Their limpid waters attract water-sports enthusiasts and swimmers. This breathtakingly beautiful environment is ideal for walking and many other outdoor activities.

This marina on Chiemsee, also known as the Bavarian Sea, is one of the finest spots in southern Bavaria for amateur yachting.

The Zugspitze, rising to a height of 2,962 m (9,718 ft), is the highest German peak.

Forests are thick and extensive, covering a major portion of the mountainous terrain.

Plants and animals of the Bavarian Alps

Southern Bavaria's varied natural scenery has remained largely unspoiled thanks to careful protection and clean air. Animals and plants occur in several bands of vegetation. While in the higher parts of the Alps only mosses and lichens grow, at altitudes of under 1,500 m (4,900 ft) there is an abundance of flora and fauna. The forests contain a wealth of plants, animals and birds, while the extensive meadows and marshes are covered in various grasses, and the clear waters of the rivers and lakes are home to many species of fish. The parks and nature reserves help to preserve endangered species.

The grey-brown Alpine cow is especially common in the Allgäu, a region known for its dairy products.

Chamois can negotiate rough terrain and steep slopes and are a common sight on mountain hikes.

Marmots peep out from mountain screes and crevasses, emitting their characteristic whistling call.

Ravens appear in large flocks over ploughed fields, searching for worms and leftover grains of corn.

Butterflies share the flowery Alpine meadows with bees, gadflies and grass-hoppers. The most colourful of the butterflies is the peacock butterfly.

Trout is the most common species of fish to be found in Bavaria's mountain streams. They thrive in the clear, unpolluted waters.

Edelweiß is an increasingly rare sight in the Alps. This protected Alpine flower is a favourite decorative motif in the Bavarian national costume.

The gentian is the "national" flower of Bavaria. It is honoured in song and is used in making the famous gentian schnapps.

Architecture of the Bavarian Alps

The architectural landscape of southern Bavaria features a large number of churches and monasteries. These noble buildings, in perfect harmony with the surrounding landscape, are topped by onion-domed towers. Although each architectural era created a legacy of fine buildings, it was during the Baroque period (the late 16th to the early 18th century) that the region flourished architecturally. New churches were built, and existing ones endowed with stunning ornamentation. In southern Bavaria architectural splendours were built in the 19th century, including the fairytale residences of Ludwig II.

Altenstadt basilica is one of the many Romanesque buildings in Bavaria.

Gothic

The Gothic style of architecture is widely represented in Bavaria, although its impact in Europe went far beyond this region. As well as in surviving town houses, the Gothic style in Bavaria is seen in fortified residences and religious buildings. A specific regional characteristic is the wide nave of Gothic churches. The oldest Gothic church was built in Laufen. The largest is the Frauenkirche in Munich, and the most resplendent is the St Martin and Kastulus in Landshut. The use of pointed arches and ribbed vaulting made it possible to create much higher, light-filled spaces. Gothic architecture reached its apogee in the mid-15th century.

The Chapel of St Sigismund in Blutenburg Castle is a typical example of late Gothic religious architecture.

Entrance to the St Ulrich and St Afra church, Augsburg

Renaissance and Mannerism

The Renaissance reached Bavaria from Italy via Augsburg, where in 1510 the Renaissance chapel of the Fugger family was built. This set the style for town houses (as at Neuburg and Augsburg). At the end of the century, Renaissance style was overtaken by Mannerism, which departed from Classical forms. One of the main Mannerist architects was Elias Holl.

The window is set under a broken pediment.

Carvings contrast with the austere façade.

The Archangel Michael overcoming Satan, bronze sculpture by Hans Reichle, displays dramatic poses typical of Mannerism.

The façade of the Arsenal at Augsburg, designed by Josef Heintz the Elder in 1607, is a fine example of Mannerism, distinguished by a flat façade and the rejection of Classical proportions.

Baroque

No architectural style left such a strong impression on southern Bavaria as did the Baroque. Its highly decorated, almost theatrical style held a special appeal, and it was expressed in skilfully articulated spaces to which abundant ornamentation was added. The first Baroque buildings were by Italian architects, but a local school was soon producing work of the highest quality. The Bavarian Baroque reached its height with the Asam brothers *(see pp70 & 72–3).*

The vaulting of Passau Cathedral is a fine example of late Baroque forms derived directly from Italy. Despite the excessive stuccowork and elaborate fresco decorations, the main architectural elements are still discernible.

The façade of the church of Berg am Laim illustrates the typical Baroque rhythm of architectural elements, accentuated by cornices, pilasters and columns.

The windows of the Neues Schloss in Schleißheim are framed and decorated with rosettes and mock-antique masks. Doorways and windows with exuberant ornamentation were highly characteristic of Baroque architecture.

Neo-Classicism

The Neo-Classical style developed in France in the 18th century. After 1806, when Bavaria proclaimed itself a kingdom, it was adapted to serve the purposes of the Napoleonic Empire Style. Neo-Classicism reached the peak of its splendour after 1816, but was confined to Munich. Ludwig I intended to rebuild the city to turn it into "Athens on Isar". To this end the court architect Leo von Klenze designed many fine buildings, with references to ancient Greece and the Italian Renaissance.

The Prinz-Carl-Palais, by the architect Karl von Fischer, is a typical example of early Neo-Classical architecture. It is fronted by an imposing portico with Ionic columns supporting a tympanum.

This capital of a column in the portico of the Glyptothek is decorated with typically Ionic scrolled volutes.

An akroterion is a decorative element often used in Classical architecture.

The tympanum of the Propyläen contains sculptures of Otto I among kings of the Greeks. Otto I abdicated before the building was completed. The people mocked: "Do not glorify the day before the sun is down – the proof is the Propyläen."

Sculptures in a style evoking the glory of ancient Greece were carved by Ludwig Schwanthaler.

Monasteries and Abbeys

A surprising feature of the Bavarian Alps is the large number of monasteries and abbeys that are to be seen here. The first Benedictine monastery was founded in the early Middle Ages. In the 11th and 12th centuries monastic establishments were built in the foothills of the Alps. The next period at which such building activity flourished was the Baroque, when medieval abbeys were rebuilt and new ones, such as Ottobeuren and Ettal, were constructed. In the 18th century, with the spirit of the Enlightenment, fine libraries with valuable collections of books were built. The secularization of more than 160 monasteries in 1803 led to the destruction of a large part of Bavarian monastic culture.

Altarpieces often take the form of large statues of saints or of one of the Church Fathers. They are a prominent feature of church interiors.

Heilig-Kreuz-Kapelle
The Chapel of the Holy Cross is one of the few monastic chapels open only to monks. Such chapels were used for gatherings and for silent prayer away from the outside world. Their decoration is no less lavish than that of the rest of the monastery.

The church interior is graced by numerous altars, and the architectural features, mouldings, paintings and furniture combine to form a unified whole.

The Library reflects the scientific and cultural aspirations of Bavarian churches. The walls are lined with decorated shelves that harmonize with the leather-bound volumes they hold.

The Kaisersaal, or imperial hall, was one of the abbey's countless reception rooms. It underlines the abbey's close association with the concept of a Christian Empire.

The ceremonial hall was designed for official gatherings.

Ottobeuren Abbey

Ottobeuren, which has been described as the "Swabian Escorial", is one of the largest monastic establishments in Europe. The church is attached to a vast complex with rows of rooms built around three courtyards, as well as numerous ancillary buildings.

Ottobeuren Abbey blends with the sub-Alpine landscape in a way that is characteristic of many Bavarian monasteries, with their red roofs and their tall belfries. In spring and summer, the entire building stands in striking contrast to the lush greenery with which it is surrounded.

The staircase, a feature of conscious pomp and elegance, shows the importance that abbeys attached to the appearance of public reception areas.

Art of the Bavarian Alps

Art in the region developed against the background of the major trends in European art. The ecclesiastical and ducal protectorate, and later that of free cities, led to the development of important artistic centres in Munich, Augsburg, Landshut and Passau. Schools of painting, sculpture and craftsmanship developed as early as the Gothic period, and the Renaissance and Mannerism also left their mark. But it was in the Baroque period that the arts of fresco, stucco and sculpture reached their peak. Folk elements meanwhile were always a feature of Bavarian art, taking the form of votive images, roadside shrines and mural paintings on village houses.

This man with a shield is a late Gothic figure from Ottobeuren Abbey.

Romanesque and Gothic Art

Romanesque art is characterized by a stylization rooted in Byzantine art. As well as the crafts and sculpture, southern Bavaria has interesting examples of mural painting. The windows of Augsburg Cathedral are among the finest in Europe. The Gothic period, which continued until about 1520, brought in a new style, primarily in the way that human figures were depicted, with flowing garments and expressive gestures. By about 1,500 Gothic painting and sculpture had their greatest exponents in Jan Polack and Erasmus Grasser.

Masks are placed at the intersections between panels.

Bas-reliefs are of allegorical and Old Testament subjects.

Door handles take the shape of lions' masks.

The Moriskentänzer is one of ten expressive carvings by Erasmus Grasser of Moriskentanz, a court dance. According to custom, the men would dance in sophisticated poses, and capture the ladies' attention with elegant gestures. These sculptures are a rare example of secular subject matter in Gothic art.

The bronze doors of Augsburg Cathedral show the influence of Byzantine art. They initially consisted of four wings, with a total of 224 reliefs. Only 35 remain today.

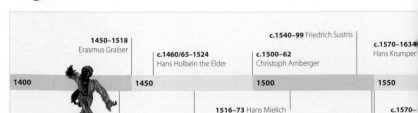

1400	1450	1500	1550
	1450–1518 Erasmus Grasser	**c.1540–99** Friedrich Sustris	**c.1570–1634** Hans Krumper
	c.1460/65–1524 Hans Holbein the Elder	**c.1500–62** Christoph Amberger	
One of Erasmus Grasser's Moriscos	**c.1435–1519** Jan Polack	**1516–73** Hans Mielich	**c.1570–1642** Hans Reichle
		1473–1531 Hans Burgkmair	**c.1548–1628** Peter Candid de Witte
		c.1550–1620 Hubert Gerhard	

Renaissance and Mannerism

The southern Bavarian Renaissance was influenced by Italy and the Netherlands, but it developed its own elements. The crafts flourished, and in sculpture and painting new themes, such as genre scenes, classical mythology and portraiture, appeared. The most prominent artists of the time were the Augsburg painters Hans Holbein the Elder, Hans Burgkmair and Christoph Amberger. Mannerism developed in the mid-16th century, its most outstanding exponents in southern Bavaria being Hans Krumper and Hans Reichle.

This ornamental cup dating from 1570–80 was made in one of Augsburg's famous goldsmiths' workshops. The work of Augsburg goldsmiths graced many churches and grand houses in Europe.

This portrait of Felicitas Welser by Christoph Amberger is typical of Renaissance portraiture in that it shows a certain rigidity of pose combined with a care to capture the sitter's individuality and accurately depict the costume. The coloration reveals a Venetian influence.

Baroque

During the Baroque period the walls of churches, monasteries and palaces were lavishly covered with stucco mouldings and *trompe-l'oeil* paintings. An important centre for such art was Wessobrunn. From the 18th century the prominent Asam brothers began working in Bavaria *(see p70)*. *Lüftlmalerei*, paintings on the walls of houses *(see p216)*, is a typically Bavarian phenomenon. Fine Rococo sculpture was produced by Ignaz Günther and Johann Baptist Straub, while the court artist François Cuvilliés refined the art of Rococo decor to perfection.

This traditional wardrobe is from the renowned furniture-making centre in Bad Tölz. The distinctive furniture made here was covered in folk paintings. Sideboards, beds and the carts associated with the St Leonard's Day festival can be seen in the town's local history museum.

This amber sculpture from the Bürgersaal in Munich by Ignaz Günther embodies all the elements of the late Baroque: pathos, levity and dynamism.

1692–1750 Egid Quirin Asam

1601–34 Georg Petel

1680–1758 Johann Baptist Zimmermann

Guardian angel by Ignaz Günther

1600

1650

1700

1609–84 Johann Heinrich Schönfeld

Portrait of Cosmas Damian Asam

1686–1739 Cosmas Damian Asam

1695–1768 François Cuvilliés

1697–1776 George Desmarées

1704–84 Johann Baptist Straub

1725–75 Ignaz Günther

Traditions of the Bavarian Alps

Bavaria is a land where old local traditions and folklore are cultivated and revered. Almost every town and village has its own local holiday, with folk bands, beer-drinking and general merriment in the streets. These events variously involve folk dancing and fire-work displays. The Catholic tradition is strong in the region, the countless religious feast days and church processions often coinciding with fairs. Many places also commemorate local historical events.

Passion Plays

Once every ten years the mountain village of Oberammergau becomes the centre of the Easter mystery plays *(Passionsspiele)* that are performed over four months from late May to early October. This tradition dates back to 1633.

At that time, so as to ward off the plague, the villagers vowed to act out scenes from the Passion of Christ. Initially these were staged outside the church, but since 1930 they have been held in a special open-air theatre with seating for 4,800. The performances, lasting from morning until late afternoon with a break in between, take place five days a week. According to tradition, the actors must be residents of Oberammergau by birth. The lavish decorations and the costumes, of which there are over 1,000, are provided by the local populace. The scenes,

accompanied by a choir and music, are performed by amateur actors in a natural and expressive way. Against the backdrop of mountains they have the realism of *tableaux vivants*.

The Passion plays have gained world renown, and tickets must be booked well in advance. A similar tradition exists in certain other Bavarian villages.

The Maypole

On 30 April each year, small groups of people can be seen beside fires, drinking beer and watching over a long, barkless tree trunk. Recovering a tree trunk stolen by the inhabitants of the neighbouring village is rewarded by a large number of barrels (or today, cases) of the Bavarians' favourite drink. Next day the trunk is decorated and ceremonially raised in the village square.

According to tradition, the maypole, the pride of every local community, ensures a successful year. The custom of raising the maypole, the tree of life, goes back to medieval times. Usually painted in the Bavarian colours of white and blue, maypoles are decorated with the emblems of local crafts and crowned with a large wreath. Traditions include dancing round the maypole and climbing up it to reach the prizes tied to the wreath.

Residents of a small town joining forces to raise the maypole

Landshut Wedding

In 1475, Landshut saw the wedding of Georg, son of Ludwig the Rich, and Princess Jadwiga of Poland, daughter of Casimir Jagiellon. The celebrations lasted eight days, and went down in history as one of the most sumptuous in medieval Bavaria.

Since 1903 the Landshut Wedding (Landshuter Fürstenhochzeit) has been re-enacted every four years on three weekends in June and July. About 100,000 visitors come to enjoy this historic drama. Medieval costumes are worn during the young couple's triumphal procession, which is accompanied by court dances and by tests of the skills of knights and squires.

Christ stumbling under the Cross during the Oberammergau Passion play

The Oktoberfest

This famous folk festival, the world's largest, began in 1810, when Princess Therese von Sachsen-Hildburghausen married Ludwig (later to become King Ludwig I), the heir to the Bavarian throne. Horse races were organized in a meadow on the edge of Munich, which was named the Theresienwiese in honour of the young lady. It was decided to make this a regular event, and gradually it became customary to organize agricultural shows, which were combined with equestrian events and shooting contests. To these were added roundabouts, beer tents and fireworks, thus giving rise to the present Oktoberfest (it was moved from October to late September due to the weather).

Today the Oktoberfest attracts some 6 million visitors from all over the world. Year after year the record for amounts of beer, sausages and roast chickens consumed at the festival is broken. The Oktoberfest opens with a grand procession of wagons of the city's seven main breweries accompanied by folk bands. On the stroke of noon, the city's mayor broaches a barrel of beer to open the two-week revelry surrounding the city's fair.

Singing and beer – the world-renowned Oktoberfest

The Christmas Fair

Advent, which comes from the Latin *adventus*, "the coming", is the period in the Christian calendar leading up to Christmas. It starts on the fourth Sunday before 24 December. In Bavaria this period is marked with a number of rituals.

Advent candles are lit in churches and in people's houses, and special biscuits known as *Plätzchen* are baked. In the larger towns and cities, market stalls are set up for the Christmas fairs, which are known as *Christkindlmarkt* or *Weihnachtsmarkt*. They begin with the ritual raising of a huge Christmas tree in the brightly illuminated market squares.

Wooden decorations, Nativity figures and all sorts of delicacies and gifts are displayed for sale round the tree. The air is filled with the delicious aroma of freshly baked gingerbread and roasted almonds. The celebrations include drinking hot wine (*Glühwein*) in the frosty air. St Nicholas accompanied by Knecht Ruprecht or Krampus distribute apples and nuts to children, and the holiday atmosphere is heightened by the joyful singing of carollers. The best Christmas fairs in southern Bavaria are those that are held in Munich, Augsburg and Landsberg.

Bavarian folk costume

To many people, traditional Bavarian folk costume epitomizes Bavaria. The traditional Bavarian costume is among one of the most widely celebrated and well known of the European national costumes. The traditional men's *Tracht* includes: *Lederhosen*, leather shorts held up by leather braces and sometimes tied up at the knees; the *Janker*, a waistcoat of rough cloth with bone buttons; the *Gamsbart*, a hat with a goat's hair tassel, and asymmetrically tied shoes. Women wear the *Dirndl*, a blouse with puffed sleeves, a corset, a waistcoat, a crimped skirt and an apron. Jewellery and ornaments are an important element of Bavarian costume. Men's trousers are decorated with chains with pendants and their shirts have letters, medallions, coats of arms as well as embroidery. The women wear intricate necklaces and richly decorated chokers.

Illuminated tree, the focal point of a Christmas market

Bavarian in national costume

MUNICH & THE BAVARIAN ALPS THROUGH THE YEAR

The Bavarian calendar is filled with picturesque rituals, historical spectacles, festivals and trade fairs. The type of event depends on the season, and in Bavaria they are varied indeed. The snowy winter is the season for skiers and tobogganists, while hikers enjoy walking along the scenic and well-marked trails. From springtime onwards, colourful paragliders can be spotted as they soar over mountain peaks, and the appearance of sails heralds the start of the yachting season on the lakes. The summer attracts mountaineers, hikers and watersports enthusiasts. Almost everyone can be seen during the famous Oktoberfest, which starts in the middle of September.

Spring

Spring comes early here. At the beginning of April, fruit trees are in blossom, Alpine meadows become carpeted with flowers, mostly crocuses, and the melting Alpine snow creates rushing streams. Numerous festive ceremonies mark the Easter period in Bavaria. Easter traditions centre on the symbolism of the egg. Houses are decorated with ornamental twigs with Easter eggs hanging from them, while excited children are up early searching for eggs. In May, the blossom of chestnut trees forms a canopy over reawakening beer-gardens.

Crocus from a meadow

March
Starkbierfest *(between Ash Wednesday and Good Friday)* Munich. The Festival of Strong Beer commemorates the strong ale that was drunk by Pauline monks as they observed the Lenten fast.

April
Biennale *(April/May)*, Munich. Germany's largest contemporary music festival.
Augsburger Plärrer *(two weeks after Easter)*, Augsburg. Biannual event (also held in September). The largest folk festival in Swabia, a small counterpart to the Oktoberfest.

Auer Dult (Maidult) *(from the last Saturday in April)*, Munich. Renowned fair held in the Mariahilfplatz in the city's Au district.
Internationale Jazzwoche *(last two weeks in April)*, international jazz festival that takes place in Burghausen.

May
Trachten- und Schützenumzug *(last Sunday in April/first Sunday in May)*, Passau. Large procession of folk groups and bands from Bavaria and Austria open this annual fair.
Maibaumaufstellen *(May 1)*. Virtually every Bavarian community honours the custom of Raising the Maypole *(see p32)*.
Maibockausschank *(May 1–14)*, Munich. The occasion when the strong Bockbier is broached. It begins in the Hofbräuhaus to the sounds of a children's orchestra.
Lange Nacht der Musik *(May)*, Munich. Over 400 live music events are held at 100 venues for one long night.
Fronleichnam *(Thursday after Trinity Sunday)*. According to Catholic tradition, this religious festival in honour of Corpus Christi is marked by countless processions. The most picturesque are in Lenggries and Bad Tölz.

Typical Fronleichnam (Corpus Christi) procession

Antiques for sale at the famous Auer Dult fair in Au

Average hours of sunshine

Hours   Hours

12 —   — 10

9 —   — 8

6 —   — 6

                             — 4

3 —   — 2

0 —   — 0

Jan Feb Mar Apr May Jun Jul Aug Sep Oct Nov Dec

Sunshine
The greatest number of sunny days are concentrated in the period from June to September. May can also be sunny. December is the least sunny month.

Summer

On summer days the blue skies over Bavaria reach an almost Mediterranean intensity. Cascades of flowers hang from balconies and window boxes. Bathers and watersports enthusiasts are drawn to the crystal-clear rivers and lakes. Almost every resort has its own summer festival, and these celebrations are particularly impressive when they are held by a lakeside. They feature regattas, firework displays and angling contests.

June

Stadtgeburtstag *(weekend on/ after 14 June)*, Munich. Festival commemorating the foundation of the city.
Filmfest München *(last week in June)*, Munich. One of Europe's liveliest and most important film festivals.
Tollwood Festival *(four weeks June–July)*, Munich, Olympic Park. Festival of jazz, rock and theatre, with lots of food stalls.

July

Kaltenberger Ritterspiele *(first 3 weekends in July)*, Kaltenberg Castle, near Landsberg. Jousting tournaments re-enacting medieval traditions.
Münchener Opernfestspiele *(1–31 July)*, Munich. Festival of classical opera, ballet, singing and music.
Landshuter Hochzeit *(every four years, the next in 2017)*, Landshut. Spectacle commemorating the marriage of Georg, son of

Agnes Bernauer Festspiele in Straubing

Poster for the Auer Dult fair

Ludwig the Rich, and Princess Jadwiga *(see p32)*.
Schwäbischwerder Kindertag *(mid-July)*, Donauwörth. Children dressed in historical costume re-enact important events in the history of the town.
Agnes Bernauer Festspiele *(every four years, the next in 2015)*, Straubing. Historical theatre festival telling the story of Duke Albrecht III and Agnes Bernauer, an Augsburg barber's daughter.
Memminger Fischertag *(second half of July)*, Memmingen. Trout-angling competition.

August

Auer Dult (Jakobidult) *(July/ August)*, Munich. One of three annual fairs held in the Au district of Munich.
Schleißheimer Schloßkonzerte *(July/August)*, Schleißheim. Concerts of classical music.

Gäubodenfest *(around mid-Aug)*, Straubing. Folk festival combined with an agricultural and industrial fair, Bavaria's second largest after the Oktoberfest.
Allgäuer Festwoche *(mid-August)*, Kempten. Exhibition of the Allgäu region's economic and cultural achievements, also including an important folk festival.
König-Ludwig-Feier *(24 Aug)*, Oberammergau. Festival commemorating the death of Ludwig II, who drowned in the Starnbergersee. There is singing, dancing and speeches.

Sunflowers, symbols of summer, a common sight in Bavaria

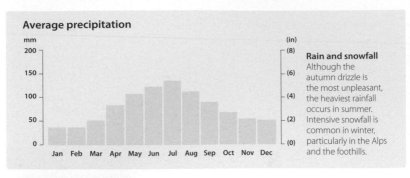

Average precipitation

mm
(in)

Rain and snowfall
Although the
autumn drizzle is
the most unpleasant,
the heaviest rainfall
occurs in summer.
Intensive snowfall is
common in winter,
particularly in the Alps
and the foothills.

One of the vast beer tents at
the Oktoberfest

Autumn

Bavarian autumns are often
warm and sunny. The forests
turn every shade of red and
gold, and mushroom-pickers
return with baskets filled
with many species of edible
fungi. The mountain pastures
echo to the sounds of herded
cows and sheep.

In autumn the sky becomes
dull and overcast, and the
shortening days are chilly and
damp. The first overnight frosts
set in, and mornings often start
with a blanket of thick fog,
which causes problems for
road and air traffic.

September
Oktoberfest *(16 days leading
up to the 1st Sunday in October)*,
Munich. The city's world-famous
folk festival, held in the
Theresienwiese fair-ground.
Sample Wiesnbeer, especially
brewed for the Oktoberfest,
accompanied by traditional

Bavarian entertainment
(see p33).
Viehscheid *(second half
of September)*. Traditional
celebration of the cattle
being brought down from
summer pastures in many
areas, including Hindelang,
Oberstdorf and Königssee.

October
Oktoberfest *(see September)*.
Auer Dult (Herbst Dult) *(third
Saturday in October)*, Munich.
The third of the annual fairs
held in the Au district of Munich.
Lange Nacht der Museen *(one
night in October, date varies)*,
Munich. About 90 of the city's
galleries and museums open
late for one evening of tours
and parties.
Medientage München
(around mid-October), Munich.
Fair dedicated to the mass
media. Discover the latest
trends in multimedia and
communications.

November
**Leonardifahrten und
Leonardiritte** *(1st Sunday
in November)* throughout
Bavaria. In many areas, such
as Bad Tölz, Schliersee,
Murnau and Benediktbeuern,
processions on horseback
or in painted carts take
place in honour of St Leonard,
regarded by Bavarians as
the patron saint of horses.
In Bad Tölz the horses
reenact Christ's journey on
the road to Calvary in a
procession after receiving a
blessing. **St Martin's Day**
(11 November) throughout
Bavaria. In almost every
town and village process-
ions are held in which
children take part, carrying
lanterns. Pretzels that
they have been given hang
from the lanterns. The
processions are often led by
a horse-rider in a long cloak
who represents St Martin.

Bavarian women in a painted cart on St Leonard's Day

Average monthly temperatures

Temperatures
Temperatures are highest in the summer, although temperatures rarely exceed 30°C (86°F). Winters are frosty and snowy, although they can be mild. The coldest temperatures are naturally in the mountains.

Winter

As autumn draws to a close, people light the candles on the Advent wreaths in their homes every week, while the smell of baking biscuits wafts through the air. At the beginning of December skiers set out on excursions, and if the lakes and canals are sufficiently thickly frozen, they are soon covered with skaters.

Winters in southern Bavaria are unpredictable. They may be icy and snowy, or mild and snow-free. December is marked by the carnival spirit. Village carnivals are colourful affairs. At events associated with driving off winter with witchcraft, masks and costumes are a common sight.

December

WinterTollwood (throughout December), Munich. A major music and arts festival held in Theresienwiese.

The Skifasching (skiing carnival) in Firstalm

Christkindlmarkt (early December to Christmas Eve), throughout southern Bavaria. A Christmas fair inaugurating the festive Christmas season with the ritual raising of the Christmas tree in the town or village square.

Sylvester (31 December). Sumptuous balls and receptions mark the New Year, which is ushered in with lavish firework displays.

January

Four Ski-Jump Tournament (1–4 January), Oberstdorf, Garmisch-Partenkirchen. Famous ski-jumping tournament. **Schäfflertanz** (Epiphany to Shrove Tuesday), Munich. The Dance of the Coopers street festival held every seven years (the next in 2019) to commemorate the passing of the plague in the 15th century.

February

Tanz der Marktfrauen (Shrove Tuesday), Munich. Market women of the Viktualienmarkt dress up and perform a dance. **Skifasching** (last Sunday of Carnival), Firstalm. Bavaria's renowned skiing carnival, including a competition for the best fancy dress. Also held in Garmisch-Partenkirchen.

Public Holidays

Neujahr New Year

Epiphany (6 January)

Karfreitag Good Friday

Ostern Easter

Maifeiertag May Day

Christi Himmelfahrt Ascension

Pfingsten Whitsun

Fronleichnam Corpus Christi

Mariä Himmelfahrt Assumption (15 August)

Nationalfeiertag German Reunification Day (3 October)

Allerheiligen All Saints (1 November)

Weihnachten Christmas (25/26 December)

Oberstdorf in winter during the Four Ski-Jump Tournament

THE HISTORY OF MUNICH AND BAVARIA

Over the centuries, despite its location in the heart of Europe, southern Bavaria gradually built up its distinct character, becoming a geographically and culturally unified entity. Although it never played a leading role, it was one of the strongest duchies in Germany. The Wittelsbach dynasty ruled Bavaria until 1918, when the Free State of Bavaria (Freistaat Bayern) was proclaimed. After World War II Bavaria opposed centralization.

Early Settlement

The first farming communities settled in southern Bavaria in the 4th millennium BC. Traces of their presence, in the form of the foundations of peasant huts, were found near Kelheim in the 1960s. During the period of the Altheim culture (about 3900–3500 BC), peasant settlements were often surrounded by fortified ditches. During the Bronze Age (1800–1200 BC) the pace of cultural development accelerated, and a wealth of items from burials and many everyday tools of that period have been discovered. During the Hallstatt period, iron began to be used in preference to bronze.

The Celts

The Hallstatt period was marked by the appearance in Bavaria of the Celts, whose origins are not clear to this day. The Celts were distinguished by their loose tribal and family ties. The Vindelici tribe of Celts settled in the territory between the rivers Inn and Lech, and their capital was Manching, near Ingolstadt. The Bavarian Celts maintained links with the Mediterranean world, particularly with the Etruscans. They imported Etruscan, and sometimes Greek, luxury goods. Many later Bavarian towns, among them Regensburg (Ratisbon), Kempten, Straubing and Passau, were founded by the Celts.

The Roman Empire

In 15 BC the Roman army, under Drusus and Tiberius, conquered the Celts and reached the Danube. This became the frontier of the Roman Empire and a fortified wall was constructed to defend it. Southern Bavaria was divided into the provinces of Raetia and Noricum. The city of Vindelicorum, today Augsburg, was founded by the Emperor Augustus, whose name it still bears. It became the administrative centre of this part of the Roman Empire.

150,000 BC	3000 BC	1500 BC	600 BC	300 BC	AD 1	AD 300

10,000 BC Start of the Neolithic period

3900–3500 BC Appearance of the Altheim culture

1600 BC Bronze Age

700–500 BC Appearance of the Hallstatt culture

15 BC Roman soldiers invade the area between the Alps and the Danube

AD 166–80 The Marcomanni launch attacks that devastate southern Bavaria

150,000–100,000 BC First human settlement in the Danube valley

2000–1800 BC Appearance of the first bronze artifacts

1200 BC Appearance of the earliest Beaker culture

500 BC First Celtic settlements in Bavaria

Gilt mask from the Roman period

AD 233–83 Fifty years of conflict between the Romans and Germanic tribes

◄ Portrait of Ludwig I, king of Bavaria (1786–1868)

The End of the Roman Empire

After two centuries of peaceful development, Raetia and Noricum were attacked by two Germanic tribes, the Marcomanni and the Alamanni. The first attacks were repulsed by Emperor Marcus Aurelius, but the province suffered destruction in the mid-3rd century by invasions and civil war. Towards the end of the 3rd century stability returned for about 100 years, but after AD 400 a new wave of Germanic invasions toppled Roman control.

Roman stele from Augsburg

From those war-torn and troubled times there are records of the activities of the early Christians – St Afra, the martyr who was burned in Augsburg, and St Severinus, who revived missionary activity in the region.

The Great Migration and Early Christianity

The origins of the Bavarians are still imperfectly known. Most historians believe that a new tribe, whom the Romans knew as the Baiovarii, appeared south of the Danube, in the area of present-day southern Bavaria, in 450–550. They are thought to have originated from a Germanic tribe centred in Boiohaemum, what is today the Czech Republic. The Baiovarii were joined by remnants of other Germanic and Celtic tribes and by Romanized people. At the same time, settlers started appearing to the west of the River Lech. The Alamanni tribes became the neighbours of the Baiovarii to the west, while to the north, the region a few dozen kilometres beyond the Danube was conquered by the Franks. This situation continued virtually unchanged to the present day, with the addition of the territories beyond the River Lech and Bavaria's acquisition of the Franconian lands after 1803.

Most of the inhabitants of the region retained their pagan beliefs for some time, and Christianity took hold only very slowly. Irish, Anglo-Saxon and Frankish missionaries started preaching in the region in the early 7th century. At the turn of the 7th century, numerous bishops were active in Bavarian lands: Emmeram in Ratisbon, Korbinian in Freising, and Rupert in Salzburg. In 739 there were bishoprics in Ratisbon, Freising, Passau and present-day Salzburg. They were set up and run by the Anglo-Saxon missionary bishop, St Boniface. It is noteworthy that the importance of their sees continued for the next millennium. A key role in the establishment of Christianity and the nurturing of cultural development from the late 7th century and throughout the 8th

Roman mosaic with hunting scenes from a villa near Westerhofen

450–550 Emergence of the Bavarian tribes	476 Fall of the Roman Empire	555 Garibald I becomes Duke of Bavaria	c. 617 First monastery founded in Weltenburg
400	**450**	**500**	**550**	**600**	**650**
400–476 Pressure from Germanic tribes overthrows Roman rule in Bavaria	482 Death of the missionary St Severinus in Bavaria		c. 630 Lex Baiuvariorum, the first book of Bavarian law, is written

Fragment from a Longobardi helmet

century was played by the many Benedictine monasteries, particularly by those of Weltenburg and Benediktbeuern.

Rule of the Bavarian Tribes

The Duchy of Bavaria was founded in the mid-6th century. The ruling Agilolfing dynasty probably orig-inated from the territories of the Merovingian state to the west, and was its vassals. The first known Duke of Bavaria was Garibald I (555–91). According to the *Lex Baiuvariorum*, the first legal code issued in those lands, the ducal throne was to belong to the Agilolfing dynasty for all time.

Being dependent on the powerful Merovingians and weaker than the Frankish dukes to the north, Bavaria's Agilolfing rulers were forced to resort to constant manoeuvring to retain their position. One of the ways in which they managed to preserve their rule was by strategic marriages with the Allaman, Longobardi and Frankish dynasties. Their activity within the state was limited to military leadership, while in peacetime they took charge of the judiciary. Despite this, the Agilolfing dukes played a major role in Bavaria's development. Not only did they lay the foundations of the future state of Bavaria by ensuring its territorial unity, but they also played an important role in championing Christianity.

The main centre of ducal and ecclesiastic power was Ratisbon, on the River Danube. The duchy itself grew slowly and by peaceful

The Cross of Tassilo from the church in Polling

means, and almost unnoticed it expanded into what was later to become Austria. Under the rule of Tassilo III (748–88), the last ruler of the Agilolfing dynasty, the duchy extended as far as Carinthia. However, the growing might of the Agilolfing dynasty and of its state alarmed the Frankish ruler Charlemagne, who defeated Tassilo in 788 and in so doing put an end to the Bavarian tribes' first state.

Bavaria lost its independence and became part of the Frankish state, while Tassilo himself was confined to a monastery.

After the division of the Frankish empire under the terms of the Treaty of Verdun in 843, Bavaria became one of the centres of the East Frankish Empire (which was the embryo of the later Germany). The Emperor Arnulf of Carinthia resided in Ratisbon at the end of the 9th century.

Initial from an illuminated manuscript, depicting the martyrdom of St Emmeram, Bishop of Ratisbon

A fibula decorated with a geometric pattern

788 Tassilo III is overthrown by Charlemagne

907 Hungarian tribes overrun Bavaria

938 Emperor Otto's campaign against Duke Eberhard of Bavaria

750	800	850	900	950	1000

739 Bishoprics established in Freising and Passau

738 St Boniface begins evangelizing Bavaria

843 Division of the Frankish empire

899 Death of Emperor Arnulf leads to a period of instability

954 Hungarian tribes invade Swabia

Friedrich Barbarossa bestowing power on the Ottonians and Wittelsbachs

The Early Middle Ages

At the end of the 8th century, rulers proceeded to unify the Bavarian tribes and founded a new duchy. Throughout the 9th century the Bavarian dukes were in conflict with the Saxons, who took the Bavarian throne in 919. These conflicts ended in their defeat, and in the 10th century the German kings decided to appoint their own vassals to the Bavarian ducal throne, or to rule the duchy directly.

The following centuries brought a degree of stability with the rule of the Welf dynasty. Duke Henry the Lion founded Munich in 1158 and with the support of Bavaria and his possessions in Saxony waged a war against the Emperor Friedrich Barbarossa. He was finally defeated in 1180, and Bavaria lost the lands east of Salzburg. The same year, Friedrich Barbarossa conferred the title of Duke of Bavaria on Otto I Wittelsbach. This powerful dynasty was to rule Bavaria right up until 1918, a record length of time for any German dynasty. The Wittelsbachs gradually built up their family possessions in central Bavaria, repelling successive attacks by rival families. In 1214 they annexed part of the Rhineland Palatinate, and by 1253 Bavaria was one of the largest ducal territories in the fragmented German empire.

The Late Middle Ages

Under Ludwig IV of Bavaria, the duchy was at the height of its powers. Ludwig added the Margravate of Brandenburg, the Tyrol and part of the southern Netherlands to Bavaria. In 1314 he became king of Germany, and 14 years later he was crowned Holy Roman Emperor. External glory was reflected in internal changes. The Emperor introduced civic and land laws, and built up an administrative system with new central institutions.

From the end of the 14th century, tax affairs were decided by representatives of three ranks: knights, clergy and burghers. From the 15th century this group assumed the form of an assembly called the Landtag or Landschaft. After the death of Ludwig IV, Bavaria was shaken by an endless succession of conflicts and local wars.

Late Gothic sculpture from Ottobeuren Abbey

1070
Bavaria is ruled by the Welfs

1180 Otto Wittelsbach is made Duke of Bavaria

c.1200 The final edition of the *Nibelungenlied* appears in Passau

1328 Ludwig IV of Bavaria becomes German emperor

1100 **1150** **1200** **1250** **130**

Romanesque stained glass from Augsburg Cathedral

1158 Foundation of Munich by Duke Heinrich der Löwe

1214 The Palatinate is incorporated into Bavaria

1255 Munich becomes the capital of the duchy

1317 Fire destroys a large part of Munich

The sons of Ludwig IV attempted to divide the state into small duchies ruled by each of them. In spite of the poverty and sacrifice brought by the resulting wars, this situation had a positive aspect. The division and rivalry of the various ducal courts encouraged the development of culture.

Landshut underwent a period of splendour and in 1475 it was the venue of the sumptuous wedding of the daughter of Casimir Jagiellon, king of Poland (see p32). However, in the Swabian territories on the River Lech, territorial disintegration continued in the 15th century. A leading role was played by the empire's principal city, Augsburg. The territory under the control of the Bishop of Augsburg also held a prime position.

Renaissance tombstone from the church in Oettingen

The Renaissance and Counter-Reformation

In 1506 the Bavarian states forced the adoption of a regulation that forbade the division of duchies: from then on, the throne passed to the eldest son. The Bavarian duchies were strengthened by the fact that their lands were not affected by the German peasants' wars of 1524–6.

The rulers of Bavaria were firmly opposed to the Protestantism that was spreading through the territories of Swabia and Franconia.

In 1530, at the imperial parliament in Augsburg, the Protestants presented the articles of their faith, known as the Confessions of Augsburg, to the Emperor. Some Bavarian Protestants were forced to renounce their faith, while the following edict of 1571 finally removed all supporters of the reformation from Bavaria. In the war of 1546–7 between Karl V and the Protestant dukes, Bavaria took the Emperor's side. The first Bavarian Jesuits fought actively against the Reformation. The great Michaelskirche in Munich was built in the late 16th-century as a symbol of Bavarian Catholicism.

In return for their allegiance to Rome, the younger sons of the Wittelsbachs were given sees in the west and north of the Empire, thus further strengthening the position of the Wittelsbachs on the German political scene.

Handing the Confessions of Augsburg to Emperor Karl V

see p32

Martin Luther, father of the Reformation

1385 The first residence in Munich is built by Duke Stephan III

1369 The population of Munich exceeds 10,000

1516 The dukes of Bavaria issue the Reinheitsgebot, the world's first decree, enforced to this day, on brewing beer

1506 The states of Bavaria issue a decree forbidding the division of the country

1517 Luther's 95 "theses" launch the Reformation

1530 Protestants submit the Confessions of Augsburg to Karl V at the imperial parliament

1555 The imperial parliament declares the Religious Peace of Augsburg

1350   1400   1450   1500   1550

The Age of Maximilian I

Duke Wilhelm V, who came to the throne in 1579, brought the state to the edge of bankruptcy, abdicating in 1598 in favour of his son Maximilian I (1573–1651). During his 54-year reign, Maximilian reorganized the administration of the state and the military, streamlined the fiscal system and reigned in a kind of early absolutism. In the face of worsening religious and political conflicts in the empire, which ultimately led to the outbreak of the Thirty Years' War, Maximilian I took charge of the Catholic camp. In 1618 he supported the Habsburgs against the rebellious Bohemian state, and Bavarian troops played a decisive role in the defeat of the Bohemians at the Battle of White Mountain in 1620.

Bust of Maximilian I

As a reward for his part in this victory, Maximilian I was given the title of Prince Elector in 1623. The lands of the Upper Palatinate, which were added to Bavaria, were subjected to a brutal regime of re-Catholicization.

During the second part of the Thirty Years' War, attacks by Swedish and Franco-Swedish forces caused a great deal of devastation and severely impoverished the country.

Finally, thanks to French support, Maximilian succeeded in retaining all conquered lands and the title of Elector at the peace congress in Münster. Pro-French policy would dominate Bavarian policy from then up until German Unification in 1871.

Maximilian's style and method of rule were emulated by later Bavarian leaders, including Duke Maximilian Montgelas and Franz Josef Strauß. Bertel Thorvaldsen's equestrian statue of Maximilian in Munich commemorates his achievements.

Dreams of Power

Maximilian II Emanuel, who married the daughter of the Polish king Jan III Sobieski, was known as the "White Knight". One of the most colourful figures in Bavaria's history, he had dreams of great conquests and of winning the crown. He allied himself with the Viennese court, and took part in the Battle of Vienna, where the Turks were defeated, in 1683. He was rewarded with the regency of the southern Netherlands. Entangled in the Wars of the Spanish Succession, he changed sides and in 1702 formed an alliance with Louis XIV. However, in 1704 the Franco-Bavarian army was defeated by Habsburg troops and Maximilian II Emanuel fled to France. Bavaria then suffered ten years of harsh Austrian rule

Maximilian Emanuel receiving a Turkish emissary after his victory at Vienna

1609 Maximilian I, Duke of Bavaria, founds the League of Catholic Rulers of the Empire

1618 An uprising in Prague sparks the Thirty Years' War

1623 The Duke of Bavaria is declared Elector of Palatinate

1648 The Peace of Westphalia ends the Thirty Years' War. Bavaria retains the lands of the Upper Palatinate won in 1620–22

1600   **1620**   **1640**   **1660**   **168**

Patrona Bavariae
from the wall of the Residenz in Munich

1620 Maximilian I is victorious at the Battle of White Mountain, fought against rebellious Bohemian states

1645–8 Swedish and French troops devastate Bavarian lands

1683 An anti-Turkish coalition led by Jan III Sobieski is victorious at the Battle of Vienna during which protests by desperate peasants were suppressed with bloodshed.

Maximilian II Emanuel did not return to the elector's throne until a peace treaty was signed in 1714. Although he was a rominent patron of the arts and a popular leader, his lengthy and turbulent rule had weakened Bavaria's position.

Rococo window arch at the Residenz in Munich

Reform, Annexation and Enlightenment

In 1740–45, despite Maximilian II Emanuel's disastrous anti-Habsburg policy, his son Karl Albrecht made a further attempt to become involved in the Austrian succession. As Karl VII, Emperor of the Holy Roman Empire, he

Rococo monstrance from Passau

was, however, unable to repel the troops of Maria Teresia. At the Treaty of Füssen in 1745, his successor Maximilian III Joseph was forced to renounce claims to the Austrian throne.

During the long and peaceful reign of Maximilian III Joseph, in which the ideology of enlightened absolutism was put into practice, there were important agricultural reforms, as well as the foundation of the Bavarian Academy of Sciences in 1759. Another development was the famous Nymphenburg porcelain factory.

The king's death in 1777 ended the direct Wittelsbach line. Emperor Joseph II's orders to annexe Bavaria caused Prussian objections and led to the accession of Karl Theodor, an indirect descendant of the ruling family of the Palatinate. Karl Theodor continued his predecessor's policy of enlightenment, while the spirit of scientific enquiry was cultivated in Bavarian abbeys, which contributed to knowledge and culture.

With the outbreak of the Napoleonic Wars (1799–1815), Bavaria tried to remain neutral but was unable to protect its possessions in the Palatinate from French occupation.

Ornamental interior of the church of Weltenburg Monastery, one of many built in the Baroque period

1714 The Peace of Rastatt between Bavaria and the Habsburg Empire		**1740** War of Austrian Succession breaks out, with Bavaria on the anti-Habsburg side	**1759** Foundation of the Bavarian Academy of Sciences	**1789** Start of the French Revolution
1700	**1720**	**1740**	**1760**	**1780**
1701–02 The Elector Maximilian II Emanuel makes an alliance with France against the Habsburgs		**1745** Peace of Füssen between Bavaria and Austria *Ornamental Rococo window of a town house in Straubing*	**1778–9** War of Bavarian Succession	

The Wittelsbach Dynasty

In 1180 Bavaria was given in lien to Otto I Wittelsbach, whose family ruled Bavaria until 1918. In 1329 the family was divided into a Bavarian and Palatinate line, which branched out even further. The Wittelsbachs occupied the German imperial throne on two occasions (in 1328 and 1742). In 1806 Napoleon proclaimed Maximilian I Joseph king. The family traditionally patronized the arts, which reached their apogee in the 19th century. The decline of the Wittelsbach dynasty began with Ludwig II, the "dilettante" king, and finally ended with the abdication of Ludwig III.

Wilhelm IV (1508–50) periodically shared his rule with his brother, Albrecht IV.

Otto II (1231–53) reformed the administrative and judicial system.

Ludwig II, the Severe (1253–94) shared power with his brother Henry XIII. He moved the duchy's capital from Landshut to Munich.

Otto I (1180–83) was the first Wittelsbach on the Bavarian throne.

Stephan II (1347–75) was one of six sons of Ludwig IV, who shared power among themselves.

Albrecht III, the Pious (1438–60) secretly married Agnes Bernauer, a baker's daughter, who was drowned in the Danube on his father's orders.

1150	1225	1300	1375	1450	15

1150	1225	1300	1375	1450	15

Ludwig I of Kelheim (1183–1231) extended Bavarian territory into the Rhineland Palatinate. He was stabbed on the bridge at Kelheim by an unknown assassin.

Johann II (1375–97), son of Stephan II, built the new Residenz in Munich with his three co-ruling brothers.

Ernst (1397–1438) ruled Bavaria for over 40 years, averting wars and conflicts.

Albrecht IV, the Wise (1467–1508) was the first humanist to occupy the Bavarian throne. He ended the influence of the Italian Renaissance.

Ludwig IV of Bavaria (1294–1347) was crowned king of Germany in 1314. He became Emperor in 1328, and this brought him into conflict with the Pope.

Maximilian II Emanuel
(1679–1726), an ambitious but
unfortunate ruler, caused Bavaria
to fall under Austrian rule.

Karl Theodor
(1777–99),
a descendant of
the Palatine
family, united
Bavaria and
the Palatinate,
which had
been separated
since 1329.

Maximilian II (1848–64),
a highly educated ruler,
was a great patron of science
and the arts.

Ludwig II (1864–86)
is remembered as an insane
ruler who had fairy-tale
residences built for him.

Wilhelm V, the Pious
(1579–97) brought Bavaria to
bankruptcy and abdicated in
favour of his son Maximilian.

Karl Albrecht
(1726–45) was
crowned king
of Bohemia,
and later
became Karl VII,
Emperor of
Germany.

Ferdinand Maria
(1651–79)
had a peace-
seeking policy.

Ludwig III (1913–18)
was the last and the
most unfortunate
king of Bavaria.

1600	1675	1750	1825	1900

1600	1675	1750	1825	1900

Maximilian I
(1597–1651)
was one of the
leaders of the
Habsburg-
Catholic faction
during the Thirty
Years' War.

Ludwig I
(1825–40) was
a lover of the
arts, antiques
and women.

Maximilian I Joseph
(1806–1825),
first king of
Bavaria, issued the
Bavarian
Constitution
in 1818.

Albrecht V
(1550–79)
founded a fine
library and also
created the first
art collection
in Germany.

Luitpold (1886–1912)
ruled the country as
prince regent on behalf
of the ailing king Otto I.

Maximilian III Joseph
(1745–77) was an aesthete
and composer, and did not
have any great political
ambitions. He was the last
of the old Bavarian line
of Wittelsbachs.

Panel with portraits of the Wittelsbach rulers of Bavaria, painted by Franz Xaver Thallmaier, 1880

Golden Age of The Wittelsbachs

The modern state of Bavaria was established at the beginning of the 19th century and it has survived more or less intact to this day. In 1803 Napoleon dissolved the German Empire's old territorial structures, and with his approval in 1803–06 Bavaria doubled its territory, incorporating the Swabian lands up to Ulm, and the Franconian lands. In 1806 Maximilian Joseph, again with Napoleon's approval, was crowned king, acquiring the title of Maximilian I Joseph.

Territorial expansion was accompanied by far-reaching internal reforms. In 1803 Maximilian I Joseph and his aide Count Maximilian Montgelas disbanded the monasteries and reorganized the country's administration. In late 1813 they deftly switched allegiance from Napoleon to the anti-Napoleonic coalition. Thus, at the Congress of Vienna they were able to retain the bulk of the territory that they had acquired with Napoleon's aid.

From 1815 to 1866 the Bavarian kings manoeuvred between the Prussians and Austrians, managing to conduct an independent foreign policy. This ended when the Prussians defeated the Bavarian-Austrian alliance.

Cartouche with Bavarian crest

In the latter half of the 19th century Bavaria made significant cultural and political advances. Education was developed and the re-established University of Munich flourished. Thanks to Ludwig I, Munich acquired impressive new parks, gardens and buildings. The visual arts and drama flourished, briefly overtaking those of Vienna and Berlin. Maximilian I Joseph's reign saw great progress in science and industry, and the emergence of "Maximilian" architecture. Ludwig I's patronage of the arts was continued by his grandson Ludwig II. In 1866 Bismarck forced Bavaria to join the Prussian camp, which was supported by groups from the state bureaucracy and Franconian Protestant quarters.

Maximilian I Joseph, king of Bavaria

1803 Montgelas dissolves the Bavarian monasteries

1813 Bavaria joins the anti-Napoleonic coalition

1818 Bavaria becomes a constitutional monarchy

1848 The revolution in Munich leads to the abdication of Ludwig I

1866 Prussian War against Austria and Bavaria

1800	1815	1830	1845	1860

1805 Bavaria forms an alliance with Napoleon

1815 At the Congress of Vienna, Bavaria retains almost all its territorial gains from the Napoleonic period

1806 Bavaria becomes a kingdom

The dancer Lola Montez, mistress of Ludwig I

After the Unification of Germany

Their country's participation on the victors' side in the Franco-Prussian war of 1870–71 won many Bavarians over to the idea of a unified Germany. Ludwig II, who ruled Bavaria at the time, increasingly avoided any involvement in politics and escaped more and more into the world of Wagner's music, tales of chivalry and fairytale castles. The day-to-day running of the country was left to an anonymous group of government officials in Munich.

When the regency was taken over by Prince Luitpold after Ludwig II's tragic death, little changed. Luitpold, a popular ruler, attempted to offset political dependency on Berlin with a liberal cultural policy which contained a distinct anti-Prussian element. Under Luitpold's rule, Munich enjoyed the highest period of cultural and artistic development that it has ever experienced. Luitpold's son and heir, Ludwig III, who was thoroughly pro-Prussian, quickly lost his popularity.

After Germany's defeat at the end of World War I, on 7 November 1918 the rule of the Wittelsbachs in Munich was overthrown, and the Free State of Bavaria (Freistaat Bayern) was proclaimed. This has been Bavaria's official name ever since. Between February and May 1919 the farleft Bavarian Soviet Republic ruled Munich and part of Bavaria. This weakened Bavaria's moderate forces and radicalized the right, which started to embrace extremist groups, such as

Old postcard painted by Fritz Bergen shows King Ludwig II, much admired among Bavarians

Hitler's. In the general ferment of the Weimar Republic, Bavaria became a bastion of stability, with a slightly dictatorial rightwing government. The failure of Hitler's attempted putsch in 1923 helped to stave off Nazism for a while, but the mild sentences imposed on the leaders of the fascist Brownshirts only helped to increase their popularity.

From 1923 to 1933 the country was ruled by the Bavarian People's Party, whose policy was to oppose that of liberal and "red" Berlin. However, attempts to weaken Prussia's position in the Reich were unsuccessful, and political and cultural decline ensued. From 1918 to 1933 Munich's position as a cultural metropolis was taken over by Berlin.

Cartoon from a 1908 issue of the satirical journal *Simplicissimus*

1870–1871
Franco-Prussian War, in which Bavaria takes part

1900 Population of Munich reaches 500,000

Art Nouveau decoration on a house in Munich

9 November 1923
Hitler's attempted putsch in Munich

| 1875 | 1890 | 1905 | 1920 |

1886 Tragic drowning of King Ludwig II in the Starnbergersee

Frieze from the Propyläen in Munich

1 August 1914
Outbreak of World War I

7 September 1918 Revolution in Munich overthrows the Wittelsbach dynasty. Bavaria is declared Freistaat Bayern.

The Castles of Ludwig II

King Ludwig II of Bavaria, fondly known as "Kini" to his subjects, has remained a cult figure to this day. With his mad fantasies and lack of interest in politics, he seemed to come from another world. The king's passions were architecture and music, and his friendship with Richard Wagner influenced his entire life. He dragged the country into financial ruin as he built one magnificent country home after another, all the while dreaming of new ones. Gradually he became withdrawn and, deemed insane, was finally removed from power. At the age of 42 he drowned in the Starnbergersee in mysterious circumstances.

This turret is reached by a spiral staircase leading from a picturesque gallery.

Ludwig II's Night Sleigh Ride
This painting by Richard Wenig, and the actual sleigh, can be seen in the Marstall-museum in Nymphenburg. The king adored his nocturnal escapades, which helped him avoid the harsh realities of daylight.

Throne Room of Neuschwanstein Castle
The Throne Room was designed in Byzantine style. It is decorated with gilded mural paintings, mosaics and a huge chandelier. A splendid gold and ivory throne planned for Ludwig II *(see p234)* was never made.

The Minstrels' Room
is a lavishly painted official reception room.

Neuschwanstein Castle

The castle was built in 1868–86. Assisted by the painter and designer Christoph Jank, Ludwig II fulfilled his vision of an old German castle, although he only lived here for 172 days.

The Linderhof Grotto
Built in the park, complete with stalactites, the grotto covers a lake 3 m (10 ft) deep. Ludwig II reached it in a gilded barge, which rocked on artificially created waves *(see pp220–21)*.

Hall of Mirrors in Herrenchiemsee Palace
This showcase gallery was built in 1879–81 along the side of the palace facing the garden. Almost 100 m (328 ft) long, it outstrips the Hall of Mirrors at Versailles, on which it is based. The ceiling frescoes glorify Louis XIV, and night-time concerts *(see p206)* were illuminated with 1,848 candles placed in the gilded candelabras and chandeliers.

Turkish Hall in Schachen
With its fountain, rich carpets, ottomans, gilded candelabra and vases, the hall of this palace conjures up *The Tales of the Thousand and One Nights (see p221)*.

The upper courtyard leads into the main part of the castle, containing the reception room and apartments.

The gatehouse, flanked by turrets and set with crenellations, is decorated with the royal coat of arms.

Ludwig's Castles

Ludwig II was obsessed with creating the perfect residence. In Alpine surroundings he built Neuschwanstein Castle *(see p244)*. His fascination with the world of the Bourbons was expressed in the Linderhof *(see pp220–21)* and Herrenchiemsee *(see p206)* palaces.

Adolf Hitler signing the Munich Agreement

In the Shadow of the Nazis

The rulers of Bavaria underestimated the danger of the burgeoning Nazi movement. The participants in Hitler's 1923 putsch were given light sentences, with Hitler spending only eight months behind bars. In 1925 the NSDAP (Nazi Party) was reactivated, and in 1926 the ban on public speeches by Hitler was lifted. By 30 January 1933 Hitler had seized power, and in March he overthrew the Bavarian government and stripped Bavaria of its autonomy. Munich became Capital of the Movement; the Führer wanted it to become the Reich's ideological and cultural centre. The first concentration camp was built in nearby Dachau. During the Winter Olympics in Garmisch-Partenkirchen and the Summer Olympics in Berlin in 1936, the Nazis were at pains to present a positive image to the world. In 1937 Hitler embarked on an overt

Concentration camp prisoner's shirt

clampdown in cultural policy. An exhibition of Degenerate Art was held in Munich, and later in other cities, its aim being to stigmatize modern "degenerate" art. The Haus der Kunst was built for annual exhibitions of German art. The large-scale redevelopment of Munich began, and the Königsplatz became the venue for Nazi rallies. In 1938 the Munich Agreement, by which Czechoslovakia was partitioned, was signed and four years later the first Allied bombs fell on Munich. Hitler was associated with Bavaria until the end of his life, frequently visiting its capital and his residence near Berchtesgaden. Relatively few Bavarians spoke out against Hitler, a notable exception being the White Rose student group, and the opposition movement did not play a significant role here. In April 1945 an attempt was made to organize the final resistance here, but Hitler's "Alpine Fortress" ultimately proved to be of no use.

Hikers at the Kehlsteinhaus restaurant, the surviving part of Hitler's residence

1934 Hitler abolishes independence of German states, including Bavaria

1 September 1939 German attack on Poland launches World War II

30 April 1945 American troops enter Munich

1 October 1946 The first elections in Bavaria bring victory to the CSU

1974 The 10th World Soccer Championship finals are held in Munich

14 June 1958 Celebrations mark Munich's 800th anniversary

1972 The 20th Olympic Games are held in Munich

1930	1935	1940	1945	1950	1955	1960	1965	1970

29 September 1938 Munich Agreement

30 January 1933 Hitler becomes Chancellor of the Reich

February 1936 – the 4th Winter Olympics are held in Garmisch-Partenkirchen

1957 The population of Munich reaches 1 million

14 September 1949 Appointment of the government of the Federal Republic of Germany

1966 Construction of the Munich U-Bahn and S-Bahn network begins

Pageant at the Oktoberfest below Bavaria, a bronze statue made by Ferdinand von Miller

Modern Bavaria

The ravages of war were less severe in Bavaria than they were in other parts of Germany. In April and May 1945 Bavaria was occupied by American troops and until 1949 it formed part of the American occupation zone. Despite a great influx of displaced people, most of Bavaria's inhabitants were spared the worst of postwar deprivation because of the agricultural strength of the region. The Federal Republic of Bavaria, set up in 1949, made efforts to take an independent position as the region with the best preserved sense of historical and geographical identity, and constantly opposed any attempts at centralization. One of the external manifestations of this trend towards autonomy was the success that the local Christian Democrats had in keeping their own organization distinct from the CDU (Christian Democratic Union), and in setting up their own CSU (Christian Social Union). It ruled Bavaria continuously from 1949. The main figure in the CSU, until his death in 1988, was the temperamental Franz Josef Strauß, an unquestioned leader of the German right.

The CSU, appealing to regional tradition even to the extent of anti-Prussian separatist sentiment, skilfully pursued a policy of industrialization after 1960. Electronics and computer manufacture developed strongly, as did the car manufacturers BMW and Audi. During the 1972 Summer Olympics, the region glittered not only with its celebrated modern architecture, but also with its openness and liberalism. The Olympic ideal of peace was, however, marred by bloodshed in an attack by Palestinian separatists.

Franz Josef Strauß

In the years leading up to the reunification of Germany, Munich was regarded as "Germany's secret capital". But 1989 and the revival of Berlin's role means that Munich and Bavaria now face fresh challenges.

FC Bayern Munich, one of the world's best soccer teams

1980 Pope John Paul II visits Altötting during his pilgrimage to Germany

1992 The opening of Munich's new airport

The BMW logo, one of the symbols of modern Bavaria

2008 Munich celebrates its 850th birthday

1980	1985	1990	1995	2000	2005	2010	2015	2020

1988 Death of Franz Josef Strauß

3 October 1990 Reunification of Germany weakens Bavaria's political role

2004 Munich hosts the EuroGames

2006 Germany hosts the FIFA World Cup. The opening ceremony is held in Munich's Allianz arena

MUNICH AREA BY AREA

Munich at a Glance   **56–57**

Old Town (South)   **58–73**

Old Town (North)   **74–89**

Around the Isar   **90–101**

The University District   **102–113**

The Museums District   **114–131**

Further Afield   **132–143**

Shopping in Munich   **144–145**

Entertainment in Munich   **146–147**

Munich Street Finder   **148–157**

Munich at a Glance

Munich is Germany's third-largest city, and before the fall of the Berlin Wall it was dubbed the "unofficial capital of the country". Another name for it was the "village with a million inhabitants". Its metropolitan bustle, prosperity and high-tech industries exist alongside a rural, traditional atmosphere. The city has many parks, including the landscaped Englischer Garten, with the pretty River Isar that flows through it, and on fine days there are splendid views of the Alps, all of which combine to give the capital of Bavaria its unique atmosphere. It is also a city of culture. Munich has many historic monuments as well as outstanding museums and art galleries and several theatres.

Alte Pinakothek
Susanna and the Elders by Albrecht Altdorfer is one of the gallery's masterpieces of German Renaissance art *(see pp122–25)*.

The Glyptothek
Peace, a Roman copy of a sculpture by Cephisodotus, is one of the many classical sculptures on display in the Glyptothek, built by Ludwig I specifically to house such works of art *(see p120)*.

Theatinerkirche
This elegant Baroque church with its twin-towered façade is a prominent feature of the city's skyline *(see p83)*.

The Museums District
(See pp114–131)

Old Town (North)
(See pp)

Old Town (South)
(See pp58–73)

Asamkirche
The interior of the Church of St Johann Nepomuk exemplifies Baroque illusionism. Space, architectural elements, stuccowork, frescoes and the interplay of light and shadow combine to create the illusion of wave-like motion *(see pp70–71)*.

| 0 metres | 750 |
| 0 yards | 750 |

◄ Aerial view of the city center from the tower of Peterskirche

Siegestor
Based on the Arch of Constantine in Rome, this is a monument to the Bavarian army. It is crowned by a statue symbolizing Bavaria riding in a chariot drawn by four lions *(see p108)*.

Bayerisches Nationalmuseum
This museum contains interiors taken from elsewhere in Bavaria and preserved in their entirety. An example is the Gothic Weberstube from Augsburg *(see pp112–13)*.

Friedensengel
The Angel of Peace, standing on the right bank of the Isar, can be seen from afar. The column, 10m (59 ft) high, is topped by a gilded bronze angel *(see p96)*.

The University District
(See pp102–113)

Around the Isar
(See pp90–101)

Maximilianeum
This building, in what is known as the Maximilian style, now houses the Bavarian parliament *(see p95)*.

The Residenz
The Brunnenhof is one of the seven courtyards in the Residenz. It takes its name from the Mannerist Wittelsbach Fountain (Brunnen) that stands in the centre *(see pp78–81)*.

OLD TOWN (SOUTH)

Three gates, the Karlstor, Sendlinger Tor and Isartor, mark the boundary of the southern part of the Altstadt (Old Town). Marienplatz is the main square in this district, and it is also the central point of the whole of Munich. Marienplatz was once a market square, and it has witnessed all of the most important events in Munich's history.

Both tourists and local people come to admire the many fine historic buildings,

including the Frauenkirche, with its distinctive outline, and Peterskirche, the city's oldest church. South of Marienplatz is the Angerviertel. Because it was safe from flooding by the River Isar, this area was chosen by the legendary monks who founded Munich and gave the city its name. Life in the Angerviertel centres around the Viktualienmarkt, which has been held here for almost 200 years.

Sights at a Glance

Buildings and Squares
1. Karlstor
7. Neues Rathaus
10. Marienplatz
11. Altes Rathaus
13. Isartor
15. Viktualienmarkt
16. Gärtnerplatz
17. Ignaz-Günther-Haus
19. Jüdisches Zentrum Jakobsplatz
21. Asamhaus
22. Sendlinger Tor

Museums
5. Deutsches Jagd- und Fischereimuseum
14. Bier-und-Oktoberfestmuseum
18. Stadtmuseum

Churches
2. Bürgersaal
4. Michaelskirche
6. *Frauenkirche pp64–5*
9. Peterskirche
12. Heiliggeistkirche
20. *Asamkirche pp70–71*
23. Allerheiligenkirche am Kreuz
24. Damenstift St Anna

Eateries
3. Augustinerbräu
10. Ehem. Stadtschreiberei

☐ **Restaurants** *p276*
1. Bratwurstherzl
2. Café Glockenspiel
3. Fisch Poseidon
4. Milagros
5. Niederlassung
6. Nürnberger Bratwurst Glöckl am Dom
7. Prinz Myshkin
8. Ratskeller
9. Riva Tal
10. Sababa
11. Stadtkantine
12. Sushi Sano
13. The Victorian House
14. Viktus
15. Weisses Brauhaus
16. Weinhaus Neuner
17. Yum

0 metres 300
0 yards 300

See also Street Finder maps 3, 4, 5 & 6

◀ Interior of the Asamkirche, Church of St Johann Nepomuk

For map symbols *see back flap*

Street-by-Street: Around Marienplatz

Ever since Munich was founded, Marienplatz has been the city's architectural and commercial hub. The geographical centre of the city is marked by the Mariensäule (Column of the Virgin), from which all distances in Munich are measured. The square and the streets around it, which have been pedestrianized since the Munich Olympics in 1972, are always full of visitors. In one hour up to 18,000 tourists and shoppers pass through this area, rising to 22,000 on Saturdays.

❶ Karlstor
This gate was retained when the old city walls were demolished in 1791.

HERZOG-WILHELM STR.

HERZOG-MAX STR.

HERZOGSPITALSTR.

NEUHAUSER STR.

KAPELLENST

EISENMANNSTR.

Asamkirche →

❷ Bürgersaal
The austere façade of this church is decorated by a statue of the Madonna and Child by Franz Ableitner set over the portal.

Neuhauser Straße
is Munich's largest shopping street. It is filled with typical 19th-century buildings and with cafés and shops that enjoy the highest turnover in the whole of Germany.

❸ Augustinerbräu
This pub, one of the oldest in Munich, has elaborate interior decoration and a picturesque beer-garden courtyard.

| 0 metres | | 100 |
| 0 yards | | 100 |

Key
— Suggested route

❹ ★ Michaelskirche
The nave of the Church of St Michael, roofed by impressive barrel vaulting, is separated from the presbytery by a triumphal arch.

⑤ Deutsches Jagd- und Fischereimuseum
The German Hunting and Fishing Museum, located in a former Augustinian church, is reached from the presbytery side.

Locator Map
See Street Finder, maps 3, 5 & 6

⑥ ★ Frauenkirche
The figure of the Madonna and Sorrowful Christ comes from a 13th-century basilica. The Baroque gates were carved by Ignaz Günther.

⑦ ★ Neues Rathaus
The figures in the New Town Hall's chiming clock enact a joust and perform the Dance of the Coopers.

⑨ Peterskirche
The high altar of the Church of St Peter is decorated with a figure of the saint carved by Erasmus Grasser. Around it are the four Church Fathers, by Egid Quirin Asam.

⑪ Altes Rathaus
The tower of the Old Town hall was reconstructed after World War II on the basis of plans dating from 1493.

Heilig-Geist-Kirche

❶ Karlstor
Karl's Gate

Karlsplatz 5. **Map** 3 A2 (5 A2). Ⓢ or Ⓤ Karlsplatz-Stachus. 🚊 16, 17, 18, 20, 21, 22, 27, 28, N16, N20, N27.

A vestige of the medieval town's fortifications, this gate stands at the western entrance to the Old Town. Originally known as the Neuhauser Tor, the gate received its present name in 1791 in honour of Elector Karl Theodor, who recommended the demolition of the old walls to enable the city to expand.

Initially, the Karlstor had three towers. The tallest of them, the central tower, was destroyed in 1857 when the gunpowder that was stored there exploded. The gate was rebuilt, to a Neo-Gothic design by Arnold Zenetti. The bronze figures in the walls of the arches were taken from the old fountain in Marienplatz in 1865.

The medieval Karlstor, seen from the Old Town

❷ Bürgersaal

Neuhauser Str. 14. **Map** 3 A2 (5 B3). **Tel** 21 99 720. Ⓢ or Ⓤ Karlsplatz-Stachus. 🚊 16, 17, 18, 20, 21, 22, 27, 28, N16, N20, N27. **Open** 8am–7pm daily. Upper church hall: **Open** May–Oct: 11am–6pm daily; Nov–Apr: during mass only.

The name of this church reflects its original purpose as the headquarters of the Marian congre-gation. It was designed by Giovanni Antonio Viscardi and consecrated in 1778. The rather austere façade fronts a two-storey interior. The **lower church** contains the tomb of

The dazzling interior of the Bürgersaal, featuring 19th-century frescoes

the beatified Rupert Mayer, a staunch fighter against the Nazis. The **upper church**, which was the main meetingplace of the Marians, glitters with Rococo stuccowork by Joseph Georg Bader and paintings by Anton von Gumpp. During World War II the interior was damaged and some of the decoration has been restored. Surviving original features include the bas-relief on the high altar by Andreas Faistenberger, dating from 1710, the famous Guardian Angel of 1763 and the group of figures crowning the pulpit by Ignaz Günther.

❸ Augustinerbräu
Augustine Brewery

Neuhauser Str. 27. **Map** 3 A2 (5 B3). **Tel** 23 18 32 57. Ⓢ or Ⓤ Karl-splatz-Stachus. 🚊 16, 17, 18, 20, 21, 22, 27, 28, N16, N20, N27. **Open** 9am–midnight. 🖉

Two adjoining houses with picturesque 19th-century façades form part of the oldest brewery in Munich. The

Alfresco seating outside the Augustinerbräu

Augustinerbräu was founded by Augustinian monks and was mentioned as early as 1328. The historic interior of the brewery hall is a fine, and rare, example of the aesthetics and atmosphere of a Munich restaurant pre-dating World War I. An unusual feature is the Muschelsaal (Shell Hall), whose walls are lined with seashells, pebbles, decorative mouldings, busts and antlers. The brewery is divided into a restaurant and beer hall, with a delightful beer garden.

❹ Michaelskirche
St Michael's Church

Neuhauser Str. 6. **Map** 3 B2 (5 B3). Ⓢ or Ⓤ Karlsplatz-Stachus. 🚊 16, 17, 18, 20, 21, 22, 27, 28, N16, N20, N27. **Open** 10am–7pm Mon & Fri; 8am–7pm Tue–Thu & Sat; 7am–10:15pm Sun

The founder of this church, built for the Jesuit order, which was active in this area from 1559 onwards, was Duke Wilhelm V. Construction began in 1585, but when the tower collapsed in 1590, it was decided to enlarge the transept and to add a choir to designs by Friedrich Sustris. The Michaelskirche, which aimed to bolster the Counter-Reformation and reinforce the Jesuits' presence, is the largest late-Renaissance religious building north of the Alps. It is reminiscent of the church of Il Gesú in Rome.

The three-tier façade, with its double doorway, is an outstanding example of Mannerist architecture. Between the pilasters there are windows and rows of niches containing the figures of Bavarian and imperial rulers engaged in the expansion and defence of Christendom. The ground floor is dominated by a bronze figure of St Michael slaying the Dragon, with a figure of Christ the Saviour on his shield, made by Hubert Gerhard in 1585. The two portals, designed by Friedrich Sustris, lead in to a strikingly spacious interior. The barrel vaulting over the nave spans the second-largest space after St Peter's Basilica in Rome. The elongated choir ends with the massive high altar, where a painting by Christoph Schwarz depicts the fall of the rebellious angels. In the crypt beneath the choir lie members of the Wittelsbach family, including Maximilian I and Ludwig II, and the church's founder. Beside the church is a monastery and a college. The latter was built in 1585–97, also by Sustris. It is known as the Alte Akademie.

Statue from the Michaelskirche

❺ Deutsches Jagd- und Fischereimuseum
German Hunting and Fishing Museum

Neuhauser Str. 2. **Map** 3 B2 (5 B3). **Tel** 22 05 22. Ⓢ or Ⓤ Marienplatz. 🚋 16, 17, 18, 20, 21, 22, 27, 28, N16, N20, N27. **Open** 9:30am–5pm Fri–Wed; 9:30am–9pm Thu. 🅿

The largest collection of field sports equipment in the world is displayed in a white Augustinian basilica. The building's ecclesiastical origins are concealed by the shops in the aisle, through which the museum is entered from the street. The church was built in the late 13th century. It was rebuilt several times, and became the first building in Munich to be decorated in the Baroque style. In 1911 it was converted into a concert hall, and in 1966 the collection of the German Hunting and Fishing Museum, founded in 1938, was moved here from Schloss Nymphenburg. The collection includes hunting weapons, bags and sleighs, and 1,000 stuffed animals and birds in re-creations of their natural surroundings. There are also trophies and pictures of hunting scenes. The angling section illustrates the development of fishing tackle, and shows numerous specimens of fish.

❻ Frauenkirche
See pp64–5.

❼ Neues Rathaus
New Town Hall

Marienplatz 8. **Map** 3 B2 (6 D3). **Tel** 23 300. Ⓢ or Ⓤ Marienplatz. 🚾 🖼 Viewing tower: **Open** Nov–Apr: 10am–5pm Mon–Fri; May–Oct: 10am–7pm daily. Clock chimes: Nov–end Feb: 11am & noon; Mar–Oct: 11am, noon & 5pm.

In the second half of the 19th century, the civic authorities decided to build new headquarters for themselves. The chosen site was the north side of Marienplatz and 24 houses were demolished to clear a large plot of land. Construction lasted from 1867 to 1909. This monumental building with its six courtyards is a prime example of German pseudo-historical architecture, in this case mock-Netherlands Gothic. The decoration of the façade abounds in sculptures alluding to Bavaria's legends and history, images of local saints and many allegorical figures. The steeple is topped by a bronze figure of the Münchner Kindl (Munich Child), the symbol of the Bavarian capital. The clock in the tower is the fourth-largest chiming clock in Europe. Every day a concert is played on its 43 bells, with coloured copper figures dancing to its rhythms. The figures dance in two scenes: a knightly tournament of honour of the wedding of Duke Wilhelm V and Renata of Lotharingia, and the Schäfflertanz, or Dance of the Coopers (see pp36–7), which is performed in the streets of Munich to this day to commemorate the passing of an epidemic of the plague in 1515–17. In the evening, in the bays of the tower's seventh storey, appear the figures of a night-watchman blowing on his horn and the Angel of Peace blessing the Münchner Kindl. The spectacular viewing tower commands a fine view of the city.

The Neues Rathaus, a highly ornamented 19th-century public building

⊙ Frauenkirche

The Frauenkirche, the largest Gothic building in
southern Germany, was built in just 20 years from
1468–88, a record time for the period. It stands on
the site of an earlier Romanesque parish church.
The imposing triple-naved brick building was
begun by Jörg von Halsbach, and was continued
after his death by Lucas Rottaler. The domes that
crown the west towers, rising to a height of almost
100 m (330 ft), were not completed until 1525.
Since 1821, the Frauenkirche has been the seat
of the archbishopric of Munich and Freysing.

View of the Church
With its twin towers, the church's distinctive
silhouette is Munich's oldest and best-known
symbol. By law, no new building that may
obscure the view of the church is allowed.

★ Emperor's Tomb
A Mannerist canopy of black marble covers the tomb
of Emperor Ludwig IV of Bavaria. The sarcophagus is
surrounded by the figures of four kneeling knights,
personifications of War and Peace, and putti.

KEY

① **The onion domes** crowning the
towers are typical of the Renaissance.

② **The façade** has a rather severe
aspect. The towers have blind
windows at their angles and are
pierced by arched doors and
windows that echo the shape of
the central portal.

Entrance

Chorhauptkapelle
This painting by Jan Polack (c.1510), in the main chapel of the choir, shows the Virgin protecting members of the patrician Sänftl family.

VISITORS' CHECKLIST

Practical Information
Frauenplatz 1.
Map 3 B2 (5 C3).
Open 7am–7pm Sat–Wed, 7am–8:30pm Thu, 7am–6pm Fri. ⏰ 2pm Tue, Thu & Sun. 🗼 Tower: Apr–Oct: 10am–5pm, except Sun and public holidays.

Transport
Ⓢ or Ⓤ Marienplatz. 🚌 19.

★ Statue of St Christopher
This carved statue, sculpted by Hans Leinberger (c.1525), is an example of the dramatic style of the late Gothic period.

★ Stalls
Like the other figures that decorate the stalls, this bust of St James was made by Erasmus Grasser.

Cathedral Interior
Legend tells that the cathedral's builder wagered with the Devil that no window could be seen from within. From the spot where the Devil made his footprint, only a wall of pillars is seen.

"Memminger Altar"
This altar was built in 1500, incorporating reliefs by Ignaz Günther and a Rococo Madonna.

Marienplatz, Munich's bustling and historic central square

❽ Marienplatz
St Mary's Square

Map 3 B2 (6 D3). Ⓢ or Ⓤ Marienplatz. 🚇 Dec.

Ever since the city was planned by Heinrich der Löwe, Marienplatz has been Munich's focal point. Until 1807 it was a marketplace. It acquired its present name in 1854, when Munich's citizens asked the Virgin Mary to protect them from a cholera epidemic. For centuries the square was the place where major public events, proclamations, tournaments and executions took place.

Today it is the venue for the famous Christkindlmarkt (Christmas Fair), which is held in the days leading up to Christmas. The square is dominated by the Neues Rathaus (New Town Hall).

Crowds of tourists and local people gather in the square every day to watch the mechanical figures on the clock tower perform their concert. The Mariensäule (Column of the Virgin) in the square was erected in 1638 in gratitude for the end of the Swedish invasion.

The golden statue of the Virgin (1593) is by Hubert Gerhard and the four putti around the plinth (1639) are by Ferdinand Murmann. The putti are shown overcoming hunger, war, heresy and pestilence. Another attraction of the square is the 19th-century Fischbrunnen (Fish Fountain), which was rebuilt after being destroyed in World War II.

❾ Peterskirche
St Peter's Church

Rindermarkt 1. **Map** 3 C, D2 (6 D3). Ⓢ or Ⓤ Marienplatz. Church: **Open** 7am–7pm daily (closed Wed pm). Tower: **Open** 9am–6:30pm Mon–Fri, 10am–6:30pm Sat, Sun & public hols (to 5:30pm in winter).

St Peter's Church, standing on the highest point of the Old Town, is Munich's earliest public building. Built in the 12th century, the basilica formed part of the monastery from which the city received it's name (*Mönchen* meaning "monks"). In 1278–94 it was replaced by a new church in the Gothic style. In the 14th century the twin towers were replaced with a single tower. In the 17th century the church was redecorated in Baroque style, and in the 18th century

The Peterskirche, with its famous tower, Munich's oldest church

was remodelled in the Rococo style. The stuccowork is by Johann Baptist Zimmermann and others. The church's famous tower, known as Alter Peter (Old Peter), has eight clocks, seven bells and a viewing gallery that offers a splendid view over the Old Town. The interior of the church has unusually lavish decoration. The high altar is crowned with a statue of St Peter (1492) by Erasmus Grasser, surrounded by the Church Fathers (1732) by Egid Quirin Asam. The choir contains five figures (1517) by Jan Polack with scenes from the life of St Peter.

Late Gothic side entrance to the Ehem. Stadtschreiberei

❿ Ehem. Stadtschreiberei
Former City Writers' Guild

Burgstraße 5. **Map** 3 C2 (6 D3). **Tel** 22 80 74 20. Ⓢ or Ⓤ Marienplatz. Restaurant: **Open** 10am–noon Mon–Sat.

A visit to Munich's oldest surviving town house is the perfect excuse to enjoy a beer and some food in a late Gothic cloistered courtyard. In 1510 the town council bought this pair of houses between Burgstraße and Dienerstraße. The house on Burgstraße, rebuilt in 1551/2, housed the offices of the city writers' guild (Stadtschreiberhaus) from 1552–1612. The house has an interesting façade with a large window in the centre. The perfectly preserved large main doorway conceals the entrance passage. To the right of the façade is a small late

Gothic side entrance framed by a donkey-back arch. The façade, which had been under restoration, was unveiled in 1964, revealing most of the restored Renaissance decoration executed by Hans Mielich in 1552. An attractive addition to the courtyard is a late Gothic tower with a spiral staircase.

⓫ Altes Rathaus
Old Town Hall

Marienplatz 15. **Map** 3 C2 (6 D3). Ⓢ or Ⓤ Marienplatz. **Closed** to visitors. Spielzeugmuseum: **Tel** 29 40 01. **Open** 10am 5:30pm daily. 🖼

The original Old Town Hall, dating from 1310, was replaced by a new one in 1464 which is known today as the Altes Rathaus (Old Town Hall). It was built by Jörg von Halsbach, who also built the Frauenkirche. The town hall was rebuilt on many occasions, most recently in 1861–4, when it acquired its present Neo-Gothic character. In 1877 and then in 1934 two gateways were cut through in order to accommodate the increasing flow of traffic.

The oldest part of the building is the tower of 1180–1200, part of the original city fortifications. Since 1983 it has housed the **Spielzeugmuseum** (Toy Museum), which as well as antique doll's houses, tin cars and copper soldiers contains a display tracing the history of the Barbie doll.

Clock on the tower of the Altes Rathaus

The Gothic interior of the Altes Rathaus survives. The ceremonial hall occupying the ground floor has wide wooden barrel vaulting, and a wall with a frieze of 96 coats of arms dating from 1478. There are plans to use this hall to exhibit the Moriscos (Moriskentänzer) that Erasmus Grasser carved in 1480. The figures currently on display here are copies of the originals that can be seen in the Stadtmuseum.

The Pentecost, by Ulrich Loth, in the Heilig-Geist-Kirche

⓬ Heilig-Geist-Kirche
Church of the Holy Spirit

Prälat-Miller-Weg 3. **Map** 3 C2 (6 D3). Ⓢ or Ⓤ Marienplatz. **Open** 8:30am–7pm daily

The Church of the Holy Spirit is one of Munich's oldest buildings, ranking in importance alongside the Cathedral and the Peterskirche. It stands on the site of a chapel, a hospital and a pilgrims' hostel. In the mid-13th century a hospital church was built here. This was replaced by a church in the 14th century. In 1724 the church was decorated in the Baroque style. The fine vaulting and stuccowork are by the Asam brothers. In 1729 a tower was added. Its Neo-Baroque façade dates from 1895, when the hospital next to the church was demolished.

The interior is a fine example of the combination of Gothic and late Baroque elements. The ceiling frescoes depict scenes from the hospital's history. The high altar was made by Nikolaus Stuber and Antonio Matteo in 1728–30 and rebuilt after World War II.

Original elements of the altar include the painting of the Pentecost (1644) by Ulrich Loth and the flanking angels by Johann Georg Greiff. The bronze figures in the vestibule (1608) by Hans Krumpper originally formed part of the tomb of Ferdinand of Bavaria.

⓭ Isartor
Isar Gate

Tal 50. **Map** 3 C3 (6 E4). Ⓢ Isartor. 🚊 Valentinmusäum: **Tel** 22 32 66. **Open** 11am–5:30pm Mon, Tue & Thu, 11am–6pm Fri–Sun.

Entry into the city from the south-east is through the Isartor. This gate is the only vestige of the city's original fortifications, and it has been preserved in its original form. The central tower was built in 1337, and in 1429–33 two eight-sided towers, connected by walls, were added. In the 19th century arcades were made in the towers. They were decorated with friezes representing the triumphal procession of Ludwig IV of Bavaria after his victory at the Battle of Ampfing (1322).

The southern tower houses the **Valentin-Karlstadt-Musäum**, a museum dedicated to the actor and comedian Karl Valentin (1882–1948), a master of the absurd who wrote theatre sketches and short films. The collections include many of his scenes, among them *The Vesuvius that Doesn't Smoke Because it is Forbidden in the Museum* and *The Hook on which the Artist Hung his Learned Profession*.

The central fortified tower of Isartor

⑭ Bier-und Oktober-festmuseum

Sterneckerstr. 2. **Map** 3 C3. **Tel** 24 23 16 07. Ⓢ or Ⓤ Isartor. 🚋 17, 18. **Open** 1–7pm Tue–Sat. 📷 📷

The building housing the Bier-und Oktoberfestmuseum was constructed under the city expansion scheme, spearheaded by Ludwig IV of Bavaria, after the great fire of 1327.

The museum covers both the history of beer and the Oktoberfest, telling the story of how the festival is an important part of Munich's tradition. Visitors can learn how beer was first made in ancient Egypt, as well as how the beer-making process developed in Munich itself. Up until 1870, beer was only brewed in the city during the winter months, as ice from the lakes was necessary for the cooling process. After the invention of refrigerators, beer began to be brewed all year round, with a rapid expansion in the number of breweries in Munich. At one time there were as many as 70 breweries in the ancient city; today just six remain.

A tankard from the Bier-und Oktoberfestmuseum

Visitors will also get to see a collection of artifacts from Oktoberfests over the years, including a vast collection of beer tankards. The museum has a restaurant serving beer and typical Bavarian snacks.

⑮ Viktualienmarkt
Food Market

Between Petersplatz and Frauenstr. **Map** 3 C3 (6 D4). Ⓢ or Ⓤ Marienplatz. 🚋 132.

This is Munich's oldest and most picturesque market. Since the beginning of the 19th century food of all kinds has been sold here – fruit and vegetables, milk, meat, the finest French wines and cheeses, fish and shellfish and exotic delicacies from all corners of the world, albeit at fairly high prices. All

A colourful stall at the popular, lively and historic Viktualienmarkt

sorts of people, from ordinary shoppers to tourists, can be seen here. Local customs include eating white sausage (Weißwürst), sipping hot soup and drinking beer in a beer-garden around a decorated maypole. The last day of the carnival is famed for the masked dance of the market women.

The fountain that was erected to commemorate various German cabaret artists, such as Karl Valentin, emphasizes the popular nature of the square.

⑯ Gärtnerplatz

Road map 3 C3 (6 D5). Ⓤ Frauenhoferstr. 🚋 16, 18. 🚌 52, 62. Gärtnerplatztheater: **Closed** for renovation until 2015. Staatstheater am Gärtnerplatz: **Tel** 21 85 19 60. Box office: **Open** 10am–6pm Mon–Fri, 10am–1pm Sat.

The hexagonal square lying at the intersection of Reichenbachstraße, Corneliusstraße and Klenzestraße is named after

The 19th-century Gärtnerplatz, a green space in the city

the prominent 19th-century architect Friedrich von Gärtner. It is the focal point of the district known as the Gärtnerplatzviertel, which was built in the second half of the 19th century. It was the first large district of purpose-built apartment blocks in Munich to be designed in a unified style.

In 1864–5 a theatre was built on the south side of Gärtnerplatz. It was designed by Franz Michael Reiffenstuel and was known as the Gärtnerplatztheater. It was a slightly less upmarket response to the courtly Nationaltheater. Its decorative façade stands out among the somewhat monotonous architecture that surrounds it and is considered by many to be the most beautiful theatre in Munich.

The **Gärtnerplatztheater** stages minor operas, operettas and musicals. Rare works are often staged, including operas that have never been performed in Munich before.

⑰ Ignaz-Günther-Haus
Ignaz Günther House

St-Jakobs-Platz 15. **Map** 3 B3 (5 C4). Ⓢ or Ⓤ Marienplatz. Ⓤ Sendlinger Tor. **Closed** to public (staircase & hall may sometimes be viewed during business hours).

Ignaz Günther (1725–75) was one of Europe's finest Rococo sculptors. He worked throughout southern Germany, but primarily in Munich. His work can be seen in the Peterskirche, Bürgersaal, Frauenkirche, the grounds of Schloss Nymphenburg and Schleißheim Palace as well as the churches and abbeys of Upper and Lower Bavaria. In

1754 he became court sculptor to the Wittelsbachs. He moved into the house on St Jakob's Platz in 1761.

The Ignaz-Günther-Haus is a very fine example of late Gothic residential architecture. It still has its small courtyard with a central fountain. The reception room on the first floor has an early 16th-century wooden ceiling. The façade on the side of the Oberanger contains a statue of the Virgin carved by Günther and known as the Hausmadonna. This is a copy of the original, which is housed in the Bayerisches Nationalmuseum in Munich.

The house and studio of the renowned sculptor Ignaz Günther

⑱ Stadtmuseum
Town Museum

St-Jakobs-Platz 1. **Map** 3 B3 (5 C4). **Tel** 23 32 23 70. Ⓢ or Ⓤ Marienplatz. Ⓤ Sendlinger Tor. **Open** 10am–6pm Tue–Sun. 🖼

Six adjoining buildings house the Town Museum. Two of them, the Marstall and the Zeughaus, were built in the 15th century as granaries but later became the city's stables and arsenal. During the rebellions of 1848 the citizens of Munich broke into the Zeughaus tower. However, the weapons that they found there had rusted and were useless.

In the second half of the 19th century, this arsenal building was used as a display space for the embryonic museum of local history. At this time a major campaign was under way to collect antique objects from the city's inns and attics, hospitals, orphanages, churches and pawnshops.

In addition to the 1,500 objects that were amassed in this way, a huge collection of etchings with a Munich theme was purchased. The Museum of History finally opened in 1888. As the collection grew, a total of four additional wings were added to the original buildings. The museum was given its present name in 1954.

The Stadtmuseum as it is today is divided into sections, each of which operates independently, organizing various temporary exhibitions. As well as permanent exhibitions of old weapons, crafts, folk art, townscapes and collections of posters, there are the collections of the Puppet Theatre and Museum of Musical Instruments, the Photographic Museum and the Fashion Museum.

There is also an exhibition which illustrates the history of Munich with over 400 items on display. Amateur filmmakers can view the rare film archives of the Film Museum, which enjoys international renown, especially for reconstructions of silent films.

Those interested in interior design will be drawn to the Urban Interiors section. The most valuable and intriguing items in the museum are the ten famous Moriskentänzer (Moriscos), made by Erasmus Grasser in about 1480. These were originally designed for the ceremonial hall of the Old Town.

⑲ Jüdisches Zentrum Jakobsplatz
Jewish Centre Jakobsplatz

St.-Jakobs-Platz 16. **Map** 3 B3 (5 C4). Ⓢ or Ⓤ Marienplatz. **Tel** 23 39 60 96. **Open** Jewish Museum: 10am–6pm Tue–Sun. 🖼 🔳 juedisches zentrumjakobsplatz.de 🔳 juedisches-museum. muenchen.de

The Main Synagogue Ohel Jakob, the Jewish Community Centre of Munich and Upper Bavaria, and the Jewish Museum, constitute a prestigious centre for the Jewish community at St. Jakobsplatz. Commissioned with the design of the entire complex were the Saarbrücken based architects Wandel, Hoefer and Lorch.

The **Jewish Museum** is housed in a cube-shaped, free standing building. The transparent ground floor lobby, glazed on all sides, emphasizes the museum's role as a place for open discussion. Three floors of exhibitions, plus a library and a learning centre, all offer extensive information on Jewish culture and history and highlight important aspects of contemporary Jewish life.

The Synagogue, also cube-shaped, is crowned by a light-flooded roof. The Community Centre contains the administrative department, the rabbinate, conference rooms, a kindergarden, a public full-time school, a youth and arts centre and a kosher restaurant. It is a popular venue for events. With this combination it reflects the religious, cultural and social demands of contemporary life.

Model of a shop with wax figures, an exhibit at the Stadtmuseum

⑳ Asamkirche

The Asamkirche, or Church of St Johann Nepomuk, was built in 1733–46. It was funded, designed and executed by the Asam brothers, the most famous builders and decorators of the time. Drawing on the full effects of Baroque artistic expression, they created a mysterious theatrical illusion of another world. The façade, set upon a plinth that imitates natural stone, gives no hint of the splendour within. The nave, with its low-key lighting, is full of striking architectural details, rich stuccowork and masterpieces of fresco painting.

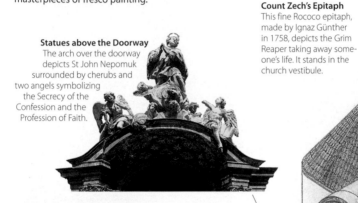

Count Zech's Epitaph
This fine Rococo epitaph, made by Ignaz Günther in 1758, depicts the Grim Reaper taking away someone's life. It stands in the church vestibule.

Statues above the Doorway
The arch over the doorway depicts St John Nepomuk surrounded by cherubs and two angels symbolizing the Secrecy of the Confession and the Profession of Faith.

Church Interior
The exquisite combination of architecture, painting, light and shadow draws attention away from the proportions of the interior. The nave is 28 m (92 ft) long and just 8.80 m (29 ft) wide, proportions that were dictated by the relatively small ground space available.

Bas-relief on the West Doors
The top left-hand carving on the doors of the west façade depicts St John Nepomuk being thrown into prison.

Entrance

★ Painted Ceiling
The ceiling is covered with accomplished *trompe-l'oeil* paintings exe-cuted by Cosmas Damian Asam in 1735. They depict scenes from the life and martyrdom of St John Nepomuk.

VISITORS' CHECKLIST

Practical Information
Sendlinger Str. 62. **Map** 3 A3.
Open 7:30am–6pm Mon–Fri,
8am–7pm Sat (to 3pm Sun).
🕓 5pm Tue, Thu & Fri; 8:30am
Wed, 10am Sun.

Transport
Ⓤ Sendlinger Tor.
🚃 16, 17, 18, 27. 🚌 52, 152.

Detail of the Gallery
The undulating gallery that encircles the interior divides the walls of the nave and the high altar into two distinct parts.

★ High Altar
The high altar contains a glass sarcophagus in which lies a robed wax figure of a prelate representing St John Nepomuk.

Pulpit
The pulpit is reached directly from the adjacent presbytery to the east. It is surrounded by a relief with scenes from the life of St John the Baptist and symbols of the Evangelists.

Façade of the Asamhaus, lavishly decorated with allegorical scenes

❹ Asamhaus

Assam House

Sendlinger Str. 61. **Map** 3 A3 (5 B4).
Ⓤ Sendlinger Tor. 🚋 16, 17, 18, 27, 28, N16, N27. 🚌 62. **Closed** to visitors.

It would be difficult to find a more unusual artist's home. While Cosmas Damian Asam decided to settle in the suburban Maria Einsiedel Palace, which he renovated, his brother Egid Quirin Asam purchased four adjoining properties on Sendlinger Straße in 1729–33. He converted them into his own residence, with a church and presbytery in addition.

This was the first time that an artist had built his own house next to a church of his own design (there was even an interior window looking from the house towards the high altar).

Egid Quirin Asam added stucco decorations to the medieval façades, depicting Christian and Classical motifs – personifications of the fine arts, poetry and music are watched over by St Joseph, patron saint of craftsmen, who is surrounded by symbols of Faith, Hope and Mercy. A relief depicting Perfection and the initials IHS crowning the entire imagery symbolize the Christian concept of heaven.

On the left the artist gives a vision of the world of Antiquity, whose ideals were adopted by Baroque artists. Thus Pallas Athenae leads a childlike figure into the world of art and science under the aegis of Pegasus, with Apollo watching over

The Asam Brothers

The fresco painter Cosmas Damian Asam (1686–1739) and the sculptor and stuccoist Egid Quirin Asam (1692–1750) were taught by their father, the painter Georg Asam, and studied briefly at the Accademia di San Luca in Rome. Cosmas Damian married twice and had a total of 13 children, while Egid Quirin remained a bachelor. They worked in partnership in Bavaria from 1714 onwards, creating masterpieces of late Baroque art in Weltenburg, Rohr, Osterhofen and Munich. They were adept at

Portrait of Egid Quirin Asam in the Asamkirche presbytery

combining architectural, sculptural and paint effects, creating what was called *theatrum sacrum*. This was based on the interaction of shapes modelled by means of light and shadow.

them all. These visions are complemented by the world of sensations, which are represented by Cupid, satyrs and fauns.

❷ Sendlinger Tor

Sendlinger-Tor-Platz. **Map** 3 A3 (5 A4).
Ⓤ Sendlinger Tor. 🚋 16, 17, 18, 27, 28, N16, N27. 🚌 62.

The southern end of the bustling thoroughfare known as Sendlinger Straße passes through a large Gothic city gate that is overgrown with vines.

The Sendlinger Tor was first mentioned in 1318 and, with the Karlstor and Isartor, this gate is all that remains of the secondary city fortifications that were built in 1285–1347 during the reigns of Ludwig II the Severe and Ludwig IV of Bavaria. An important trade

route to Italy via Innsbruck once passed along here.

The tall gatehouse that formerly stood in the centre of the Sendlinger Tor was demolished in 1808. The octagonal tower which then functioned as a gatehouse dates from the end of the 14th century. In 1906, because of the increasing volume of traffic, the three arches were converted into a single large arch, with pedestrian arches made through the side towers.

Beyond the gate is Sendlinger Tor Platz, a square named after the gate. It is one of Munich's crossroads, with pedestrian subways leading to the metro station. The Sonnenstraße, which continues from here, was the first 19th- century thoroughfare to be built along the course of the old city walls.

The medieval Sendlinger Tor, now overgrown with vines

Its name, meaning "sun street", reflects its bright, open design compared with the narrow, shady passages of the Old Town. Sendlinger-Tor-Platz has a park on the west side with St Matthew's Church rising over it.

Baroque tombstone set into the façade of the Allerheiligenkirche

㉓ Allerheiligenkirche am Kreuz
All Hallows' Church

Kreuzstr. 10. **Map** 3 A3 (5 B4).
Ⓤ Sendlinger Tor, Karlsplatz-Stachus. **Open** 8am–8pm daily.

All Hallows' Church was built in 1478 by Jörg von Halsbach, and was the first cemetery church in the parish of St Peter. In the past, four streets converged here, hence the name "am Kreuz" ("at the crossing").

The church's bare brick walls, Gothic vaults and tall steeple make it a prominent landmark in Kreuzstraße. The interior was refurbished during the Baroque era, so that the only vestiges of its Gothic appearance are the web vaulting over the nave, fragments of a fresco of Christ in a mandorla and a crucifix made by Hans Leinberger in 1520.

Fine examples of the transitional style of art that developed between the Mannerist period and led into the Baroque can be seen in the tomb of the banker Gietz (1627) by Hans Krumpper, and in the depiction of the Virgin appearing before St Augustine on the high altar, which was created by Hans

Rottenhammer in 1614. Today Allerheiligenkirche is a Uniate (Greek Catholic) church.

㉔ Damenstift St Anna
Church of St Anne

Damenstiftstr. 1.
Map 3 A2 (5 B3).
Ⓤ Karlsplatz-Stachus, Marienplatz. **Open** 8am–8pm daily.

Baroque doorway of the Damenstift St Anna

Princess Henrietta of Savoy, founder of the Theatine Church, brought the Salesian order of sisters to Munich in 1667. During the 18th century the order acquired its own church, which was designed by the Gunetzrhainer brothers. In time the convent passed into the hands of an order of aristocratic ladies, hence the name "Damenstift". Today the building houses a high school for girls. The façade is in the late Baroque style, as is the opulent decoration of the interior, which was executed

by the Asam brothers. After suffering total destruction during World War II, the painting inside the church was restored in sepia, as black-and-white photographs were the only existing record of the original decorative scheme. The paint-ings depict the oath of angels, the Glory of St Mary and St Anne, and the concert of angels (above the gallery). The realistic group of the Last Supper to the right of the high altar is unusually lifelike. The life-sized statues sitting at the table and gesticulating were probably copied from Spanish originals. This single-nave church, with side chapels behind mighty arches and a presbytery at one end, is a typically Baroque attempt to combine the centrally planned church with the elongated model.

The intersecting interior spaces of the Baroque Damenstift St Anna

OLD TOWN (NORTH)

The northern part of the Old Town (Altstadt) was once defined by the fortified city walls. Today it is enclosed by the Altstadtring (ring road). The principal thoroughfares traversing the Old Town are Theatinerstraße and Residenzstraße. West of Theatinerstraße is the old Kreuzviertel district, with Promenadeplatz its hub.

The Old Town has modern shopping streets, and also many fine 17th- and 18th-century palaces and churches – two of them being the Theatinerkirche and Dreifaltigkeitskirche.

To the east lies the former Graggenau district. At the Alter Hof (Old Court), the first seat of the Wittelsbach family, there is a maze of medieval streets and buildings, among which is the Hofbräuhaus, Munich's most renowned brewery. The majestic Residenz overlooks the Hofgarten (Palace Gardens).

Max-Joseph-Platz, a stately square surrounded by fine Neo-Classical buildings, marks the beginning of the grand Maximilianstraße, which is a practical example of 19th-century ideals of integral town planning.

Sights at a Glance

Churches

6 Theatinerkirche (St Kajetan)
7 Salvatorkirche
13 Dreifaltigkeitskirche

Museum

11 Literaturhaus

Garden

23 Hofgarten

Eatery

18 Hofbräuhaus

Theatres

20 Münchner Kammerspiele im Schauspielhaus

Historic Buildings

1 *Residenz (pp78–81)*
3 Eilles-Hof
4 Palais Preysing
5 Feldherrnhalle
8 Erzbischöfliches Palais
9 Palais Porcia
10 Palais Neuhaus-Preysing
12 Künstlerhaus
15 Palais Töerring-Jettenbach
16 Münzhof
17 Alter Hof
21 Marstall
22 Bayerische Staatskanzlei

Streets and Squares

2 Max-Joseph-Platz
14 Promenadeplatz
19 Maximilianstraße

☐ Restaurants *pp276–7*

1 Austernkeller
2 Bar München
3 Dallmayr
4 Due Passi
5 Ederer
6 Eisbach
7 Garden Restaurant
8 Kulisse
9 Le Stollberg
10 Mark's Restaurant
11 Restaurant Pfistermühle
12 Spatenhaus an der Oper
13 Tavernetta
14 Trader Vic's
15 Zum Franciskaner

See also Street Finder maps 3, 4, 5 & 6

◀ The famed Hofbrauhaus brewery in Munich city center

For map symbols *see back flap*

Street-by-Street: Around the Residenz

The Residenz is set in the most elegant part of Munich, an area characterized mainly by the Wittelsbach residences, numerous Baroque palaces and the fine silhouettes of the Theatinerkirche and the opera house. The streets leading to the Altstadtring are lined with cafés and shops selling luxury goods. This area is also the centre of Munich's cultural life, with several theatres as well as concert and banqueting halls within the residences themselves.

7 Salvatorkirche
Until the end of the 18th century this old chapel stood in the middle of the city cemetery. It is now a Uniate church.

6 ★ Theatinerkirche
The Baroque coat of arms on the façade of the Theatine Church, designed by Ignaz Günther, features the crests of Bavaria and Saxony.

8 Erzbischöfliches Palais
The façade of the Archbishop's Palace was decorated by the great stuccoist Johann Baptist Zimmermann.

3 Eilles-Hof
The arcades of this enchanting late Gothic courtyard, hidden behind the Residenzstraße, are an oasis of peace.

2 Max-Joseph-Platz
This monument to Maximilian I Joseph was erected in the square ten years after the king's death. He had opposed it, believing that the pose did not convey sufficient majesty.

Key

— Suggested route

❺ Feldherrnhalle
This hall was built in 1841–44 in honour of Johann Tilly and Karl Philipp von Wrede, the Bavarian field marshals after whom it is named. Their statues stand inside the loggia.

Locator Map
See Street Finder maps 3, 4, 5 & 6

❹ Preysing-Palais
This was the first late Baroque palace in Munich to be decorated with Regency elements. It is also the first work of the court architect Joseph Effner.

❶ ★ Residenz
The wooden carvings that decorate the interior of the Residenz's Cuvilliés-Theater feature allegories of the arts and mythology.

| 0 metres | 50 |
| 0 yards | 50 |

The Nationaltheater doubles as the National Opera. It was famed for operas by Richard Wagner staged here for Ludwig II.

❶ Residenz

The Residenz was the home of the Wittelsbach dynasty up until 1918. The buildings date back to 1385, when the Neuveste was built in the part of Munich enclosed by city walls. In the 16th century the Antiquarium and another wing were added, creating the Grottenhof courtyard. The Kaiserhof was added in the 17th century. After rebuilding in the Baroque and Rococo periods, the ensemble was enclosed by Königsbau and Festsaalbau in the 19th century.

★ Hofkapelle
The Princely Chapel, with intricate ceiling stuccowork, was designed by Hans Krumpper in 1601–3.

Patrona Bavariae
The 17th-century façade is decorated with a bronze statue of St Mary, patron saint of Bavaria, by Hans Krumpper.

Grottenhof
The courtyard contains a grotto decorated with volcanic crystals and colourful seashells, and a gilded bronze sculpture of Mercury.

KEY

① **Kaiserhof**

② **Apothekenhof**

③ **Cuvilliés-Theater** is the Residenz's old theatre. It is one of the finest Rococo theatres in the world.

④ **Brunnenhof**

Nibelungensäle
This mural by Julius Schnorr von Carolsfeld, showing Hagen von Tronje defeating Siegfried, is one of the paintings of the *Nibelungenlied*.

★ **Antiquarium**
Built in 1569–71, this great hall is the largest Renaissance ceremonial hall north of the Alps, and the oldest surviving part of the Residenz.

VISITORS' CHECKLIST

Practical Information
Max-Joseph-Platz 3.
Map 3 C1. **Tel** (089) 29 06 71.
Open Apr–mid-Oct: 9am–6pm daily; mid-Oct–Mar: 10am–5pm daily.
Cuvilliés-Theater: **Open** Apr–Jul: 2–6pm Mon–Sat, 9am–6pm Sun & public hols; Aug–mid-Sep: 9am–6pm; mid-Sep–mid-Oct: 2–6pm Mon–Sat, 9am–6pm Sun & public hols; mid-Oct–Mar: 2–5pm Mon–Sat, 10am–5pm Sun & public hols.
Staatliche Münzsammlung: Residenzstr. 1 **Tel** 22 72 21.
Open 10am–5pm Tue–Sat.

Transport
U Odeonsplatz. 100. 19.

② ③ ④

ntrance

★ **Schatzkammer**
This 17th-century ornamental cup is made of rhinoceros horn and gold-plated silver. It can be admired here alongside numerous other works of art.

★ **Schatzkammer**
The crown and orb of the Bavarian kings were made by Martin Guillaume Biennais in 1806 when Bavaria was recognized as a kingdom and Maximilian I was proclaimed king. However, the coronation itself did not take place.

Exploring the Residenz

A thorough exploration of this unusual palace takes a few days. The first parts to see are the three monumental façades and the many courtyards that are open to the public. The interior of the Residenz is open to the public as the Residenzmuseum. There is separate admission to the Schatzkammer and the Cuvilliés-Theater. Due to on-going restoration, there are always some parts of the museum that are closed to the public.

The Grottenhof, which exudes an air of cool Mannerist elegance

The Courtyards

The courtyard that lies on the side of the Residenzstraße features two Mannerist door ways with figures representing the four cardinal virtues: Justice, Prudence, Fortitude and Temperance.

The south doorway leads into the Kapellenhof (Chapel Yard). It is enclosed by the Residenz's tower, built in 1615. The Grottenhof (Grotto Court) is visible through the gates to the right. This Mannerist courtyard, designed by Friedrich Sustris, encloses the Perseus Fountain.

The north doorway leads to the Kaiserhof, the centre of that part of the Residenz that was built in Maximilian style in the early 17th century. This leads in turn to the monumental Apothekenhof, which is closed on its northern side by Festsaalbau (Ceremonial Hall Wing) of 1835–42.

Parallel to the Antiquarium is the elongated octagonal Brunnenhof, with the famous Wittelsbach Fountain by Hans Krumpper and Hubert Gerhard (1611–23). It shows Otto I surrounded by personifications of the rivers of Bavaria.

Museums and Rooms

Access to the Residenzmuseum is from Max-Joseph-Platz and through Königsbau, built by Leo von Klenze in 1826–35. Visits start from the vestibule and the two garden halls leading to the Ahnengalerie (Ancestral Gallery) with its lavish stuccowork. and 121 portraits of the Wittelsbachs. After passing François Cuvilliés' porcelain

Tureen from the Silberkammern

The Grüne Galerie, an example of Rococo interiors at their finest

cabinet, visitors reach the Grottenhof and the Antiquarium, the oldest part of the Residenz, which was built in 1568–71 for Prince Albrecht V. The first floor once housed a library and a richly decorated reception hall containing classical sculpture. The final room on this floor is the Schwarzer Saal (Black Hall) of 1590, with *trompe-l'oeil* paintings on the ceiling. It in turn leads to the Gelbe Treppe (Yellow Stairs), where there is a statue of Venus Italica by Antonio Canova, and rooms in which European and Oriental porcelain and Persian divans are displayed.

Beyond the bedrooms of Maximilian III Joseph and his wife, designed by Cuvilliés in 1763, is the Allerheiligengang (All Saints Passage). It is decorated with 18 paintings by Carl Rottmann, which were moved here from the Hofgarten arcades in 1966. The Charlottentrakt that leads away from here is named after Princess Karoline Charlotte Auguste von Bayern, daughter of Maximilian I Joseph, who once lived in the Residenz. Next is the 17th century Trierzimmer (Trier Room). The ceiling was painted by Peter Candid and others and the walls are hung with tapestries dating from 1604–15. The St Georgs-Rittersaal (Knights' Hall) leads to the Reiches Zimmer (Rich Room), built in the 1730s to a design by Cuvilliés, with early Rococo decoration. These rooms also include the Grüne Galerie (Green Gallery), Paradeschlafzimmer (Parade Bedroom) and Spiegelkabinett (Mirrored Cabinet).

Other notable rooms include the Ahnengalerie (Ancestral Gallery) and Porzellankabinett (Porcelain Cabinet), Reiches Zimmer (Rich Room), Päpstliches Zimmer (Pope's Room), the Nibelungensäle and the large collections of European porcelain that are exhibited

The Reiche Kapelle, a masterpiece of encrusted ornamentation

in the seven Porzellankammern (Porcelain Rooms). Also accessible is the lavishly decorated Hofkapelle, designed by Hans Krumpper in 1601–14. It is adjacent to the Paramentenkammern, a treasury of liturgical objects. The royal staircase leads to the Reliquienkammer, which contains an interesting collection of reliquaries from the different workshops of the Augsburg monasteries.

The Reiche Kapelle is a true masterpiece of religious Mannerist architecture. The private oratory of Maximilian I, it was built in 1607 by Hans Krumpper and sparkles with coloured marble, stuccowork, stone plaques and terracotta reliefs, and scagliola (imitation marble).

The Silberkammern and Hartschiersaal nearby house 3,500 pieces of silver plate from the Wittelsbach Service, made in the 18th and 19th centuries. The Steinzimmer (Stone Rooms) beyond are named after their stone walls.

A visit to the 17th-century part of the Residenz ends in the Vierschimmelsaal (Hall of the Four White Horses) and the Kaisersaal (Imperial Hall), where there is a statue of Tellus Bavarica (1594), which once crowned the circular church in the Hofgarten.

Schatzkammer

In 1565, Albrecht V ordered that the jewels of the Wittelsbachs were not to be sold after his death. This led to the creation of a treasure house. To it Elector Karl Theodor added the contents of the Palatinate treasury from Heidelberg, Düsseldorf and Mannheim. Later, religious works of art confiscated after the secularization of the knightly orders, and the insignia of the newly founded kingdom of Bavaria were added.

Decorative chain made in 1575

Highlights include the royal insignia, the cyborium (covered cup) of Arnulf of Carinthia (c. 890), the

Figure of St George (1597), inlaid with precious stones

Rappoltsteiner Cup (1540), a statue of St George (1597) and royal insignia of 1806.

Cuvillies-Theater (Altes Residenztheater)

Europe's finest surviving Rococo theatre was designed in 1751–53 by François Cuvilliés in collaboration with Johann Baptist Straub and Johann Baptist Zimmermann.

The predominantly gold and red wood carvings on the balconies, royal loggia and proscenia still survive. The first performance of Mozart's *Idomeneo* took place here in 1781. Destroyed in World War II, the theatre was rebuilt in the Apothekenhof, using the surviving original carvings.

East Asian Collection

The collection of East Asian art comprises of over 500 porcelain objects and some lacquer items. Most of the pieces on display were acquired around 1700 by Elector Maximilian Emanuel.

The earliest porcelain wares in the collection are the blue and white bowls and plates made in China around 1600, during the period of the Ming dynasty. The collection also contains items of Japanese and Chinese Imari porcelain.

Among others, items with mounts of finely chased fire-gilt bronze are of special note. The mounts were commissioned from craftsmen in Paris and were intended to enhance the richness of the objects.

Coin Collection

The Residenz contains the largest coin collection in the world. Its nucleus originated in a collection formed by Albrecht V and Ludwig I. It contains coins and medals dating from all periods and originating from all over the world. Seals, weights and banknotes also form part of the display.

The Neo-Classical National Theatre at Max-Joseph-Platz

❷ Max-Joseph-Platz

Map 3 C2 (6 D2). Ⓢ Marienplatz.
Ⓤ Odeonsplatz, Marienplatz.
🚋 19. Nationaltheater: **Tel** 21 85 19
20. **Open** 10am–7pm Mon–Sat
(tickets for performances can also be
obtained). 🎫 guided tours only.

During the 1820s, Karl von
Fischer and Leo von Klenze laid
out a grand square outside the
Residenz, flanking it with the
monumental façades of Neo-
Classical buildings: Königsbau
to the north, the National
Theatre to the east, and the
arcaded Töerring-Jettenbach
Palace to the south. The latter is
now an exclusive residence and
also houses high-end stores.

In the square is a statue of
Maximilian I Joseph, the first
king of Bavaria, who drew up the
Bavarian constitution, the first in
Germany, in 1818. The statue
was created by Leo von Klenze
and Christian Daniel Rauch.

The building of the **National
Theatre**, which doubles as
the National Opera, is modelled
on a Greek temple. The interior
also obeys Classical canons.
The large circular auditorium
is decorated predominantly
in purple, gold, ivory and sky
blue. It is surrounded by five-
tiered galleries, with the royal
box in the centre. The National
Theatre became famous for
its performances of Wagnerian
operas. It was here that *Tristan
und Isolde, Die Walküre* and
Rheingold were first performed.
Today it is the venue for
opera festivals. Next door is
the Residenztheatre.

❸ Eilleshof

Residenzstr. 13 (also accessible from
the side of Theatinerstr. 40–42).
Map 3 C2 (6 D2). Ⓤ or Ⓢ
Marienplatz. Ⓤ Odeonsplatz. 🚋 19.

Between the Residenzstraße,
Perusastraße and Theatinerstraße
runs a network of narrow
passages that are filled with
small shops and cafés. The
peace in this area is broken
only by the music of
street musicians.

One of the most impressive
courtyards in this part of the
city is the mid-16th century
Eilles-Hof, which once formed
part of a monastery. The yard
is surrounded by glazed arched
cloisters with late Gothic
balustrades. It is one of the
last surviving arcaded courtyards in Munich. Nearby is the
award-winning shopping area,
Fünf Höfe *(see p144)*.

❹ Palais Preysing

Residenzstr. 27. **Map** 3 C1 (6 C2).

On an irregular plot
of land between
Theatinerstraße and
Residenzstraße, which
leads to Odeonsplatz,
Count Emanuel Graf
von Preysing built the
first Rococo palace in
Munich. It was
designed by the
court architect
Joseph Effner and
built in 1723–8.
Novel designs were
used for the three

sides of the palace (the fourth
adjoins Feldherrnhalle). For the
first time exuberant mouldings
covered the entire façade,
partially obscuring the architectural divisions of the building.

The finest example of rich
Baroque design at the palace
is the grand staircase, in the
centre of the north wing. It
is reached today via an internal
passage that was once a hall
and is now lined with elegant
shops. The staircase has
decorative balustrades and is
supported by giant Caryatids,
and the walls are covered with
lavish stuccowork. No succeeding
late Baroque palace has such a
wealth of interior decor.

Palais Preysing, an example of early
Baroque exterior decoration

❺ Feldherrnhalle
Field Marshals' Hall

Odeonsplatz. **Map** 3 C1 (6 C2).
Ⓤ Odeonsplatz. 🚋 53.

On the site of the Schwabinger
Tor, a medieval watchtower,
the architect Friedrich von
Gärtner raised a building that
blends perfectly with the old
and new towns between
which it stands. The aim had
been to create a focal point
that would close off
Ludwigstraße and
give the irregular
Odeonsplatz a
more ordered
appearance. At the
request of Ludwig I
a loggia in honour of
the heroes of Bavaria
was built, modelled on
the famous Loggia dei
Lanzi in Florence.
The Feldherrnhalle
was completed in

Statue of Count Tilly in the
loggia of the Feldherrnhalle

For hotels and restaurants in this region see pp266–7 and pp276–9

Hitler and the Feldherrnhalle

On 8 November 1923, Adolf Hitler announced the start of the "people's revolution" in the Bürgerbräukeller and ordered the takeover of the central districts of Munich. The following day, a march of some 2,000 people acting on his orders was stopped by a police cordon outside the Feldherrnhalle in Residenzstraße. Four policemen and 16 of Hitler's supporters were shot. The marchers were dispersed, and Hitler fled to Uffing am Staffelsee, but was arrested and imprisoned. When Hitler finally came to power in 1933, he turned what became known as the *Hitler-Putsch* ("revolt") into a central element of the Nazi cult.

The accused in the trial against the participants in the *Hitler-Putsch* of 1923

Cuvilliés and his son, who finished the work in 1765. The distinctive form of the church brought considerable variety to Munich's cityscape. The huge domes of the towers are 70 m (230 ft) high. The volutes on the towers are inspired by those of Santa Maria della Salute in Venice.

The Cuvilliés' late Baroque façade is brought forward and broken up by pilasters and scrolled cornices. It also has niches with the figures of Ferdinand and Adelaide, Maximilian and Kajetan, the patron saint of the church. The portico contains a cartouche with coats of arms, including those of Bavaria and Saxony.

The white interior, which contrasts with the black confessionals and pulpit, is decorated with stuccowork, allegorical figures and putti. The main altar is flanked by twisted columns.

The crypt contains the tombs of the dukes and kings of Bavaria, among them the founders of the church and their son Maximilian Emanuel and his wife Therese Kunigunde Sobieska.

1844. It consists of an open hall 20 m (65 ft) high with a triple arcade approached by a stairway in the central span. The statues of lions flanking the stairway were added in 1906. The niches in the arcade contain statues of Count Tilly, a renowned military leader in the Thirty Years' War, and of Count von Wrede, a marshal of the Bavarian Napoleonic era. There is also an allegorical memorial to the Bavarian army of Ferdinand von Miller the Younger, built in 1892.

❻ Theatinerkirche (St Kajetan)

St Cajetan's Church

Theatinerstr. 22. Ⓢ Marienplatz. Ⓤ Odeonsplatz. 🚊 19. **Open** 7am–7:30pm daily.

To celebrate the birth of their long-awaited son in 1662, the Elector Ferdinand Maria and his wife Henriette Adelheid von Savoyen ordered the construction of a church and monastery for the Theatine order. It was designed by Agostino Barelli of Bologna, who wanted it to be the finest and most highly decorated temple.

Work began in 1663. The church was also designed for use as a court chapel. It was based on Sant'Andrea della Valle in Rome. Thus a building of pure Roman Baroque form

rose in Munich. It is a barrel-vaulted cruciform basilica with an apse, a dome over the crossing and arcades opening onto side chapels. From 1675 work was supervised by Enrico Zucalli, who completed the dome, designed the interior and added twin towers which had not formed part of Barelli's original design. Almost 100 years later, the completion of the façade was entrusted to

The Baroque Theatinerkirche, one of Munich's finest buildings

The Salvatorkirche, with the Literaturhaus in the foreground

❼ Salvatorkirche
Church of the Saviour

Salvatorplatz 17. **Map** 3 B1 (5 C2).
🅄 Odeonsplatz. 🚋 19. 🚌 100.
Open 10am–8pm daily.

In the late 15th century, the population of Munich increased greatly, and the existing cemeteries at Frauenkirche and Peterskirche were no longer sufficient. A new cemetery was created near the city walls, and cemetery chapels were built – the Allerheiligenkirche am Kreuz for the parish of St Peter and the Frauenkirche for that of St Mary.

Salvatorkirche was completed in a single year (1493–4). It was built by Lukas Rottaler, who brought the Gothic style to Munich. The combination of brick, stone and terracotta, the intricate fan vaulting and the delicate division of the walls give the church a distinctive elegance. The whole is complemented by a slender tower ending in a steeple. Vestiges of late Gothic frescoes can be seen over the north door.

In 1829 Ludwig I donated the church to the Orthodox community. The iconostasis (screen) at the end of the nave is in Romanesque style, and the combination of Gothic architecture with Greek Orthodox furniture creates a unique effect. A plaque on the outer wall commemorates those who lie in the cemetery. They include the painter Hans Mielich, the composer Orlando di Lasso, and the architects François Cuvilliés and Johann Baptist Gunetzrhainer.

❽ Erzbischöfliches Palais
Archbishops' Palace

Kardinal-Faulhaber-Str. 12.
Map 3 B1 (6 D2). 🅂 🅄 Marienplatz, Odeonsplatz. 🚋 19.
Closed to visitors.

This palace, which consists of four wings enclosing a courtyard, was commissioned by the Elector Karl Albrecht and built by François Cuvilliés in 1733–7. It became the seat of the archbishops of Munich and Freising in 1821. It is the only surviving urban palace built by Cuvilliés.

The building is fronted by finely moulded pilasters. The tympanum contains the crest of Count von Holnstein, Karl Albrecht's illegitimate son, the division across the coat of arms indicating his illegitimate status. A bas-relief over the doorway depicts the Virgin surrounded by cherubs.

The interiors of the palace were completed in about 1735 by Johann Baptist Zimmermann to a design by Cuvilliés. They are among the finest examples of late Baroque decoration in Munich. The courtyard contains a statue of Venus by Johann Baptist Straub.

Monumental sculpture on the façade of the Palais Porcia

❾ Palais Porcia

Kardinal-Faulhaber Str. 12.
Map 3 B2 (5 C2). 🅂 Marienplatz.
🅄 Marienplatz, Odeonsplatz. 🚋 19.
Closed to visitors.

The Palais Porcia was Munich's first four-winged Italianate Baroque palace. It was built for the Fugger family in 1693–4 by the architect Enrico Zucalli.

The façade is based on that of Bernini's Palazzo Odescalchi in Rome. The rusticated lower storey, which is pierced by a columned doorway, is surmounted by two upper storeys that are divided by pilasters.

In 1733 the Elector Karl Albrecht dedicated the palace to his sweetheart, Princess Porcia. The interior was remodelled in the Rococo style to a design by François Cuvilliés, with the involvement of Johann Baptist Zimmermann. The balustrade of the balcony was replaced by an ornamental grille.

In 1819 the palace was acquired by the Museum

Medallion with the Virgin above the entrance to the Erzbischöfliches Palais

Literary Society, and in 1820 the rear wing was extended by the addition of a ballroom and a concert hall designed by Leo von Klenze.

Over the following century the building was an important centre of musical life in Munich. In 1934 it housed the Bayerische Hypotheken- und Wechselbank. Bombing raids in 1944 unfortunately destroyed the Rococo interior. However, the general design of the vestibule was restored in 1952, and the Rococo statue of Bellony was moved here from the Archbishops' Palace.

❿ Palais Neuhaus-Preysing

Prannerstr. 2. **Map** 2 B1 (5 C2).
Ⓢ Marienplatz. Ⓤ Marienplatz, Odeonsplatz. 🚋 19.
Closed to visitors.

This palace was built in 1737, probably by Karl Albrecht von Lespilliez. A small attic was added during the Neo-Classical period.

The building is currently owned by Hypo Vereinsbank. The interior was completely destroyed during World War II, although the façade somehow survived. The palace was restored and renovated in 1956–8.

A little further along the same street are two fine late Baroque palaces, also probably designed by Lespilliez: the Palais Seinsheim at No. 7, built in 1764, and the Palais Gise at No. 9, built in 1765.

The SiemensForum

The Siemensforum is a showcase that the electronics giant Siemens has built in Munich, and also in Berlin, Zurich, Vienna and Milan. Its purpose is to provide a forum for discussion and information on modern technological advances. As well as organizing congresses, events and exhibitions, the Munich Siemensforum contains a permanent exhibition taken from the Siemens-Museum. The museum was built in 1916 in Berlin to commemorate the 100th anniversary of the birth of Werner von Siemens, the inventor and engineer who founded the company. The museum moved to Munich in 1954.

The history section includes exhibits of the first telegraphic devices, such as the Morse transmitter. The modern section displays modern electronics and microelectronics, which are presented using the latest multimedia technology.

The Siemensforum is closed for renovation until the end of 2015.

The SiemensForum, an impressive display of modern technology

⓫ Literaturhaus

Salvatorplatz 1. **Tel** 29 19 340.
During exhibitions: **Open** 10am–7pm Mon–Fri, 10am–6pm Sat–Sun.

Munich's great literary traditions and its influential position in the European publishing market were marked by the opening of the Literaturhaus in 1997.

This monumental building, which blends with the closely aligned façades of town houses and the outline of the Salvatorkirche, dominates Salvatorplatz. Until the beginning of the 20th century this was the site of the city market. In 1887 a large school building designed by Friedrich Löbel was built here, its open ground floor fulfilling the function of a market hall up until 1906.

In 1993 the building, which had been partially destroyed during World War II, underwent renovation and re-opened as the Literaturhaus.

The present building skillfully combines the period style of the lower storeys with a light steel and glass structure for the two upper storeys. These provide a breathtaking view on to the dome of the Theatinerkirche and the city's rooftops.

The Literaturhaus is the home of literary institutions and foundations that organize literary conferences and seminars as well as readings, concerts and receptions.

Part of the ground floor hall is occupied by an interesting display area where temporary exhibitions are held. There is a library on the first floor.

One of the institution's great attractions is the literary café. Its decor includes an impressive installation by the American artist Jenny Holzer devoted to the Bavarian poet and novelist Oskar Maria Graf.

Façade of the Palais Neuhaus-Preysing with its rich Rococo stuccowork

The Künstlerhaus, built in northern German Renaissance style

⓬ Künstlerhaus
Artists' House

Lenbachplatz 8. **Map** 3 A1 (5 B2).
Tel 59 91 840. Ⓢ or Ⓤ Karlsplatz-
Stachus. 🚋 16, 17, 18, 19, 27, 28, N16,
N27. 🚌 N40, N41. Inner Courtyard:
Open only during events.

The Künstlerhaus, on the
south-ern side of Lenbachplatz,
was designed by Gabriel von
Seidl and built in 1892–1900. This
attractive building, with wings
set around an inner courtyard,
is in mock northern German
Renaissance style, which is
characterized by stepped gables
and bronze decoration.

The Munich painter Franz von
Lenbach made a great contribu-
tion to its completion. Having
collected funds, he set to work
on the interior. The rooms are
decorated in Italian Renaissance
and Art Nouveau styles.

Despite wartime destruction,
the vestibule and the Venetian
Room – which today houses a
restaurant – have been preserved.
The Künstlerhaus is now the
headquarter of an art foundation
with the same name. Small
exhibitions, workshops and
concerts are also held here.

⓭ Dreifaltigkeits-
kirche
Church of the Holy Trinity

Pacellistr. 6. **Map** 3 B1 (5 B2). Ⓢ &
Ⓤ Karlsplatz-Stachus. 🚋 19.
Open 7am–7pm daily.

In the war of the Spanish
Succession (1700–14) the
townswoman Anna Maria
Lindmayr had a vision in
which the city was consumed
by the flames of war. To ward
off such disaster, the burghers
pledged to build a church.

Work began in 1711, and the
result is an unusually interesting
piece of architecture. The design,
inspired by the Roman architecture of Francesco Morrominiego,
is by Giovanni Antonio Viscardi,
and construction was supervised
by Enrico Zucalli and Johann
Georg Ettenhofer. It was
completed in 1718.

The broken façade is set
with a multitude of columns,
pilasters and cornices, and
windows of different shapes
are set in surprising places.
A niche in the upper storey
contains a statue of St Michael
by Joseph Fichtl. The plan
combines elongated and
centralized schemes.

High altar of the Dreifaltigkeitskirche

The interior is profusely
decorated with stuccowork
and with paintings by Cosmas
Damian Asam. The high altar
(1717) has a painting of the Holy
Trinity, to whom the church is
dedicated, by Andreas Wolff
and Johann Degler. The Rococo
tabernacle of 1760 is by Johann
Baptist Straub.

⓮ Promenadeplatz

Map 3 B2 (5 C2). Ⓤ Marienplatz. 🚋 19.

This elongated rectangular
square, whose origins date back
to the Middle Ages, was once
the site of the salt market, and
storehouses for salt and the
customs house stood here. At
the end of the 18th century, the
buildings were demolished and
the square was planted with
linden trees. Fine palaces and
town houses also rose up all
round the square.

The square, whose present
name dates from 1805, is
decorated with 19th-century
statues of well-known local
and regional figures.

On the northern side is the
Bayerischer Hof, a high-class
hotel, where many famous
people have stayed. In addition
to the main building, in the
Maximilian style, the adjoining
Palais Montgelas also forms part
of the hotel. It was designed for
the king's minister and the
creator of modern
Bavaria by the architect
Joseph Emanuel von
Herigoyen (1811–13).
The decoration is by
Jean-Baptiste Métivier.
The grand interior has
been preserved,
including the Royal
Hall, Montgelas Hall
and Library, all in Empire
style. It was beside the
building on Kardinal-
Faulhaber-Straße that
Kurt Eisner, first president
of the Bavarian Republic,
was shot in 1919.
Situated on the other
side of the square,
at No. 15, is the house
belonging to the
architect Johann Baptist
Gunetzrhainer.

For hotels and restaurants in this region see pp266–7 and pp276–9

The Neo-Renaissance loggia of the Palais Töerring-Jettenbach

⓯ Palais Töerring-Jettenbach

Residenzstr. 2. **Map** 3 C2 (6 D2). Ⓢ or Ⓤ Marienplatz. Ⓤ Odeonsplatz. 🚋 19.

The Baroque palace that originally stood on this site was at odds with ideas of town planning that had inspired the creation of Max-Joseph-Platz, particularly after the Neo-Classical wing of Königsbau and the Opera House were built.

In 1835–8 Ludwig I commissioned Leo von Klenze to rebuild the original palace, extending it and creating a façade based on that of the Ospedale degli Innocenti in Florence. The Baroque doorway was moved inside, as were two of the nine sculptures by Johann Baptist Straub (the remaining seven are in the Bayerisches

Nationalmuseum). The new arcade-style loggia was painted in ochre, contrasting with the red walls behind. This aristocratic palace, once home to a post office, is now an exclusive residence and also houses high-end stores.

⓰ Münzhof

State Mint

Hofgraben 4. **Map** 3 C2 (6 E3). Ⓢ or Ⓤ Marienplatz. 🚋 19. Courtyard: **Open** 8am–4:15pm Mon–Thu, 8am–2pm Fri.

Two ducal seats in Munich are associated with Albrecht V – the Alter Hof and the mid-14th century Neuveste (now destroyed), which were separated by a stable building. Designed by the architect Bernhard Zwitzel of Augsburg, they were built by Wilhelm Egkl.

The courtyard was surrounded by a three-storey loggia housing the stables and coach-houses. They also contained Albrecht V's library and some of the earliest collections of art in Europe. Despite a marked adherence to the Italian Renaissance, the building shows Albrecht's own interpretation.

When it was rebuilt in the 19th century as the state mint, it was given a Neo-Classical east façade. The north façade, meanwhile, is in the Maximilian style.

⓱ Alter Hof

Old Residence

Burgstr. 8. **Map** 3 C2 (6 D3). Ⓢ or Ⓤ Marienplatz. 🚋 19.

The first fortified residence built for the Wittelsbachs within the walls of Munich was constructed in 1253–5. The purpose was to protect them not only from outside invaders, but also from rebellious citizens. In 1328–47 the Alter Hof was the residence of Emperor Ludwig IV of Bavaria. In the second half of the 14th century construction began on a larger residence, and gradually the seat of power was moved there.

From the 14th century the Alter Hof only housed the duchy's administrative offices. This delightful residence is a rare example of medieval secular architecture. The west wing ends with a gatehouse decorated with the crests of the Wittelsbachs, and it retains its original Gothic character. Another original feature is the distinctive bay window known as the Monkey Tower. According to legend, when Ludwig IV was a baby he was carried off by a monkey from the royal menagerie. The monkey climbed to the top of the tower, and it took a long time for it to be coaxed into returning the child.

Monkey Tower in Alter Hof

Renaissance triple-tier arcades create an orderly sense of space in the Münzhof

The Hofbräuhaus – the best-known address in Munich

⑱ Hofbräuhaus

Platzl 9. **Map** 3 C2 (6 E3). **Tel** 29 01 36 100. Ⓢ Isartor or Ⓤ Marienplatz. 🚋 19. **Open** 9am–11:30pm daily. 🖥

Munich's greatest tourist attraction, and the epitome of the Bavarian lifestyle, is the Hofbräuhaus. An inn, it formed part of the Royal Brewery that was founded by Wilhelm V in 1589. The opening ceremony of the inn in 1830 was attended by Ludwig I. Extended on numerous occasions, the building was given its present Neo-Renaissance exterior in 1896.

The ground floor contains the Schwemme, a large hall with a ceiling painted in 1971. The hall can hold 1,000 drinkers seated at long tables, strains of folk music audible over the talking and laughter.

On the first floor is the vaulted Festsaal, a ceremonial hall seating 1,300, and many smaller side-rooms known as *Trinkstuben*. In summer the beer-garden, with chestnut trees and a bubbling fountain, is a popular place. Every day 10,000 litres (17,600 pints) of beer are consumed here.

⑲ Maximilianstraße

Map 3 C2 (6 D, E2). Ⓤ Odeonsplatz. Ⓢ or Ⓤ Marienplatz. 🚋 19.

When he came to power, Maxmilian I Joseph continued the passion for building that had gripped his father Ludwig I. His wish to make his own archi-tectural mark on Munich

manifested itself in Maximilianstraße. Built in 1852–5, this was a reaction to the outmoded Neo-Classicism of Ludwig-straße. Maximilianstraße was built to connect the Residenz and the Old Town with the green areas along the banks of the Isar. It is divided into two parts, the showpiece square closed off by the Maximilianeum, and the commercial part within the Old Town. The division is further accentuated by the modern ring road. Today, this luxurious boulevard is one of the world's most exclusive and expensive streets.

Friedrich Bürklein, who designed the thoroughfare, created a novel architectural and decorative scheme that combined English Gothic with Italianesque arcades and depended on new skeleton construction methods. The arcades of the imposing Neo-Gothic buildings contain Munich's luxury shops such as Bulgari, Laroche, Hermès, Armani and the eccentric local men's fashion designer the late Rudolph Moshammer.

The famous Kempinski Vier Jahreszeiten hotel and the Ethnographic Museum are the only buildings not designed by Bürklein.

The opera house, the theatre, the many art galleries, where private views are a social event, and the clientele of the bustling cafés combine to create a thriving urban atmosphere in the area.

⑳ Münchner Kammerspiele im Schauspielhaus
Munich Chamber Theatre

Maximilianstr. 34–35. **Map** 4 D2 (6 F3). **Tel** 23 39 66 00. Ⓤ Lehel. 🚋 19. Box office: **Open** 10am–6pm Mon–Fri, 10am–1pm Sat.

The Schauspielhaus is one of the few surviving Art Nouveau theatres in Germany. It was built in 1900–01 and adjoins the backs of two buildings in Maximilian style. The architect was Richard Riemerschmid and the modern stage equipment was created by Max Littmann.

The interior is also in Art Nouveau style. The walls of the auditorium are bright red with ornamental outlines. The green ceiling has six stucco beams and imaginative floral strands lit by spotlights in the shape of flower buds. The typical Art Nouveau device of softening lines with floral motifs can be seen everywhere – around the stage and the balconies and on door handles. The decorative stage curtain was made in 1971. Equally imaginative and colourful are the foyers on the two floors and the ticket office.

The theatre, which was originally named the Schauspielhaus (Playhouse), was renowned for the controversial works performed there, such as Frank Wedekind's *The Awakening of Spring*. The theatre's avant-garde traditions continued in the postwar period.

The interior of the Art Nouveau-style Munich Chamber Theatre

The imposing façade of the Bavarian State Chancellery

㉑ Marstall
Royal Stables

Marstallplatz 4. **Map** 3 C1 (6 E2). **Tel** 21 85 20 28. **U** Odeonsplatz. 🚌 19.

Leo von Klenze's first majorwork on the Residenz was the royal stables, on which he worked from 1817 to 1822. The large hall-like building is based on Renaissance and Baroque palace architecture.

The row of semi-circular windows is topped by medallions depicting horses' heads. Busts of Castor and Pollux, the sons of Zeus who (particularly in the case of Castor) were excellent horsemen, crown the columns at the entrance. The reliefs on the gates depicting the epic battle between the Lapiths and the Centaurs were made by Johann Martin von Wagner in 1821.

Medallion from the Marstall

Today the Marstall houses the Marstalltheater, which is known for its experimental performances combining theatre with dance and music.

㉒ Bayerische Staatskanzlei
Bavarian State Chancellery

Map 4 D1 (6 F1). **U** Odeonsplatz. 🚌 100.

After a dispute between the city council and the government that went on for almost 30 years, the Bavarian State Chancellery was finally completed in 1992. A design proposed in the 1980s, by which the ruins of the former army museum at the end of the Hofgarten would be linked to a modern architectural complex, seemed too invasive to most of Munich's residents. It interfered with green areas, and the wings of the new building would mean the demolition of the 16th-century garden wall. After protests and litigation brought by the town council, supported by art historians and building conservationists, the government altered the original plans.

㉓ Hofgarten
Palace Garden

North side of the Residenz. **Map** 3 C1 (6 E1). **U** Odeonsplatz. German Theatre Museum: Galeriestr. 4A. **Open** 10am–4pm Tue–Sun.

The Hofgarten is one of the largest Mannerist gardens north of the Alps. It was laid out in front of the north wing of the Residenz in 1613–17. The geometrically designed gardens are divided by two straight main paths that intersect at right angles. At the intersection is the polygonal Hofgartentempel, or Temple of Diana, built by Heinrich Schön in 1615. The figure of Diana crowning the cupola was completed by Hubert Gerhard in 1594 (the present one is a copy). In 1623 Hans Krumpper remodelled the figure, transforming it into a symbol of Bavaria and adding putti bearing the ducal insignia.

The garden is bounded to the west and north by a gallery built in the reigns of Albrecht V and Maximilian I. The art gallery built in the north of the garden in 1781 was the precursor of the present Alte Pinakothek and Neue Pinakothek. The rooms now house an art gallery and the **German Theatre Museum**, the oldest of its kind in Europe. Its collections illustrate the history of drama in all parts of the world.

The triumphal arch of the entrance gate is Leo von Klenze's first work in Munich. The carvings are by Ludwig Schwanthaler and the frescoes, by Peter Cornelius, depict the history of the Wittelsbachs and Bavaria. The northern arcades feature landscapes by Richard Seewald of 1962. South of the gardens rises the imposing Festsaalbau, with von Klenze's huge doorway of 1835–42.

The Mannerist Temple of Diana in the centre of the Hofgarten

AROUND THE ISAR

The Isar, the river that flows through Munich, is quite attractive in the stretch between two bridges, the Luitpoldbrücke (Prinzregentenbrücke) and Corneliusbrücke. The Praterinsel and Museumsinsel, two islands linked to the city by several foot-bridges, also contribute to a striking townscape.

The main attractions that draw visitors to this part of Munich are in the area of the Luitpoldbrücke, Maximiliansbrücke and Ludwigsbrücke. On the steep right bank of the Isar are the Maximilansanlagen, green

areas densely planted with trees and favourite places for walks and cycle rides.

The Maximilianstraße leads to the Maximilianeum, the great parliament building, which appears to be drawn like a theatre curtain across this wide thoroughfare. Everything exudes an air of dignity. Here is the monument to Maximilian II, the Ethnographical Museum and the Upper Bavarian government building. This section of the Maximilianstraße is flanked by Lehel, the fashion quarter, one of Munich's prettiest districts.

Sights at a Glance

Churches

① Pfarrkirche St Anna
② Klosterkirche St Anna
⑩ St-Nikolai-Kirche

Museums and Galleries

④ Völkerkundemuseum
⑥ Alpines Museum
⑧ Villa Stuck
⑭ *Deutsches Museum*
  see pp98–101

**Historic Buildings
and Monuments**

③ Regierung von Oberbayern
⑤ Monument to Maximilian II
⑦ Maximilianeum
⑨ Friedensengel
⑫ Müllersches Volksbad
⑬ Ludwigsbrücke

Other Sights

⑪ Gasteig

Restaurants *pp277–8*

1 Dukatz
2 Gandl
3 Goa
4 Käfer Schänke
5 Königsquelle
6 Nektar
7 Nero
8 Wirtshaus in der Au

See also Street Finder maps
4 & 6

◀ The impressive clock tower of Müllersches Volksbad

For map symbols *see back flap*

Street-by-Street: Along Maximilianstraße

Maximilian II, with the aid of his court architect Friedrich Bürklein, translated his vision of urban planning into reality in the Maximilianstraße. Designed in what became known as the Maximilian style, it opens out from the Old Town into a kind of forum flanked by monumental buildings. It is completed by a circus with a monument of the king contemplating his creation. The scheme is dominated by the Maximilianeum, the Bavarian parliament building, on the opposite side of the river.

Haus der Kunst

ST.-ANNA-STR.

BÜRKLEINSTR.

❸ Regierung von Oberbayern
These Neo-Gothic buildings house the government of Upper Bavaria.

ST.-ANNA-STR.

PFARRSTR.

Residenz

MAXIMILIANSTR.

❷ ★ Klosterkirche St Anna
The niche in the finial of St Anne's church holds a statue of its patron saint.

❺ Monument to Maximilian II
This statue, 13 m (42 ft) high, was carved by Ferdinand von Miller, to a design by Kaspar von Zumbusch, in 1875. The king, whose great ambition was to be a professor rather than a monarch, is surrounded by figures symbolizing Peace, Liberty, Justice and Strength.

❹ Völkerkundemuseum
The rich collection of the Ethnographical Museum illustrates the culture and everyday life of non-European peoples.

STEINSDO

0 metres 100
0 yards 100

Key

━ Suggested route

The Isar, although flanked by embankments, retains its woodland charm.

❶ Pfarrkirche St Anna
The monumental apse of St Anne's Church, built in Neo-Romanesque style, was painted by Rudolf von Seitz in 1892. It shows the Holy Trinity surrounded by St Mary, St Anne and the Apostles.

Locator Map
See Street Finder maps 4 & 6

The Maximiliansbrücke
was built in 1904–6 to a design by Friedrich von Thiersch that incorporates Neo-Romanesque decoration. The figure of Athena expresses the idea of Munich as Athens on the Isar.

❼ ★ Maximilianeum
This tympanum in the façade of the Maximilianeum contains scenes of the foundation of the abbey and the knight house in Ettal by Ludwig IV of Bavaria in 1330.

Friedensengel

❻ Alpines Museum
This museum is dedicated to the Alps and mountaineering displays, including equipment from 1900.

Neo-Romanesque doorway of Pfarrkirche St Anna

❶ Pfarrkirche St Anna

Parish Church of St Anne

St-Anna-Platz 5. **Map** 4 D2. **U** Lehel. 🚋 18, 19. **Open** 8am–6pm daily.

A competition for the design of a parish church for the Lehel district was held in 1885. The winner was Gabriel von Seidl. Work began in 1887, continuing until 1892. The design of the church is based on that of the Romanesque imperial cathedrals of the Rhineland, in the great German nationalist style that was prevalent after 1871.

The monumental triple-nave basilica has a square plan, the transept and apse ending in a chapel and the west front having a large tower and a Neo-Romanesque doorway. The interior is decorated with late 18th- to early 19th- century wall paintings. An interesting feature is the hybrid iconography in the figure of Christ on the west front, dating from 1910, in which He is depicted on horse-back holding a bow and an olive branch.

❷ Klosterkirche St Anna

Abbey Church of St Anne

St-Anna-Platz 21. **Map** 4 D2 (6 F2). **U** Lehel. 🚋 18, 19. **Open** 6am–7pm daily.

In 1725 Lehel, then still a suburb, was settled by an order of Hieronymite monks. A monastery church was built here in 1727–33. Designed by Johann Michael Fischer, it was a real architectural jewel for the city: Munich's first Rococo religious building. The oval interior is lined with scalloped niches that are separated by arches supported on pilasters. The interior decoration was executed by the Asam brothers. The ceiling paintings, which glorify St Anne, were executed by Cosmas Damian Asam and completed in 1730. In 1737 the Asam brothers completed the high altar and most of the side altars, their stuccowork and paintings harmonizing with the fluid forms of the interior. The pulpit and tabernacle, by Johann Baptist Straub, date from around 1756.

Cartouche from the Klosterkirche St Anna

After suffering war damage, the interior was restored on the basis of a record of colour photographs.

❸ Regierung von Oberbayern

Upper Bavaria Government Building

Maximilianstr. 39. **Map** 4 D2 (6 F3). **S** Isartor. **U** Lehel. 🚋 18, 19.

This monumental building, the seat of the government of Upper Bavaria, is one of the finest examples of the Maximilian style. The eponymous king, Maximilian II, strove to create a new archi-tectural style, distancing himself from the severe Classicism of his father, Ludwig I. The result was an eclectic mixture of elements drawn from such diverse styles as English Gothic and Moorish architecture.

Solid and imposing, the Regierung von Oberbayern was built in 1856–64 to a design by Friedrich Bürklein. The façade, 170 m (558 ft) long, was conceived as part of the grand new city plan. It is vertically divided into 17 bays of arched windows arranged above an imposing arcade. Its strong horizontal lines and its ornamentation are highly reminiscent of those of English Gothic cathedrals. Indeed, the pseudo-ecclesiastical appearance of the building was designed to underline its civic importance and dignity. This symbolism is further reinforced by the large statue of Justice that crowns the building.

❹ Völkerkunde-museum

State Museum of Ethnography

Maximilianstr. 42. **Map** 4 D2 (6 F3). **Tel** 21 01 36 100. **S** Isartor. **U** Lehel. 🚋 18, 19. **Open** 9:30am–5:30pm Tue–Sun. 🗙

The building that was eventually to become the State Museum of Ethnography was built in 1859–65 to a design by Eduard Riedel. It is in the Maximilian style and the façade is set with eight figures personifying the virtues of the Bavarian people: Patriotism, Diligence, Magnanimity, Piety, Loyalty, Justice, Courage and Wisdom.

The building was originally intended to house the collections of the Bavarian National Museum. From 1900 to 1923 it served as the first main building of the Deutsches Museum. Since 1926 it has been the home of

Part of the façade of the Upper Bavaria Government building

Caryatids flanking the entrance to the Völkerkundemuseum

the State Ethnographic Museum, the second largest in Germany after that of Berlin.

The collection itself dates from 1782, when curiosities from the collections of Bavarian rulers were displayed in the galleries of the Residenz. The museum collection now consists of some 150,000 pieces relating to the life and culture of non-European peoples. The Far East (China and Japan), South America (Peru) and East and Central Africa are particularly well represented.

Because of the size of the collection, many exhibits are displayed on a rotating basis.

❺ Monument to Maximilian II

Rondo Maximilianstr. **Map** 4 D2. 🚋 19.

As you walk along Maximilianstraße you pass a circus that has at its centre a statue of Maximilian II, patron of the arts and industry, and inspirer of the new architectural style to which he gave his name. Maximilian II conceived the urban planning of this part of the city. The monument was erected by the citizens of Munich in homage to their ruler and in honour of the monarchy.

The bronze statue, designed by Kaspar Zumbusch and cast in 1875, stands on a red marble plinth surrounded by personifications of the four royal virtues.

Four putti hold the coat of arms of the four tribes of Bavaria: the Franconians, Bavarians, Swabians and Palatines.

❻ Alpines Museum

Museum of the Alps and Mountaineering

Praterinsel 5. **Map** 4 E3. **Tel** 21 12 240. **Open** 1–6pm Tue–Fri, 11am–6pm Sat–Sun. 🖾

The museum stands in scenic parkland in the southern part of Praterinsel, one of the islands in the Isar in central Munich. The building that it occupies, dating from the late 19th century, was presented to the German-Austrian Mountaineering Association in 1938.

The museum's exhibits illustrate both the scientific and the aesthetic aspects of the Alps. The displays, with a geological section on Alpine rocks and minerals, relate to their exploration and study, and include many paintings and drawings of Alpine scenery.

The museum also houses the world's largest library of books on Alpine subjects, and has a mountaineering archive. An information centre serves the needs of mountaineers intending to set out on expeditions into the Alps.

A book from 1897, Alpines Museum

❼ Maximilianeum

Max-Planck-Str. 1. **Map** 4 E2. Ⓤ Max-Weber-Platz. 🚋 15, 16, 19, 25. 🚌 190, 191.

The largest building on Maximilianstraße is, not surprisingly, the monumental Maximilianeum. It was built as a commission from Maximilian II by Friedrich Bürklein in 1857–74 and stands on an elevation on the right bank of the Isar.

The building is the headquarters of a royal fund that gave gifted school students the opportunity to study at university without paying fees. Since 1949 it has also been the seat of the Bavarian parliament (and until 1999 the Bavarian senate).

It took 17 years to complete the Maximilianeum, progress being hampered by the sloping terrain of the river bank. The focal point of the slightly concave façade is the tall, triple-arched projecting entrance, topped by the figure of an angel. Wings, arcaded in their lower storey, extend on either side. The terracotta façade is decorated with busts and statues, while coloured mosaics on a gold background fill the semi-circular blind windows over the upper storey. The interior is decorated with historical and allegorical paintings by Wilhelm and Friedrich von Kaulbach.

The Maximilianeum, seat of the Bavarian parliament

Die Sünde, a portrait of sin by Franz von Stuck, in the Villa Stuck

❽ Villa Stuck

Prinzregentenstr. 60. **Map** 4 F1. **Tel** 45 55 510. **U** Prinzregentenplatz, Max-Weber-Platz. ⭐ 15, 16, 19, 25, N16. 🚌 100, 190, 191. **Open** 11am–6pm Tue–Sun, 11am–10pm 1st Fri of month.

Franz von Stuck (1863–1928), the talented son of a miller from Lower Bavaria, made a giddy career for himself in Munich. He not only achieved great success as a painter, sculptor and graphic artist, but also became a professor at the Academy of Fine Arts, was given an aristocratic title and earned himself the title "prince of art".

In 1897–8 Stuck built himself a magnificent home, to which a large studio was added in 1913–14. Both the architectural conception and the interior decoration of the house were his own work. In it, he combined Neo-Classical, Art Nouveau and Symbolist elements, thus underlining his tenet that art and life were connected.

The house contains finely decorated reception rooms which, after the artist's death, were used for meetings by Munich's high society. The walls of the drawing rooms and studios are covered with mosaics and paintings in a Pompeian style. As well as ostentatious furniture, there are examples of Stuck's own sculpture. The museum also has an Art Nouveau display and hosts visiting exhibitions.

❾ Friedensengel
Angel of Peace

Prinzregentenstr. **Map** 4 F1. ⭐ 16. 🚌 100.

High on the right bank of the Isar stands the Angel of Peace, a monument raised to mark 25 years of peace after the Franco-Prussian War of 1870–71, in which Germany was victorious.

Commissioned by the city council, the monument was designed by the architect Jacob Möhl in 1891 and built in 1896–9 by Heinrich Düll, Max Heilmeier and Georg Pezold. It stands on the Maximilian Terraces, which are supported by a wall pierced by three niches. The central niche is in the form of a grotto that acts as a backdrop to the fountain. The monument is flanked by a stairway with a decorative balustrade. The plinth, on a tall podium, is in the form of an open hall with caryatids and columns. It contains portraits of the rulers and generals of the Franco-Prussian War.

The Angel of Peace

The monument was modelled on the Erechtheum on the Acropolis in Athens. Inside the hall, gold mosaics depicting the allegories of Peace, War, Victory and Culture cover a pedestal from which rises a Corinthian column 38 m (125 ft) high. The golden figure of the angel, 6 m (19 ft) high and crowning the column, imitates the Greek statue of Nike Paioniosa on Mount Olympus.

❿ St-Nikolai-Kirche
Church of St Nicholas

Innere Wiener Str. 1 **Map** 4 E3. **S** Rosenheimer Platz. ⭐ 16, N16. **Open** daily.

Beside the Gasteig Culture Centre, in the middle of a small, tranquil wood, stands the little church of St Nicholas. Its white-washed walls and onion dome bring to mind the churches of rural Bavaria. The building, first mentioned in 1313, was originally part of a leper hospital. It was rebuilt in the Renaissance and Baroque periods. After suffering destruction in World War II, it was restored and a late Baroque altar from Garmisch was added. Adjoining the church is the Altöttinger Kapelle, a chapel with an arcaded ambulatory. It is a copy of the famous church at Altötting. Originally built in Baroque style, it has been given several facelifts since then, the latest being in 1916. The Crucifixion group once formed part of an ancient Calvary. The modern crucifix standing amid the Baroque figures replaces the 18th-century original one that was destroyed during World War II.

The tiny Church of St Nicholas, which has a provincial atmosphere

The Modernist, fortress-like Gasteig Cultural Centre

⓫ Gasteig

Rosenheimer Str. 5. **Map** 4 E4. **Tel** 48 09 80. Ⓢ Rosenheimer Platz. 🚋 16, N16. **Open** 8am–11pm daily. Library: 10am–7pm Mon–Fri, 11am–4pm Sat.

Gasteig Cultural Centre is one of the largest of its kind in Europe. Built from 1978 to 1985, it covers more than 23,000 sq m (247,300 sq ft) and stands on the site of the Bürgerbräukeller, the beer hall where Hitler survived an attempt on his life when a bomb was planted there in 1939. The beer hall was demolished in the 1970s.

The modern glass, steel and brick building dominates the surrounding area like a fortress. It houses three major institutions: the Volkshochschule (an adult education centre), the municipal library, the Munich Philharmonic Orchestra and the Academy of Music and Theatre Munich..

The semicircular concert hall, with seating for 2,400, is lined with wood to enhance the acoustics. Besides the three other halls – the Carl Orff performance hall, the Small Concert Hall and the Black Box chamber theatre, there are many smaller auditoriums, workshops and rooms, which offer huge scope for variety and are a focal point in the cultural life of Munich.

The complex contains a large forum where sometimes major performances take place, and where there are also shops, restaurants and cafeterias. The east entrance is graced by a fountain in the shape of an enormous wind instrument.

⓬ Müllersches Volksbad

Müller Baths

Rosenheimer Str.1. **Map** 4 E3. **Tel** 23 61 50 50. Ⓢ Isartor. 🚋 16, 18. 🚌 132. **Open** 7:30am–11pm daily (to 5pm Mon); sauna: 9am–11pm daily.

Anyone who is keen on swimming or interested in interior design should visit this complex. It was built in 1897–1901 by the engineer Karl Müller to an architectural design by Carl Hocheder. At the time the baths – the first public baths in Munich – were considered to be the finest in Germany.

The men's and women's pools were originally separate. In addition to the many relaxation rooms, showers and baths, there is also a barrel-vaulted men's swimming pool, a domed ladies' swimming pool, a Roman bath and an Art Nouveau café. In the basement is a grooming centre for dogs.

The whole building reflects the new concepts of hygiene that were coming into vogue in the late 19th century, together with an interest in Roman bathing traditions. From an architectural point of view, the building is notable for the Neo-Baroque, Art Nouveau and Moorish elements that it incorporates.

The tower of the Müllersches Volksbad

⓭ Ludwigsbrücke

Zweibrückenstr./Rosenheimer Str. **Map** 4 D3 (6 F5). Ⓢ Isartor. Ⓤ Rosenheimer Platz, Isartor. 🚋 16, 18.

The history of Munich began at Ludwigsbrücke in 1158, when Heinrich der Löwe destroyed the toll bridge over the Isar belonging to the Bishop of Freising. Prince Heinrich wished the Salzstrasse, the salt route that had existed since Roman times, to cross the Isar near the place where Benedictine monks had established a settlement. He therefore built a new toll bridge, and the settlement became a centre of trade, having trading rights and issuing its own coinage.

The present bridge dates from 1935. It is decorated with figures personifying Industry and River Navigation (these were made in 1892 for the previous bridge) and Art (made in 1979).

Beside the bridge, on Museumsinsel, is the Fountain of Father Rhine, built in 1897–1902 by the sculptor Adolf von Hildebrand. The bronze statue of Father Rhine originally formed part of the fountain that stood outside the theatre in Strasbourg. When it was brought to Munich, it was placed in the centre of a fountain and was surrounded by putti standing on plinths.

⑭ Deutsches Museum

The Deutsches Museum, one of the world's oldest and largest museums of technology and engineering, draws over 1.4 million visitors each year. It was founded in 1903 by Oskar von Miller, an engineer. The collections cover most aspects of technology and the museum is also home to the world's largest library of technology. The museum has two other branches in Munich – the Verkehrszentrum for urban transport and the Flugwerft Schleissheim on the history of aviation.

Exterior of the Museum
The building combines Neo-Baroque, Neo-Classical and modern elements.

Decorative Arts
This plate with the portrait of a lady from Ludwig I's "Gallery of Beauties" is an example of reproduction techniques applied to porcelain. The ceramics section illustrates the development of faience, stoneware and porcelain.

Second floor

★ Physics
Galileo's workshop features a large collection of the scientific equipment used by the famous astronomer and physicist to establish the basic laws of mechanics.

First floor

★ Pharmaceuticals
Among the exhibits in this section is a model of a human cell magnified 350,000 times and graphically illustrating how it functions.

Museum Guide

The museum's 20,000 exhibits are displayed over six floors. While those on the lower floors include sections on chemistry, physics, and aeronautics, those on the middle floors relate to the decorative arts. The upper floors are devoted to astronomy, computers and microelectronics.

Main entrance

Ground floor

Sixth floor

Fifth floor

Fourth floor

Third floor

VISITORS' CHECKLIST

Practical Information

Museumsinsel. **Map** 4 D4.
Tel 21 791. **Open** 9am–5pm daily
(on-going restoration, call ahead).
🎫 (children under 6 free). 🖊
📷 ♿ 🎧 by arrangement (21 79
252). 🌐 **deutsches-museum.de**

Transport

🚇 Frauenhoferstr. 🚉 Isartor.
🚊 16, 18. 🚌 132.

Telecommunications

The Philips camera of 1967 was
one of the first colour television
cameras in the world.

★ **Musical Instruments**

The keyboard instruments
room contains the earliest
southern German organ
and a 17th-century
highly decorated
harpsichord.

Key to Floorplan

- ☐ Design and Technology
- ☐ Centre for New Technology
- ☐ Kids' Kingdom
- ☐ Physics, Chemistry and Pharmaceuticals
- ☐ Musical Instruments
- ☐ Decorative Arts
- ☐ Time, Weights and Measures
- ☐ Automation, Microelectronics and Telecommunications
- ☐ Astronomy
- ☐ Agriculture and Geodesy
- ☐ Aviation
- ☐ Miscellaneous

Kids' Kingdom is an area where children
between the ages of 3 and 8 can learn
about science and technology in a fun
and imaginative way. There are many
exciting exhibits, including a giant guitar,
a fire engine and an electric light cinema.
It lives up to its name because adults can
only enter with the child's permission.

Exploring the Deutsches Museum

To view all the exhibits on every floor in detail would take a whole month since the entire route through the museum is 17 km (10.5 miles) long. With more than 50 sections on offer, it is best to concentrate on just a few areas. The attractive way in which the exhibits are laid out is very effective, and there are plenty of items that visitors can operate themselves, so this is a museum that children will enjoy too. There are also regular demonstrations of working machinery and film shows.

Design and Technology

The museum contains displays of such classic aspects of engineering as machine-building, mining, metallurgy, and hydraulic and civil engineering. The display of machines and turbines features many pro-totypes and the first diesel engine. The demonstra-tions of high-voltage currents and artificial lightning are particularly impressive, as is the re-creation of a mine.

Figures of miners at work in a re-created coal mine from c.1925

Physics, Chemistry and Pharmaceuticals

The physics and chemistry section is outstanding. There are fascinating reconstructions of the laboratories of great scientists and also a collection of the original instruments used in some of the greatest scientific discoveries, as well as many pieces of prototype apparatus.

The exhibits are complemented by interesting demonstrations of the latest technology in optics, nuclear physics and chemistry. In the pharmaceuticals section the exhibits graphically illustrate

the different biochemical processes that take place in the human body.

Musical Instruments

This section is displayed in chronological order, with over 1,800 instruments on display. The centrepiece of the key-board instruments section is the earliest harpsichord, which was made in 1561.

On the first floor are wind, stringed and percussion instruments. There are also music machines and modern electronic keyboards located on the second floor, displayed in a walk-in storage area. Regular tours take place, as well as concerts on specific musical themes.

Decorative Arts

The decorative arts are illustrated by a number of thematic displays. The section opens with glass and ceramics manufacturing techniques from the earliest times to the present.

There is an exhibition of paper manufacturing and printing technology, including an impressive display of industrial textile machinery.

The exhibition of the development of film and photography begins with Daguerre's original equip-ment from 1839 and ends with digital technology.

The display of technical toys goes all the way from simple building blocks to the most sophisticated modern modelling kits. On the same floor is a realistic re-creation of Altamira Cave, in Spain, with its Stone Age paintings.

A quadrant (an instrument for measuring azimuths) made in 1760

Time, Weights and Measures

A fine display of clocks and watches illustrates the problems of measuring time. The clocks begin with the simplest forms, such as sundials and sand-clocks, and progress to highly intricate and lavishly deco-rated mechanical clocks. There are also gigantic clock-tower mechanisms and elaborately ornamented grandfather clocks from various periods, as well as more modern clocks and watches.

The weights and measures section illustrates the unifica-tion of measurements, and shows various types of measuring equipment.

An Augsburg clock with the figure of a dancing bear, 1580–90

Astronomy

With over 180 exhibits, the astronomy section explores such major and still incompletely understood questions as the structure of the universe and the nature of solar energy. It also charts the development of this field of human enquiry with a variety of measuring instruments and models of spaceships, and with models of solar systems and galaxies. It also addresses the problems of radiation and the enigma of black holes. In the observatory visitors can view the stars through giant telescopes.

A highly ornamental brass calculating machine from 1735

Automation, Microelectronics and Telecommunications

The purpose of this section is to illustrate the genesis and development of modern technology. It opens with the first calculating machines, developed by Blaise Pascal (1642), Gottfried von Leibniz (1700) and Anton Braun (1735), and the first computer, the earliest built by Konrad Zuse in 1941. There is also an interesting display of the latest information technology.

The development of microelectronics is illustrated with models of the simplest diodes, transistors, resistors, condensers and semiconductors. The importance of crystals in semiconductors and other aspects of modern electronics is also illustrated.

For non-specialists, the use of high-tech applications in everyday life is of particular interest. Broadcasting and the disseminating of information, by means of radio, television, fibre optics and computers, also have important displays.

The Zeiss Planetarium

One of the world's best-equipped planetariums occupies the sixth floor of the museum. An artificial sky is created by a Zeiss computer-controlled projector. The dome, 15 m (49 ft) across, is used for the projection of images of the sun, the moon and the planets, along with 8,900 stars and 25 constellations and nebulae. You can watch the movements of heavenly bodies as they change position through the year and view them from different points on the earth, and listen to detailed explanations of the universe. It is a treat to experience a clear, starry sky. Presentations available vary and tickets for the Zeiss Planetarium are sold separately.

Agriculture and Geodesy

This section illustrates the development of farming equipment from the simplest tools to ploughs and modern farm machinery. The geodesic displays show methods of measuring the earth and the development of topography, from early surveying equipment and maps and globes to modern satellite surveying.

Centre for New Technology

The Centre is a platform from which technological experts can share their knowledge with a wider public on subjects as diverse as research on climate change to biomedical discoveries and inventions. The Centre hosts permanent exhibitions as well as temporary presentations. An exhibition on permanent display is Nanotechnology and Biotechnology. This exhibition examines the ultra-miniscule side of our world, looking at genome research and cancer treatments amongst other subjects. There is also a small exhibition on Robotics, which illustrates the development and potential of modern robots.

The Centre for New Technology also contains three laboratories. At the interactive DNA visitors' laboratory you can take part in modern research and even examine your own genetic matter.

Due to the nature of the technological world, the exhibits here are ever-changing, aiming to provide an up-to-date resource on the very latest discoveries.

A laboratory pod in the Centre for New Technology

THE UNIVERSITY DISTRICT

The area to the north of the Old Town is a varied district in terms both of its architecture and its atmosphere. Ludwigstraße is lined exclusively with elegant Neo-Classical buildings, most of them government offices and public buildings, including the Bavarian State Library and the university.

West and north of Ludwigstraße the atmosphere changes completely. The buildings here are in a variety of styles spanning the 19th and 20th centuries. The area abounds in trendy shops, bookshops and pubs and it is filled with crowds of young students. Full of history and local colour, this area, known as Schwabing, is fascinating to visit. Leopoldstraße, its bustling main boulevard, comes as a great contrast to Ludwigstraße.

To the east of Schwabing is the Englischer Garten, with the museums of Prinzregentenstraße on its southern side. The park is a welcome oasis to the footsore visitor and to those seeking a moment's peace. Here you can rest among abundant greenery, sunbathe (even nude), cool off in the water or enjoy a cold beer in the beergarden at the Chinese Tower.

Sights at a Glance

Churches
5 Ludwigskirche

Museums and Galleries
11 Archäologische Staatssammlung
12 Sammlung Schack
13 Bayerisches Nationalmuseum pp112–13
14 Haus der Kunst

Historic Buildings
4 Bayerische Staatsbibliothek
6 Ludwig-Maximilians-Universität
7 Siegestor
8 Akademie der Bildenden Künste
9 Pacelli Palais
10 Art Nouveau house in Ainmillerstraße

Streets and Squares
1 Wittelsbacherplatz
2 Odeonsplatz
3 Ludwigstraße

Restaurants pp278
1 Cohen's
2 Huckebein Essen & Trinken
3 Kytaro
4 Reitschule
5 Sangeet
6 Vanilla Lounge

0 metres 400
0 yards 400

See also Street Finder maps 2, 3, 4 & 6

◀ Magnificent frescoes adorn the interior of Ludwigskirche

For map symbols *see back flap*

Street-by-Street: Along Ludwigstraße

Sightseeing in this part of the city is fascinating for some but less appealing for others. The district's monumental Neo-Classical architecture was designed to a unified urban plan. There are no shops or pubs here. Instead the Ludwigstraße is lined with palaces whose façades are reminiscent of Italian Romanesque or Renaissance architecture, and the long avenue is punctuated by large squares. It is hard to imagine that the bustling, culturally varied Schwabing district is just next door.

❻ Ludwig-Maximilians-Universität
The university building, looking onto Amalienstraße, has an eclectic façade with an arcaded lower storey.

❶ ★ Wittelsbacherplatz
The Palais Ludwig Ferdinand on Wittelsbacherplatz was built by Leo von Klenze and was his residence for 25 years. Today, it serves as the headquarters of Siemens AG.

The Monument to Maximilian I
by the Danish sculptor Bertel Thorvaldsen is based on the style of equestrian statues of the Italian Renaissance.

❷ Odeonsplatz
The focal point is the Feldherrnhalle on the south side.

❸ Ludwigstraße
This stretch of the street is flanked by monochrome façades in Italian Renaissance style.

Schwabing

ADALBERTSTR.

LUDWIGSTR.

VETERINÄRSTR.

The 19th-century architecture between Ludwigstraße and the Englischer Garten is as varied as the colourful Schwabing district.

Locator Map
See Street Finder maps 2, 3, 4 & 6

UNIVERSITY DISTRICT

❼ Siegestor
This triumphal arch is decorated with bas-reliefs depicting scenes of battles fought by the Bavarian army. The reliefs, by Johann Martin von Wagner, show the Bavarian troops dressed in the uniforms of Classical antiquity.

❺ ★ Ludwigskirche
St Ludwig's Church was built in the Italian Romanesque style. The façade, with its triple-arched entrance, is watched over by figures of Christ and the four Evangelists by Ludwig Schwanthaler.

Key

— Suggested route

0 metres   100
0 yards   100

❹ Bayerische Staatsbibliothek
A long flight of steps leads to the entrance of the Bavarian State Library. The balustrade is decorated with statues of Thucydides, Homer, Aristotle and Hippocrates by Ludwig Schwanthaler.

The Palladian façade of Arco-Zinneberg Palace on Wittelsbacherplatz

❶ Wittelsbacherplatz

Map 3 C1 (6 D1). **U** Odeonsplatz. 🚌 100.

This square is situated on Briennerstraße, one of the city's most elegant streets, which leads off from Odeonsplatz. Wittelsbacherplatz was laid out in the 1820s to a design by Leo von Klenze, and is one of Munich's finest squares. It is lined on three sides by Neo-Classical palaces, and the square itself is laid with paving slabs and stones arranged to form various patterns.

Von Klenze lived in the Ludwig-Ferdinand Palais on the north side of the square. From 1878 the palace belonged to Duke Ludwig Ferdinand, after whom it was named. It is now owned by the Siemens corporation.

On the west side of the square is Arco-Zinneberg Palace, also designed by Leo von Klenze, which today houses upmarket shops. To the east is the Odeon and the Palais Méjean, which was rebuilt after being destroyed in World War II.

In the centre of the square stands a monument to the Elector Maximilian I. It was designed by the prominent Danish Neo-Classical sculptor Bertel Thorwaldsen and was unveiled in 1839.

❷ Odeonsplatz

Map 3 C1 (6 D1). **U** Odeonsplatz. 🚌 100.

In the early 19th century, when the Schwabinger Tor was demolished, a decision was made to impose order on the haphazard arrangement of buildings to the north of the Residenz and the

Theatinerkirche. In 1817 Maximilian I Joseph approved Leo von Klenze's plan for the Odeons-platz, unaware that its orig-inator was in fact his son, Ludwig I. The heir to the throne wished to create a magnificent square marking the start of the main thoroughfare to the northern districts and also acting as a triumphal entry point into Munich.

The Odeonsplatz takes its name from the Odeon, a concert hall built by Leo von Klenze in 1826–8 as a counterpart to the Leuchtenbergpalais of 1816–21. Set back from the square, both buildings serve to elongate it.

The equestrian statue of Ludwig I flanked by personifications of Religion, Art, Poetry and Industry in the centre of the square was created by Max Widmann in 1862. It faces the side of the square containing the Market Hall of

Monument to Ludwig I on Odeonsplatz

1825–6 and the arch leading to the palace court. On the side of the Old Town, the square is bounded by the Feldherrnhalle.

❸ Ludwigstraße

Map 2 D5, 2 E5. **U** Odeonsplatz, Universität. 🚌 100, 154.

One of the most splendid city streets in Europe is Ludwigstraße. It was built from 1815 to 1852, the general plan and the first group of buildings being designed and completed by Leo von Klenze. The street begins at Odeonsplatz, whose Italian Renaissance-style palaces harmonize perfectly with the buildings at the begin-ning of Ludwigstraße. In 1827 the project was taken over by Friedrich von Gärtner, who was responsible for the buildings north of Theresien-straße, which he gave Romanesque and Byzantine elements.

The principal buildings on this part of the street are the Bavarian State Library, Ludwigskirche and university buildings. In the mid-19th century, the Feldherrnhalle and Siegestor were added, at the south and north ends of the street respectively. In building this triumphal route, Ludwig I departed from the city's planning rules to satisfy his aesthetic and political ideals.

The Odeon concert hall before it was destroyed in 1944

The fountain in the centre of Professor-Huber-Platz at Ludwig-Maximilians-Universität

❹ Bayerische Staatsbibliothek

Bavarian State Library

Ludwigstr. 16. **Map** 2 E5. **Tel** 28 63 82 322. Ⓤ Odeonsplatz, Universität. 🚌 100. **Open** 8am–midnight Mon–Sun. ♿ phone in advance.

The Bayerische Staatsbibliothek, Germany's second largest library after the German national library in Leipzig, has its origins in the collections of books that were amassed by Duke Albrecht V and Wilhelm V in the 16th century. It was enhanced from 1663, when the Elector Friedrich Maria ordered that one copy of every new book published in Bavaria or published by a Bavarian abroad should be kept in the library. An enormous addition to the royal collection of books – particularly of early editions – was made when the Jesuit order was disbanded in 1773 and again when the monasteries were dissolved in 1803.

Today the Bayerische Staatsbibliothek contains almost 10 million volumes, including 95,900 manuscripts, 29,000 maps and almost 62,100 current periodicals.

The library was the first architectural project undertaken by Friedrich von Gärtner, who started in 1832 and completed it in 1843. The building echoes the style of Italian Renaissance palaces. The great interior staircase is flanked by figures of Classical sages carved by Ludwig Schwanthaler and overlooked by figures of the library's founders, Albrecht V and Ludwig I.

Statue of Hippocrates outside the library

❺ Ludwigskirche

St Ludwig's Church

Ludwigstr. 20. **Map** 2 E5. Ⓤ Universität. 🚌 154. **Open** 8am–8pm daily (except during services).

Its façade set with pointed twin steeples, St Ludwig's Church is in sharp contrast to the neighbouring Staatsbibliothek. It was built in the Italian Romanesque style by Friedrich von Gärtner in 1829–43. The niches in the façade contain figures of Christ and the four Evangelists. The wings connect the church to the presbytery and to Friedrich von Gärtner's house. The interior is decorated with Italian Renaissance-style paintings by Peter von Cornelius and his pupils. The painting of the Last Judgment is the second largest in the world after Michelangelo's in the Sistine Chapel.

The Neo-Romanesque façade of St Ludwig's Church

❻ Ludwig-Maximilians-Universität

Ludwig Maximilian University

Geschwister-Scholl-Platz / Professor-Huber-Platz. **Map** 2 E4. **Tel** 21 800. Ⓤ Universität. 🚌 154. **Open** 6:15am–10pm Mon–Fri, 8am–6pm Sat. ♿

This institute of higher education is named in honour of its first sponsors.

In 1472 Ludwig der Reiche (the Rich) founded a Jesuit Studium Generale in Ingolstadt. In 1771 it became a university. Maximilian I Joseph moved it to Landshut in 1800 and in 1826 Ludwig I transferred it to Munich. The university has been located on Ludwigstraße since 1840.

Today there are some 50,000 students. The noisy crowds of young people ensure that the streets in the vicinity are always full of life. The university's assembly hall and seminar rooms are set round two quadrangles. The latter are named after Hans and Sophie Scholl and Professor Kurt Huber, who together founded the White Rose movement that opposed Hitler. In 1943 members of the group distributed anti-Nazi leaflets at the university, an event that is commemorated by the "fossilized" sheets of paper in the paving of the main building's courtyard. The group was arrested and most of its members were executed.

The monumental Siegestor, crowned by the personification of Bavaria

❼ Siegestor
Victory Gate

Ludwigstr. **Map** 2 E4. Ⓤ Universität. 🚌 154.

Following the early 19th-century fashion for erecting triumphal arches, Friedrich von Gärtner designed the Siegestor for Ludwig I. The monument was built in 1843–50, and with its three grand arches it echoes the architecture of the Feldherrnhalle *(see pp82–3)*. The building stands on Ludwigstraße at the junction with Leopoldstraße, Schwabing's fine main street.

The design of the Siegestor is based on the Arch of Constantine in Rome. It honours the Bavarian army and its role in the country's victory against Napoleon. The arch is covered in bas-reliefs depicting battle scenes, medallions, personifications of the Bavarian provinces, and figures of Victory at the top of the columns. The arch is crowned by the figure of Bavaria riding in a chariot drawn by four lions. The inscription that was added in 1958 states that the arch, which is "dedicated to victory, destroyed during the war", appeals for peace.

Passing through the Siegestor and entering Leo-poldstraße,

there is a notable change of atmosphere. The architectural uniformity of Ludwigstraße is replaced by stylistic variety in houses of the late 19th and early 20th centuries. The cafés, restaurants, music shops, bookstores, cinemas and discos here make for a vibrant atmosphere that persists into the small hours. This is the heart of the renowned Schwabing district.

❽ Akademie der Bildenden Künste
Academy of Fine Arts

Akademiestr. 2. **Map** 2 E4. **Tel** 38 520. Ⓤ Universität. 🚌 154. ♿ **Closed** to the public.

During the 19th century Munich was one of the most important centres of painting, although it was regarded as being rather conservative.

Munich's artistic community developed around the Academy of Graphic Arts, which was founded in 1808. Many painters who subsequently became famous studied here, including the Germans Wilhelm Leibl and Franz Marc, the German-Swiss Paul Klee, the Russian-born Wassily Kandinsky, and the Italian Giorgio de Chirico.

The Academy of Graphic Arts was originally housed in the Jesuit College of Michaelskirche, moving to its present location in 1886. The architect of the new building was Gottfried Neureuther, who based his design on that of a three-storey Italian palazzo.

The imposing façade is pierced by a series of arched windows and the building is approached by a driveway leading to a grand staircase, with equestrian statues of Castor and Pollux.

❾ Pacelli Palais

Georgenstr. 8–10. **Map** 2 E3. Ⓤ Universität, Giselastr. 🚌 27, 28, N27. **Closed** to the public.

This grand city palace provides an opportunity to compare two distinct architectural styles that were prevalent in Munich around 1900. The right-hand half of the building is in a late historical style, with columns, tympanums, small towers, carved loggias and sculptures. The flat but colourful Neo-Classical decoration on the left-hand half is typical of the Munich Art Nouveau style. It is now a private residence.

Art Nouveau decoration on the Pacelli Palais

❿ Jugendstilhaus in der Ainmillerstraße
Art Nouveau House

Ainmillerstr. 22. **Map** 2 E2. Ⓤ Giselastr. 🚌 144, 154, N40, N41. 🚋 27, 28, N27. **Closed** to the public.

The house at Ainmillerstraße 22 was the first residential building in Munich to be given an Art Nouveau (Jugendstil) façade. It was designed by Ernst Haiger and Henry Helbig in 1899–1900. The intricate scheme features decorative floral and mock-antique motifs.

Highly ornamental terracotta frieze on a window at the Akademie der Bildenden Künste

For hotels and restaurants in this region see pp266–7 and pp276–9

Schwabing

At the end of the 19th century Schwabing was well known as a bohemian district inhabited by writers and avant-garde artists. *Simplicissimus*, an anti-authoritarian satirical magazine, and the Elf Scharfrichter cabaret associated with it, were both located here. Many writers' cafés determined the atmosphere of the district. It had its heyday in the years preceding World War I, when the writers Thomas Mann and Frank Wedekind and the artists Wassily Kandinsky and Paul Klee lived here. Paradoxically, after 1918, it became the favourite haunt of Adolf Hitler, who set up the offices of the *Völkischer Beobachter* newspaper here. After 1945 the district strove to revive its former glory with the help of local artists and students.

The suburbs of Munich are seen here in a painting by Wassily Kandinsky. The Russian-born painter lived in Schwabing from 1902 to 1914, becoming a German citizen in 1927.

Art Nouveau window decoration on the house at Leopoldstraße 77 is a fine example of the trend for geometrical Art Nouveau typical of houses in Schwabing.

Artists from Schwabing formed the avant-garde Neue Künstlervereinigung in Munich in the early 1900s. This photograph was taken on the balcony of Kandinsky's house at No. 36 Ainmillerstraße. It shows, from left to right: Maria and Franz Marc; Bernhard Koehler, Kandinsky (seated), Heinrich Campendonk and Thomas von Hartmann. In 1911, the Der Blaue Reiter group was established in Munich, with Kandsinky at the forefront.

This front door decoration on the Jugendstilhaus in Ainmillerstraße shows Art Nouveau asymmetry and symbolism. It reflects local artistic bohemian culture, in which the legendary Countess Reventlow, who propounded a free, erotic lifestyle, was a leading figure.

Englischer Garten

The Englischer Garten (English Garden) is so named because it is naturalistically laid out, in the manner of English landscaped grounds. One of Europe's largest city parks, it came into existence thanks to the vision of Sir Benjamin Thompson, an American officer on whom the Elector Karl Theodor bestowed the title Count von Rumford. As Bavaria's Minister of War, he ordered that the swampy terrain around the Isar be developed for military use. It became a municipal park, with many landscaped features designed by Rumford, Reinhold von Werneck and Friedrich Ludwig von Sckell, in 1789. Today the park is a valued green area for the people of Munich.

The Eisbach, despite the chilly water, is an excellent place to practise surfing.

The Chinese Tower was built in 1789–90 as a viewing tower and bandstand. One of the city's most famous beer-gardens is laid out around it.

The paths through the park are usually busy with cyclists and walkers.

The grassy areas are crowded with sunbathers in summer.

The Monopteros is a Neo-Classical building designed by Leo von Klenze and offering a panoramic view of the city.

ENGLISCHER GARTEN

The Rumford Memorial, built by Ludwig Schwanthaler in 1795, features a relief portrait of the count and a bas-relief depicting Bavaria favoured by Abundance.

Scenic streams wind among the trees and shrubs. One of the streams feeds the large artificial lake known as the Kleinhesseloher See, lying north of the Chinese Tower.

0 metres 200
0 yards 200

⓫ Archäologische Staatssammlung

Archaeological Museum

Lerchenfeldstr. 2. **Map** 4 E1.
Tel 21 12 402. 🚋 18. 🚌 100.
Open 9:30am–5pm Tue–Sun. ♿

The Archaeological Museum, at the southern end of the Englischer Garten, is a modern glass and steel construction consisting of six blocks arranged in chequer-board formation. Formerly known as the Museum of Prehistory, it is one of the largest regional museums of archaeology in Germany.

The collections date back to the foundation of the Bavarian Academy of Sciences in 1759. The exhibits, which span a period of time from as early as 100,000 BC to AD 800, are chronologically presented in three separate sections: Pre-historic, Roman and Early Medieval.

Implements and jewellery, coins and religious artifacts illustrate the history of human settlement in Bavaria. There is a rich collection of Roman exhibits, including bronze masks from Eining, the Straubing Treasure and many mosaics from Roman baths. A popular attraction is the mummified body of a 16th-century woman that was discovered in marshland.

⓬ Sammlung Schack

Prinzregentenstr. 9. **Map** 4 E1.
Tel 23 80 52 24. 🚌 100. 🚋 18.
Open 10am–6pm Wed–Sun (to 8pm 1st and 3rd Wed in month). 🖼

This interesting collection of 19th-century paintings was formed by Friedrich von Schack (1815–94), a wealthy baron from Mecklenburg. As well as an art collector, he was a man of letters, a translator and a traveller. In 1857 Schack bought a palace near the Propyläen, where he housed his art collection. Von Schack's main interest lay in contemporary Munich painters, and he often sponsored young

Façade of the Neo-Classical Haus der Kunst

artists. Under the terms of his will, von Schack's art collection was bequeathed to the Emperor Wilhelm II, who then decided to give the collection a home in Munich, commissioning a building especially for it. Designed by Max Littman and completed in 1910, the Schack-Galerie has a Neo-Classical façade and is similar to the Berlin castle of the collection's founder, who is praised in an inscription on the façade.

In 1939, the Sammlung Schack was merged with the Bavarian State Art Collection. In 17 halls, it presents German painting from the late Romantic period. Among the 270 paintings are works by Moritz von Schwind, including Turnip-counter and King Olch and Anselm Feuerbach's Portrait of a Roman Woman and Paolo and Francesca. Also of interest are the paintings by Karl Spitzweg, Franz von Lenbach and Hans von Marées.

A Celtic staff, probably for use in rituals

Façade of the Schack-Galerie, based on von Schack's Berlin castle

⓭ Bayerisches Nationalmuseum

See pp112–13.

⓮ Haus der Kunst

Art House

Prinzregentenstr. 1. **Map** 4 D1. **Tel** 21 12 71 13. **Open** 10am–8pm daily (until 10pm Thu). **Closed** 24 & 31 Dec. ♿

At the end of World War II, the palatial Haus der Kunst housed a collection of modern art. Built between 1933 and 1937, the Neo-Classical building is the work of architect Paul Ludwig Troost; Adolf Hitler laid the foundation stone and the building became the model for the nascent National Socialist architecture.

The museum, known as the House of German Art under the Nazi regime, opened its doors in July 1937 with a display of propaganda art, proclaimed by the Nazis as "truly German". At the same time "The Exhibition of Degenerate Art", opened in the Hofgarten Arcades, now the German Theatre Museum *(see p89)*. Several of the masterpieces were denigrated and ridiculed by the public during the opening. The "Great German Art Exhibition", housed here, displayed the work of officially approved artists.

In 2002, the National Collection of Modern and Contemporary Arts moved into the Pinakothek der Moderne *(see pp120–21)*. Today, while housing no permanent collections of its own, the museum showcases temporary exhibitions of the world's major contemporary artists and photographers.

⑬ Bayerisches Nationalmuseum

In architectural terms, the Bavarian National Museum was intended to embody the idea of a 19th-century artistic shrine. It was built by Gabriel von Seidl in 1894–1900, and features a mixture of styles that expresses the richness and variety of the collections within. The decoration of the interior was devised with the exhibits in mind. The nucleus of the collection is that of the Wittelsbachs, which Maximilian II donated to the country in 1855. One of Germany's largest history museums, its collections span Classical antiquity to the 19th century.

Model of Munich
Commissioned by Albrecht V, this wooden model was made by Jakob Sandtner in 1570.

Bauernstube (Farmhouse Parlour)
These pieces of traditional furniture were made by Anton Perthaler of Lower Bavaria in the late 18th century.

First floor

Ground floor

★ **Judith with the Head of Holofernes**
This alabaster figure was made by Conrad Meit in 1515, with the figure of Judith being depicted as a nude.

Main entrance

★ **Christmas Crib**
This 18th-century Neapolitan crib forms part of the largest and most important collection of its kind in the world.

Basement

Harpsichord

This harpsichord in the Musical Instruments Hall was made in Paris in 1754 by Jean Henri Hemsch.

★ St Mary Magdalene

This statue of the saint borne by angels was made by Tilman Riemenschneider in 1490–92 for an altarpiece.

Museum Guide

The collections are laid out on three floors connected by grand staircases. The basement contains a collection of Christmas cribs and a section devoted to folk art. Painting, sculpture and crafts up to the 18th century are exhibited on the ground floor. The upper floor contains collections of musical instruments, porcelain and Biedermeier art.

Gothic Hall

Laid out like a church, the hall contains religious art and tombstones of around 1500, including paintings by Jan Polack.

Romanesque Sculpture

Sculpture and architectural details dating from the first half of the 13th century and originating from the Wessobrunn Benedictine monastery fill this sculpture hall.

Key to Floorplan

- Ethnographic, Pottery & Furniture
- Cribs
- Gothic
- Renaissance
- Thematic exhibition, including musical instruments and porcelain
- 19th-Century Art and Jugendstil
- Baroque and Rococo
- Non-exhibition space

THE MUSEUMS DISTRICT

A competition for an architectural design to embellish the area along the Royal Route between the Residenz and Schloss Nymphenburg was announced in 1807. The winning design was one jointly produced by Friedrich Ludwig von Sckell and Karl von Fischer, although it was later modified by Leo von Klenze.

The axis of this area, known as the Maxvorstadt, is Briennerstraße. Maximilian I Joseph and Ludwig I dreamed of turning Munich into a city of the arts, commissioning the Alte Pinakothek and Neue Pinakothek, and grand buildings on Königsplatz. The 19th-century painter Franz von Lenbach had an imposing villa (now an art gallery) built on the square. The omnipresence of art here is underscored by the district's many private galleries, antique shops and bookstores.

Sights at a Glance

Museums and Galleries
3 Staatliche
   Antikensammlungen
5 Glyptothek
6 Galerie im Lenbachhaus
7 Paläontologisches Museum
8 *Alte Pinakothek pp122–5*
9 *Neue Pinakothek pp126–9*
10 Museum "Reich der Kristalle"
11 Pinakothek der Moderne
12 Museum Brandhorst

Historic Buildings
4 Propyläen
13 Palais Pinakothek
16 Justizpalast

Churches
2 Basilika St Bonifaz

Streets and Squares
1 Karolinenplatz
14 Lenbachplatz
15 Karlsplatz

Gardens
17 Alter Botanischer Garten

Other Sights
18 Löwenbräukeller

☐ **Restaurants** *pp278*
1 Königshof
2 Rilano No. 6

See also Street Finder maps 1, 3 & 5

0 metres 250
0 yards 250

◀ *The Great Last Judgement* by Peter Paul Rubens, Alte Pinakothek

For map symbols *see back flap*

Street-by-Street: Around Königsplatz

Several days are needed for a thorough exploration of this part of the city. The many museums here contain world-class art – from prehistoric to modern. On Königsplatz, Greek and Roman sculpture can be seen in the Glyptothek, and Classical and other antiquities in the Antikensammlungen. The Alte Pinakothek, Neue Pinakothek and Pinakothek der Moderne nearby contain some of the richest collections of European painting in the world. The Lenbachhaus is renowned for works by the Blaue Reiter group. Those interested in natural history will enjoy the Palaeontology Museum.

❼ Paläontologisches Museum
One of the most impressive exhibits in the museum is the cast of a mammoth skeleton from the early Tertiary period.

Galerie im Lenbachhaus
The Lenbachhaus interior sets in its context the bourgeois lifestyle of Franz von Lenbach, the famous late 19th-century portraitist.

❹ Propyläen
The frieze decorating the side towers of the Propyläen, with motifs and scenes from the Greek War of Independence, is by Ludwig Schwanthaler.

❸ Staatliche Antikensammlungen
Among the museum's treasures is a collection of antique art and artifacts.

❷ Basilika St Bonifaz
This church contains the tomb of Ludwig I.

❺ ★ Glyptothek
The Glyptothek's Ionic colonnade with pediment is flanked by statues of great artistic figures from Classical antiquity: Hephaestus, Prometheus, Daedalus, Phidias, Pericles and Emperor Hadrian.

❾ ★ Neue Pinakothek
After viewing this modern museum's impressive collection of paintings ranging from 1780 to 1910, visitors can relax on the terrace, with its pools of water.

Locator Map
See Street Finder map 1

❽ ★ Alte Pinakothek
Giovanni Battista Tiepolo's painting *The Adoration of the Magi* is one of the most important 18th-century works of Viennese art.

❶ Karolinenplatz
In the centre of this square, which was named in honour of Karolina, stepmother of Ludwig I, stands a large obelisk commemorating the 30,000 Bavarian soldiers in Napoleon's army who died during his Russian campaign.

Old Town

0 metres   100
0 yards   100

Key
— Suggested route

The Amerika Haus on Karolinenplatz

❶ Karolinenplatz

Map 1 C5, 3 A1. 🚊 27, 28, N27.

Maximilian I Joseph, who continued the development of Munich that was begun by his predecessor Karl Theodor, focused his attention on the area around Briennerstraße. The Royal Route connecting the Residenz with Schloss Nymphenburg was opened up, and it became the focal point of the development of this suburb, which was named Maxvorstadt in the king's honour.

In 1809–12 a square was built at the junction of Briennerstraße and Barerstraße. This square was Karolinenplatz, the first star junction in Munich. Designed by Karl von Fischer, it was modelled on the Place de l'Étoile in Paris. In the centre of the square stands a bronze obelisk 29 m (95 ft) high, designed by Leo von Klenze and cast from Turkish guns captured at the Battle of Navarino in 1827. The obelisk commemorates the 30,000 Bavarian soldiers who died during Napoleon's Russian campaign of 1812.

On the south side of the Karolinenplatz is the Staatssammlung für Anthropologie und Paläoanatomie, the only anthropological collection of its kind in Germany, with a curious assortment of skulls. On the southwestern side is the Amerika Haus, an American cultural centre, which was built in 1955–7.

❷ Basilika St Bonifaz

Basilica of St Boniface

Karlstr. 34. **Map** 3 A1, 5 A1. **Tel** 55 17 10. **Open** 7am–7pm daily. 🚊 27, 28, N27.

The Basilica of St Boniface, which was commissioned by Ludwig I, functioned as the parish church of the Maxvorstadt but was later dedicated to the Benedictine monks who moved to Munich. The church, which takes the form of an early Christian basilica, was built in 1835–48 by Georg Friedrich Ziebland.

Behind the portico, which is supported by Ionic columns, are three arched doorways. The central one is flanked by statues of St Peter and St Boniface, and the arch is crowned by a portrait of the architect himself – a rare occurrence – in medieval dress. The location of the church and monastery at the rear of the Kunstausstellungsgebäude (now the Antikensammlung) illustrates contemporary ideas about architecture, in which religion was to be linked with art and science, as represented by the Benedictine order.

The basilica, which was built after the destruction brought by World War II, carries no memory of the original

Central section of the façade of the Basilika St Bonifaz

double-aisled church, which had colourful paintings and an open-beam roof supported on 66 monolithic columns. Of its furnishings, the white marble tomb of Ludwig I survives, with the tombstone of his wife Therese behind it.

❸ Staatliche Antikensammlungen

The National Collection of Antiquities

Königsplatz 1. **Map** 1 B5. **Tel** 59 98 88 30. 🚇 Königsplatz. 🚊 27, 28, N27. **Open** 10am–5pm Tue–Sun (to 8pm Wed). 🎨

In 1838 Ludwig I, temporarily at loggerheads with the court architect Leo von Klenze, commissioned Georg Friedrich Ziebland to design the southern side of the Königsplatz. The king wished for an exhibition hall that would adjoin the Benedictine monastery and Basilica of St Boniface at the rear. The building, completed in 1848, was modelled on the design of a late Classical Greek temple, its proportions differing from those of the Glyptothek on the opposite side of the square. Over the large colonnaded portico is a tympanum containing a figure of Bavaria as patroness of art and industry. From 1898 to 1916 the hall housed the gallery of the Munich Secession (Art Nouveau movement), after which it was taken over by the Neue Staatsgalerie. Since 1967 it has housed the National Collection of Antiquities.

Greek kylix (drinking vessel), Staatliche Antikensammlung

This impressive collection includes an important assemblage of Greek and Etruscan vases, plus fine pottery and glass, bronze and terracotta figures and jewellery. The core of the collection was donated by Ludwig I, who was a passionate collector and an ardent admirer of the ancient world.

❹ Propyläen

Map 1 B5. **Ⓤ** Königsplatz.
🚍 27, 28, N27.

From 1815, Ludwig I and Leo von Klenze planned the layout of the Royal Square, or Königsplatz, west of Karolinenplatz. The latter was laid out as an almost perfect square, with the Glyptothek and what is now the Antikensammlungen facing one another on opposite sides. To the west of the square was a gate built by Leo von Klenze in 1854–62, named the Propyläen.

According to the designs of the king and the architect, the buildings on three sides of the square would each represent one of the orders of architecture. The Propyläen would represent the Doric order, the Glyptothek the Ionic, and the exhibition hall the Corinthian.

The Propyläen was based on the Propylaeum in Athens, which consists of a central entrance way crowned by a grand tympanum and flanked by towers. Munich's Propyläen was intended to function as the western gate into the city, the Neo-Classical equivalent of the medieval Isar Gate.

When, however, the city's development rendered it superfluous, Ludwig I and von Klenze emphasized the Hellenistic character of the Propyläen, turning it into a kind of monument to the Greek War of Liberation against Turkey (1821–9). In so doing they strove to underline the connection between Bavaria and the newly independent Greek state (Otto I Wittelsbach, son of Ludwig I, was its first ruler).

Leo von Klenze (1784–1864)

After Karl Friedrich Schinkel, Leo von Klenze is considered to be the most prominent representative of the Neo-Classical movement in 19th-century German architecture. In the reign of Ludwig I, his constant if fussy patron, von Klenze was responsible for the new face of Munich, designing such buildings as the Alte Pinakothek, the forum of the Königsplatz, the Residenz, the Ruhmeshalle and Ludwigstraße. He was responsible for planning Munich as the new Athens, as well as the Walhalla near Ratisbon, the Befreiungshalle in Kelheim and the New Hermitage in St Petersburg.

Bust of the architect crowned with laurel

❺ Glyptothek

Glyptoteca

Königsplatz 3. **Map** 1 B5. **Tel** 28 61 00. **Ⓤ** Königsplatz 🚍 27, 28, N27.
Open 10am–5pm Tue–Sun (to 8pm Thu). 🖼

The idea of building a museum to house Greek and Roman sculpture originated in 1805, when Ludwig I, the future king, was on his first tour of Italy. In 1816, Leo von Klenze was assigned the task of designing a museum for his collection. It was named the Glyptothek, from the Greek word *glypte*, meaning "carved stone". It is regarded as von Klenze's finest Neo-Classical work.

The museum's hall contains the world's finest collection of antique sculpture. Prize exhibits include Archaic figures from the Temple of Aphaia on Aegina of 500 BC, the famous Barberini Faun of 220 BC and the Rondanini Alexander of 338 BC.

❻ Galerie im Lenbachhaus

Lenbachhaus Art Gallery

Luisenstr. 33. **Map** 1 B5. **Tel** 23 33 20 00. **Ⓤ** Königsplatz. **Open** 10am–6pm Tue–Sun. **Closed** 24 Dec. 🖼

The portraitist Franz von Lenbach (1836–1904) commissioned Gabriel von Seidl to build him a grand residence behind Königsplatz. Completed in 1891, the house and its garden are in the style of an Italian suburban villa, with Renaissance and Baroque elements.

In 1924 the property was bought by the municipality for use as an art gallery. The exhibition area contains galleries in which Munich painting from the Gothic to the Art Nouveau periods is displayed, the 19th and early 20th centuries being well represented with works by Karl Spitzweg, Wilhelm Leibl and Lovis Corinth. The museum is also renowned for its fine paintings by artists of the Blaue Reiter group, which was active in Munich from 1911 to 1914 *(see p219)*. In 1957 Gabriele Münter, Wassily Kandinsky's partner up to 1914, gave her collection of pictures from his defining Munich and Murnau period. A building designed by Norman Foster has been added to the gallery. An exhibition hall, which is part of the Lenbach gallery, can be seen at the Kunstbau space underneath Königsplatz U-Bahn station.

Propyläen, Leo von Klenze's grand city gate in the Neo-Classical style

❼ Paläontologisches Museum

Palaeontology Museum

Richard-Wagner-Str. 10. **Map** 1 B5. **Tel** 21 80 66 30. Ⓤ Königsplatz. **Open** 8am–4pm Mon–Thu, 8am–2pm Fri, 10am–4pm first Sun of the month. ♿

Since 1950, the Bavarian palaeontological collection has occupied an eclectic building dating from 1899–1902. Built by Leonhard Romeis as a crafts school, there are decorative motifs in the main entranceway. The main hall is an arcade with a glass roof, where skeletons of large animals are exhibited.

The displays are divided into various thematic groups. Skeletons found in Bavaria include a mas-todon, woolly rhinoceros and giant tortoise. Fossilized palm trees show the existence of a tropical climate here in prehistoric times.

❽ Alte Pinakothek

See pp122–25.

❾ Neue Pinakothek

See pp126–9.

❿ Museum "Reich der Kristalle"

Mineralogy Museum

Theresienstr. 41 (entrance in Barer Straße). **Map** 1 C5. **Tel** 21 80 43 34. Ⓤ Theresienstr. 🚊 27. **Closed** 31 Dec & Shrove Tue. ♿

The exhibits here are part of the great collection of the Mineralogische Staatssammlung, which originated with collections of rocks and minerals found in the 18th century. The museum owes its valuable collection to Duke Maximilian von Leuchtenberg, who supervised mineral extraction in Siberia. His collection was added to that of the Bavarian Academy of Sciences in 1858.

The present museum is in a modern building. Visitors can enjoy colourful mineral formations from all over the world, and study their structure.

⓫ Pinakothek der Moderne

The Pinakothek der Moderne opened in 2002 as one of the world's largest museums of modern art. Its vast collection contains works from the 20th and 21st centuries and is intended to complement the nearby Alte Pinakothek and Neue Pinakothek. The museum has outstanding artworks, from Cubism (with works by Pablo Picasso and Georges Braque), the Neue Sachlichkeit and paintings by Giorgio De Chirico and Max Beckmann through to Pop Art, Photorealism and the Junge Wilde movement of the 1980s. The gallery also houses Die Neue Sammlung – The International Design Museum.

★ **Still Life with Geraniums** (1910)
This painting is by Henri Matisse and shows his bold use of colour and lack of detail, which is typical of his style.

★ **The Falling Man** (1915)
This bronze cast of a naked youth by Wilhelm Lehmbruck mirrors the artist's shocked feelings about World War I. It was originally part of a monument entitled *Suffering of Mankind*.

Ground Floor

Proust's Armchair (1978)
Designed by Alessandro Mendini, this piece is one of 60,000 objects that illustrate the history of design.

The central rotunda is over
30 metres in diameter

First Floor

VISITORS' CHECKLIST

Practical Information
Barer Straße 40. **Map** 1 C3.
Tel 23 80 53 60.
w pinakothek-der-moderne.de
Open 10am–6pm Tue–Sun (until
8pm Thu). €10, €1 on Sun.

Transport
Ⓤ Königsplatz. 100. 27, 28.

Pinakothek der Moderne
This vast concrete and glass building was
designed by Munich architect Stephan
Braunfels, whose goal was to create a
spacious, transparent structure.

Gallery Guide

*The collections are laid out over
three floors. The basement level is
home to The International Design
Museum, from here stairs lead
down to the Danner Rotunda. The
ground floor contains exhibition
rooms for architecture and works
on paper. A leading collection of
painting, sculpture and new
media is located on the first floor.*

North
entrance

South
entrance

Basement

Key to Floorplan

- ☐ Painting and sculpture
- ☐ Design
- ☐ Works on paper
- ☐ Architecture
- ☐ Non-exhibition space

The Danner Rotunda Home to
innovative jewellery, including
this gold bracelet, *Goldfinger*
(1969), by Bruno Martinazzi.

❽ Alte Pinakothek

The Alte Pinakothek, one of the world's most famous
art galleries, opened in 1836. It is a building in the Italian
Renaissance style, designed by Leo von Klenze. The
history of its collections goes back to the Renaissance,
when Wilhelm IV the Steadfast (ruled 1508–50) decided
to adorn his residence with historic paintings. His
successors were equally keen art collectors and, by
the 18th century, an outstanding collection of 14th-
to 18th-century paintings had been amassed.

**St Luke Painting the
Madonna** (c.1484)
This painting by the
Netherlandish artist Rogier
van der Weyden is one
of his most widely
copied works.

★ The Battle of Issus (1529)
This famous painting by
Albrecht Altdorfer depicts
the decisive moment in
Alexander the Great's victory
over the Persians.

★ Pietà (c.1490)
The rich, contrasting colours, strong effects
of light and shadow and homogeneous
composition of this painting are typical of
the later work of Sandro Botticelli.

Portrait of Karl V (1548)
This portrait of the emperor in
Augsburg, once attributed to Titian,
was in fact painted by Lambert
Sustris who worked in his studio.

Main entrance

Key to Floorplan

- ⬜ German painting
- ⬜ Netherlandish painting
- ⬜ Flemish painting
- ⬛ Dutch painting
- ⬜ Italian painting
- ⬜ Spanish painting
- ⬛ French painting
- ⬜ Non-exhibition space
- ⬜ Special exhibition space

Gallery Guide

*The collections are laid out on two floors. The ground floor is
occupied mainly by Flemish painting from the 16th and 17th
centuries. On the first floor are works by German painters as well as
Dutch, Netherlandish, Flemish, French, Italian and Spanish paintings.*

Peasants Playing Cards
(c.1625–49)
This is an expressive, semi-satirical scene from Flemish peasant life painted by Adriaen Brouwer.

VISITORS' CHECKLIST

Practical Information
Barer Straße 27. **Map** 1 C5.
Tel 23 80 52 16.
w **alte-pinakothek.de**
Open 10am–6pm Wed–Sun
(until 8pm Tue). €9, €3 on Sun,
children under 18 free.

Transport
U Königsplatz. 100.
27, 28, N27.

★ The Deposition
(c.1633)
In this dramatic painting, Rembrandt consciously challenges Rubens' idealised version of Christ's sacrifice by focusing on the pained expressions of the other figures in the composition.

Italian Baroque painting
is represented by such masters as Tiepolo and Guido Reni.

Portrait of the Marquise de Pompadour (1756)
One of the finest French Rococo paintings by François Boucher.

First floor

Adoraton of the Magi
(c.1502)
This scene by Hans Holbein the Elder forms part of an altarpiece from Kaisheim.

Land of Cockaigne (1567)
The Flemish artist Pieter Brueghel painted this visual satire on the mythical land of plenty, condemning gluttony and indolence.

Exploring the Alte Pinakothek

After World War II, the Alte Pinakothek was rebuilt by
Hans Döllgast. The entrance hall, ticket office, bookshop
and cafeteria are on the ground floor, as are the section
on German Gothic painting, the Breughel Room and the
temporary exhibitions gallery. The collections on the first
floor are grouped according to the great national schools.
The larger paintings are exhibited in the main rooms,
and smaller ones in the side galleries.

*The Abduction of the Daughters of
Leukippos* (1618) by Rubens

Four Apostles (1526), a pair of panels by
Albrecht Dürer

German Painting

The Alte Pinakothek is
renowned for its important
collection of German late
Gothic and Renaissance art.
The section opens with a
collection of paintings by the
Cologne School, from the
Master of St Veronica (c.1420),
to the fine altar of St Bartholomew
(1500–10), which anticipates
the Renaissance. Late 15th-
century painting is represented
by Michael Pacher's *Altar of
the Church Fathers*, with a bold
handling of perspective.

The collection of paintings by
Albrecht Dürer documents the
development of his work from
a *Self-Portrait* of 1500 to the *Four
Apostles* of 1526. Two paintings
by Matthias Grünewald show a
strong Renaissance influence,
as does the *Crucifixion* (1503)
by Lucas Cranach the Elder.
Albrecht Altdorfer of Regensburg,
a painter of the Danube School,
is represented by his *Battle of
Issus* with its pioneering use
of landscape.

Mannerism is exemplified by
the allegories by Hans Baldung
Grien and Hans von Aachen's

Allegory of Truth. Painting of the
17th century includes works by
Adam Elsheimer and Johann Liss.

Netherlandish Painting

This school, which split into
the Flemish and Dutch schools
at the end of the 16th century,
is introduced by the fine works
of Rogier van der Weyden,
particularly his Cologne Altarpiece
with the famous *Adoration of
the Magi*.

Hans Memling's *Seven Joys
of the Virgin* depicts scenes
from the life of Christ in an
extensive symbolic landscape.
A glimpse of the grotesque
world of Hieronymus Bosch is
given by a fragment of his *Last
Judgement*, while a completely
different climate bathes Pieter
Breughel's *Land of Cockaigne*.
An outstanding example of
the assimilation of Italian
Renaissance style is *Danae*
by Jan Grossaert.

Flemish Painting

The largest collection of works
by the great 17th-century
painter Peter Paul Rubens
can be seen here. They range
from the intimate *Rubens
and Isabella Brandt in the
Honeysuckle Bower* (1609),
painted to celebrate the artist's
marriage, to *The Abduction
of the Daughters of Leukippos*
and *The Battle of the Amazons*
in the High Baroque style. Here
also are the large-scale *Last
Judgement, Fall of the Rebel
Angels* and *Women of the
Apocalypse,* as well as sketches
for the scenes from the life
of Marie de Medici.

This section also includes
paintings by Rubens' pupils
Anthony van Dyck and Jacob
Jordaens, and the peasant
scenes of Adriaen Brouwer,
the most notable of which is
Peasants Playing Cards.

The Adoration of the Magi (c.1455) by Rogier van der Weyden

Dutch Painting

The gallery's rich collection of 17th-century Dutch art represents the Golden Age of Dutch painting. It includes an outstanding series of Passion scenes by Rembrandt that were executed in the 1630s and are important examples of the Baroque style.

Outstanding among the wealth of portraits is a self-portrait by Carel Fabritius and the *Portrait of Willem van Heythuysen* by Frans Hals.

Landscape painting is represented by the work of Jacob van Ruisdael and by the town-scapes and river scenes of Han van Goyen. Among the genre painters, Jan Steen, Gabriel Metsu and Gerard Terborch are particularly noteworthy names.

Portrait of Willem van Heythuysen (1625–30) by Frans Hals

Italian Painting

Such is the comprehensive nature of the gallery's collection that it is possible to make a thorough study of Italian painting here. Most of the early works came to the gallery thanks to Ludwig I's infatuation with the art of this particular period.

Paintings of the 14th century include Giotto's *Last Supper*. Florentine art, which flowered a century later, is represented by the religious paintings of Fra Filippo Lippi and Dominico Ghirlandaio. Other highlights include Leonardo da Vinci's *Madonna and Child* (c.1473), Perugino's *Vision of St Bernard* and works by Raphael,

The Annunciation (c.1473) by Antonello da Messina

out-standing among which is the *Madonna dei Tempi* (1507).

The Venetian School is represented by Titian's *Crown of Thorns* and Tintoretto's series of battle scenes glorifying the Gonzaga family. Great works of the 18th century include the religious canvases of Tiepolo and the fascinating Venetian townscapes of both Canaletto and Francesco Guardi.

Spanish Painting

Although it is smaller than other sections in the gallery, the collection of Spanish painting is no less interesting and includes works by the major masters of the Spanish School. The dramatic *Disrobing of Christ* by El Greco is one of three versions of this famous work. There are also paintings by Diego Velázquez, as well as the Mannerist scenes from the *Legend of St Catherine* by Francisco de Zurbarán, one of his finest works.

Also of interest are Murillo's paintings, in particular his genre scenes depicting street urchins in Seville. Other notable works include studio paintings by the lesser-known Claudio José Antonílez of about 1670.

French Painting

Despite their political connections with France, the Wittelsbachs did not collect French art on a large scale. The museum has three small paintings by Nicolas Poussin that, as early works, are not representative of his mature style. The work of Claude Lorrain is better documented, exhibits including his melancholic *Banishment of Hagar*.

By contrast, 18th-century French painting is well represented, most of the works having been acquired with the help of various banks. Noteworthy among them are paintings by Jean-Baptiste Pater and Nicolas Lancret, followers of Antoine Watteau, and Jean-Marc Nattier's excellent *Portrait of the Marquis of Baglion*. The work of François Boucher is generously represented, from the exquisite *Portrait of the Marquise de Pompadour* to his intimate study of the young Louise O'Murphy, mistress of Louis XV.

The eroticism of the Rococo age is illustrated by sketches by Jean-Honoré Fragonard, while Jean-Baptiste Greuze's moralistic *Grievance of Time* heralds the sentimentality of Neo-Classicism.

Disrobing of Christ (c.1585) by El Greco

❾ Neue Pinakothek

The Neue Pinakothek, which contains
19th-century paintings displayed in a building
designed by August von Volt, opened in 1853.
From 1909 to 1914, under the curatorship of
the art historian Hugo von Tschudi, the collection
of academic paintings was extended in an
avant-garde direction. The building itself was
destroyed during World War II, and between
1976 and 1981 a new gallery, designed by
Alexander von Branca, was constructed. Today
the museum's exhibits consist primarily of
German, French and English paintings dating
from 1780 to 1910.

Girl with Straw Hat (1835)
This portrait is typical
of Friedrich Von
Amerling's work of the
Biedermeier period.

**Heroic Landscape
with Fishermen**
(1818)
In this Romantic
painting by Théodore
Géricault, the Neo-
Classical landscape
is bathed in a
romantic light.

**I Lock My Door Upon
Myself** (1891)
This evocative painting
by Fernand Khnopff, a
co-founder of the Groupe
des XX ("Group of Twenty"),
was inspired by the work
of Christina Rossetti.

Ground floor

Basement

Main entrance

Restaurant and
cafeteria

Disabled access

Gallery Guide

*The collections are arranged
in 22 halls and 11 rooms. The
recommended route for visitors,
tracing a figure of eight, takes the
collections in chronological order.
The halls, of varying size, height
and level, are arranged around
two inner courtyards.*

★ **Italia and Germania** (1828)
This painting by Friedrich Overbeck looks back to the Renaissance.

Still Life with Asparagus
(c.1885/90)
The artist Karl Schuch remains underrated to this day. His painting of asparagus spears was influenced by the work of Édouard Manet.

★ **Seni before the Corpse of Wallenstein** (1855)
This illustration by Carl Theodor von Piloty of a scene from Schiller's famous play enjoyed enormous popularity during the 19th century.

Play of the Waves (1883)
Arnold Böcklin interpreted this mythological scene in a subtly erotic Neo-Baroque manner.

★ **Breakfast in the Studio** (1868)
This outstanding painting by Édouard Manet, with strongly contrasting dark and light tones, dates from the end of his pre-Expressionist period.

Key to Floorplan
- Neo-Classicism
- Art at the Court of Ludwig I
- Early Romantic Art
- History painting
- Böcklin, Marées and late Realism
- Impressionism
- Symbolism and Art Nouveau
- Art from 1800
- French Romanticism and Realism
- Biedermeier and Early Realism
- Temporary exhibitions
- Non-exhibition space

Exploring the Neue Pinakothek

The Neue Pinakothek is admirably designed for visitors. The recommended route for viewing the collections starts and ends in a large hall, and can easily be extended or shortened. Glass roofs allow the rooms to be illuminated by natural light. The varied rhythm of the itinerary and the size and height of the rooms, which are situated at different levels, keep the experience interesting and full of stimulating variety.

Church Ruins in the Forest (1831) by Caspar David Friedrich

Neo-Classicism and Early Romanticism

The sculptures of Paris by Antonio Canova and of Adonis by Bertel Thorvaldsen show these artists' different approaches to Neo-Classicism. Ascetic Neo-Classicism was also shaped by Jacques-Louis David with his *Portrait of the Comtesse Sorcy de Thélusson* (1790). Neo-Classical landscape painting is represented by German painters including Jacob Philipp Hackert.

Also on display is a series of melancholy landscapes by the German Romantic painter Caspar David Friedrich. The Dresden school of landscape painters is represented by Carl Gustav Carus and Johan Christian Dahl, among others. *Heroic Landscape with Fishermen* by Théodore Géricault imbues the Neo-Classical landscape with a Romantic atmosphere. The paintings of Eugène Delacroix, such as *Valentine Dying* (c.1826) and *The Death of Ophelia* (1838) treat the Faustian and Shakespearean themes so beloved of the Romantic painters.

The Nazarenes and Biedermeier

The gallery's body of Nazarene paintings formed the basis of its collection when it first opened in 1853. *Italia and Germania*, the allegory by Friedrich Overbeck in which the two figures sit in a sisterly embrace, expresses the artistic relationship between the two nations. Joseph Anton Koch's paintings *Heroic Landscape with Rainbow* (1812) and *View of the Environs of Olevano* (1830) combine Romantic impulses with the religious mood characteristic of the Nazarenes.

Although they are artistically quite different, the genre paintings of the Austrian artist Ferdinand Waldmüller and the fairy-tale cycles of Moritz von Schwind (such as *Symphony*) both express a specific urban view of happiness in line with the Biedermeier style's *Gemütlichkeit* (domestic harmony).

Realism and Late Romanticism

In the early 20th century the Neue Pinakothek started to acquire French paintings of the Realist school, whose origins date from about 1850.

The Poor Poet (1839) by Carl Spitzweg

Don Quijote (1868) by French artist Honoré Daumier

The gallery's acquisitions from that time include studies by Camille Corot, notably some of his Italian vignettes. There is also a collection of works by Gustave Courbet, among which images of rocks in landscapes predominate. The contrast between different paintings by the caricaturist Honoré Daumier is superb: while *Dramatist on Stage* (1860) shows the world of Parisian theatre, his incomparable *Don Quijote* (1868) conveys the symbolic character of the knight from La Mancha. With his satirical *The Poor Poet* (1839), Carl Spitzweg created almost a cult character in Germany.

History Painting

Historical subjects were a favourite theme in the 19th century. This section opens with Wilhelm von Kaulbach's vast canvas *The Destruction of Jerusalem* (1846), in which the sacking of the city by the Emperor Titus is given an allegorical setting. Kaulbach also painted canvases showing the virtues of Ludwig I, who was a prominent patron of the arts. Historical painting is represented to a significant degree by Carl Theodor von Piloty, with his famous *Seni before the Corpse of Wallenstein* (1855) and

For hotels and restaurants in this region see pp266–7 and pp276–9

the much later *Thusnelda in the Triumphal Procession of Germanicus* (1873), a Neo-Baroque vision of what was seen as Germanic virtues.

Böcklin, Marees and Late Realism

After the unification of the German Empire in 1871, German art fragmented into various movements. Hans von Marées of the Rhineland sought new ways of treating Classical themes. The Neue Pinakothek houses his principal works, including the triptych *Hesperides II* (1884) and *Three Riders* (1887).

Anselm Feuerbach's superb handling of colour expresses a tragic interpretation of Classical themes, as in his *Medea* (1870), while Arnold Böcklin's world of Classical mythology is in harmony with Neo-Baroque trends (as in his *Play of the Waves*). Here also is a substantial collection of works by the Munich Realist Wilhelm Leibl, including *Portrait of Mrs Gedon* (1869), as well as paintings by Carl Schuch and Wilhelm Trübner.

Hesperides II (1884/87) by Hans von Marées

Boys on the Beach (1898) by Max Liebermann

Impressionism and Post-Impressionism

With regard to Impressionist painting, what the Neue Pinakothek lacks in quantity it makes up for in the importance of its collection. Mention should be made of masterpieces by Édouard Manet, such as *Barque at Argenteuil* (1874), Claude Monet's *Bridge at Argenteuil* (1874) and in particular of Paul Cézanne's *The Railway Cutting* (1870). In the latter, a milestone in his artistic development, the

artist shows for the first time his tendency to endow natural forms with geometric shapes. Edgar Degas' delightful *Woman Ironing* (1869) is accompanied by a number of his portraits and statuettes of dancers. The gallery also has paintings by Auguste Renoir, Camille Pissarro and Alfred Sisley.

German Impressionists are also well represented. On display are early works by Adolph von Menzel and paintings by Lovis Corinth, Max Slevogt and Max Liebermann, including his carefree *Boys on the Beach*. The room containing paintings by Paul Signac inaugurates the gallery's Post-Impressionist section. Paul Gauguin is represented by works from his Breton period as well as by *The Birth* (1896), a classic painting from his Tahitian period. Most notably, the Neue Pinakothek has a representative collection of works by Vincent van Gogh. Prominent among them are *Sunflowers* (1888) and two landscapes: *View of Arles* (1889) and *Plain at Auvers* (1890). All three paintings express the artist's delight in the beauty of the sun, the sky, flowers and crops.

Symbolism and Art Nouveau

The interaction between the two artistic movements Symbolism and Art Nouveau is illustrated by *I Lock My Door Upon Myself* by Fernand Khnopff. James Ensor's expressive *Masks* and paintings by Edvard Munch and Maurice Denis can also be seen here.

Of equal interest are works by artists such as Pierre Bonnard and Édouard Vuillard who continued the Impressionist tradition. The erotic and eschatological themes typical of Symbolism can be seen in Egon Schiele's *Agony* (1902), for example. The *Portrait of Margarethe Stonborough-Wittgenstein* (1905) by Gustav Klimt comes at the end of the Neue Pinakothek's exhibits.

Sunflowers (1888) by famous painter Vincent van Gogh

The modern and colourful façade of Museum Brandhorst

⑫ Museum Brandhorst

Theresienstr. 35a. **Map** 1 C5.
Tel 23 80 52 286. **U** Universität.
🚋 17, 28, N27. 🚌 100.
Open 10am–6pm Tue–Sun
(until 8pm Thu).
W museum-brandhorst.de

Opened in 2009, Museum Brandhorst is home to the Brandhorst collection; an extensive and important collection of modern and contemporary art. Commissioned by the Bavarian government, the museum lies adjacent to the Pinakothek der Moderne.

Many of the leading art figures of the late 20th century – among them Joseph Beuys, Gerhard Richter and Damien Hirst – are shown here. With more than 60 works by abstract painter Cy Twombly, the gallery provides a retrospective of this artist's development. The museum building is impressive, with 23 different coloured panes of glass.

⑬ Palais Pinakothek

Türkenstr. 4. **Map** 3 B1. **U** Odeonsplatz.
🚌 100. **Closed** to the public.

Formerly known as Dürckheim Palais, the palace was built in 1843–4 for the chief steward of the court, Count Georg Friedrich von Dürckheim-Montmartin, the palace was designed by Friedrich Jakob Kreuther. Up until 1909 the building housed the Prussian Embassy. The modern building of the bank next door to the palace creates a strong sense of aesthetic dissonance.

The façade of the palace, with its distinctive brick and terracotta reliefs, makes

reference to early Italian Renaissance architecture. The main entrance, which was originally centrally placed on the building, was moved to the right in 1912. The palace is a classic example of the transitional style of architecture that links the work of Friedrich von Gärtner and the Maximilian style.

Statue on the Wittelsbacher Brunnen on Lenbachplatz

⑭ Lenbachplatz

Map 3 A1. **S** and **U** Karlsplatz/
Stachus. 🚋 16, 17, 18, 19, 20, 21, 27,
28, N27, N28.

This irregularly shaped square lies between Maximiliansplatz, the Alter Botanischer Garten and Karlsplatz. The buildings that line it are typical of the late 19th century and are laid out irregularly around the square, creating a set of contrasting perspectives.

On the west side stand the law courts (Justizpalast) and on the south side rises the bizarre outline

of the Künstlerhaus. On the north side is the **Stock Exchange** (Börse). Built in 1868–98, it is an example of pompous Neo-Baroque, its splendour reflecting the power of the financial institution within. The neighbouring **Bernheimerhaus**, at No. 6, was built in 1889. It was regarded as the ultimate residential building in Munich, a novelty at the time being the exposed iron structure of the ground floor and the huge picture windows.

On the east side of the square is Munich's finest fountain, the **Wittelsbacher Brunnen**, built by Adolf von Hildebrand in 1893–5 to commemorate the completion of the city's new water-supply system. The fountain symbolizes both charity and the destructive power of water. It is dominated by two allegorical figures – a youth on a steed, and a woman seated on a bull.

⑮ Karlsplatz

Map 3 A1 (5 A2). **S** and **U**
Karlsplatz/Stachus. 🚋 16, 17, 18, 19,
20, 21, 27, 28, N27, N28.

After the city's fortifications were blown up in 1791 on the orders of Karl Theodor, a vast square was laid out on the western side of the Old Town. It was named Karlsplatz in honour of the ruler, as was the gate called the **Karlstor**. The square also had a popular name – Stachus – which is still used today. It refers to the most popular inn in Munich,

People relaxing beside the fountains of Karlsplatz

which since 1759 has stood on the southwest side of the square. In 1899–1902 the architect Gabriel von Seidl added two wings, known as the Rondelbauten, to the Karlstor. These Neo-Baroque buildings, with two tower-shaped projections, have shops in their ground-floor arcades.

The large fountain in the centre of the square is a favourite meeting place, and there is a major shopping centre beneath the square.

Detail of the ornamental attic of the Justizpalast

⓰ Justizpalast

Law Courts

Elisenstr. 1a. (Karlsplatz) Prielmayerstr. 7. **Map** 3 A1 (5 A2). **Tel** 55 9/ 01. Ⓢ and Ⓤ Karlsplatz/Stachus. 🚋 16, 17, 18, 19, 20, 21, 27, 28, N27, N28.

On the northwest side of Karlsplatz stands one of the best-known late 19th-century landmarks in Munich. The law courts, built in 1891–98 by Friedrich von Thiersch, are an example of pure Neo-Baroque architecture, with discreet Neo-Mannerist elements.

The building's great novelty at the time was its vast steel and glass dome, which acted as a skylight. The interior – particularly the main hall and the main stair-way, which are directly beneath the dome – has an extraordinary wealth of detail in its design.

West of the Justizpalast are the Neues Justizgebäude (New Law Courts). Built in 1906–08, also by Thiersch, they are in the Neo-Gothic style and have a clocktower and gables.

⓱ Alter Botanischer Garten

Old Botanical Garden

Map 3 A1 (5 A1). Between Elisen- and Sophienstr. Ⓢ and Ⓤ Karlsplatz/Stachus, Hauptbahnhof. 🚋 16, 17, 18, 19, 20, 21, 27, 28, N27, N28. 🚌 100.

Visitors to Munich who find themselves in need of respite from the bustle of the city centre will find a sanctuary in the Old Botanical Garden north of the Justizpalast. Laid out on a semi-circular plan in 1804–14, they were designed by Ludwig von Sckell, who was also responsible for the Englischer Garten.

The entrance to the garden is through an early Neo-Classical gate built by Emanuel Joseph von Herigoyen in 1811 and bearing a Latin inscription by Goethe. In 1854 the greenhouse was demolished to make space for the Glaspalast. Modelled on London's Crystal Palace, it was built to house the First Industrial Exhibition. The Glaspalast burned down in 1931, destroying at the same time an exhibition of German Romantic painting.

In 1914 a new botanical garden was laid out in Nymphenburg, and the Old Botanical Garden was converted into a municipal park. A restaurant (today the Park Café) was built in 1935–7, as well as an exhibition hall designed by Oswald Bieber. The sculptor Josef Wackerle created the Neptune Fountain, which has a figure based on Michelangelo's David. The café garden, shaded by exotic trees, is an ideal place to relax and enjoy a cold beer.

The Neptune Fountain in the Old Botanical Garden

⓲ Löwenbräukeller

Stiglmaierplatz 2 /Nymphenburger-straße. **Map** 1 A5. **Tel** 54 72 66 90. Ⓤ Stiglmaierplatz. 🚋 20, 21, 22, N20. **Open** 10am–midnight daily.

Visitors entering the city from the west along Nymphenburgerstraße will see from afar the marble statue of the lion that crowns the Löwenbräukeller on Stiglmaierplatz. This famous Munich brewery has its own inn, which is large enough to hold 4,000 drinkers.

The picturesque brewery and inn were built in 1883 by Albert Schmidt and were refurbished by Friedrich von Thiersch at the turn of the 19th and 20th centuries. The sides of the octagonal tower are decorated alternately with the brewery's emblem – a white griffin – and the city's coat of arms. The tower rises above an arcaded entrance hall with a roof terrace.

In summer drinkers are drawn to the beer garden shaded by large chestnut trees.

The building of the world-famous Löwenbräukeller

FURTHER AFIELD

Many of Munich's attractions lie outside the city centre and, thanks to a highly efficient transport system, they are easily reached. To the north, for instance, is the famous Olympiapark and the BMW factory's modern complex of buildings. To the west lies the Nymphenburg district, with its palace, park and botanical gardens. Southwest of the Old Town is Theresienwiese, where the famous Oktoberfest is held, and unfailing attractions to the south are the Hellabrunn Zoo, in Thalkirchen, and the Bavaria Film Museum, in Geiselgasteig. To the east are some master-pieces of religious architecture – the great Mariä Himmelfahrtskirche in Ramersdorf, and Michaelskirche in Berg am Laim.

Sights at a Glance

Palaces and Historic Buildings
1 Nymphenburg pp134–7
11 Grünwald
12 Asam-Schlössl
16 Blutenburg

Museum
4 BMW Museum
13 Deutsches Museum Verkehrszentrum

Districts
7 Berg am Laim
8 Ramersdorf

Parks and Open Spaces
2 Botanischer Garten
3 Olympiapark
9 Tierpark Hellabrunn
14 Theresienwiese

Others
5 Hypo-Hochhaus
6 Au
10 Bavaria-Filmstadt
15 Neue Messe München

Key
- Central Munich
- Outskirts of Munich
- Motorway
- Major road
- Minor road
- Railway line

◄ The ultramodern BMW administration tower and museum

For map symbols see back flap

❶ Nymphenburg

After the birth in 1679 of Maximilian Emanuel, the heir to the throne, his father, Duke Ferdinand Maria, presented his wife with a suburban palace. The queen named it Nymphenburg (Nymphs' Castle) and supervised the building work that ensued. Max Emanuel continued his mother's work, creating with architects Joseph Effner and Enrico Zucalli one of the finest palaces and gardens in Europe. Later, buildings were added around the courtyard fronting the palace. In the 1800s the formal French gardens were converted into a landscaped park incorporating the existing canals.

★ Amalienburg
Built by François Cuvilliés, the Amalienburg was a small hunting lodge. Its circular hall was covered with fine shellwork, and the windows and mirrors created the illusion of great space.

★ Marstallmuseum
This museum contains coaches, carriages and sleighs that once belonged to Bavarian rulers, including Ludwig II's coronation coach, and portraits of his favourite horses.

KEY

① **The Porzellanmanufaktur** has produced fine porcelain since 1761. The factory's chief designer was Franz Anton Bustelli.

② **The façade of the Palace** is 600 m (1,968 ft) wide and broken up in typically Baroque style. It is perfectly complemented by the geometric layout of the formal gardens.

③ **The Museum Mensch und Natur** is dedicated to the structure of the earth and the workings of the human body.

④ **The orangery** was, at the time it was built, the first in Germany to be heated by hot water.

Garden
The formal French garden at the rear of the palace, with an 18th-century canal, forms the main axis of the entire palace and its gardens.

VISITORS' CHECKLIST

Practical Information
Nymphenburg: **Tel** 17 90 80.
W schloesser.bayern.de
Open 1 Apr–15 Oct: 9am–6pm daily; 16 Oct–31 Mar: 10am–4pm daily. 🗓 📷 Museum Mensch und Natur: **Open** 9am–5pm Tue–Fri (until 8pm Thu); 10am–6pm Sat, Sun & public hols.
W musmn.de

Transport
U Rotkreuzplatz, then
🚋 12, 17. 🚌 51.

Badenburg
The bathing hall and the first heated tiled pool are surrounded by a viewing gallery.

★ Pagodenburg
This pavilion was used for receiving visitors and for relaxation. The ground floor is covered with 2,000 Dutch Delft tiles depicting figures and landscapes.

Magdalenenklause
This folly, built as a chapel in a grotto with hermits' cells, reflects the Baroque idea of withdrawal from courtly life into a world of peace and contemplation.

Schloss Nymphenburg

The oldest part of the palace is the central section, built in 1675 in the form of an Italianate villa. In 1702 Maximilian Emanuel commissioned the construction of side pavilions, which were connected to the villa by galleries. Soon after 1715, when Joseph Effner took charge of building work on the palace, the Steinerner Saal (Audience Hall) with stunningly lavish interior decoration was built, along with the other rooms in the wings, and the stables and orangery.

Italianate Villa
The façade of the oldest, 17th-century wing of the palace, facing the garden, is fronted by a double stairway supported on three arches.

★ Schönheitengalerie
Ludwig I commissioned Joseph Stieler to paint portraits of the city's beautiful women. The Gallery of Beauties was hung with portraits of noblewomen, dancers, towns-women and "Helene Sedlmayr, the Beauty of Munich", a cobbler's daughter.

★ Royal Bed
The royal bedchamber in the south wing of the palace is decorated with fine paintings and filled with mahogany furniture, including the Royal Bed, where Ludwig II was born.

Portrait of Karl Albrecht as Emperor Karl VII
This majestic portrait was produced in the studio of the court painter George de Marées in 1742. The pendant is the portrait of the Empress Maria Amalia, which hangs in the same room.

KEY

① **Balustrades** decorated with vases line the stairways leading to the palace gardens.

Paintings
The walls and ceilings of the palace halls are covered with colourful paintings framed with stuccowork. The finest is the ceiling of the Steinerner Saal, in which mythological scenes are shown in idyllic garden settings.

VISITORS' CHECKLIST

Practical Information
Schloss Nymphenburg;, Eingang 1.
Tel 17 90 80. **W** **schloesser. bayern.de Open** 1 Apr–15 Oct: 9am–6pm daily; 16 Oct–31 Mar: 10am–4pm daily.

Transport
 Hauptbahnhof, then 16, 17, N16. Rotkreuzplatz, then 12.

Lackkabinett
This corner cabinet with Chinese motifs is exquisitely decorated with black lacquer on wood panelling. The Chinese theme is reinforced by the Rococo painting of the ceiling.

Entrance

Vorzimmer
This anteroom in the north part of the palace is richly decorated in French Regency style. Paintings, stuccowork and wood carvings cover the walls, while the ceiling is decorated with Classical subjects.

★ Steinerner Saal
Upon entering the palace, visitors walk into a spacious hall with windows on either side decorated in a resplendent Rococo style.

❷ Botanischer Garten

Botanical Garden

Menzingerstr. 12. **Tel** 17 86 13 10.
🚋 17. **Open** Feb, Mar & Oct:
9am–5pm; Apr & Sep: 9am–6pm;
May–Aug: 9am–7pm; Nov–Jan:
9am–4:30pm. Greenhouses:
Open 9am–4pm.

North of the gardens of Schloss Nymphenburg, new botanical

The Botanical Garden with its stunning variety of plants

gardens were laid out in 1909–14. Covering 0.22 sq km (0.08 sq mile) and containing over 14,000 species of plants growing in artistic arrangements, this is one of the finest botanical gardens in Europe.

Entry to the garden is through the Botanical Institute, which is fronted by the colourful Schmuckhof (Decorative Yard). Passing through it visitors see a section on ecology and genetics, followed by a rose garden and a plantation of rhododendrons and protected species, and of medicinal plants and crops. There is also an arboretum with rare trees. Beyond this is a section illustrating the vegetation of meadows, plains, swamps and sandy and arctic environments.

The impressive **greenhouses** shelter tropical plants, cacti and fruit trees, unusual orchids and giant water lilies.

Vehicles displayed at the BMW Museum

❹ BMW Museum

Olympiapark 2. **Tel** 0180 211 88 22.
🅄 Olympiazentrum.
Open 10am–6pm Tue–Sun. 🅿 ♿
BMW Welt: Olympiapark 1.
Open 9am–6pm daily.

In the early 1970s, the BMW car manufacturing group built a series of ostentatious structures that went some way to rival the architectural development of the neighbouring Olympiapark.

The designer in charge of the concept, Karl Schanzer of Vienna, used the idiom of architectural symbolism.

❸ Olympiapark

Munich's Olympic Park was built for the 20th Olympic Games, which the city hosted in 1972. The modern complex of sports facilities overlies an area formerly used as drill grounds and later as an airfield. The artificial lake is fed by the Nymphenburg Canal and the hills were made from the rubble removed from the city after World War II. The whole complex is dominated by the Olympic Tower.

② Olympiahalle
The sweeping roofs, designed by the architect Günter Behnisch, form a canopy of steel netting and acrylic slabs supported on masts up to 80 m (260 feet) high.

GEORG-

Olympic

ERNST-CURTIUS-WEG

SPIRIDON-LOUIS-RING

Werner-von-Linde-Halle

Olympia-stadion
①

TONI-MERKENS-WEG

OLYMPIAP

① Olympiastadion
The main Olympic stadium can hold 60,000 spectators.

He envisaged the 19-storey office building that dominates the complex as resembling the four cylinders of a car engine. The building, clad in silver aluminium, has a ground plan in the form of a clover leaf.

At the foot of the building, and counterbalancing its imposing structure, is what could be described as a shrine – the BMW Museum. Built in concrete and taking the form of a bowl 41 m (135 ft) across, this windowless, silver-painted structure contains exhibits illustrating the history of the factory's production. A spiral ramp connects five platforms where the first cars, including the famous Dixi, are displayed, along with motorbikes, racing cars of the 1950s and 1960s, the modern BMW range and futuristic prototypes. There are also film and slide shows.

Nearby is **BMW Welt** in an impressive modern building, holding the world's largest permanent BMW exhibition.

❺ Hypo-Hochhaus

Arabellastr. 12. **Tel** 3780. 🚇 Richard-Strauss-Str. **Closed** for renovation until 2017.

Unlike many other major cities throughout the world, central Munich is not overshadowed by forests of skyscrapers housing the headquarters of banks, tall buildings and hotels. Munich's

Hypo-Hochhaus's silver-clad futuristic headquarters

modern urban agglomerations have been built outside the Mittlerer Ring (ring road). One example of this is Arabella Park, a group of multi-functional exclusive residential developments, hotels and office buildings. The buildings of the HypoVereinsbank AG were built here in 1975–81 to designs by Walter and Bea Betz.

The architects achieved a unique effect. The 114-m (375-ft) skyscraper consists of three blocks of different sizes that are joined by gigantic rings supported by four cylindrical towers. The glazing and the silver panels covering the exterior of the buildings create an effect of levity and cool elegance.

It is worth walking round the building to experience the unusual metamorphosis of forms that is produced from different viewpoints. Despite its architectural significance, Hypovereinsbank's headquarters is a typical example of the megalomania of major financial institutions today.

Tips for Drivers

Getting there:
🚇 Olympiazentrum.
Start: Hans-Braun-Brücke.
Length of tour: 2 km (1.25 m).
Stopping-off places: At Olympiahalle and Olympiaturm.

⑤ Olympia-Eissportzentrum
Like the Swimming Hall, the skating rink and ice-hockey stadium is open to the public.

④ Olympiaturm
The Olympic Tower commands a fine view over the city and – when the weather is fine – a panoramic view over the Bavarian Alps.

③ Schwimmhalle
The Swimming Hall is one of the finest in Europe. The complex comprises five pools, saunas, a jacuzzi and a diving platform, as well as a grassed relaxation area.

0 metres 150
0 yards 150

Key
— Suggested route

For map symbols see back flap

Colourful Italian crockery at the Auer Dult fair

❻ Au

Map 4 D5. 🚊 25, 27. 🚋 52. 🏛 Auer Dult: Mariahilfplatz. Maidult: starts around 1 May; Jakobidult: starts Sat after 25 Jul; Herbstdult: starts third Sat in Sep.

Up until the 15th century, the district of Au was part of the floodplain of the River Isar, and it was only after the river was controlled that people started to settle here. Au was incorporated into Munich in 1854. Until the early 20th century, the poorer population of the city lived in Au, and picturesque cottages typical of old Munich can still be seen there today.

Three times a year, for nine days, the heart of the Au transforms into Munich's biggest traditional fair for household articles, antiquities and old books. This local event goes back to the 14th century. The atmospheric **Auer Dult** starts on the first weekend in May, at St Jacob's Day and in the week after kermess. In addition to the many stalls with antiquities, books, pottery and every kind of household stuff there are some nostalgic shooting galleries, merry-go-rounds, and food stalls, as well as a beer tent.

The square with the fair is dominated by the Maria-Hilf-Kirche, a Neo-Gothic brick church built by Joseph Ohlmüller and Georg Ziebland in 1831–39. It was the first instance of the Gothic revival in southern Germany.

❼ Berg am Laim

🚇 Josephsburg. 🚊 19. 🚋 146. Michaelskirche: Clemens-August Str. 9a. **Open** 8am–6pm daily.

The name Berg am Laim reflects its position: along Harlbacher Bach is an elongated hill *(Berg)*, from which clay *(Lehm)* was extracted.

By the beginning of the 18th century, the area had been taken over by Clemens Joseph, Bishop of Cologne, who founded the Brotherhood of St Michael here. His successor, Clemens August, ordered the construction of **Michaelskirche**. For this he commissioned the most prominent figures of his time: the architect Johann Michael Fischer, the painter and stuccoist Johann Baptist Zimmermann and the sculptor Johann Baptist Straub. Work lasted from 1737 to 1751 and the result was one of the finest Rococo churches in Germany.

While the twin-towered façade is the quintessence of late Baroque style, the interior has Rococo furnishings and paintings. The painting of St Michael overcoming Satan on the high altar (1694) is by Johann Andreas Wolff, and the figures of putti and angels are ascribed to Ignaz Günther. The pulpit, crowned with a statue of St Michael bearing the Bavarian flag, is by Benedikt Haßler. The dome and ceiling are painted with scenes from the life of St Michael. In 1941–3 over 300 Jews from Munich were rounded up by the church and the monastery before being deported to a concentration camp. A modest memorial is dedicated to them.

The pulpit in Michaelskirche in Berg am Laim

❽ Ramersdorf

🚇 Karl-Preis-Platz and Innsbrucker Ring. St Maria Ramersdorf: Ramersdorfer Str. 6. **Open** 7:30am–7pm.

Ramersdorf is one of Munich's industrial centres. In the midst of small factories, garages and a close network of streets is an oasis of peace: the village church of **St Maria Ramersdorf**. This is one of the oldest pilgrimage churches in Bavaria. Since the 14th century processions of people have made their way here to worship a relic of the Holy Cross that is kept in a precious monstrance. Since 1465 another object of worship has been the figure of the Madonna Enthroned carved by Erasmus Grasser. While the exterior of the church has retained its Gothic character, the interior is Baroque. The Gothic cloisters are decorated with stucco-work and have 17th-century altars. The cemetery is worth a visit, as is the Alter Wirt, an inn dating from 1663 that was frequented by pilgrims and travellers on the road between Salzburg and Augsburg.

The Baroque interior of the pilgrimage church in Ramersdorf

❾ Tierpark Hellabrunn

Munich's zoo was established in 1911. It has over 4,800
animals representing 480 species and covers an area of
3.6 sq km (1.38 sq miles). The species are arranged by
continent and by their geographical occurrence. The
design of the enclosures, which recreate natural
environments, makes Hellabrunn one of the most
beautiful zoos in the world. The zoo specializes in
breeding animals that are under threat of extinction.

VISITORS' CHECKLIST

Practical Information
Tierparkstr. 30. **Tel** 62 50 80.
Open 9am–6pm daily (Nov–Mar:
9am–5pm). 🎨 ♿ ✏️
ⓦ zoo-munich.de

Transport
Ⓤ Thalkirchen. 🚌 52.

Elephants
The elephants live in a hall covered
by a dome of reinforced concrete,
the first of its type in the world.

Isar Entrance

TIERPARKSTRASSE

① EUROPE

AMERICA

SIEBENBRUNNERSTRASSE

②
③
④
⑤
⑥

AUSTRALIA

⑦

Flamingo
Entrance

⑪
⑫

HARLACHINGER BERG

⑨   ⑧

⑬   ⑩

ASIA

AFRICA

⑭

⑮

⑯

HOCHLEITE

Isar

Alpine Ibex
These protected
animals are rarely seen
in the wild. In the zoo,
they live in a rocky
paddock planted with
Alpine vegetation.

The Kiang is a wild
ass from Tibet that
lives in herds.

**The mhorr
gazelle** no
longer exists in
the wild.

The Gardens
The animals are not the only
attraction here. The layout of
the zoo includes peaceful areas
for walking and relaxation.

Key

① Touch Paddock
② Pelicans
③ Przewalski's horse
④ Alpine ibex
⑤ Chimpanzees
⑥ Aquarium
⑦ Elephants
⑧ Jungle House
⑨ Lions
⑩ Gazelles
⑪ Siberian tigers
⑫ Rhinoceros
⑬ Mesopotamian deer
⑭ Kiang
⑮ Children's Zoo
⑯ Penguins

★ Rhinoceros
The sheer size and primitive shape
of these animals never fail to fas-
cinate. They live in the zoo in a
re-created natural environment.

| 0 metres | 150 |
| 0 yards | 150 |

For map symbols see back flap

The realistic reconstruction of the U-boat from the film *Das Boot*

⑩ Bavaria-Filmstadt

Geiselgasteig. Bavariafilmplatz 7.
Tel 64 99 20 00. Ⓤ Silberhornstr,
Wettersteinplatz (some distance
away). 🚋 25. Ⓢ Rosenheimer
Platz (some distance away).
Open Apr–Oct: 9am–6pm; Nov–Mar:
10am–5pm, daily. 🎦 .
Ⓦ **filmstadt.de**

Commonly known as
Hollywood on the Isar, Bavaria-
Filmstadt is one of Europe's
major film studios.

Set up in 1919, they were
originally located in the Stachus
district. Among the prominent
people who have worked here
have been famous directors
such as Orson Welles and
Ingmar Bergman. Every year
scores of films for the big screen
and television are made at
the Filmstadt ("cinema city"),
which opened to the public
in 1981.

The 90-minute tour of the
studios takes visitors on a
miniature railway and on
foot, through some fascinating
film sets.

Entering the 57-m (187-ft)
reconstruction of the U-boat
used in the Oscar-winning
film *Das Boot* is an unforgettable
experience. Another lasting
impression is made by the backdrops used in the production
of *Asterix and Obelix*, set in the
age of the Romans and Gauls.

Another major attraction is
Bullyversum, an interactive,
3-D adventure into the world
of film. The attraction is named
after, and stars, the German
comedian, actor and director,
Michael "Bully" Herbig.

⑪ Grünwald

Grünwald Burg. Grünwald Zeillerstr. 3.
Tel 64 13 218. Ⓤ Silberhornstr. 🚋 25.
Ⓢ Rosenheimer Platz. 🚌 224, 271,
391. **Open** 10am–5pm Wed–Sun.
Closed 31 Oct–mid-Mar.

Grünwald, on the southern
outskirts of Munich, is one
of the city's most exclusive
villa suburbs. It is also a good
starting point for walking
and cycling tours. The district's
greatest attraction is Burg
Grünwald, a well-preserved
medieval castle whose origins
go back to the 12th century. In
1270 the building came into
the possession of the Wittelsbachs. In the 15th century a
gatehouse was constructed:
its stepped gable is set with
11 coats of arms, those of
Bavaria at the apex and those
of Poland and Jerusalem
among the others further
down. From 1602 to 1857
the castle accommodated a
prison and a gunpowder store.

Grünwald Burg's Gothic gatehouse, set with
coats of arms

The archaeological collections
housed here illustrate the
history of the castle and of
Roman art in Bavaria. There
are lapidariums and frescoes,
a kiln and a reconstruction
of a Roman kitchen.

⑫ Asam-Schlössl

Thalkirchen. Maria-Einsiedel-Str. 45.
Ⓤ Thalkirchen. 🚌 135.

In 1724 Cosmas Damian Asam
acquired a 17th-century
property in the Isar valley. He
intended to use it as an out-of-
town residence and studio.

With the help of his brother
Egid Quirin Asam, Cosmas
Damian rebuilt the house
that he had bought, con-
verting the second floor
into a spacious studio lit by
a huge semicircular window.
The house was named Maria
Einsiedel in honour of the
Swiss pilgrimage church that
the brothers had decorated.
The artist covered the façade
of his new home with paintings. He decorated the third
floor with a statue of Moses
bearing the Ten Command-
ments, and a painting of the
antique sculpture known as
The Borghese Fencer.

The building houses a
restaurant serving delicious
German dishes.

⑬ Deutsches Museum Verkehrszentrum

Theresienhöhe 14a. **Tel** 500 806 762.
Ⓤ Theresienwiese. **Open** 9am–5pm
daily. **Closed** 1 Jan, Good Friday, 1
May, 1 Nov, 24, 25 & 31 Dec. 🅿
Ⓦ **deutsches-museum.de/
verkehrszentrum**

The historic exhibition halls
on Theresienhöhe house
the transport section of the
Deutsches Museum. This
huge collection ranges from
the very first motorcar to the
ICE-Experimental train and
features interactive displays
that illustrate the past, present
and future of worldwide
travel and mobility.

⑭ Theresienwiese

Theresienhöhe 16. **U** Theresienwiese.
Ruhmeshalle, Bavaria: **Tel** 29 06 71.
Open Apr–15 Oct: 9am–6pm daily.
🎪 Oktoberfest Sep–Oct (16 days).

The events that took place in
Munich on 17 October 1810
had far-reaching consequences.
This was the day on which
the marriage of Therese von
Sachsen-Hildburghausen and
Ludwig I, the future king, took
place. To mark the occasion,
horse races, a cattle fair and
a folk festival were held in
meadows outside the city. The
folk celebrations were repeated
in following years, and this
custom continued to grow
and eventually became the
Oktoberfest *(see p33)*, the
largest folk festival in the world.
The festival grounds were
named Theresienwiese in
honour of the bride.

The folk festival is not,
however, the only attraction
of Theresienwiese. On an
elevated ridge with a grand
stairway stands the Neo-Classical
Ruhmeshalle (Hall of Fame),
built by Leo von Klenze in 1848–
53. It is an open hall fronted by
48 Ionian columns and containing the busts of 77 prominent
Bavarians. In front of the hall
stands a gigantic figure of Bavaria
as a Germanic goddess carrying
a sword and an oak wreath
and accompanied by a lion. This
unusual work by Leo von Klenze
and Ludwig Schwanthaler, which
stands 18 m (59 ft) high, was
the first monumental cast iron
figure to be made. It predates
New York's Statue of Liberty
by some 30 years. Visitors can
view the city from a platform
in the figure's head.

The main entrance to the Neue Messe, with the flags of many nations

⑮ Neue Messe München

Am Messesee 2. **U** Messestadt-West,
Messestadt-Ost.

In 1992 the international
airport at Riem was closed
and the site, where building
work took place from 1995 to
1998, was transformed into a
huge exhibition area.

This was the Neue Messe
München, which came to
stand as an example of
modern functional yet
elegant architecture. It
was designed by Bystrup,
Bregenhoj & Partners,
architects from
Copenhagen, the
winners of the
international com-
petition that was
announced in 1991.

A sequence of
17 halls is arranged
along the Atrium,
an arterial axis 600 m
(1,968 ft) long. The
main entrance is
flanked by the
multi-functional
ICM (International
Congress Centre
Munich) building. The entire
covered area of 200,000 sq m
(50 acres) stands in front of a
large lake. Major international
events that are held in the

Neue Messe include
an information and tele-
communications fair, a
fashion show, a crafts show
and a mineralogy congress.

⑯ Blutenburg

Blutenburg. **S** Obermenzing
(some distance away). 🚌 143, 160.
Internationale Jugend-bibliothek:
Tel 89 12 110. **Open** 2–6pm Mon–Fri.

On a man-made island in
the River Würm stands
Blutenburg, a small hunting
lodge surrounded by
greenery and water.
From 1425 the lodge
belonged to the
Wittelsbachs and its
residents included
Duke Albrecht III, his
son Sigismund, the
later Princess Henriette
Adelaide, Therese
Kunigunde Sobieska
and Maximilian I
Joseph.

The lodge now
houses the **Inter-
nationale Jugend-
bibliothek**. Containing
over 500,000 volumes
in 110 languages, the library is
the largest collection of children's
and young people's literature in
the world and is under the
patronage of UNESCO.

The only original part of
the lodge that still stands is St
Sigismund's Chapel (1488), built
by the architects of Munich's
Frauenkirche. The frescoes on its
exterior walls are among the few
surviving examples of late Gothic
mural painting. The interior of the
chapel, covered with intricate rib
vaulting, contains some treasures of religious art, including
altarpieces of 1491 by Jan Polack
and late Gothic sculptures and
stained glass.

The doorway
of Blutenburg's
Gothic chapel

The great statue of Bavaria fronting the Ruhmeshalle in Theresienweise

SHOPPING IN MUNICH

Munich often claims to be Germany's richest and most sophisticated city and when it comes to shopping you are sure not to be disappointed. The key shopping areas are dotted around the centre of the city. You can conveniently walk around the pedestrianized central area, with numerous options for taking a break for lunch or a coffee. Not to be missed is the visual and gourmet treat of the Viktualienmarkt food market, the classic department store Ludwig Beck and some of the smaller speciality shops tucked away in side streets. In the less commercial shopping streets, shops tend to open late morning or in the afternoon only.

Main Shopping Areas

Munich's key luxury shopping street is Maximilianstraße and those streets connected to it, Theatinerstraße, Briennerstraße and Residenzstraße. Here you will find all the top international brands and jewellery shops. For more affordable shops head to the central pedestrianized area between Kaufingerstraße, Neuhauserstraße and Marienplatz. Here you will find family shops, large chains, mid-market fashion, souvenirs and department stores. For less conventional areas with small specialist boutiques and local designers seek out the Glockenbachviertel around Hans-Sachs Straße, or streets radiating out from Gärtnerplatz, home to the Art Nouveau State Theatre and relaxed cafés. Schwabing is the young Bohemian area with a variety of casualwear and jeanswear shops, plus fashion boutiques and plenty of laid-back bistros and coffee bars.

Department Stores and Shopping Centres

The most famous department store in Munich is **Ludwig Beck**, which has a particularly impressive Christmas decorations department in December. **Galeria Kaufhof** is another large national department store chain offering several floors of goods. Shopping Centres (*Einkaufspassagen*) are also aplenty. **Fünf Höfe** (the five courtyards) is central and upmarket. It sits between Theatiner, Maffei, Kardinal-Faulhaber and Salvator streets and mixes shopping, art and culture with cafés including a great café/restaurant attached to the Kunsthalle Art Museum. Munich has three other large shopping centres. **Olympia-Einkaufszentrum** (OEZ) is vast with over 140 shops on two levels, **Perlacher Einkaufspassage** (PEP) has over 110 shops and the **Riem Arcaden** is home to the largest branch of H&M, a huge Lego store, C&A and Ludwig Beck Fashion.

Pedestrianized shopping area in central Munich

Fashion

Munich has a wide variety of shops for clothes and accessories. For Munich-style chic try boutiques such as **Theresa** which has the best choice of designer fashion and accessories, **Trachten Angermaier** at the Viktualienmarkt, which offers the pick of top brands and **Off & Co** in Schwabing for fashion items for both men and women. Hohenzollernstraße in Schwabing is a good place to shop for youth-styled street fashion and trainers. For traditional Bavarian Loden costumes take a look in **Lodenfrey**.

Children's Shops

Munich is a stylish and expen-sive city and parents love to dress their children accordingly. This means there are some good shopping opportunities for kids' clothing and toys, mainly in the department stores and C&A. A large central shop for mother and baby is **Schlichting**, as well as

The exclusive shopping centre, Fünf Höfe

One of the city's regularly held flea markets

Thierchen Kindermode for original hand-made clothing. **Noemi & Friends** is a lovely kids' beauty salon-cum-accessories shop and is a haven for girls, big and little. **Die Puppenstube** is also good for old-fashioned toys and gifts.

Flea Markets

Flea markets are popular, especially at the weekends. Most take place on Saturday, some every two weeks and most only from spring to late autumn. The key ones around Munich are **Zenith Flohmarkt** (open 6am–6pm Thu–Sat) at Lilienthalallee, **AntikPalast**

also at Lilienthalallee (open 10am–5pm Fri–Sat, 11am–5pm Sun), and **Flohmarkt Riem**, the largest flea market in Bavaria, at the trade show grounds.

Food Shopping

Viktualienmarkt *(see p68)* is a huge produce market, selling fruit, vegetables, spices, meat, poultry, fish, preserves and flowers. Open daily, it is a feast for all the senses and a permanent fixture. *Bio* is the German word for organic and Germans have always been enthusiastic about organic produce. **Basic Bio** is a good organic supermarket in the city centre. For a selection

of gourmet treats head to **Dallmayr** or **Käfer**, the city's top delicatessens, while butchers' shops sell the famous Bavarian white sausages.

Christmas Market

Munich holds a traditional Christmas market *(Christkindlmarkt)* from the first week of Advent until Christmas Eve. The market is a great tourist attraction and special trips are organized from all over Europe. Wooden stalls sell a huge variety of handcrafted decorations, in particular delicately carved wooden mangers and tree decorations, in addition to candles, ornaments, food and mulled wine *(see p37)*.

Christkindlmarkt, Munich's Christmas market

DIRECTORY

Department Stores and Shopping Centres

Fünf Höfe
Theatinerstraße. **Map 3 C1.** 🔲 fuenfhoefe.de

Galeria Kaufhof
Kaufingerstraße 1–5. **Map 3 B2. Tel** (089) 231851. 🔲 galeria-kaufhof.de

Ludwig Beck
Marienplatz 11. **Map 3 C2. Tel** (089) 7236910. 🔲 ludwigbeck.de

Olympia Einkaufszentrum
Hanauer Straße 68. 🔲 olympia-einkaufszentrum.de

Perlacher Einkaufspassage
Thomas-Dehler-Straße 12. 🔲 einkaufscenter-neuperlach.de

Riem Arcaden
Willy-Brandt-Platz 5. 🔲 riem-arcaden.de

Fashion

Lodenfrey
Maffeistraße 7. **Map 3 B2.** 🔲 loden-frey.com

Off & Co
Belgradstraße 5. 🔲 offandco.com

Theresa
Maffeistraße 3. **Map 2 B4.** 🔲 mytheresa.com

Trachten Angermaier
Rosental 10. **Map 3 B3.**

Children's Shops

Die Puppenstube
Luisenstraße 68. **Tel** (089) 2723267.

Noemi & Friends
Marktstraße 13, Schwabing. **Tel** (089) 340 86150. 🔲 noemiandfriends.de

Schlichting
Maximilianstraße 35. **Map 4 D2.** 🔲 schlichting.de

Thierchen Kindermode
Hans-Sachs-Straße 15. 🔲 thierchen.net

Flea Markets

AntikPalast
Lilienthalallee 29. 🔲 antikpalast-muenchen.de

Flohmarkt Riem
Am Messeturm. **Tel** (089) 960 51632. 🔲 flohmarkt-riem.com

Zenith Flohmarkt
Lilienthalallee. **Tel** 0173 683 5152. 🔲 zenith-muenchen.de/flohmarkt

Food Shopping

Basic Bio
Westenriederstraße 35. **Map 3 C3. Tel** (089) 242 0890. 🔲 basic-ag.de

Dallmayr
Dienerstraße 14–15. **Map 3 C2.** 🔲 dallmayr.de

Käfer
Prinzregentenstraße 73. 🔲 feinkost-kaefer.de

Viktualienmarkt
Petersplatz-Frauenstraße. **Map 3 B–C3.**

ENTERTAINMENT IN MUNICH

Munich is best known for the Oktoberfest, the Olympic grounds and Hofbräuhaus, but it also has an international reputation as a city of culture. There are 56 theatres, three large orchestras and one opera house. Munich has the rich and the powerful of its past to thank for creating and preserving its many splendid venues. This cultured metropolis on the Isar caters to all tastes, from traditional to modern, whether in theatre, music or film. There are several festivals during the year, as well as various sporting events, when the city attracts thousands of visitors from all over the world.

Entertainment Guides and Tickets

Munich Found is the best events magazine and the **Munich Tourist Board** has comprehensive listings of events happening all over Munich. Also, be sure to check the Thursday edition of *Süddeutsche Zeitung* and the daily *Münchner Merkur*.

Tickets can be booked at box offices, by phone or in person. There are also two **Zentraler Kartenverkauf** ticket kiosks in the Marienplatz underground concourse, or use the **Nationaltheater** at Marsstallplatz for tickets to the state opera, ballet and orchestra, or the Munich Opera Festival.

Theatre, Opera and Classical Music

State theatres are subsidized and tickets, therefore, are very reasonably priced. The Bavarian State Orchestra, Opera and Ballet all perform at the **Nationaltheater**. The **Deutsches Theater** offers musicals and shows, while the **Prinzregententheater** is home to the Bavarian State Opera and a concert hall. The Art Nouveau

Staatstheater am Gärtnerplatz *(closed until 2015)* presents opera, ballet, operetta, musicals and the Symphony Orchestra. **Gasteig Culture Center** is a world-class concert hall, home to the Munich Philharmonic Orchestra. The city also hosts an opera festival in July.

Music and Dance

The **Pasinger Fabrik** offers a good programme of jazz, chansons and café theatre. There are numerous dance events and dance clubs. Big name artists, such as James Blunt, Massive Attack and The Rolling Stones, tend to perform at the **Circus Krone Bau**, **Zenith Kulturhalle**, **Olympiahalle** and the **Olympic Stadium**.

Munich's world-famous folk festival, Oktoberfest

Film

As the centre of the German film industry Munich offers 76 cinemas and a college for film and television. The **Bavarian Film Studios** offers tours of their studios daily at 1pm. The **Munich Film Festival** in July boasts over 200 films on 15 screens, almost all of them German, European or world premieres.

Festivals

Munich's most famous festival is the **Oktoberfest**. For the last two weeks of September it takes over a dedicated fairground, Theresienwiese, with beer tents, traditional Bavarian brass bands, people dressed in traditional Bavarian costume (*Trachten*), fairground rides and the famous iced gingerbread hearts, *Lebkuchen*.

There is also the **Tollwood Festival** in July and December, which has music, food, a circus, performances in tents and a craft fair.

Munich also celebrates the *Dult* on three occasions throughout the year. *Dult* is the old word for street fair or market and there are traditional stalls and merry-go-rounds all over the city. Carnival or *Fasching* is celebrated throughout Munich with parties, processions and dressing up, but it is not as important here as in other cities.

The imposing Nationaltheater on Max-Joseph-Platz

Munich's ultramodern Allianz Arena

Sport

Most Münchners love the out-doors. Many make regular trips to the not too distant Alps. Running, skiing, rollerblading, cycling, Nordic walking and football are all very popular. The English Garden in the city centre is a huge park where people cycle, run or go walking.

Munich has two football teams: FC Bayern Munich and TSV 1860 München, also known as "the Lions". The **Allianz Arena** is the fantastic stadium built for the 2006 World Cup. It is an architec-tural marvel which lights up in various colours. For Bayern Munich merchandise head to the **FC Bayern Shop** in the Arena. The shop website gives details of other stores located at Central Station and the Hofbräuhaus.

Other key sporting events are the Bavarian International Tennis Championships (ATP tournament), the BMW International Golf Open and Munich Blade Night, on Monday evenings from April to September, when rollerbladers take over the streets.

Runners will enjoy the Media Marathon and also the Münchner Stadtlauf (city run). A sport unique to Munich is surfing on the River Isar at the weirs.

Kids' Entertainment

Children will love Kids' Kingdom – **Kinderreich** – in the Deutsches Museum *(see pp98–101)*. The area is designated for children and has giant interactive water games, plus a real fire engine. Adults can only enter with their children. Several playgrounds can be found along the River Isar in the city centre, but the best is **Spielzone Ost Westpark Sendling** which can be reached by the underground. The **Sea Life Olympiapark** centre is also an excellent outing, as is the zoo at **Tierpark Hellabrunn**.

Close encounter at Sea Life Olympiapark, Munich

DIRECTORY

Entertainment Guides and Tickets

Munich Tourist Board
🔳 muenchen.de

Nationaltheater
(box office)
Marsstallpaltz 5. **Map 3** C2. **Tel** 21 85 19 20.

Zentraler Kartenverkauf
Tel 0180 54 818181.
🔳 muenchenticket.de

Theatre, Opera and Classical Music

Deutsches Theater
Schwanthalerstr. 13. **Map 1 E4. Tel** (089) 552 340.

Gasteig Culture Center
Rosenheimerstr. 5.
Tel (089) 480980.

Nationaltheater
Max-Joseph-Platz. **Map 2** B4. **Tel** (089) 21851920.

Prinzregententheater
Prinzregentenstr. 12. **Map 3** D3. **Tel** (089) 21851920.

Staatstheater am Gärtnerplatz
Gärtnerplatz 3.
Tel (089) 202411.

Music and Dance

Circus Krone Bau
Marsstraße 43. **Map 1 E3. Tel** (089) 5458000.
🔳 circus-krone.de

Olympiahalle and Olympic Stadium
Spiridon-Louis-Ring 21.
Tel (089) 54 818181 (tickets).
🔳 olympiapark-muenchen.de

Pasinger Fabrik
August-Exter-Str. 1.
Tel (089) 82929079.

Zenith Kulturhalle
Lilienthalallee 29.
🔳 zenith-die-kulturhalle.de

Film

Bavarian Film Studios
🔳 filmstadt.de

Munich Film Festival
🔳 filmfest- muenchen. de

Festivals

Oktoberfest
🔳 oktoberfest.de

Tollwood Festival
🔳 tollwood.de

Sport

Allianz Arena
🔳 allianz-arena.de

FC Bayern Shop
🔳 shop.fcbayern.de

Kids' Entertainment

Kinderreich
Deutsches Museum, Museumsinsel 1. **Tel** (089) 21791. 🔳 deutsches-museum.de

Sea Life Olympiapark
Willi-Daume-Platz 1.
Tel (089) 45 00 00.
🔳 sealifeeurope.com

Spielzone Ost Westpark Sendling
Preßburger Straße.

Tierpark Hellabrunn
Tierparkstr. 30. **Tel** (089) 625 080. 🔳 zoo-munich.de

MUNICH STREET FINDER

Map references given for historic buildings and other sights throughout the chapter on Munich refer to the maps included on the following pages only.

The key map below shows the area of Munich covered by the *Street Finder*. Buildings and monuments in pink are star sights that are covered in detail in the chapter; those in brown are sights

and places that are worth seeing. Streets shown in yellow are closed to traffic.

The *Street Finder* maps include U-Bahn and S-Bahn stations as well as main car parks, hospitals, police stations, tourist information centres and taxi ranks in Munich. The word *Straße (Str.)* indicates a street, *Platz* a square, *Brücke* a bridge and *Bahnhof* a railway station.

0 metres 750
0 yards 750

Key

- ◼ Major sight
- ◻ Place of interest
- **U** U-Bahn station
- **S** S-Bahn station
- 🚓 Police station
- *i* Tourist information
- ✚ Hospital
- ✝ Church
- — Pedestrianized street

Scale of Maps 1–4

0 metres 200
0 yards 200
1:11,750

Scale of Maps 5–6

0 metres 150
0 yards 150
1:7,000

Street Finder

A

Ackerstraße	4 D5
Adalbertstraße	1 C3
Adelgundenstraße	
	4 D2, D3
Adelheidstraße	1 B3
Adolf-Kolping-Straße	5 A3
Agnesstraße	1 B2, C3
Ainmillerstraße	2 D2, E2
Akademie der	
Bildenden Künste	2 D4
Akademiestraße	2 D4, E4
Albanistraße	3 C5
Albertgasse	3 B2, 5 C3
Alexandrastraße	4 E1
Alpines Museum	4 E3
Alte Pinakothek	1 C5
Alter Botanischer	
Garten	3 A1, 5 A1
Alter Hof	3 C2, 6 D3
Altes Rathaus	3 C2, 6 D3
Altheimer Eck	3 A2, B2,
	5 B3
Am Einlaß	3 B3, 5 C5
Am Gasteig	4 E3
Am Glockenbach	3 A5
Am Gries	4 E1, F1
Am Kosttor	3 C2, 6 E3
Am Platz	3 C2, 6 E3
Amalienstraße	2 D4, D5
Amiraplatz	3 B1, 6 D1
Angererstraße	1 C1
Annakirche	4 D2
Ansbacherstraße	1 C2
Ansprengerstraße	2 D1
Antikensammlungen	1 B5
Apianstraße	1 C1
Archäologische	
Staatssammlung	4 E1
Arcisstraße	1 C3, C4,
	C5, B5
Arcostraße	3 A1, 5 A1
Arndtstraße	3 A5
Arthur-Kutscher-Platz	2 F1
Asamhaus	3 A3, 5 B4
Asamkirche	3 A3, 5 B4
Asamstraße	3 C5
Auenstraße	3 A5, B5
Auerfeldstraße	4 E5
Augsburger Straße	3 A3,
	5 A5
Augustenstraße	1 B4,
	B5, A5
Aventinstraße	3 C3,
	6 E5

B

Baaderplatz	3 C3, 6 E5
Baaderstraße	3 B4, C4
	6 E5
Balanstraße	4 F5
Baldeplatz	3 A5
Baldestraße	3 A5
Barbarastraße	1 A2

Barer Straße	1 C4, C5,
	3 A1, 5 B2
Basilika St. Bonifaz	
	3 A1, 5 A1
Bauerstraße	1 B2, C2
Baumstraße	3 A5
Bayerische	
Staatsbibliothek	2 E5
Bayerisches	
Nationalmuseum	4 E1
Bazeillesstraße	4 F5
Beichstraße	2 F2
Belgradstraße	2 D1, D2
Bereiteranger	3 C5
Bismarckstraße	2 E1, F2
Blumenstraße	3 A3, B3,
	5 B5, C5
Blütenstraße	2 D4
Boosstraße	3 C5
Bordeauxplatz	4 F4
Boschbrücke	4 D4
Bräuhausstraße	3 C2, 6 E3
Brienner Straße	1 A5, B5,
	5 C1, 6 D1
Bruderstraße	4 D1
Bürgersaalkirche	3 A2,
	5 B3
Burgstraße	3 C2,
	6 D3
Bürkleinstraße	4 D2, 6 F2
Buttermelcherstraße	3 C3, 6 D5

C

Cherubini-Straße	2 D1
Clemensstraße	1 B1, C1,
	2 D1, E1
Corneliusbrücke	3 C4
Corneliusstraße	3 B3,
	C4, 5 C5
Cranachstraße	1 A3

D

Dachauer Straße	1 A4
Daimlerstraße	1 C3
Damenstiftstraße	
	3 A2, 5 B3
Degenfeldstraße	2 D1
Destouchesstraße	1 B1,
	C1, 2 D1, E1
Deutsches Museum	3 C4
Dienerstraße	3 C2, 6 D3
Dillisstraße	2 F2
Drächslstraße	4 D5, E5
Dreifaltigkeitskirche	
	3 B1, 5 B2
Dreifaltigkeitsplatz	
	3 C3, 6 D4
Deutches Jagd- und	
Fischereimuseum	
	3 B2, 5 B3
Dultstraße	3 B3, 5 C4

E

Eduard-Schmid-	
Straße	3 C4, C5,B5
Ehem. Stadtschreiberei	
	3 C2, 6 D3
Eilles Hof	3 C2, 6 D2
Eisenmannstraße	3 A2,
	5 B3
Elisabethplatz	2 D3
Elisabethstraße	1 A2,
	B2, C2
Elisenstraße	3 A1, 5 A2
Emanuelstraße	1 C2
Englischer Garten	
	2 F3, F4, F5
Enhuberstraße	1 B4
Entenbachstraße	3 C5
Erhardtstraße	3 C4
Erich-Kästner-Straße	1 C1
Erich-Mühsam-Platz	2 E1
Erzbischöfliches Palais	
	3 B1, 6 D2
Ettstraße	3 B2, 5 B2, B3
Europaplatz	4 F1

F

Falckenbergstraße	6 E3
Falkenstraße	3 C5, 6 D5
Falkenturmstraße	3 C2,
	6 E3
Fallmerayerstraße	1 C1
Färbergraben	3 B2,
	5 C3
Feilitzschplatz	2 F1
Feilitzschstraße	2 F2
Feldherrnhalle	3 C1,
	6 D2
Fendstraße	2 F2
Finkenstraße	3 B1, 5 C1
Fischerweg	4 D5
Fliegenstraße	3 A3,
	5 A5
Franziskanerstraße	
	4 E4, E5
Franz-Joseph-Straße	
	2 D3
Franz-Josef-Strauß-Ring	
	4 D1, 6 F1
Franzstraße	2 F2, 6 D4
Frauenkirche	3 B2,
	5 C3
Frauenlobstraße	3 A4
Frauenplatz	3 B2, 5 C3
Frauenstraße	3 C3,
	6 D4
Fraunhoferstraße	3 B4
Freystraße	2 F1
Friedensengel	4 F1
Friedrichstraße	2 D3
Fuchsstraße	2 F1
Fürstenfelder Straße	3 B2,
	5 C3
Fürstenstraße	2 D5

G

Gabelsbergerstraße	
	1 A4, B5, C5
Galerie im	
Lenbachhaus	1 B5
Galeriestraße	3 C1, 6 E1
Gärtnerplatz	3 B3, C3,
	6 D5
Gasteig	4 E3
Gebsattelstraße	4 D5, E5
Gedonstraße	2 F3
Georgenstraße	1 A3, B3,
	C3, 2 D3, E3
Germaniastraße	2 F1
Geschwister-	
Scholl Platz	2 E4
Gewürzmühlstraße	4 E2
Geyerstraße	3 A5
Giselastraße	2 E3, F3
Glückstraße	2 D5
Glyptothek	1 B5
Gohrenstraße	2 F1
Görresstraße	1 A3, B3
Grütznerstraße	4 F3
Günther Haus	3 B3,
	5 C4

H

Habsburgerplatz	2 D2, E2
Habsburgerstraße	2 D3
Hackenstraße	3 B2, B3
	5 B4
Hahnenstraße	2 E5
Haimhauserstraße	2 F1, F2
Hans-Sachs-Straße	3 B4
Haus der Kunst	4 D1,
	6 F1
Heiliggeistkirche	3 C2, 6 D4
Herrnstraße	3 C2, 4 D2,
	6 E3, F4
Herzog-Max-Straße	
	3 A2, 5 B2
Herzog-Rudolf-Straße	
	4 D2, 6 F2, F3
Herzogspitalstraße	
	3 A2, 5 A1, A2
Herzogstraße	1 B1, C1,
	2 D1, E1
Herzog-Wilhelm-Straße	
	3 A2, A3, 5 A3, A4
Hesseloher Straße	2 F1
Heßstraße	1 A3, A4,
	B4, C4
Hildegardstraße	3 C2, 4 D2,
	6 E3, F3
Hiltenspergerstraße	1 B1,
	B2, B3
Hochbrückenstraße	3 C2,
	6 E3, E4
Hochstraße	4 E4, D4, D5
Hofbräuhaus	3 C2, 6 E3
Hofgartenstraße	3 C1, 4 D1,
	6 D1, E1
Hofgarten	3 C1, 6 E1

Hofgraben 3 C2, 6 D2, D3
Hofstatt 3 B2, 5 B3
Hohenstaufenstraße 2 D3
Hohenzollernplatz 1 C2
Hohenzollernstraße 1 B2, C2,
2 D2, D3
Holzhofstraße 4 E3, E4
Holzstraße 3 A4
Hotterstraße 3 B2, 5 B3

I

Ickstattstraße 3 B4
Im Tal 3 C2, C3,
6 D3, D4, E4
Infanteriestraße 1 A2, A3
Innere Wiener
Straße 4 E3, F3
Isabellastraße 1 C2, C3
Isartor 3 C3, 6 E4
Isartorplatz 4 D3, 6 E4
Ismaninger Straße 4 F2

J

Jahnstraße 3 B4, A4, A5
Jakob-Klar-Straße 1 C2
Johannisplatz 4 F3
Josephspitalstraße 3 A2,
5 A3, B4
Josephsplatz 1 B3
Josephstraße 1 B3, C3
Jugendstilhaus 2 E2
Jugendstraße 4 F3
Jungferntürmstraße 3 B1,
5 C1
Justizpalast 3 A1, 5 A2

K

Kabelsteg 4 E3
Kaiserplatz 2 E2
Kaiserstraße 2 D2, E2
Kammerspiele 4 D2,
6 F3
Kanalstraße 4 D3, 6 F4
Kapellenstraße 3 A2,
5 B2, B3
Kardinal-Faulhaber-
Straße 3 B1, B2, 5 C2
Karl-Scharnagl-Ring
4 D1, D2, 6 F2, F3
Karlsplatz 3 A2, 5 A2
Karlstraße 1 A5, 5 A1
Karlstor 3 A2, 5 A3
Karl-Theodor-Straße
2 E1
Karmeliterstraße 3 B2,
5 B2, C2
Karolinenplatz 1 C5
Katharina-Von-
Bora-Straße 3 A1, 5 A1
Kathi-Kobus-Straße 1 A2
Kaufingerstraße 3 B2, C2,
5 C3, 6 D3
Kaulbachstraße 2 E3,
E4, E5
Kellerstraße 4 E3, E4, F4
Keuslinstraße 1 B3

Kirchenstraße 4 F3
Kisskalt-Platz 2 F3
Klenzestraße 3 C3, B4,
B5, 6 D5
Klosterkirche
St. Anna 4 D2
Knöbelstraße 4 D2,
6 F3, F4
Knollerstraße 2 F2
Kohlstraße 3 C3, C4,
6 E5
Kolosseumstraße 3 B4
Kolumbusstraße 3 B5
Königinstraße 2 F3, F4,
E4, E5
Königsplatz 1 B5
Konradstraße 2 D3
Kreuzkirche 3 A3, 5 B4
Kreuzstraße 3 A3,
5 B4
Kunigundenstraße 2 F1
Künstlerhaus 3 A2, 5 B2
Kurfürstenplatz 2 D2
Kurfürstenstraße 2 D2,
D3, D4

L

Landschaftstraße 3 C2,
6 D3
Landstraße 4 D3, 6 F4
Ledererstraße 3 C2, 6 E3
Lenbachplatz 3 A1, 5 B2
Leopoldpark 2 E3
Leopoldstraße 2 F1, F2,
E2, E3, E4
Lerchenfeldstraße 4 E1
Liebherrstraße 4 D3,
6 F4, F5
Liebigstraße 4 D1, E1
Lilienstraße 4 D4, D5
Lindwurmstraße 3 A3,
5 A5
Lothringer Straße 4 F4, F5
Lothstraße 1 A3
Löwengrube 3 B2, 5 C2
Ludwig-Maximilians-
Universität 2 E4
Ludwigsbrücke 4 D3, 6 F5
Ludwigskirche 2 E5
Ludwigstraße 2 D5, 6 D1
Luisenstraße 1 C4, B4, B5
Luitpoldbrücke 4 F1

M

Maderbräustraße 3 C2, 6 D3
Maffeistraße 3 B2, 5 C2,
6 D2
Mandlstraße 2 F2, F3
Mannhardtstraße 4 D3,
6 F4
Mariahilfplatz 4 D5
Mariahilfstraße 3 C5
Maria-Josepha-
Straße 2 F2, F3
Mariannenbrücke 4 D3
Mariannenplatz 4 D3

Maria-Theresia-
Straße 4 F1, F2
Marienplatz 3 B2, 6 D3
Marienstraße 3 C2,
6 E3, E4
Marktstraße 2 F1, F2
Marschallstraße 2 F1
Marstall 3 C1, C2, 6 E2
Marstallplatz 3 C1, C2,
6 E2
Marstallstraße 3 C2,
6 E3
Martiusstraße 2 E3
Massmannstraße 1 A4
Maxburgstraße 3 A2, B2,
5 B2
Maximiliansbrücke 4 E2
Maximiliansplatz 3 B1,
5 B1, C1
Maximilianstraße 3 C2, 4 D2,
6 D2, E2, E3, F3
Max-Joseph-Platz 3 C2,
6 D2
Max-Joseph-Straße 3 B1,
5 B1
Max-Planck-Straße 4 E2, F3
Max-Weber-Platz 4 F3
Meillerweg 4 E3
Metzgerstraße 4 F3
Metzstraße 4 F4
Michaelskirche 3 B2,
5 B2
Milchstraße 4 F4
Mittermayrstraße 1 C1
Möhlstraße 4 F1
Moltkestraße 2 E1
Morassistraße 4 D3,
6 E5, F5
Morawitzkystraße 2 E1
Muffatstraße 2 E1
Müllersches Volksbad 4 E3
Müllerstraße 3 A4, B4,
B3, 5 A5, B5, C5
Münzhof 3 C2, 6 E3
Münzstraße 3 C2, 6 E3
Museum "Reich
der Kristalle" 1 C5
Museumsinsel 4 D4

N

Neue Pinakothek 1 C4
Neues Rathaus 3 B2, 6 D3
Neuhauser Straße 3 A2,
B2, 5 A2, B3
Neureutherstraße 1 C3
Neuturmstraße 3 C2, 6 E3
Nikolaiplatz 2 F2
Nikolaistraße 2 F2
Nordendstraße 2 D2, D3, D4
Nußbaumstraße 3 A3,
5 A4, A5

O

Oberanger 3 A3, B3, 5 B5
Occamstraße 2 F1, F2
Odeonsplatz 3 C1, 6 D1
Oettingenstraße 4 E1

Ohlmüllerstraße 3 C5
Ohmstraße 2 E3, F4
Orleansstraße 4 F5
Ottostraße 3 B1, A1,
5 C1, B1, A2

P

Pacelli Palais 2 E3
Pacellistraße 3 B1, 5 B2
Palais Porcia 3 B1, 5 C2
Palais Neuhaus-
Preysing 1 B1, 5 C2
Palais Törring-
Jettenbach 3 C2, 6 D2
Paläontologisches
Museum 1 B5
Palmstraße 3 A5
Pariser Platz 4 F4
Pariser Straße 4 F4, F5
Perusastraße 3 C2, 6 D2
Pestalozzistraße 3 A4, A5
Peterskirche 3 C2, 6 D3
Petersplatz 3 C3, 6 D4
Pfarrstraße 4 D2
Pfisterstraße 3 C2, 6 E3
Pilotystraße 4 D1, 6 F1
Pinakothek
der Moderne 1 C5
Platz der Opfer des
Nationalsozialismus
3 B1, 5 C1
Pöppelstraße 4 D5
Prannerstraße 3 B1, 5 C2
Praterinsel 4 E3
Praterwehrbrücke 4 E2
Preysing Palais 3 C1,
6 D1, D2
Preysingplatz 4 E3
Preysingstraße 4 E3, F3
Prielmayerstraße 3 A2, 5 A2
Prinz-Ludwig-Straße 1 C5
Prinzregentenstraße 4 D1,
E1
Professor-Huber-Platz 2 E4
Promenadeplatz 3 B1,
B2, 5 C2
Propyläen 1 B5
Pündterplatz 2 D1
Pütrichstraße 4 E4, F4

Q

Quellenstraße 4 D4, D5

R

Rablstraße 4 E4, E5
Radlsteg 3 C3, 6 E4
Rankestraße 1 C1
Regerstraße 4 D5
Regierung von
Oberbayern 4 D2, 6 F3
Reichenbachbrücke 3 C4
Reichenbachplatz 3 B3,
6 D5
Reichenbachstraße 3 C3, B4,
6 D4, D5
Reisingerstraße 3 A4

Reitmorstraße 4 E1, E2
Residenz 3 C1, C2,
6 D2, E2
Residenzstraße 3 C1, C2,
6 D1, D2
Rheinbergerstraße 2 D5
Riggauerweg 4 E4
Rindermarkt 3 B2, 5 C3
Robert-Koch-Straße 4 E2
Rochusberg 3 B1, 5 C1
Rochusstraße 3 B1,
5 B2, C2
Römerstraße 2 D2
Rosenheimer Platz 4 E4
Rosenheimer Straße 4 E4,
F4, F5
Rosenstraße 3 B2, 5 C3
Rosental 3 B2, B3, 5 C4
Roßmarkt 3 A3, 5 B5
Rottmannstraße 1 A5
Rumfordstraße 3 C3,
6 D5, E5

S

St-Anna-Platz 4 D1
St-Anna-Straße 4 D1, D2
St Nikolai 4 E3
Salvatorkirche 3 B1, 5 C1
Salvatorplatz 3 B1, 5 C1
Salvatorstraße 3 B1,
C1, 6 D2
Sandstraße 1 A4, A5
Schack-Galerie 4 E1
Schackstraße 2 E4
Schäfflerstraße 3 B2,
5 C2
Schellingstraße 1 A3, B3,
B4, C4, 6 D4
Schleißheimer Straße B1, B2,
B3, A3, 1 A4
Schlosserstraße 3 A2,
5 A3
Schmidstraße 3 A3, B3,
5 B4

Schnorrstraße 1 C4
Schönfeldstraße 2 E5
Schornstraße 4 E5
Schraudolphstraße 1 C3, C4
Schweigerstraße 4 D5
Schwere-Reiter-
Straße 1 A2
Schwindstraße 1 B3, B4
Sckellstraße 4 F3
Sedanstraße 4 F4
Seeaustraße 4 E1
Seestraße 2 F2
Seitzstraße 4 D1,
6 F1, F2
Sendlinger Straße 3 B3, A3,
5 B4, C4
Sendlinger Tor 3 A3, 5 A4
Siebertstraße 4 F1
Sieboldstraße 4 E5
Siegesstraße 2 F2
Siegestor 2 E4
Siegfriedstraße 2 E1
Simon-Knoll-Platz 4 E5
Sonnenstraße 3 A2, A3,
5 A3, A4
Sophienstraße 3 A1,
5 A1, A2
Sparkassenstraße 3 C2,
6 D3
Sporerstraße 3 B2, 5 C3
Staatskanzlei 4 D1, 6 F1
Stadtmuseum 3 B3, 5 C4
Steinheilstraße 1 B4
Steinsdorfstraße 4 D3
Steinstraße 4 F4
Stephansplatz 3 A4
Sternstraße 4 E2
Stiglmaierplatz 1 A5
Stollbergstraße 4 D2,
6 F3, F4

T

Tassiloplatz 4 F5
Tattenbachstraße 4 E1, E2

Tengstraße 1 C2, C3
Thalkirchner Straße 3 A3,
A4, 5 A5
Theatinerkirche 3 C1,
6 D1
Theatinerstraße 3 C1, C2,
6 D1, D2
Theo-Prosel-Weg 1 A2
Theresienstraße 1 A4, B4,
C4, C5, 6 D5
Thiemestraße 2 F3
Thierschstraße 4 E2, D2,
D3, 6 F4
Thomas-Wimmer-
Ring 4 D2, D3,
6 F3, F4
Trautenwolfstraße 2 E3,
F3
Triftstraße 4 E1, E2
Türkenstraße 1 C5, 2 D5,
D4, D3

U

Unertlstraße 1 C1, 2 D1
Universität 2 E4
Unsöldstraße 4 D1
Unterer Anger 3 B3, 5 B5
Ursulastraße 2 F2
Utzschneiderstraße 3 B3,
6 D4

V

Veterinärstraße 2 E4
Viktoriastraße 2 D1, D2
Viktor-Scheffel-
Straße 2 D2
Viktualienmarkt 3 B3,
C3, 6 D4
Villa Stuck 4 F2
Völkerkunde-
Museum 4 D2, 6 F3

W

Wagmüllerstraße 4 E1
Wagnerstraße 1 B5

Wallstraße 3 A3,
5 A5, B5
Wedekindplatz 2 F2
Wehrsteg 4 D3
Weinstraße 3 B2, 6 D3
Weißenburger
Platz 4 F4
Weißenburger
Straße 4 F4
Werneckstraße 2 F2
Westenriederstraße 3 C3,
6 D4, E4
Westermühlstraße 3 A4,
B4, B5
Widenmayerstraße 4 F1,
E1, E2
Wilhelmstraße 2 E1, E2
Winzererstraße 1 B1, B2,
A2, A3
Wittelsbacherbrunnen 3 A1,
5 B1
Wittelsbacherplatz 3 C1,
6 D1
Wittelsbacherstraße 3 A5,
B5
Wolfgangsplatz 4 E5
Wormserstraße 1 B2
Wörthstraße 4 F4
Wurzerstraße 6 F2, E2

Z

Zenneckbrücke 4 D4
Zentnerstraße 1 B2, B3
Zentrum für
außergewöhnliche
Museen 3 C3, 6 E4
Zeppelinstraße 3 C5,
4 D5, D4
Zieblandstraße 1 B3, C4
Zweibrückenstraße 4 D3, 6 F4, F5
Zwingerstraße 3 C3, 6 E4

THE BAVARIAN ALPS AREA BY AREA

The Bavarian Alps
   at a Glance   160–161
Upper Bavaria (North)   162–177
Lower Bavaria   178–197
Upper Bavaria (East)   198–209
Upper Bavaria (South)   210–225
The Allgäu   226–241
Northern Swabia   242–259

The Bavarian Alps at a Glance

The Bavarian Alps have much to offer tourists. Well endowed with ski lifts and shelters, the Alps offer ideal conditions for skiers, while the many lakes draw watersports enthusiasts and ice-skaters. The mountainous regions of the Bavarian Forest are a delight, both for their primeval natural surroundings and for the affordable prices to be found here. Many of the region's towns and villages contain buildings of great splendour and architectural importance.

Augsburg
Because of its many canals which are crossed by bridges, this town is known as the Venice of the North *(see pp252–57).*

Ottobeuren
The Rococo stalls of this renowned Benedictine church are part of the overall decorative scheme *(see p232).*

Wallerstein

Nördlingen · Monhei

Donauwörth ·

Lauingen · Höchstädt · Rain

Leipheim · **SOUTHERN SWABIA** *(See pp242–59)*

Neu-Ulm · Gersth

Augsburg ·

Neuschwanstein
This castle is the embodiment of Ludwig II's idea of a roman-tic seat of power. It has a fantastical setting, and its design, particularly that of the towers, was the model for the Disneyland's fairy-tale castle *(see pp234–35).*

Fürstenfel

Landsberg am Lech

Memmingen

THE ALLGÄU *(See pp226–41)*

Kempten · Marktoberdorf · Schongau

Murn

Wasserburg

Garm Parte

Linderhof
The gardens surrounding Ludwig II's favourite palace were modelled on those of Versailles. The fountains and cascades add a magical dimension *(see p220).*

Oberammergau
Like many others here, this house, built in 1775, is covered with *Lüftlmalerei.* Oberammergau is the centre of this type of *trompe-l'oeil* decoration *(see p220).*

◀ Picturesque view of Burghausen with its castle in the background

Altmühl
Picturesquely set on a hill, Prunn Castle overlooks the River Altmühl with its wooden bridge – the oldest and longest in Europe *(see p187)*.

Hallertau
This region is renowned for its hop plantations, which supply the country's brewing industry, so satisfying the Bavarians' demand for beer, their favourite drink *(see p163)*.

Viechtach

Zwiesel

Bogen   Regen

Kelheim   Metten

Abensberg   Deggendorf

Ingolstadt

Tittling

Dingolfing   Vilshofen

LOWER BAVARIA   Obernzell
(See pp178–97)

UPPER   Landshut   Passau
ARIA (NORTH)   Moosburg
ee pp162–77)

Freising   Pfarrkirchen

Eggenfelden

rschleißheim   Erding   Pocking

arching   Dorfen

Haag   UPPER BAVARIA   Mühldorf

München   (EAST)

ering   Ebersberg   *(See pp198–209)*

erg

Rott am Inn   Traunreut

R BAVARIA
SOUTH)   Freilassing
e pp210–25)

Miesbach   Bernau

Bad Tölz   Anger

Lenggries

0 kilometres   30

0 miles   30

Herrenchiemsee
Bavaria's largest palace, with the most extensive grounds, features sculpture created for Ludwig II *(see p206)*.

Schwarzeck
Schwarzeck is one of the many hiking and skiing stations around Berchtesgaden, reached by a steep and winding road *(see p204)*.

UPPER BAVARIA (NORTH)

Consisting of flat countryside traversed by the river valleys of the Danube and its tributaries the Isar, Iller, Paar and Altmühl, this region of Upper Bavaria (Oberbayern) is not as varied as the south. However, it has plenty of historic monuments, as at Eichstätt and Freising, and architectural gems such as the palace at Schleißheim.

During the Jurassic period, 150 million years ago, a lagoon existed at the northern edges of this region. This became what is today the valley of the meandering River Altmühl, the location of the third largest nature reserve in Germany. Many Jurassic fossils have been unearthed here, particularly in the area around Eichstätt.

More recent history concerns Dachau, a charming little town just 25 km (15.5 miles) northwest of Munich. Its name has become synonymous with one of the earliest concentration camps to be set up in Germany, in 1933. The camp is still surrounded by barbed wire and guard towers still stand. The site functions as a museum of the Nazis' cruel system of forced labour and extermination in which millions of victims of the Third Reich lost their lives. It is preserved as a memento and a warning to present and future generations.

The northern part of Upper Bavaria is mainly farmland. Extensive asparagus plantations stretch out around Schrobenhausen, while in a region between the rivers Amper and Danube, an area known as Hallertau, endless forest-like plantations indicate the large-scale production of the hops that are used in the brewing of beer, Bavarians' favourite drink. Hallertau forms part of the Hopfenstraße, or German Hop Trail. Along the way lies Ingolstadt, whose main claim to fame nowadays is the Audi car plant.

Here, too, are many fine historic buildings. The imposing outlines of castles tower over towns such as Beilngries, Eichstätt, Ingolstadt and Neuburg, on the northern fringes of this region. There is also a wealth of ecclesiastical buildings, the most prominent among which are the churches and abbeys at Scheyern, Indersdorf and Fürstenfeldbruck.

The imposing Baroque façade and formal gardens of the Neues Schloss in Schleißheim

◀ Painted ceiling of the Great Hall in Neues Schloss, Schleißheim

Exploring Upper Bavaria (North)

Any exploration of the northern part of Upper Bavaria should take in the Baroque Neues Schloss at Schleißheim, the grandest building in the area, set in extensive parkland. Equally interesting is the town of Freising, with its fine cathedral and the Diözesanmuseum, which contains one of the most resplendent collections of religious art in Germany. Nature-lovers looking for particularly beautiful countryside should head for the Altmühltal or the region of Hallertau, where hop plantations stretch to the horizon.

Getting Around

Several roads traverse northern Upper Bavaria. Motorways A9 and A93 lead to the north of Germany via Nuremberg and Regensburg. Motorway A8 leads west to Stuttgart, the A92 heads east to Lower Bavaria, and the A96 leads to the southwest. The S-Bahn local rail network and Deutsche Bahn national rail network provide links between towns. Franz-Josef-Strauß Airport, near Freising, provides air links with other cities in Germany and the rest of the world.

The grand Baroque staircase of the Neues Schloss in Schleißheim

For map symbols see back flap

Neuburg, a town overlooking the River Danube

Sights at a Glance

1. Eichstätt pp166–8
2. Beilngries
3. Ingolstadt pp170–71
4. Neuburg an der Donau pp172–3
5. Pfaffenhofen
6. Scheyern
7. Freising
8. Erding
9. Sankt Wolfgang
10. Schleißheim pp176–7
11. Dachau
12. Kloster Indersdorf
13. Fürstenfeldbruck

Key

⬛⬛⬛ Motorway

▬▬▬ Main road

═══ Minor road

━━━ Scenic route

━━━ Main railway

━━━ Minor railway

❶ Eichstätt

Eichstätt, a see and centre of religious life since 741, is probably one of the prettiest towns in Bavaria. It stands in an exceptionally scenic location in the valley of the River Altmühl. The town's appearance was largely determined by 30 years of work by Maurizio Pedetti and Gabriel de Gabrieli, a prominent architect of the first half of the 18th century who was also active in Vienna. The town's unique atmosphere is further enhanced by the Catholic university and its students.

Tenement houses lining Marktplatz

🏛 Marktplatz

Marktplatz, north of the cathedral, is the focal point of the burghers' district. It is surrounded by the houses of prominent merchants, and these magnificent abodes alternate with modest craftsmen's houses. On the west side of the square stands the town hall, whose tower dates from 1444. The façade and upper part of the tower were built in 1823–4.

Eichstätt's other squares – Residenzplatz, Domplatz and Leonrodplatz – were also key elements in the urban planning of the town. Residenzplatz is

The magnificent tomb of St Willibald in the cathedral

one of the finest squares in the whole of Germany. It lies south of the cathedral and has a trapezoid shape. The two-storey buildings that line the square were originally part of the chapterhouses that were designed by Gabriel de Gabrieli.

Domplatz, with the cathedral on its southern side, is laid out on the site of the former cemetery.

On Leonrodplatz stands the church and former Jesuit abbey, as well as the former cathedral deaconry.

🏛 Dom St Salvator und St Willibald

Domplatz.

Eichstätt's cathedral has a late-Gothic nave and presbytery, the latter flanked by twin Romanesque towers. The Baroque façade was built by Gabriel de Gabrieli in 1716–18.

The Gothic cloisters on the south side of the cathedral adjoin the presbytery. The west wing of the cloisters contains a double-naved moratorium containing the Gothic tombs of priests, chaplains and benefactors of the cathedral. Distinctive among the many works of art to be seen in the

cathedral is the statue of St Willibald, who became the first bishop of Eichstätt in the 8th century. The statue, carved in the late Gothic style, was made in 1514 by Loy Hering. In 1745 Matthias Seybold built the two-sided Pappenheimer altar with a canopy to cover the statue of the saint and the tomb containing his relics. This altar is located on the elevated part at the west end of the cathedral.

🏛 Fürstbischöfliche Residenz

Residenzplatz 1. **Tel** (08421) 700.
🕐 7:30am–noon & 2–4pm Mon–Wed, 2–5:30pm Thu, 7:30am–noon Fri.

The former bishop's residence, which adjoins the cathedral on its southern side, was built in 1700–27 to a rectangular plan with a central courtyard. The interior has decorative stuccowork and Rococo frescoes, and features a fine Rococo staircase and Hall of Mirrors, from the 1700s. The Residenz houses the district administration.

The main staircase of the former bishop's residence

🏛 Schutzengelkirche

Ostenstr.

This former Jesuit church was built in 1617–20 under the direction of Hans Alberthal. Having suffered destruction in 1634, in the course of the Thirty Years' War, it was rebuilt in 1660. The interior was lavishly decorated by Franz Gabriel and Johann Rosner, among others, in the first half of the 18th century.

For hotels and restaurants in this region see pp267–8 and p279

Romanesque rotunda inside the Kapuzinerkirche

To the south of the church are the buildings of the former Jesuit College, dating from the 17th and 18th centuries, with two courtyards and cloisters. The college is now used as a seminary.

🏛 Kloster Notre Dame du Sacré Coeur

Notre Dame 1. **Open** Apr–Oct: 9am–5pm Mon–Fri, 10am–5pm Sat & Sun, Nov–Mar: 9am–noon & 2–4pm Mon–Thu, 9am–noon Fri. Informations-zentrum Naturpark Altmühltal· **Tel** (08421) 98 760.

This convent was built for a foundation established in 1711 for the education of young girls. Work on the convent began in 1712, and on the church in 1719, both to designs by the architect Gabriel de Gabrieli.

The church has a centralized plan. The façade is divided by huge pilasters and decorated with a sculpture of the Immaculate Conception above the portal. The headquarters of the information centre for Altmühl Valley National Park are housed in the church.

🏛 Kapuzinerkirche Kreuz und zum Heiligen Grab

Kapuzinergasse 2. **Tel** (08421) 6001 400. **Open** Daily during daylight

This modest church of the Capuchin monks was built in 1623–5 and enlarged in 1905. To the south of the nave stands an oval stone-built Romanesque rotunda crowned by an open gallery and a dome supported on tall, slender columns. It was built in 1160 in imitation of the Church of the Holy Sepulchre in Jerusalem.

VISITORS' CHECKLIST

Practical Information
Road map C2. 🏘 13,000.
ℹ️ Domplatz 8, (08421) 600 1400. 🔳 **eichstaett.de**
🎭 Fliegerfest (May/Jun), Burgfest auf der Willibaldsburg (Jul/Aug), Brauereifest (Aug), Volksfest (Aug/Sep).

Transport
🚌 🚉 Bahnhofplatz 17.

🏛 Fürstbischöfliche Sommer Residenz

Ostenstr. 24.

The former bishop's summer residence, also designed by Gabriel de Gabrieli, dates from 1735–7. The ground and upper floors and narrow side galleries now house the offices of the Catholic university. The residence is set in geometrically laid out parkland that merges into a landscaped park descending in terraces to the River Altmühl.

The Baroque façade of the former bishop's summer residence

Eichstätt Town Centre

① Marktplatz
② Dom St Salvator and St Willibald
③ Fürstbischöfliche Residenz
④ Schutzengelkirche
⑤ Kloster Notre Dame du Sacré Coeur

Klosterkirche St. Walburg

MARKTPLATZ
GABRIELISTRASSE
MARKTGASSE
DOMINIKANERGASSE
LOY-HERING-GASSE
PFAHLSTRASSE
PFARRGASSE
WIDMANNGASSE
LEUCHTENBERGSTRASSE
AM SALZSTADEL
LUIPOLDSTRASSE
DOMPLATZ

← *Bahnhof 200 m (220 yards)*
Willibaldsburg

② Dom St Salvator und St Willibald

PATER-PHILIP-JENINGEN-PLATZ

Kloster Notre Dame de Sacré Coeur ⑤

WOHLMUTHGASSE
AM GRABEN

RESIDENZ-PLATZ

③ Fürstbischöfliche Residenz

OSTENSTRASSE

LEONROD-PLATZ

Schutzengel-kirche ④

Fürstbischöfliche Sommer Residenz & Kapuzinerkirche Hl. Kreuz und zum Heiligen Grabkirche

0 metres — 100
0 yards — 100

Key to Symbols *see back flap*

⌂ Klosterkirche St. Walburg
Westenstr.

This church was built on the spot where the relics of St Walburg were buried in 875. The present monastery dates from 1629–31. In the chapel behind the high altar is St Walburg's tomb, the church's most holy feature and the object of pilgrimages. The chapel, which contains numerous votive images placed there in gratitude to the saint, is decorated with intricate wrought-iron grilles. The altarpiece consists of Gothic carvings depicting St Walburg, his parents and his brother, St Willibald.

⊞ Willibaldsburg
Burgstr. 19. Jura-Museum: **Tel** (08421) 29 56, (08421) 47 30. **Open** Apr–Sep: 9am–6pm, Tue–Sun; Oct–Mar: 10am–4pm Tue–Sun. Museum für Ur- und Frühgeschichte: **Tel** (08421) 89 450. **Open** Apr–Sep: 9am–6pm Tue–Sun; Oct–Mar: 10am–4pm Tue–Sun.

This castle, on a hill northwest of the town centre, overlooks the Altmühl river valley. It can be reached by car through a tunnel 63 m (206 ft) long. The castle has an elongated design and is surrounded by 17th century fortifications. From 1353 to 1725 it was the seat of bishops but was partly demolished in the 19th century. The present approaches to the castle were built in the first half of the 17th-century. The castle walls contain the ruins of a residence built for

Bishop Martin von Schaumberg (1560–90).

The western section of the hill is occupied by a three-winged building with central cloisters, and a main building with small towers. Both were built by Elias Holl, who was brought to Eichstätt by Bishop Konrad von Gemmingen in 1609. Together with Augsburg town hall, they are regarded as Germany's most important late Renaissance buildings.

The north wing houses the **Jura-Museum**, with a rich collection of fossils from the Jurassic period. The south wing contains the **Museum für Ur- und Frühgeschichte** (Museum of Prehistory and Early History), with fascinating displays.

❷ Beilngries

Road map D2. 🏘 9,000. 🚌 🚊
ℹ Hauptstr. 14, (08461) 84 35.
🌐 **beilngries.de**

The best way to reach Beilngries is by road or boat from Kelheim along the scenic Altmühl valley. The town still has a section of its defensive walls, which are set with nine towers and reinforced by a fosse (moat). Among the historic buildings on Hauptstraße is the late 16th-century house at No. 25,

Romanesque tower, a vestige of the medieval castle outside Beilngries

known as the **Kaiserbeckhaus**, which has a cantilevered upper storey supported on corbels.

The imposing Neo-Baroque **Pfarrkirche St Walburga** was built in 1912–13 to a design by Wilhelm Spannagl. The span of its vaulting and the ingenuity of its circular windows are impressive.

On a steep hill outside the town once stood a medieval castle, vestiges of which are two tall Romanesque **towers** flanking the gatehouse. In 1760–4 the castle was converted into the **Bishop's hunting lodge**. Its main decorative motifs are deer, which led to its being called Schloss Hirschberg ("Deer Mountain"). The Imperial Hall and the Knights' Hall are decorated with paintings by Michael Franz and have Rococo stuccowork. The palace chapel, built with material from the walls of the Romanesque castle chapel, was designed by Alexander von Brancas in the 1980s.

❸ Ingolstadt
See pp170–71.

❹ Neuburg an der Donau
See pp172–3.

Fossils from the Jurassic Era

About 150 million years ago, the region of the Altmühl river valley in northern Upper Bavaria and southern Franconia lay beneath a shallow lagoon that was separated from the open Jurassic sea by a reef of

corals and sponges. Today collectors search quarries for fossils of ammonites, small crustaceans, insects and marine plants. For a modest sum impressive specimens can also be purchased from the quarry workers. A rich collection of fossils is on view in the Jura-Museum in Willibaldsburg castle in Eichstätt.

A fossil of *Archaeopteryx lithographica* in the Jura-Museum in Eichstätt

---

❺ Pfaffenhofen

Road map D3. 🔼 25,000. 🚍 🚊
ℹ️ Hauptplatz 47, (08441) 49 15 11.
🌐 pfaffenhofen.de

The town, situated on the
River Ilm, lies at the western
extremity of the hop-growing
region. It was once surrounded
by fortifications set with 17
towers and pierced by four
gates. Around the pleasant
square stands the Gothic
St Johannes-Baptist-Kirche
and a Neo-Gothic **town hall**.
A tall, square tower with a
steeple stands beside the
church presbytery. The
Mesnerhaus, a residential
house dating from 1786,
contains a **museum** with a
sizeable collection of art
dating from the 16th to
the 19th centuries.

**🏛 Museum im
Mesnerhaus**
Scheyrer Str. 5. **Tel** (08441)
27 442 or (08441) 3722.
Open only by prior
arrangement.

Soaring Gothic tower of St Johannes-
Baptist-Kirche, Pfaffenhofen

❻ Scheyern

Road map D3. 🔼 4,200. 🚍 🚊 in
Pfaffenhofen. ℹ️ Ludwigstr. 2, (08441)
80 640.

Scheyern lies southwest of
Pfaffenhofen. In 1119, when the
seat of the Scheyern family was
converted into a monastery, it
was occupied by monks of the
Benedictine order. After the first
wave of the dissolution of the

Façade of the Benedictine monastery in Scheyern

monasteries, the Benedictines
left but returned in 1837 at the
request of Ludwig I.

The triple-nave basilica
of **Mariä Himmelfahrt** was
remodelled in the Baroque
style in 1768–9, with decorative
mouldings by the Wessobrunn
stuccoists. The Chapel of the
Holy Cross contains a Baroque
altar with a late Renaissance
crucifix of 1600. The centrepiece of the tabernacle is a
Byzantine relic of the True Cross,
which is kept in a magnificent
monstrance made by Johann
Georg in 1738.

❼ Freising

Road map D3. 🔼 45,000. 🚍 🚊 Ⓢ
ℹ️ Marienplatz 7, (08161) 54 122.
🌐 freising.de

The seat of a bishopric from
720, the town was for centuries
the residence of the bishops of
Freising and Munich. The hill
on which the **cathedral** stands
is known as Mons Doctus
(Learned Mount). The cathedral
dates from the mid-13th
century, with the
cloisters added in the
15th century. It was
remodelled in 1723–4
with the involvement
of the Asam brothers
(see p72).

An outstanding
feature of the interior
is a Pietà of 1492 by
Erasmus Grasser and
Gothic stalls dating
from 1485–8. The
Romanesque crypt
contains a column
known as the
Bestiensäule, which
is decorated with

carvings symbolizing the fight
against evil. Beside the crypt is
the Maximilianskapelle, with
stuccowork and paintings by
Hans Georg Asam.

The late Gothic **cloisters**
feature paintings by Johann
Baptist Zimmermann of 1717
and tombstones dating from
the 15th to the 18th centuries.
The cloisters are linked to the
Gothic **Benediktuskirche** of
1345, and a stunning Baroque
cathedral library designed by
François Cuvilliés.

The Gothic **Johanniskirche**, in
front of the cathedral, is linked
to the **bishop's residence**,
which has fine Renaissance
cloisters. On the cathedral hill
is the **Diözesanmuseum**, the
largest museum of religious
art in Germany.

In the town at the bottom
of the hill are the church of
St Peter und Paul, designed
in the early 18th century by
Giovanni Antonio Viscardi,
with paintings by Johann
Baptist Zimmermann, and
the late Gothic **St-Georg-
Kirche**, with a Baroque
tower, as well as the
Neo-Renaissance
town hall of 1904–05.
On Weihenstephan hill
stands the world's
oldest **brewery**,
founded in 1040.
The Benedictine
monastery now
houses certain
departments of
Munich's Technical
University.

Oriel window of
Freising town hall

🏛 Diözesanmuseum
Domberg 21. **Tel** (08161) 48
790. **Open** 10am–5pm
Tue–Sun.

❸ Ingolstadt

Ludwig the Rich founded Bavaria's first university here in 1472. Initially a centre of humanism, it later became a focal point of the Counter-Reformation. In the 16th century Ingolstadt was the largest fortified town in southern Germany, and was defended by Swedish soldiers during the Thirty Years' War. It suffered severe bomb damage during World War II but was restored soon after. Today Ingolstadt is known principally for the Audi cars manufactured here and for its oil refinery. However, it has some noteworthy buildings.

Alte Anatomie, now the Deutsches Medizinhistorisches Museum

The Baroque interior of the Asamkirche Maria de Victoria

🏛 Museum Mobile

Audi Forum Ingolstadt, Ettinger Strasse 60. **Tel** (0800) 283 4444. **Open** 9am–6pm daily. 🅿

With its "museum mobile", the Audi Forum is a delight for car enthusiasts. More than 80 Audi cars, motorbikes and bicycles are on display and the history of the automobile is documented in fascinating detail.

🔼 Asamkirche Maria de Victoria

Neubaustraße. **Open** Nov–Feb: 1–4pm Tue–Sun; Mar–Oct: 9am–noon, 1–5pm Tue–Sun (May–Oct: daily). 🅿

This hall was built in 1732–6 as the meeting place of the Marian students' association. The stuccowork is by Egid Quirin Asam, and the painting by his brother Cosmas Damian Asam, who exploited the various points of perspective as he covered the ceiling with extensive frescoes. The sacristy contains a famous monstrance of 1708 by the Augsburg goldsmith Johannes Zeckl, depicting the defeat of the Turks at the Battle of Lepanto in 1571.

🔲 Kreuztor and City Walls

The city walls, together with their semicircular towers, were built from 1362 to 1440. Of the four original city gates, only the western one, known as the Kreuztor, survives. It is considered to be one of the finest of its kind in Germany.

The Taschenturm, a tower with stepped gables, also survives. Of the fortification towers, built from 1539 to 1579 and demolished in 1800, only the ruins of casemates and bastions still stand today. Fortifications begun in 1823 are dotted around the town.

🔼 Liebfrauenmünster

Bergbräustr./Kreuzstr. 1.

This great 15th-century church with diagonally set twin towers is one of the largest Gothic brick buildings in Bavaria.

The high altar, completed in 1572, commemorates the centenary of the foundation of Ingolstadt's university. The altar, 9 m (30 ft) high, incorporates 91 paintings by Hans Mielich. Other features of the interior are the Renaissance stalls and pulpit, the Gothic and Renaissance stained glass, and the monument to Johannes Eck, Martin Luther's greatest opponent, who died in 1543.

🔲 Alte Anatomie

Anatomiestr. 18/20. Deutsches Medizinhistorisches Museum: **Tel** (0841) 305 2860. **Open** 10am–5pm Tue–Sun. 🅿

This fine Baroque building, completed in 1723, originally housed the university's Department of Medicine and is now home to a museum of medical history. The pleasant courtyard has a garden where medicinal herbs are grown.

The Gothic Kreuztor, Ingolstadt's western gate

🏛 Neues Schloss

Paradeplatz 4. Bayerisches
Armeemuseum: **Tel** (0841) 93770.
Open 8:45am–5pm Tue–Sun. 🏛

The Neues Schloss (New Castle)
was built in the first half of the
15th century. Set with corner
towers, the two-storey castle
has the appearance of an
impregnable stronghold. A
Renais-sance gateway leads into
the inner courtyard. Today the
castle houses the **Bavarian
Army Museum**, with displays
of items captured in the wars
against the Turks.

🏛 Herzogskasten

Hallstr. 4.
This ancient castle, standing on
the southeastern corner of the city
walls, was built in 1255. The oldest
secular building in Ingolstadt, it

The Neo-Renaissance Altes Rathaus, with
its elaborate gable

was a ducal residence until it was
superseded by the Neues Schloss,
which was built in the 15th
century. The castle then was
converted into a granary. Rising
two storeys high, it has a very tall
roof with a Gothic stepped gable.
It now houses a library.

VISITORS' CHECKLIST

Practical Information
Road map D2. 🗺 117,000.
🛈 Altes Rathaus, Rathausplatz 4,
(0841) 30 53 030.
🌐 **ingolstadt-tourismus.de**
email: **touristinformation@
ingolstadt.de**
🎭 Ingolstädter Bürgerfest
(first weekend in Jul).

Transport
🚌 🚉 (0841) 93 41 825.

🏛 Altes Rathaus

Rathausplatz 2.
The elegant town hall was
lavishly remodelled in the
Neo-Renaissance style by
Gabriel von Seidl in 1882–3.
Its sculptural decoration was
designed by Lorenz Gedon.
The building incorporates a
former residence.

🏛 Moritzkirche

Hieronymus Str. 3.
Begun in the mid-14th century
and completed in 1489, the
church is a Gothic basilica with
a 14th–15th-century watchtower known as the Pfeifturm.
The hospital nearby,
completed in 1434, served as
the main university building
from 1472 to 1800.

The Neues Schloss, an elegant and imposing residence

Ingolstadt City Centre

① Asamkirche Maria de Victoria
② Kreuztor and City Walls
③ Liebfrauenmünster
④ Alte Anatomie
⑤ Herzogskasten
⑥ Neues Schloss
⑦ Altes Rathaus
⑧ Moritzkirche

0 metres 200
0 yards 200

For map symbols *see back flap*

❹ Neuburg an der Donau

Situated on the River Danube (Donau), Neuburg is considered to be one of Bavaria's most beautiful towns. The atmosphere from the time when it flourished as a ducal residence lives on in the streets and squares of the Obere Stadt (Upper Town). These are rivalled by the Obere Vorstadt, an early centre of the Counter-Reformation, which has an Ursuline convent as well as patricians' town houses and the palaces of the court elite. Along the Danube lies the Englischer Garten, a park traversed by the road to the 16th-century castle of the Wittelsbachs in nearby Grünau.

Oberes Tor, gateway to the Upper Town

🏛 Oberes Tor and Town Walls

In the 14th century Obere Stadt was enclosed by walls, towers and galleries. Considerable vestiges of the upper town remain, notably Oberes Tor, the main gate. It was rebuilt in 1530, when it was flanked by circular towers and top-ped with a Renaissance gable.

🏛 Peterskirche

Amalienstr. 40.
The church stands on the site of the oldest church in Neuburg, first mentioned in 1214. It was designed by Johann Serro of Graubünden and built in 1641–6. The triple-nave open interior is decorated with Baroque painting and stuccowork.

🏛 Amalienstraße

Of the many fine gabled houses that line this street, two are especially worthy of note. One is the Eybhaus, the old post office, built in 1720 and located next to Weveldhaus, and the other the Court Pharmacy, first mentioned in 1713. Both have ornamental gables. Equally elegant are the 17th and 18th-century houses that can be seen in Herrenstraße.

🏛 Stadtmuseum im Weveldhaus

Amalienstr. A19. **Open** Mar–Dec: 10am–6pm Tue–Sun. **Closed** Jan–Feb.
The two-storey late Gothic Weveldhaus was built in the 16th century, and was redecorated in 1715 by Gabriel de Gabrieli, who added a fine Baroque portal. The building houses a museum that contains many artifacts relating to the history of the town and the surrounding area.

🏛 Karlsplatz

There are few town squares in Bavaria more charming than Karlsplatz. Surrounded by trees, it has a Mariensäule (Column of the Virgin) and a fountain in the centre. The square is dominated by the façade of Hofkirche, which occupies its entire eastern side. The square boasts exquisite proportions and fine, elegant

Baroque doorway of the Weveldhaus on Amalienstraße

buildings. On the northern side of the square stands the Renaissance town hall of 1603–09. Its double exterior stairway leads to the grand entrance on the first floor. Beside it stands the Taxishaus (named after the von Thurn und Taxis family). It was completed in 1747 and its façade is decorated with elaborate poly-chrome stuccowork. Further on is the Zieglerhaus, with fine wrought-iron grilles and an elegant gate.

On the west side of the square is the pleasantly proportioned and decorated Lorihaus and the library building, its Rococo façade facing onto Amalienstraße. Built in 1731–2, it was furnished in 1802 with furniture from the Kaisheim monastery library.

Mariensäule on Karlsplatz

🏛 Hofkirche

Karlsplatz 10.
The former Hofkirche (Court Church) was founded by the Protestant rulers of Neuburg in reaction to the building of the Jesuit Michaelskirche in Munich. Work began in 1608 but was interrupted by the death of Philip Ludwig. In 1617 his Catholic successor brought the Jesuits to Neuburg and donated the church to them. It was completed in 1627.

The late Renaissance building, with a flat façade and a central octagonal domed tower, was decorated with fine stuccowork in 1616–18. The paintings by Peter Paul Rubens that once graced the altar are now in the Alte Pinakothek in Munich. Some particularly interesting features of the presbytery are the ducal loggia and the stairway to the crypt, the dukes' final resting place. A passage connects the church to the neighbouring castle.

Ornate interior of Pfarrkirche Mariä Himmelfahrt

🏠 Schloss

Residenzstr. 2. **Tel** (08431) 64430. **Open** 10am–5pm Tue–Sun. 🖼 Schloss museum: **Open** Apr–Sep: 9am–6pm Tue–Sun; Oct–Mar: 10am–4pm Tue–Sun.

The history of Neuburg Castle goes back to Roman times, when the fort of Venaxamodorum stood here. It has been in the possession of the Wittelsbach family since the 13th century. The present-day castle was built in 1530–45 and was redecorated in the Renaissance style in 1667–70. It has a pentagonal outline and is set with two circular towers that look onto the Danube.

The attractive Renaissance courtyard is surrounded by a double-tiered gallery. The west side of the courtyard has sgraffito decorations and two stone figures of dukes, probably dating from the second half of the 17th century. The west wing has a Renaissance chapel with galleries and ceiling frescoes painted by Hans Bockberger in 1543. These were plastered over in 1616, when Protestant fervour celebrated its triumph over Catholicism, but they were uncovered again in 1934–51.

An underground passage beneath Neuer Bau, the north wing, leads from the Danube to Obere Stadt. The Baroque grottoes are open to visitors.

VISITORS' CHECKLIST

Practical Information
Road map C2. 🚗 28,000. 🚶 Ottheinrichplatz. A118, (08431) 55 240. 🎉 Schlossfest (in odd years, Jun/Jul); Volksfest (Jul); Kartoffelwochen (Oct). 🌐 **neuburg-donau.de** email: **tourist@neuburg-donau.de**

Transport
🚉

🏠 Former Jesuit College

Am Unteren Tor.
This 17th-century college building has a modest but imaginatively designed façade. On the third floor is the former assembly hall, which is renowned for its excellent acoustics.

Stone figures in the arcaded courtyard of the Schloss

Neuburg Town Centre

① Oberes Tor and Town Walls
② Peterskirche
③ Amalienstraße
④ Stadtmuseum Weveldhaus
⑤ Karlsplatz
⑥ Hofkirche
⑦ Schloß
⑧ Former Jesuit College

0 metres 100
0 yards 100

For map symbols *see back flap*

The Landshuter Tor in Erding, crowned by a Baroque dome

❽ Erding

Road map D3. ⚡ 34,000. 🚌 🚇 ⑤
ℹ Landshuter Str. 1, (08122) 40 80.
🔳 erding.de

This town is bounded by the rivers Fehlbach and Sempt, which join in the south of the conurbation. The historic buildings are grouped along two intersecting axes: Landshuterstraße, which culminates in the elongated Schrannenplatz, and the streets of Lange Zeile.

At the west end of Schrannenplatz is the Gothic **Johanneskirche**, built in the late 14th to early 15th centuries. It has an unusual layout, with the presbytery facing east. Outside the presbytery stands a tall, 10-storey **belfry**, its façade decorated with friezes and blind windows. Inside the church the most interesting feature is the larger-than-life figure of Christ on the Cross, carved by Hans Leinberger in about 1525.

On the opposite side of Landshuterstraße stands the Gothic town gate known as the **Landshuter Tor**, or Schöner Turm. Flanked by towers, its façade is divided by rows of arched blind windows and it is covered by a shingle-clad Baroque dome, making it one of the most outstanding town gates in southern Bavaria. At Landshuterstraße 1 is the former **residence** of the counts of Preysing, dating from 1648, which is now the town hall. Opposite stands the Gothic **Hospital Church of the Holy Spirit**, while at No. 3 Schrannenplatz is the 14th-century **Frauenkirche**.

❾ Sankt Wolfgang

Road map E4. ⚡ 4,400. 🚌 🚇 St Wolfgang. Hauptstr. 9, (08085) 18 80.
🔳 st-wolfgang-ob.de

The town is named in honour of St Wolfgang, the Bishop of Ratisbon (Regensburg), who was canonized in 1052. According to legend the saint, while on his way to Mondsee monastery, discovered a spring with miracle-working waters here.

In the early 15th century a **chapel** was built over the spring. **Wolfgangskirche** was built to the south of the chapel in 1430–77. This two-nave, web-vaulted church is an outstanding example of late Gothic Bavarian brick architecture. The foundations contain the Stone of St Wolfgang, a piece of red marble bearing what is said to be the saint's footprint. Substantial fragments of the original Gothic altar of about 1485 also remain. There is also a carving of St Wolfgang with St George and St Sigismund by Heinrich Helmschrot of Landshut (or his studio), and

Statue of St Wolfgang

paintings of scenes from the life of St Mary. In the elongated northern nave, and a few steps higher up, is the original **chapel** with the miracle-working spring, which attracts pilgrims. In the early 18th century it was decorated with fine stuccowork with acanthus motifs. The small figure of St Wolfgang that stands on the Rococo altar was made in 1470 and is said to have miraculous powers. Before the altar is a deep covered well. Visitors can lie down beside it and drink its curative water using a ladle.

The town hall is another interesting building. It was originally a presbytery, built by Johann Baptist Gunetzrhainer.

❿ Oberschleißheim

Road map D3. ⚡ 12,000. ⑤
ℹ Freisinger Str. 15, (089) 315 61 30.
🔳 oberschleissheim.de

This town is best known for its three impressive **palaces** (see pp176–7), set in the gardens of the Hofgarten. But also of interest is the **Flugwerft Schleißheim**, a museum located on one of the oldest aerodromes in Germany. Part of the Deutsches Museum, the museum is located in restored buildings dating from 1912–19, in an exhibition hall and on the apron. Some 50 aircraft and helicopters are on display. There is also an exhibition illustrating the development of flight and of space flight.

Otto Lilienthal's aeroplane, built in 1894, Flugwerft Schleißheim

The gardens of the Renaissance castle in Dachau

⓫ Dachau

Road map D4. 🚊 42,000. ⑤ 🚃
ℹ️ Konrad-Adenauer-Str. 1, (08131) 75 286 or 75 287. 🅦 dachau.info
🎭 Dachauer Volksfest (Aug).

Set on a steep hill, this picturesque little town on the River Amper has a panoramic view of nearby Munich, although it is best known as one of the sites of the Holocaust.

In 1933 the first Nazi **concentration camp** was set up here and it was in use up until 1945, during which time 30,000 prisoners perished here. The site of the camp was opened to the public as a place of remembrance in 1965.

One of the buildings contains the **KZ-Gedenkstätte Dachau**, a museum which documents the history of the concentration camps and the crimes against humanity that were committed here before and during World War II.

On the hill at the edge of the town, a **palace** was built on the site of a 15th-century castle as a summer residence for the Wittelsbachs. Of the original four wings constructed in 1558–77, only the southwest wing remains. The ceremonial hall on the first floor, which survives, was decorated in 1564–5 by Hans Wissreuter.

The focal point of the town is a triangular plaza on which the town hall and the church stand. Hans Krumpper's late Renaissance **Jakobskirche** was built in 1624–5. It incorporates an earlier presbytery with a fine tower dating from about 1425 and extended in 1676–8 with the addition of a dome.

⓬ Kloster Indersdorf

Road map C3. 🚃 ⑤ 🚃 Markt Indersdorf. ℹ️ Markt Indersdorf, Marktplatz 1, (08136) 93 40.
🅦 markt-indersdorf.de

This former Augustinian abbey built in the early 11th century stands on the north bank of the River Glonn. Vestiges of a 12th century triple-nave Romanesque basilica with a twin-towered façade and Gothic remodelling are discernible in the later **Klosterkirche Mariä Himmelfahrt**. The latter was lavishly furnished during the 18th century. Franz Xaver Feichtmayr the Elder added the interior Rococo stuccowork in 1754–6, and the paintings of scenes from the life of St Augustine were executed by Matthäus Günther, assisted by Johann Georg Dieffenbrunner.

The extensive **abbey buildings** of 1694–1704, designed by Antonio Riva, are set around two courtyards south and east of the church.

Gate and guard tower of Dachau concentration camp

Gothic Madonna in Fürstenfeldbruck's Baroque church

⓭ Fürstenfeldbruck

Road map C4. 🚊 33,000. ⑤ 🚌
ℹ️ Hauptstr. 31, (08141) 280.
🅦 fuerstenfeldbruck.de 🎭 Volks- und Heimatfest (Jun–Jul); Brucker Altstadtfest (Jul); Leonhardifahrt (Oct–Nov); Christkindlmarkt (Dec); Luzienhäusischwimmen (13 Dec).

The finest and most important building in the town is the former **Cistercian abbey**, situated on the way to Augsburg and built in 1263–90. Its establishment was funded by Ludwig II, the Severe, after the execution of his wife Maria of Brabant, who was unjustly accused of infidelity. In 1691–1754, remodelled by Giovanni Antonio Viscardi, it became one of the largest Baroque abbeys in Bavaria.

The monumental façade of **Klosterkirche Mariä Himmelfahrt** conceals an interior of fine stuccowork by Pietro Francesco Appiani, vaulting lavishly painted by Cosmas Damian Asam and a high altar of 1760–62 designed by his brother Egid Quirin Asam.

The monastery, its interior decorated with stuccowork and painting in 1924, now houses a police college and museum. Many historic town houses line the main street. The old town hall, refurbished in 1866–8, features paintings dating from 1900.

On St Lucy's Day, in memory of the flood of 1725, children float model houses illuminated with candles across the Amper, which flows through the town.

Schleißheim Palace

Originally intended to rival the splendour of Versailles, the palace at Schleißheim was the architectural setting for the imperial ambitions of Maximilian Emanuel. The architect was Enrico Zucalli, and work started in 1701. It was then interrupted, but restarted in 1717 under the direction of Joseph Effner, who deviated from the original plans. The 330-m (1,082-ft) long Neues Schloss has an overpoweringly lavish interior, which was decorated by Cosmas Damian Asam and Johann Baptist Zimmermann. Today, as well as admiring the elaborate interior decoration, visitors can see the palace's outstanding gallery of Baroque painting.

Doors
The doors leading into the vestibule were carved by Ignaz Günther in 1736 and are counted among his masterpieces.

Altes Schloss
In the late 16th century Wilhelm V built himself Altes Schloss. Heinrich Schön the Elder remodelled it in 1616–23, with mouldings and paintings by Peter Candid. It was rebuilt after World War II and houses two branches of the Bavarian National Museum.

KEY

① **A gateway with clock tower** built in about 1600 leads into the courtyard in front of the Altes Schloss.

② **Canals** of Lustheim form the axis of the park layout. In front of Neues Schloss the water flows into a basin with a cascade and fountains.

★ **Neues Schloss**
The vestibule, decorated with fine stuccowork and frescoes, leads into a Rococo dining-room on one side and to a grand staircase on the other.

★ Schloss Lustheim
This small Baroque palace was built as a love nest for Maximilian Emanuel and his first wife. It now houses a collection of Meissen porcelain.

VISITORS' CHECKLIST

Practical Information
Map D3. Altes Schloss, Neues Schloss & Schloss Lustheim:
Tel (089) 31 58 720.
🅦 schloesser-schleissheim.de
Open Apr–Sep: 9am–6pm Tue–Sun; Oct–Mar: 10am–4pm Tue–Sun.

②

0 metres   150
0 yards   150

Maximilian Emanuel

In 1701 the Elector Maximilian Emanuel ordered the extension of Schleißheim and the rebuilding of Nymphenburg. Defeat in the war against Austria caused work to be temporarily suspended, so that he did not see its completion. Despite this his patronage brought Bavaria into the mainstream of the high Baroque, giving the Wittelsbach family a name for splendour and prestige.

★ Park
This is the only Baroque park in Germany that has survived in its original form. It is characterized by canals and pathways that mark out geometrical patterns of greenery.

LOWER BAVARIA

Lower Bavaria (Niederbayern), bordering Austria and the Czech Republic in the east, is both a distinct cultural entity and a separate administrative area. With an agriculture-intensive south and mountainous north and east, it is an oasis of peace. Its fine Baroque buildings leave an indelible impression on the visitor. With none of the bustle of big cities, towns like Landshut and Passau have retained an old-world flavour.

Lower Bavaria encompasses most of the Bayerischer Wald (Bavarian Forest), which includes a nature reserve and a national park. Increasing numbers of holiday-makers are appreciating the unspoiled natural environment here. As recently as the 1960s, out-of-the-way villages delighted visitors with their tumbledown thatched cottages. Today such sights are confined to the open-air museums of the Museumsdorf Bayerischer Wald and the Freilichtmuseum Finsterau.

The local people, known for their hospitality and friendliness, work in the region's forestry, tourist and glassware industries. Calm and restrained, they have a strong sense of their own worth. When Franz Xaver Krenkl, a Lower Bavarian, beat the royal carriage on its journey to Munich in his own cart, his comment was simply "Wer ko der ko" ("He who can, can"). From the

Benedictine monastery at Weltenburg to the town of Kelheim the River Danube flows between high limestone cliffs overgrown with dense mixed foliage. On both sides of the river unique rock formations create fantastic shapes, and they have been named accordingly. Sailing along this stretch of the Danube is an unforgettable experience, as is the view down onto the river from the gallery around the Neo-Classical Liberation Hall in Kelheim. A canal completed in 1992 joins the Danube at Kelheim, providing a waterway link with the Main and the, Rhine using a stretch of the River Altmühl. This valley is as magical as that of the Danube.

Initiatives to industrialize Lower Bavaria have resulted in the construction of two modern factories in Dingolfing, where the famous BMW cars are produced.

Passau's beautiful Old Town, on the banks of the River Danube

◀ Ornate altar of the church of Mariä Himmelfahrt, Rohr

Exploring Lower Bavaria

Landshut is the capital of Lower Bavaria. Every four years tourists come for the Landshut Wedding, a great historical spectacle held at the foot of Trausnitz castle *(see p35)*. Passau, at the confluence of the Danube, Inn and Ilz rivers, is equally picturesque. From here the "Asam Trail" begins, taking in the churches that the Asam brothers *(see p72)* decorated in Aldersbach, Osterhofen, Straubing, Rohr and Weltenburg. The piety of the local people can be seen in the many pilgrimage churches, the best known being at Bogenberg, known as the Mount Athos of Lower Bavaria, and Geiersberg, near Deggendorf.

Bavarian coat of arms on the town gate in Vilshofen

Barrage on the River Altmühl at Haidhof

For map symbols *see back flap*

Getting Around

Lower Bavaria borders Austria and the Czech Republic. Three motorways pass through the region. The A92 links Landshut and Deggendorf, following the course of the River Isar, and the A3 links Regensburg and Passau, along the course of the River Danube. Regensburg can also be reached by A93. The railway network is sparse but there is a good bus service.

Sights at a Glance

1. *Landshut pp182–5*
2. Rohr
3. Weltenburg
5. *Straubing pp188–9*
6. Bogenberg
7. Metten
8. Sankt Hermann

10. Museumsdorf Bayerischer Wald
11. *Passau pp192–3*
12. Fürstenzell
13. Ortenburg
14. Sammarei
15. Aldersbach

16. Vilshofen
17. Osterhofen

Tours
4. Altmühl Valley
9. Nationalpark Bayerischer Wald

Key

- Motorway
- Main road
- Minor road
- Scenic route
- Main railway
- Minor railway
- International border
- △ Summit

The stone-built "Hochbrücke" viaduct (1612) at Dingolfing

0 kilometres 15

0 miles 15

Exploring Landshut

Landshut, like Munich, lies between a fork in the River Isar. It stretches out between Trausnitz castle, which is set on a vantage point, and the Cistercian abbey of Seligenthal. The central conurbation is concentrated around two wide parallel streets that function as squares lying on a north-south axis. They are known as Altstadt and Neustadt.

Landshut is perhaps the most quintessentially German of all Lower Bavarian towns. With its historic buildings spared damage during World War II, the town has retained the atmosphere of its earlier days of glory.

🏛 Jesuitenkirche
Spiegelgasse.

The Church of St Ignatius, located on the southern road leading out of Neustadt, was formerly part of a Jesuit monastery. Designed by the Jesuit architect Johannes Holl, it was built from 1631 to 1641. The interior features a fine Baroque high altar dating from 1663.

Side entrance to the impressive Gothic Jodokkirche

🏛 Jodokkirche
Jodokgasse.

This Gothic triple-nave brick basilica, built in 1338–1450, was dedicated to St Jodok, the son of a Breton duke who lived in the 7th century and who became a pilgrim and hermit. In the mid-19th century the church was restored to its original Gothic appearance and was furnished in Baroque style.

Stone reliefs on the Gothic altar in Martinskirche

🏛 Martinskirche
Altstadt 68. **Tel** (0871) 92 21 780.
Open 7:30am–6:30pm daily (to 5pm Oct–Mar). **Closed** 10:30am–3pm Mon & Fri.

Three architects collaborated on the building of this Gothic church. One of them was Hans von Burghausen, whose tombstone, dated 1432, is built into its southern wall. At 131 m (430 ft) high, the brick church tower is the tallest in the world; the steeple was added in 1500. The tower commands a splendid view of the town and of the castle and its gardens. The interior of the church abounds in priceless Gothic furnishings.

🏛 Dominikanerkirche
Regierungsplatz.

The Church of St Blasius, part of the former Dominican monastery, was built in 1271–1384 in the form of a triple-nave Gothic basilica. The interior was remodelled in the Rococo style by Johann Baptist Zimmermann and decorated with lavish stucco-work. The Neo-Classical façade was added in 1805.

🏛 Spitalkirche
Heilige-Geist-Gasse.

The late Gothic Church of the Holy Spirit and the building of the former hospital located opposite stand on the northern end of Altstadt. The triple-nave church was built by Hans von Burghausen in 1407–61.

The interior features fan vaulting and there is an ambulatory around the presbytery. On the northern side of the presbytery stands a large tower. The entrance to the church, in the west front, is a tall, ornamental portal fronted by a porch whose corners are set with low towers.

⊞ Stadtresidenz
Altstadt 79. **Tel** (0871) 92 41 10.
Open Apr–Sep: 9am–6pm Tue–Sun; Oct–Mar: 10am–4pm Tue–Sun. 🖼

This residence, in the Italian Renaissance style, consists of two adjacent buildings.

The Deutscher Bau, built in 1536–7, has a Neo-Classical façade dating from about 1780 on the side looking onto Altstadt. A museum of local history was laid out here in 1935.

The Italienischer Bau, built in 1537–43, has a fine arcaded courtyard. The building's façade, looking onto Ländgasse, is decorated with a large cartouche bearing the coat of arms of Ludwig X of Bavaria, for whom it was built. Inside visitors can see the fine reception halls, which occupy two floors, and admire the beautiful Renaissance frescoes depicting mythological scenes.

Spitalkirche, on the road leading from Altstadt

Burg Trausnitz

This castle, whose history began in the year 1204, was the seat of the von Bayern-Landshut branch of the Wittelsbach family. It was extended in the 14th and 15th centuries, and was converted into a residence in 1568–79. In 1961 a fire destroyed the northwest wing, but painstaking restoration has allowed it to re-open to visitors. The late Romanesque chapel and the original staircase were spared.

VISITORS' CHECKLIST

Practical Information
Burg Trausnitz 168. **Tel** (0871) 92 41 10. **Open** Apr–Sep: 9am–6pm daily; Oct–Mar: 10am–4pm daily. 🖼
W burgtrausnitz.de

Transport
🚌 7 (to Kalcherstraße).

★ Narrentreppe
The Fools' Staircase is decorated with lifesize figures from the Commedia dell'Arte painted in 1578 by Padovano. They commemorate the shows performed by an itinerant Italian theatre troupe for Wilhelm V.

St-Georgs-Rittersaal
The walls of this hall are hung with tapestries illustrating the exploits of Duke Otto Wittelsbach woven to designs by Peter Candid in Paris in 1618.

Arcaded courtyard

Alte Dürnitz
This spacious two-nave hall is situated on the ground floor and features arches supported on palmate pillars.

The Castle
A steep flight of steps leads up to the castle and its gardens. The castle commands a fine view of the whole town and the valley of the River Isar.

❷ Rohr

Road map D2. 🚌 🚊 Abensberg.
ℹ️ Marienplatz 1, (08783) 96 080.
Abbey: **Tel** (08783) 96 000.
Asamkirche: **Open** 6am–8pm daily.
📷 🅿️ 🌐 **kloster-rohr.de**

This abbey dates from the
12th century. In the first quarter of the 13th century, when
the church and **abbey** were
transferred to the Benedictines,
the buildings were remodelled
in the Baroque style.

Asamkirche is renowned
for its stuccowork and the high
altar of 1723 by Egid Quirin
Asam. The altar was built in
the form of a theatrical stage
with wings. The sculptural
group on the altar depicts
the Assumption of the Virgin.
It embodies the idea of a
Theatrum Sacrum and is
one of Asam's masterpieces
in this genre.

The high altar of the church of Mariä
Himmelfahrt in Rohr

❸ Weltenburg

Road map D2. 🚌 🚊 Kelheim.
🚢 Monastery: **Tel** (09441) 20 41 36.
📷 Tours should be pre-booked. 🅿️
🌐 **klosterschenke-weltenburg.de**

This Benedictine **monastery**
complex, dating from the
early 7th century, stands in a
picturesque setting on a terrace
beside the Danube.

The Asam brothers added to the
complex the splendid Baroque
Georgs- und Martinskirche, which
was completed in 1716. Cosmas
Damian was responsible for the
architectural designs and the
paintings, and Egid Quirin Asam

A boat trip through the Danube Gorge from Weltenburg to Kelheim

built the fine high altar and
the statue of St George slaying
the Dragon.

There is a beer-garden in
the cloisters where visitors can
sample the monastery's beer.
Boat trips through the Danube
Gorge to Kelheim also depart
from a quay nearby.

❹ Straubing

See pp188–9.

❺ Bogenberg

Road map F2. 🚶 9,800. 🚌
🚊 Bogen. ℹ️ Bogen, Stadtplatz 56,
(09422) 50 51 09. 🌐 **bogen.de**

Rising above the small town
of Bogen, the Bogenberg,
or "Mount Athos" of Lower
Bavaria, was once a Celtic
sacred place. Since the Middle
Ages it has been a place of
pilgrimage. Standing on the
top is the Gothic **Hl. Kreuz und
Mariä Heimsuchung**, which
commands an excellent view

Angel and candles in the pilgrimage
church of Bogenberg

over the Danube valley.
Pilgrims come here to honour
the miraculous statue of the
pregnant Virgin Mary, dating
from around 1400, which is
clothed in a 17th-century dress
and embroidered cloak. Dozens
of votive candles flicker in
the presbytery.

According to an ancient
custom, at Pentecost the
strongest man from the nearby
village of Holzkirchen brings to
the church a great candle –
Die lange Stang – up to 100 kg
(220 lb) in weight and 13 m
(40 ft) long.

❼ Metten

Road map F2. 🚶 4,200. 🚌 🚊
ℹ️ Krankenhausstr. 22, (0991) 99 80
50. 🌐 **markt-metten.de**

The local **Benedictine
abbey** was founded in about
766. In 1830, after it had been
appropriated as a result of the
dissolution of the monasteries,
it was returned to its
industrious owners.

Michaelskirche, which
has been rebuilt several times
since its foundation in the
Romanesque period, was
remodelled in 1712–29. The
twin-towered façade outlines
two circular chapels. The interior
has paintings and a high altar
by Cosmas Damian Asam.

The most exquisite part
of the abbey is the library,
built in 1722–9 and decorated
with stuccowork by Franz Josef
Holzinger. It is one of the finest
library buildings in the world.
A remarkable pair of Atlases
support the low vaulted ceiling.

❹ Altmühl Valley

The River Altmühl winds scenically from central Franconia, meandering through the northern part of Upper Bavaria and through Lower Bavaria before flowing into the Danube. The Altmühltal Naturpark, in the river valley, is one of the largest and finest nature parks in Germany. This tour takes visitors along the estuary, ending with the famous canal that connects the River Danube with the Main and the Rhine.

Tips for Drivers

Tour length: About 20 km (12 miles).
Stopping-off points: There are cafés or bars at each of the places along the route. The larger towns have restaurants and some also offer accommodation.

⑤ Schloß Prunn
This castle, looking as if it had grown from the rocks, houses a museum. The longest wooden bridge in Europe, over the Altmühl, is visible from the terrace.

⑦ Rosenburg
This castle is a centre for the breeding of birds of prey and contains a museum of falconry equipment. Displays with birds of prey, including eagles, are held here every day.

⑥ Riedenburg
The local Crystals Museum is famous for having the world's largest cluster of rock crystal. It weighs 7.8 tonnes and comes from Arkansas in the United States.

Kelheimwinzer

Saal

Regensburg

16

Ingolstadt

③ Randeck
A road running to the foot of the mountain leads to the ruins of an 11th-century castle, which was rebuilt several times, with the town of Essing at its feet.

① Kelheim
The Liberation Hall, built by Friedrich von Gärtner and Leo von Klenze in 1842–63, commemorates the defeat of Napoleon.

④ Essing
A narrow street leads to a delightful market square, while a medieval gate leads through to the wooden bridge (the longest in Europe) over the former course of the River Altmühl.

Key

▬ Suggested route

⋯ Other road

② Tropfsteinhöhle
These caves, off the road to Essing, were inhabited during the Stone Age. The temperature inside stays at a constant 9° C (48° C), regardless of external conditions.

0 kilometres   10

0 miles   10

❺ Straubing

Standing on the south bank of the Danube in the fertile Gäuboden, Straubing pulsates with life. The medieval appearance of the Old Town has survived basically unchanged, bearing a faithful resemblance to the wooden model made in 1568 by Jakob Sandtner and now on view in the Bayerisches Nationalmuseum in Munich. A copy can be seen in the Gäubodenmuseum. Every year in August the town holds the Gäubodenvolksfest, a folk festival second in size only to Munich's Oktoberfest.

The Stadtturm (city tower) in the centre of the town square

🏛 Ludwigsplatz and Theresienplatz

The pedestrianized market square resembles a long, wide avenue cutting through the heart of the Old Town. It is pleasant to wander through the large garden between closely packed stalls and crates full of colourful flowers, fruit and vegetables, and admire the historic buildings. The Stadtturm, or tower, offers a sweeping panorama of the town, the Gäuboden and the Bavarian Forest. A Neo-Classical gate built in 1810 divides the market square into two, with Ludwigsplatz on the eastern side and Theresienplatz on the western.

Ludwigsplatz and Theresienplatz have two foun-tains dedicated to the town's patron saints, St Jacob (1644) and St Tiburtius (1685). On Theresienplatz stands a column built in 1709, featuring gilt figures of the Holy Trinity.

Opposite the town gates on the south side of the square is the two-storey **town hall**, its two wings enclosing a courtyard. The town hall was created in 1382, when two adjacent Gothic houses were conjoined behind a single façade. The stepped gable, however, dates from the 19th century.

🏛 Karmelitenkirche

Albrechtsgasse 20.
This spacious triple-nave Gothic church with a tower was partly remodelled in about 1700 by Wolfgang Dientzenhofer. The lavish 17th and 18th-century furnishings successfully harmonize with the later Baroque decoration.

Baroque interior of Ursulinenkirche

In the church is the tomb of Duke Albrecht II. His son, Albrecht III, secretly married Agnes Bernauer, who was the beautiful daughter of a barber from Augsburg. When he found out Albrecht II ordered the drowning of Agnes in the Danube in 1435. Every four years in June/July amateur actors re-create this historical tragedy in the Agnes- Bernauer-Festspiele.

🏛 Ursulinenkirche

Burggasse 9.
This church, which forms part of an Ursuline convent, was built and decorated by the Asam brothers in 1736–41. In their inspired collaboration, Egid Quirin Asam created the architectural design and Cosmas Damian Asam painted the frescoes and the altarpieces (see p72).

🏰 Herzogsschloss

Schlossplatz 2B. **Tel** (09421) 94 43 07. 🚗 access for pre-booked guided tours only.
The castle, on the Danube, has an irregular plan and an inner courtyard. Its earliest parts date from the 14th century. The Bernauerturm on the northwestern corner is the turret from which Agnes Bernauer is said to have been thrown into the Danube. The castle is home to tax offices, but special guided tours can be arranged.

🏛 Gäubodenmuseum

Fraunhoferstr. 9. **Tel** (09421) 97 41 10. **Open** 10am–4pm Tue–Sun. 🚗
This local history museum was founded in 1845. Its most renowned exhibit is the Römerschatz, or Roman Treasure, which was discovered in 1950 and which caused a sensation among academics. It is the largest collection of Roman parade armour to have been found anywhere in the former Roman Empire. The collection includes highly ornamental helmets with visors, shin-guards and metal masks for horses.

View of the Herzogsschloss from the Danube

VISITORS' CHECKLIST

Practical Information
Road map E2. 45,000.
Theresienplatz 20, (09421)
94 43 07. Fax: (09421) 94 41 03.
straubing.de
email: **tourismus@straubing.de**
Internationales Jazz-Festival
(July), Gäubodenvolksfest (Aug),
Agnes-Bernauer-Festspiele
(every four years, next
in July 2015).

Transport
Bahnhofplatz.

⬆ Basilika St Jakob
Pfarrplatz 1a.

This is one of Bavaria's largest and most magnificent Gothic churches. Building begun in 1400 and was not completed for almost a century. The forest of columns in the extraordinarily tall interior support 18th-century barrel vaulting.

The church has preserved its Gothic statues and paintings, including an image of the Mother of God ascribed to Hans Holbein, Baroque paintings and sculptures by the Asam Brothers, and tombstones. The 15th-century stained glass windows are the church's finest elements, giving the church interior a unique atmosphere.

⬆ Kirche St Peter
Petersgasse. 50b.

Peterskirche, a Romanesque basilica dating from around 1200 whose steeples were

Gothic stained-glass window in Basilika St Jakob

enlarged in the 19th century, is one of the finest churches of its kind in Lower Bavaria. Among the interior features are a Romanesque Crucifix and a Gothic Pietà dating from about 1340.

The church cemetery is an interesting place to explore, as it is one of the oldest in Germany. It contains three Gothic chapels. One of them, the Bernauerkapelle, was built by Duke Ernst as penance for Agnes Bernauer's murder in 1435. Her symbolic tombstone can be seen within. The walls of the Totenkapelle, built in 1486, bear a cycle depicting the Dance of Death that was painted in 1763 by Felix Hölzl.

Straubing Town Centre

① Ludwigsplatz and Theresienplatz
② Karmelitenkirche
③ Ursulinenkirche
④ Herzogsschloss
⑤ Gäubodenmuseum
⑥ Basilika St Jakob

0 metres 50
0 yards 50

For map symbols see back flap

Wooden chapel and Baroque church at Sankt Hermann

❽ Sankt Hermann

Road map F2. 🚌 🚉 Regen.
ℹ️ Bischofsmais, Hauptstr. 34 (09920)
94 04 44. 🌐 **bischofsmais.de**

Just outside Bischofsmais, on the site of the oldest hermitage in the Bavarian Forest, stands a group of three ecclesiastical buildings.

In about 1320 St Herman, a Benedictine monk from the Niederalteich monastery, lived here. His cult began in the 17th century, when pilgrimages were made to places that were associated with him.

The **Brunnenkapelle**, a small domed Baroque rotunda with a niche for the miracle-working spring, was built in 1611. **Hermannskirche**, a Baroque pilgrimage church, was built in 1653–4.

The **Einsiedeleikapelle** was added in 1690. It is a wooden chapel built in memory of the saint's hermitage. Its western part, the Hermannszelle (Herman's Cell), is full of wooden legs and crutches left here by pilgrims, in thanks for the miracle cures they received.

❿ Museumsdorf Bayerischer Wald

Road map G2. 🚌 🚉 Tittling.
Tel (08504) 84 82. **Open** week before Easter–Oct: 9am–5pm daily; Museum grounds only: Nov–Mar: 9am–5pm daily. 🌐 **museumsdorf.com**

Near Tittling, on the west side of the road from Grafenau to Passau, this open-air museum is one of the largest in Europe. Here over 140 buildings dating from the 18th and 19th centuries have been erected on a 200,000-sq m (50-acre) site. As well as traditional cottages with all their furnishings, visitors can

see mills, forges, sawmills and also the oldest public school building in Germany.

Near the museum, in an **inn** dating from 1829, traditional Bavarian specialities are on offer. Visitors to the inn include prominent German figures, including the former chancellor Helmut Kohl and the writer Friedrich Dürrenmatt.

The museum is in the Dreiburgenland, so named after the three castles, **Saldenburg**, **Fürstenstein** and **Englburg**. They are well preserved but are not open to the public.

⓫ Passau

See pp192–5.

⓬ Fürstenzell

Road map G3. 🏘️ 7,700. 🚌
🚉 Passau. ℹ️ Marienplatz 7, (08502)
80 228. 🌐 **fuerstenzell.de**

Founded in 1274, the **Cistercian abbey** here reached the height of its artistic development in the 18th century (closed to the public).

Marienkirche, built in 1738, was designed by Johann Michael Fischer, with stuccowork by Johann Baptist Modler and Johann Georg Funk and

The 19th-century inn at the Museumsdorf Bayerischer Wald

Marienkirche, Fürstenzell

elaborate ceiling paintings by Johann Jakob Zeiller. The interior features Baroque and Rococo altars, the high altar by Johann Baptist Straub, and a fine Rococo pulpit. The Gothic tombs of the Cistercian abbots and the abbey's founders, which were transferred here from the medieval church, are also of interest.

The **monastery**, situated south of the church, was remodelled in 1674–87, and extended after 1770. The Festsaal (State Room), with frescoes of 1773 in the late Viennese Neo-Classical style, is outstanding.

The monastery library was decorated in about 1760. Together with the monastery library in the town of Metten nearby, it is the finest example of artistic patronage by the Cistercian order in Germany. The interior is lined with a gallery supported on alternating Tuscan columns and herms (head of Hermes on a stone pillar). The bookcases are decorated with Rococo putti, fencing figures and Atlases carved by Joseph Deutschmann.

🏛️ Marienkirche

Tel (08502) 91 150. **Open** 8am–6pm daily. 📷 by arrangement.

❾ Nationalpark Bayerischer Wald

This excursion leads through the Nationalpark Bayerischer Wald, established in 1970 and the first national park in Germany. It is an extensive hilly area of forests, woodland, swamps and meadows, picturesque lakes and interesting rock formations that combine to create unique landscapes inhabited by many species of birds and animals. The Hans-Eisenmann-Haus is the main information centre in the area.

③ Finsterau
The Freilichtmuseum Finsterau is not far from Finsterau, a village with overflowing window boxes, where there is a working smithy and a bakery selling fresh bread.

④ Hans-Eisenmann-Haus
A scenic forest road leads to the house. From here visitors can go to the Pflanzenfreigelände, a reserve with over 500 plant species, or take a trip to the Tierfreigelände, a reserve for wild animals.

⑤ St Oswald
The Waldgeschichtliches Museum illustrates the life and culture of the "forest people". The abbey and church of St Oswald were rebuilt in the Baroque style in 1876. The Brünnlkapelle stands beside a miracle-working spring.

② Mauth
The village glassworks, the Glasbläserhof Mauth, are fascinating. Glass-blowers can be seen at work and visitors may try their hand at this difficult art.

0 kilometres 15
0 miles 15

Tips for Drivers

Tour length: 50 km (31 miles)
Stopping-off points: There are bars and restaurants in Freyung, Finsterau, in the open-air museum and at Hans-Eisenmann-Haus.

① Freyung
Schloß Wolfstein contains a hunting and fishing museum. The Schramlhaus (at Abteistraße 6), with the Heimatmuseum, is also worth a visit.

Key
▬▬ Suggested route
⋯⋯ Other road

⑪ Passau

Passau is one of the oldest and most beautiful towns in Bavaria. Nestling in the hills at the confluence of three rivers, it is divided into three districts interconnected by 15 bridges. The Old Town lies on a peninsula between the Danube and the Inn, while Innstadt lies beside the Inn and Ilzstadt beside the Ilz. Passau's fine buildings give it its charm and magic, while the southern wind, felt both in the climate and the art, lends an Italian atmosphere.

Towers of the Dom St Stephan – Passau's great Baroque cathedral

⊞ Domplatz

In 1155 the cathedral chapter acquired a plot of land between the cathedral and the western section of the city walls with the aim of building on it chapterhouses arranged around a large square. What were the originally modest chapterhouses were later remodelled in a more ostentatious Baroque style.

Distinctive among them is the Lamberg Chapterhouse, at No. 6 Domplatz, on the west side of the square. Rebuilt in 1724, the chapterhouse is also known as **Lamberg Palace** for its magnificent façade, which is decorated with fine mouldings. The old chapterhouses at Nos. 4 and 5, known as the Barbarahof and Kanonikatshof Starzhausen, today accommodate the presbytery and the seminary.

The square itself features a monument to the Bavarian king, Maximilian I Joseph, and was created by Christian Gorhan the Younger in 1824.

⬆ Dom St Stephan

Domplatz 1.

The original cathedral, set on the highest point in the town, was destroyed in the Great Fire of 1662. It was rebuilt in 1668–77 by Carlo Lurago, who created the largest Baroque church north of the Alps, incorporating the surviving Gothic presbytery and transept into the new scheme.

The elegant towers can be seen from afar. The interior contains a stunning wealth of stuccowork and other ornamentation added in 1677–85 by Giovanni Battista Carlone, and paintings by Carpoforo Tencalla.

The burial chapels on the north side of the cathedral include the Gothic Herrenkapelle, which was built in about 1300 for the members of the cathedral chapter and which contains an enormous Romanesque Crucifix dating from about 1190.

Passau Cathedral is famous for its magnificent organ, one of the largest in the world. Occupying the Baroque organ loft, it was built in 1924–8 and refurbished in 1979–81. Organ recitals take place every day at noon from May to October.

⬆ Neue Residenz

Residenzplatz 8. Treasury and Diocesan Museum: **Tel** (0851) 39 33 331. **Open** 2 May–31 Oct: 10am–4pm Mon–Sat. ⬚

The new Bishop's residence, which occupies the south side of Residenzplatz, was built in 1713–30 to plans by Domenico d'Angeli and Antonio Beduzzi. It was refurbished in 1764–71 by Melchior Hefele of Vienna, with stuccowork by members of the local Modler family, the addition of a Neo-Classical façade and interior decoration in the late Baroque style.

The design and decoration of the vestibule and staircase are particularly successful. The reception rooms contain large collections of artifacts from the **Diocesan Museum** and Cathedral **Treasury**, some of which can also be seen in the cathedral.

The full splendour of the Dom St Stephan's Baroque interior

The pediment over the façade of the Neue Residenz

🏛 Alte Residenz

Theresienstr. 18.

The Old Residence, whose buildings are crowded into a small area between the cathedral and a hillside, is an important landmark visible from the River Inn. The residence probably stands on the site of a bishopric mentioned in 1188. The medieval buildings have been remodelled over the ages, and their present uniform appearance dates from 1680.

The reception rooms were decorated in the 18th century, but soon afterwards the bishopric was moved to the New Residence. The buildings now house the Landgericht, or provincial court.

🏛 Residenzplatz

This square acquired its grand stately character in the Baroque period. Later, stuccowork façades were added to the houses that line it. Particularly noteworthy are the houses at No. 1, built in 1725–30, and

No. 13, built in about 1700. The Neo-Baroque fountain on the square was built by Jakob Bradl in 1906.

🏛 Michaelskirche

Michaeligasse 25.

In terms of architectural importance, the former Jesuit church is second only to Passau's cathedral. It was built and decorated in 1665–77 by members of the Carlone family. Its fine twin-towered façade makes it a distinctive feature

The Schaiblingsturm, part of Passau's medieval defences

VISITORS' CHECKLIST

Practical Information
Road map G3. 🗺 50,000.
ℹ Rathausplatz 3, (0851) 95 59
80. 🔳 passau.de 📅 Maidult
(May, every two years); Festspiele
Europäische Wochen (Jun/Jul);
Herbstdult (Sep).

Transport
🚉 🚢

of the city's skyline. The lavish interior includes a high altar of 1712 by Christoph Tausch of Breslau, side altars of about 1677 and a pulpit and organ loft built in 1717–20.

The former Jesuit college, which was built in 1613–25, is now used as a high school. The courtyard that is enclosed on three sides by the wings of the building has been recently closed off on its northern side by a glazed passage. At the end of the east wing is a tall octagonal tower that once housed an observatory.

🏛 Schaiblingsturm

The 14th-century Schaiblingsturm, on the bank of the River Inn, is a vestige of the old city fortifications. In centuries gone by the tower protected the port on the important salt route.

Passau City Centre

① Paulskirche
② Domplatz
③ Dom St Stephan
④ Alte Residenz
⑤ Neue Residenz
⑥ Residenzplatz
⑦ Passauer Glasmuseum
⑧ Altes Rathaus
⑨ Michaelskirche
⑩ Schaiblingsturm
⑪ Kloster Niedernburg
⑫ Waisenhaus
⑬ Museum Moderner Kunst
⑭ Veste Niederhaus
⑮ Salvatorkirche
⑯ Veste Oberhaus

0 metres   200
0 yards   200

For map symbols *see back flap*

The Veste Oberhaus and below it the Veste Niederhaus, overlooking the Danube

🎏 Waisenhaus

Innkai.

This former orphanage, a two-storey building with an inner quadrangle, was built in 1750–62 to a design by Michael Schneitmann. The north wing contains a chapel whose façade and interior feature fine stuccowork executed by Giovanni Martin Luraghi in 1753.

🎏 Kloster Niedernburg

Jesuitengasse.

Originally a Benedictine abbey, this was founded in about 740 on the site of the Roman Kastell Boiodurum. The present abbey church, which replaces an earlier one built in the early 11th century, is an example of an early Romanesque basilica with two towers and a transept. The presbytery was rebuilt in the Gothic style in the 15th century and the interior was redecorated in the Baroque style after it was damaged by fire in 1662 and 1680.

The south transept contains a Romanesque tombstone marking the tomb of the abbess, St Gisela, who was the sister of Emperor Henry II and widow of St Stephen, king of Hungary. In 1420 a sarcophagus with openwork sides was built over the tomb.

🎏 Salvatorkirche

Ferdinand-Wagner-Str.

Standing on the site of a synagogue, this former pilgrimage church, is associated with a pogrom in 1477 against the Jews, sparked off by their alleged sacrilege against the Host. On the west side the church is joined to the rock where the Veste Oberhaus stands. Before a tunnel was made between the upper and lower forts in 1762, the church was accessible only by boat. It is now used as a concert hall.

🎏 Veste Oberhaus and Veste Niederhaus

Oberhaus 125. Oberhausmuseum Passau: **Tel** (0851) 49 33 50. **Open** mid-Mar–mid-Nov: 9am–5pm Mon–Fri, 10am–6pm Sat–Sun & public hols. **Closed** mid-Nov–mid-March (open 26 Dec–6 Jan: 10am–4pm). 🎏

Work on the imposing Oberhaus (Upper Castle) began in 1219, initiated by the bishop Ulrich II. It is set on a rocky outcrop known as St Georgsberg, on the bank of the Danube opposite the Old Town. The main castle consists of Gothic buildings and a chapel. The Niederhaus (Lower Castle) is connected to the Oberhaus by a gallery descending from the polygonal tower. Work on the Niederhaus,

on a spit of land between the rivers Danube and Ilz, began in 1250. Both castles, which have been extended and fortified over time, symbolize the power of the church over the town.

The Oberhaus now houses a historical museum. On the route to the Observatoriumsturm (observatory tower) is the Passauer Tölpel (Fool of Passau), a huge head with a mocking expression. This is the remains of a statue of St Stephen of about 1370 that fell from the cathedral during the Great Fire of 1662.

The Niederhaus, whose present apperance dates from about 1444, was the home of the painter Ferdinand von Wagner from 1890 to 1907. He filled the interior with antique furniture and his own paintings. A private residence, it is closed to visitors.

🎏 Altes Rathaus

Rathausplatz. **Tel** (0851) 39 60. **Open** Apr–6 Jan: 10am–4pm daily. 🎏

The Town Hall stands on the site of the former Fish Market alongside the Danube. By the annexation of houses standing between Schrottgasse and Marktgasse, the town hall was constantly enlarged up until the 19th century. The original tower, which was demolished in 1811, was replaced in 1890–91 by a fine Neo-Gothic tower designed by Heinrich

The Altes Rathaus, with Neo-Gothic tower

von Schmidt. It is encircled by a gallery and has a steep sloped roof. Floodmarks on the façade show the high levels reached by the Danube at various times. Entering the building from the side facing Schrottgasse, visitors pass through a late Gothic carved portal of 1510.

The town hall's interior and three courtyards date from the 16th and 17th centuries. The halls, open to the public, contain historical paintings by Ferdinand von Wagner.

🏛 Passauer Glasmuseum

Am Rathausplatz. **Tel** (0851) 35 071. **Open** 10am–7pm daily. 🖾

Housed in the former Wilder Mann hotel, Passau's museum of glass contains over 30,000 pieces of decorative and household glassware from the 18th to the 20th centuries.

The large collection of Bohemian glassware and the glass made in the workshops of the Bavarian Forest are remarkable. There is also an interesting section on Art Nouveau glass.

Captivated by the museum's exhibits, the writer Friedrich Dürrenmatt called it "the most beautiful glass museum in the whole world".

🏛 Paulskirche

Rindermarkt.

The parish church of St Paul was built in 1663–78 on the site of a medieval church that was destroyed by the Great Fire of 1622. The stuccowork in the interior was executed in 1909. The façade's tall, picturesque tower, rising over the Rindermarkt, is a prominent Passau landmark.

🏛 Museum Moderner Kunst

Bräugasse 17. **Tel** (0851) 38 38 790. **Open** 10am–6pm Tue–Sun. **Closed** 24, 25, 31 Dec & Good Friday. 🖾

Located in one of the old town's most beautiful houses, Passau's Museum of Modern Art exhibits art from the 20th and 21st centuries. There are regular international exhibitions of different modern artists.

🏛 Universität

Innpromenade, Innstr., Augustinergasse.

In 1972 the buildings of the former **Augustinian monastery**, founded in about 1070 and turned into barracks in 1803, were converted into a newly founded university. Further buildings were added to the side of the monastery facing the river. These are joined by the **Geisteswissenschaften I** building, constructed in 1976–81 to a design by Werner Fauser. This reinforced concrete structure is rendered in red plaster and combines regional architectural elements with modern spatial concepts.

The **Nikolakloster**, today a seminary, still has its original Romanesque crypt, although the entire building was remodelled in the Gothic style in 1348 and again in the Baroque style in 1716–17. The church furniture was moved to the parish church in Vilshofen in 1803.

🏛 Wallfahrtskirche Mariahilf

Mariahilfberg 3.

This pilgrimage church, set on the hill known as Mariahilfsberg, dominates the River Inn and Passau's Innstadt district. It commands a fine view of the city and the Dreiflüsseeck – the confluence of the three rivers.

The Capuchin church and monastery, completed in about 1630, are reached by a covered flight of 321 steps. The object of pilgrimage is a copy of a painting of the Madonna and Child by Lucas Cranach the Elder which has been venerated since 1622 (see p192). The original painting was acquired from a gallery in Dresden by Leopold, Bishop of Passau in 1611. In 1650 the painting was moved to the Jacobskirche in Innsbruck, where it remains to this day.

The strikingly austere interior of Wallfahrtskirche Mariahilf features a silver eternal lamp made by Lucas Lang and presented by the Emperor Leopold I in 1676 on the occasion of his marriage in Passau.

🏛 Römermuseum Kastell Boiotro

Lederergasse 43. **Tel** (0851) 34 769. **Open** 10am–4pm Tue–Sun. **Closed** mid-Nov–mid-Apr. 🖾

This Roman fort was built in about AD 280. From then until about 400 it was used by Roman soldiers, and in about 460 St Severinus built his cell in the ruins. Excavated in 1974, the ruins together with the finds unearthed here are open to visitors.

Picturesque houses on the banks of the Danube

Art Nouveau vase in the Glasmuseum

The imposing buildings of the Wallfahrtskirche Mariahilf

⑬ Ortenburg

Road map F3. 🗻 7,000. 🚌
🚆 Vilshofen or Passau. 🚇 Marktplatz
11, (08542) 16 421. 🌐 **ortenburg.de**

This Renaissance **palace**,
which is set on a ridge, was
built in about 1567 on the
site of a medieval castle
belonging to the Bavarian
von Krailburg-Ortenburg
family. Joachim, one of the
family members, brought
the Reformation to the town
in 1563, and ever since then
Ortenburg has been a
Protestant enclave within
Catholic, Counter-Reformation
Lower Bavaria.

The palace is today in private
ownership, but it contains a
museum that is open to the
public. Visitors can also see
such features as a fine late
Renaissance panelled ceiling
dating from around 1600 in
the castle chapel, the remnants
of *trompe-l'oeil* frescoes on
the wall of the Knights' Hall
and a torture chamber. The
well outside the palace, which
descends to a depth of 55 m
(180 ft), supplied the townspeople with water up
until 1927.

The presbytery of the
late Gothic **church**, which
has been a Protestant
church since 1563, contains
the splendid tombs of the
owners of Ortenburg in
the 16th and 17th centuries.

🏛 **Schlossmuseum Ortenburg**
Tel (08542) 12 00. **Open** Apr–Oct:
10am–5pm Tue–Sun.

The chapel in Sammarei's church,
bedecked with votive images

⑭ Sammarei

Road map F3. 🗻 300. 🚌
🚆 Vilshofen or Passau.
🛈 Ortenburg, Marktplatz 11,
(08542) 16 421. 🌐 **sammarei.de**

Sammarei has one of the
most remarkable pilgrimage
churches in the whole of
southern Germany.

An old wooden **chapel**
miraculously survived the
fire that destroyed the neighbouring house of Cistercian
monks from Aldersbach. The
chapel was subsequently
enclosed within the late Renaissance church of **Mariä
Himmelfahrt**, occupying part
of the presbytery. The construction of this stone-built
church was supervised by
Isaak Bader the Elder, a court
architect from Munich, and
work began in 1629. While
the church was completed in
1631, the interior decoration
was not finished until 1650.

The ambulatory that was
created between the walls of
the chapel and the presbytery
of the church are completely
covered with Baroque votive
images, as are the walls of the
chapel itself.

The chapel is separated
from the nave by a fine high
altar of 1645, which acts as a
kind of iconostasis.

The chapel's late Rococo
altar contains the miraculous
image that is venerated by
pilgrims to the church. It is a
copy of the original *Madonna
and Child* ascribed to Hans
Holbein the Elder in the church
of Jakobs- und Tiburtiuskirche
in Straubing.

Baroque façade of the Mariä Himmelfahrt
church, Aldersbach

⑮ Aldersbach

Road map F3. 🗻 4,300. 🚌
🚆 Vilshofen. 🛈 Klosterplatz 1,
(08543) 96 100. 🌐 **aldersbach.de**

Work on the **Cistercian
monastery** in the town began
at the end of the 17th century.
It was remodelled by Dominikus
Magzin in the first half of the
18th century, when it became
the church of **Mariä
Himmelfahrt**.

The interior, which is lit by
large windows, is decorated
with exquisite paintings and
stuccowork executed by Egid
and Cosmas Damian Asam in
1718–20, the first time that the
brothers had collaborated on
a project *(see p72)*. Among the
most outstanding features
are the choir borne by angels
in wide flowing garments, and
the *trompe-l'oeil* paintings on
the ceiling over the nave.

The high altar, dating from
1723, is Matthias Götz' masterpiece. The pulpit, of 1748,
and the stalls, of 1762, are by
Joseph Deutschmann.

Courtyard of the Renaissance palace in Ortenburg

⑯ Vilshofen

Road map F3. ⚏ 16,500. 🚌
ℹ️ Stadtplatz 27, (08541) 20 81 12.
🅆 **vilshofen.de**

Founded in 1206 where the Vils, Wolfach and Pfudrach meet the Danube, Vilshofen centres around Stadtplatz. This long street is lined with colourful houses that were built after the great fire that destroyed the town in 1794.

The parish church of **St Johannes der Täufer**, built in the late 14th century, with two naves, was rebuilt in 1803–04. Its fine Baroque decoration was executed in the 18th century, and was originally intended for the Nikolakirche in Passau. The decoration was later transferred to this church.

Another notable feature of the town is the late Gothic **Barbarakirche**, built in the second half of the 15th century, and the **Mariähilfskirche**, a former pilgrimage church built in 1611 by Antonio Riva. The Mariähilfskirche is decorated with stuccowork and frescoes executed by northern Italian artists, among whom was Giovanni Petro Camuzzi.

The **gate tower** was built in 1643–7. It was designed by Bartholomäus Viscardi in the Mannerist style and has greyish-white tones and an onion dome. It has come to symbolize the town.

The high altar at the Asambasilika in Osterhofen

The most prominent building in Vilshofen is the **Benedictine abbey** of Schweiklberg, designed by Michael Kurz and built in 1909–11. The church has two Art Nouveau steeples.

The gate tower at the end of the Straßenmarkt in Vilshofen

⑰ Osterhofen

Road map F2. ⚏ 11,600. 🚌
🚌 Altenmarkt. ℹ️ Stadtplatz 13, (09932) 40 30. 🅆 **osterhofen.de**

This small Bavarian town, whose history goes back almost six centuries, boasts a jewel of Baroque archi-tecture, the **Asambasilika**.

The church was built in 1726 on the site of a medieval Premonstratensian church. Its appearance is the result of a collaboration between the architect Michael Fischer and the Asam brothers. While its exterior is somewhat austere, with the façade merging with a wing of the monastery, the decorative scheme of the interior is phenomenal.

The unusual shape of the single-nave interior is created by its oval side chapels and serpentine walls. The architec-ture, painting and stuccowork, fused into a single entity, are highly distinctive, both as an ensemble and as individual elements.

While the extensive ceiling frescoes by Cosmas Damian Asam create an illusion of extensive space, Egid Quirin Asam's stuccowork blurs the boundaries between reality and illusion. Absorbing the exquisite artistry and admiring the artists' skill can take some time (*see p72*).

The Asambasilika made a profound impression on Pope John Paul II, who visited Osterhofen during his pilgrimage to Germany in 1980.

The Bavarian Forest

The area between the Danube, Regen and Chamb and the Czech border is covered by one of the largest woodlands in Europe. Once Bavaria's most destitute region, it now draws tourists with its stunning scenery and low prices. The region is renowned for its locally made glass and crystal, its hiking trails and skiing areas. The heart of the Bavarian Forest is the densely wooded National Park Reserve.

A historic Alpine house in the open-air museum at Finsterau

Exploring Upper Bavaria (East)

The town of Rosenheim on the River Inn could be regarded as the capital of this region. Although not well endowed with historic features, it is well worth a visit in late summer, when the local folk (beer) festival takes place. While it vies with Munich's Oktoberfest, it has a much more authentic, local atmosphere. There are historic towns on the river Inn, Wasserburg and Rott, the latter containing the grave of the Christian Democrat leader Franz Josef Strauß. The towns in the Salzach and Traun valleys are also worth exploring. The towns of Tittmoning and Laufen, with their captivating southern atmosphere, are very underrated.

Castle courtyard in Burghausen

Sights at a Glance

1. Altötting
2. Burghausen
3. Tittmoning
4. Laufen
5. Anger
6. Bad Reichenhall
7. Maria Gern
8. Berchtesgaden
9. Königssee
10. Ramsau
11. Ruhpolding
12. Reit im Winkl
13. Aschau
14. Herrenchiemsee
16. Stein an der Traun
17. Kloster Seeon
18. Amerang
19. Wasserburg am Inn
20. Rott am Inn
21. Bad Aibling
22. Neubeuern

Excursion

15. Around Chiemsee

Key

═══ Motorway

═══ Main road

····· Minor road

─── Scenic route

─•─ Main railway

─── Minor railway

▬▬▬ International border

△ Summit

0 kilometres   10

0 miles   10

Lüftlmalerei, Bavarian *trompe-l'oeil* decoration, on a house in Neubeuren

Getting Around

Only one motorway, the A8, crosses eastern Bavaria. From Munich, it runs on to Salzburg and Linz in Austria, linking up near Neubeuren with a section of the A38 to Innsbruck. However, there is no problem getting around in the region, as it has a good network of major and minor roads. All the larger towns and the most frequently visited areas, such as the Berchtesgadener Land and Chiemsee, are easily reached by train.

The Martersäulewin Bernau

Burghausen Castle, the longest castle in Europe

❶ Altötting

Road map F4. 🚞 12,500. 🚌
ℹ️ Kapellplatz 2a, (08671) 50 62
19/38. 🌐 **altoetting.de**

This town, established in the 8th century, is one of the earliest Christian sites in Europe. It is also the earliest place of pilgrimage in Bavaria, and is called the Heart of Bavaria by some. Every year about half a million pilgrims come here to pay their respects to the Black Madonna. This early 13th-century statue is kept in the **Heilige Kapelle** (Holy Chapel) which stands in the centre of a large square. The chapel, with a Carolingian apse and a Gothic nave, is surrounded by an ambulatory whose walls are covered with votive images. Pilgrims holding crosses inch up to it on their knees. Pope John Paul II paid a visit to the shrine during his pilgrimage to Germany in 1980.

The treasury of the late Gothic **Stiftskirche** contains valuable votive offerings from the Holy Chapel. The most highly prized of these is the

Goldenes Rössl (Golden Steed) of 1404, a masterpiece of French goldwork. The crypt contains the mortal remains of Johann Tilly, the renowned military leader in the Thirty Years' War.

Another feature of interest is the **Panorama** re-creating the view from the hill of Golgotha in Jerusalem. It is located in a building dating from 1902–03, and was made by Gebhard Fugel and Joseph Krieger.

🏛 Panorama

Gebhard–Fugel–Weg
10. **Tel** (08671) 69 34.
Open Mar–Oct: 10am–
5pm daily; Nov–Feb:
11am– 2pm Sat & Sun.

Environs

Two km (1.5 miles) north, on the River Inn, is **Neuötting**. Notable buildings here include the Gothic Nikolauskirche, designed by Hans von Burghausen, and the late Gothic Annakirche completed in 1515.

❷ Burghausen

Road map F4. 🚞 18,000. 🚌 ℹ️
Stadtplatz 112, (08677) 887 140/141.
🌐 **burghausen.de** 🎷 Jazz Festival
(May); Historisches Burgfest (Jul).

Situated on the River Salzach, which forms the border with Austria, Burghausen is famous for having the longest **castle** in Europe. With its six court-yards, the castle stretches some 1,051 m (3,448 ft) along a ridge between the river and Wöhrsee. The castle was built in 1025 and rebuilt in 1490. The main castle (Hauptburg) contains several **museums**, including a local history and a photographic museum. In the rooms that are open to the public, German paintings and furniture are on display.

Angel in Burghausen's
Schutzengelkirche

The Old Town, between the castle and the river, has an old-world atmosphere. The market square is surrounded by what are Burghausen's finest buildings: the Gothic **Jakobskirche**, with a Baroque tower, the **town hall**, the mid-16th-century **old Bavarian government building**, with a Renaissance courtyard, the **Schutzengelkirche** of 1731–46, and many historic houses.

On the north side of the square is the Jesuit **Josefskirche** of about 1629 and the **Marienbrunnen**, a mid-17th-century fountain.

Arcade on the the market square in Neuötting

For hotels and restaurants in this region see p268 and pp280–81

❸ Tittmoning

Road map F4. 🚉 6,000. 🚌
🚉 Laufen, Burghausen. **ℹ** Stadtplatz
1, (08683) 70 07 10. **W** tittmoning.eu

The entrance to this little town
on the River Salzach is through
a gate in the town walls. The
market square is lined with
colourful houses with bay
windows and wood carvings.
Among them is the tall **town
hall**, its tower and façade dating
from 1711–12. The hill above
the town, the summit crowned
by a 13th-century **castle**, gives
a fine view of the surrounding
countryside and the Alps. The
Maria Ponlach pilgrimage
chapel of 1617 is reached by
a road round the castle that
follows a ravine overlooking
the River Ponlach.

Iron bridge at Laufen, crossing over the
border with Austria

❹ Laufen

Road map F4. 🚉 6,000. 🚉
ℹ Tathausplatz 1, (08682) 89 87 49.
W stadtlaufen.de

Set on a bend in the
RiverSalzach, this town has a
southern, almost Italian feel.
It was originally a Roman
settlement, and flourished
during the Middle Ages. Entry
into the town is through two
medieval **gates**. The streets
are lined with arcaded houses
with oriels and concave roofs
typical of the region.

The 14th-century **parish
church** is the oldest single-
nave Gothic church in
southern Germany. With

Column of St Mary in Anger's main square

its huge roof and late
12th-century Romanesque
tower, it dominates the town.

North of the church is the
Dechantshof, the old archbishop's castle, which contains
plaques from the church. Its
staircase is decorated with the
portraits of bishops. The four-
winged **castle,** with an inner
courtyard, was built in 1606–08
by Vincenzo Scamozzi.

❺ Anger

Road map F5. 🚉 4,300. 🚌 🚉
ℹ Dorfplatz 4, (08656) 98 89 22.
W anger.de

Ludwig I deemed Anger the
prettiest village in Bavaria. Much
of its charm has been eroded by
the arrival of a motorway and
commercial development,
but it still has a delightfully
situated late Gothic **church**.
The large square, which is lined
with interesting houses, has a
column with the statue of
St Mary in the centre.

Environs

Two km (1.5 miles) to the north
is **Höglwörth,** a tiny former
Augustine abbey built in the
12th century on an island in a
lake covered with water lilies.

❻ Bad Reichenhall

Road map F5. 🚉 17,100. 🚉
ℹ Wittelsbacherstr. 15, (08651) 60 60.
W bad-reichenhall.com

The town has been known
for its salt since Celtic and
Roman times, and in the
mid-19th century it became
an important spa. Noteworthy
buildings include the **St Zeno**

a former Augustinian
monastery dating from the
first half of the 12th century.
Although it was remodelled
after the Gothic period, it
retains its original Romanesque
portal, which features two
lions supporting the columns.

Gradierwerk, the inhalation
house in the Kurpark built in
1909–10, gives an idea of how
salt used to be produced by
evaporation. In the **Alte Saline**,
the old saltworks, which date
from 1836–51, Ludwig I
ordered a salt **museum** to be
built. The exhibits include old
salt-making equipment. The
saltworks' marble enclosures
date from 1524–36 and,
together with an underground
passage, were designed by
the sculptor Erasmus Grasser.

🏛 Alte Saline mit Salzmuseum

An der Salinenstr. **Tel** (08651) 70 02
146. **Open** May–Oct: 10am–11:30am
and 2–4pm daily; Nov–Apr: 2–4pm
Tue–Fri and the first Sunday in
the month.

The Gradierwerk in Bad Reichenhall's
spa park

Maria Gern church seen against snowy Alpine peaks

❼ Maria Gern

Road map F5. 🚌 🚃 Berchtesgaden.
ℹ Berchtesgaden, Königseer Str. 2,
(08652) 96 70.

This pilgrimage church is in a serene and picturesque setting among woodland pastures. Built in 1708–10, its pink pilasters on the exterior make a pleasing contrast with the white walls and the steep polygonal roofs harmonize with the Baroque onion dome of the tower.

The interior is decorated with stuccowork by Joseph Schmidt. The walls of the presbytery are hung with votive images spanning the 12th to the 20th centuries, and the altar has a beautiful wooden carving of the Madonna by Wolfgang Huber before which the faithful pray for forgiveness.

The **Ölbergkapelle** below the church dates from 1710.

❽ Berchtesgaden

Road map F5. 🏔 7,700. 🚌 🚃
ℹ Maximilianstraße 9, (08652) 94 45
300. 🌐 berchtesgadener-land.com

The area known as Berchtesgadener Land enjoys an excellent climate. The town is set in beautiful Alpine scenery on the River Ache at the foot of the Watzmann, which at 2,713 m (8,900 ft) is Germany's second highest peak.

The town is an ideal base for hikes throughout the region but with its old-world charm it also has plenty to offer. Here are houses with walls decorated with *Lüftlmalerei* (*see p217*). One of them, the **Gasthof zum Hirschen**, an inn dating from about 1600, has paintings depicting monkeys parodying human vices. Another interesting building is the Gothic **Franziskanerkirche**, while a major attraction is the nearby saltworks – the **Salzbergwerk und Salzmuseum**. A little way from the town is the **Kehlsteinhaus**, also known as Hitler's Eagle's Nest (*see p205*). An interesting excursion follows the scenic **Roßfeld-Panoramastraße**, which winds its way along hairpin bends to a height of 1600 m (5,249 ft).

The **Königliches Schloss**, formerly an Augustinian monastery and now owned by the Wittelsbach family, contains a museum with an interesting collection of furniture, paintings and Gothic woodcarving. The adjoining **church** was remodelled in the Gothic style, although it retains its original Romanesque portal. The façade with its rose window and two towers were added in 1864–8. The Romanesque cloisters, unusual in southern Germany, date from the 12th century.

🏛 Salzbergwerk und Salzmuseum
Bergwerkstr. 83. **Tel** (08652) 60 020.
Open May–Oct: 9am–5pm daily;
Nov–Apr: 11am–3pm daily.

🏛 Königliches Schloss
Schlossplatz 2. **Tel** (08652) 94 79 80.
Open 16 May–15 Oct: 10am–noon &
2– 4pm Sun–Fri; 16 Oct–15 May:
11am–2pm Mon–Fri. 🎟 11am & 2pm.

A jetty on Königssee

❾ Königssee

Road map F5. ℹ Berchtesgaden,
Maximilianstr. 9, (08652) 94 45 300.
🌐 nationalpark-berchtesgaden.de

With its crystal-clear water and fjord-like setting between mountain ridges, Königssee is Bavaria's loveliest lake. The area also forms part of a national park.

The electric-powered boats that are used on the 8-km (5-mile) lake take visitors to the pilgrimage church of **St Bartholomä**, built in about 1700 and set on a peninsula below the eastern escarpment of the Watzmann. Nearby is a well-frequented inn. The boat trip offers views of awesome rock formations, enchanting little spots, waterfalls and echoing cliffs that throw back the sound of the boat's horn. The trip goes all the way to the northern end of Königssee, from where **Obersee** can be reached on foot.

The town of Berchtesgaden, nestling in an Alpine valley

The main street in Reit im Winkl, a popular tourist resort

❿ Ramsau

Road map F5. 🚠 1,900. 🚌
🚉 Berchtesgaden. 🛈 Im Tal 2,
(08657) 98 89 20. 🇼 ramsau.de

This resort town, nestling amid wooded mountain slopes, has one of the most photographed churches in the world – the **Pfarrkirche St Sebastian**, dating from 1512. Its picturesque cemetery, which was laid out in 1658, contains tombstones spanning the 17th to the 20th centuries. The church is situated above a stream, and stands out wonderfully against the magnificent backdrop of the Reiteralpe.

⓫ Ruhpolding

Road map E5. 🚠 6,400. 🚌 🚉
🛈 Hauptstr. 60, (08663) 88 060.
🇼 ruhpolding.de

Ruhpolding attracts a high volume of tourists. It is overlooked by **Georgskirche**, built in 1738–54 with highly decorated altars and a pulpit dating from the same period. The right-hand altar features a small Romanesque figure of the Virgin Enthroned, with large almond-shaped eyes, dating from about 1200. Above the church is the old **cemetery**, which has a Baroque chapel and tombstones dating from the 18th and 19th centuries.

The old Renaissance **hunting lodge** houses the **Heimatmuseum**, which has a collection of furniture, glass and jewellery spanning the 17th to the 19th centuries. Also on display in the

museum is a collection of fossils and interesting minerals that were found in the surrounding mountains. Among the displays at the **Museum für Bäuerliche und Sakrale Kunst** (Museum of Folk and Religious Art) is a fine collection of church ornaments, as well as royal jewels and crowns.

🏛 **Heimatmuseum**
Schlossstr. 2. **Tel** (08663) 41 230. **Open** 10am–noon Tue–Fri. **Closed** Nov–Dec.

🏛 **Museum für Bäuerliche und Sakrale Kunst**
Roman-Friesinger-Str. 1. **Tel** (08663) 5078. **Open** 9:30am–noon & 2–4pm Tue–Sat, 9:30am–noon Sun. **Closed** 25 Oct–25 Dec.

⓬ Reit im Winkl

Road map E5. 🚠 2,400. 🚌
🚉 Marquartstein. 🛈 Dorfstraße 38, (08640) 80 027. 🇼 reitimwinkl.de

This small town, at an altitude of almost 700 m (2296 ft), may not have any buildings of historic interest, but it is still a very popular tourist resort. Picturesquely set in the middle of the forest, with its colourful storybook houses and narrow streets, it is easy to see why the place is so appealing. Many people come here, especially in winter, as the area has the best snow cover in the Bavarian Alps. The town is also filled with visitors in summer, especially hikers using it as a base for day trips into the surrounding area or even into the whole Berchtesgadener Land. The road to Ruhpolding, about 24 km (15 miles) in length, is exceptionally scenic. Forming part of the Alpine Route, it winds among lakes which, when seen from above, resemble a necklace of green beads strung on either side of the road that traverses spectacularly beautiful mountain scenery.

The Madonna of Ruhpolding

Kehlsteinhaus – "The Eagle's Nest"

Set on the summit of Kehlstein, this stone building resembling a mountain shelter is known as the Adlerhorst (Eagle's Nest). It was given to Hitler by Martin Bormann on behalf of the Nazi Party in 1939 and became the Führer's favourite residence. The building was attached to the summer residence built in 1933 and is situated on the slopes of Obersalzberg. The approach to Kehlsteinhaus is a masterpiece of engineering. First, a road with stunning views passes through five tunnels, after which there is an elevator whose shaft is cut into the rock. The last stage of the trip is a ride up in a high-speed elevator, which is taken by the thousands of tourists who come here.

Hitler's famous "Eagle's Nest"

Road leading towards the Alps near Aschau

⑬ Aschau

Road map E5. 🚠 5,500. 🚌 🚉
ℹ️ Kampenwandstr. 38. **Tel** (08052)
90 490. **W** aschau.de

In the centre of this small
town, set against fine
mountain backdrops, stands
a twin-towered **church**.
Originally built in the Gothic
style, it was rebuilt in the
Baroque period and in the
early 18th century was
decorated with stuccowork
and paintings of scenes
of the life of St Mary. Beside
the church is the small
Kreuzkapelle, built in the
mid-18th century, while
opposite, at Kirchplatz 1, is
an old **inn**, built in 1680 and
today named the Post Hotel.

Environs
From Aschau a road leads
south towards **Schloss
Hohenaschau**, which, set
on a height, is visible from
a distance. This mighty
12th-century fortress was
decorated in the Baroque style
in the 17th century,
although its medieval
walls still survive. The
reception hall on the
second floor was
decorated in 1682–4
with Baroque mouldings.
The grounds are also
worth exploring;
the castle is home to
a falconry and there
are regular birds of
prey demonstrations.

🏰 **Schloss Hohenaschau**
Tel (08052) 90 490. 🕐 only
guided tours: 1:30 & 3pm Tue,
Thu, Sun & hols; 10 & 11:30am
Wed & Fri (closed Sat). 🅿️

⑭ Herrenchiemsee

Road map E4. 🚉 to Stock. 🚌
W herrenchiemsee.de

Herreninsel, the largest island
in Chiemsee, has been settled
since prehistoric times. Thanks
to Ludwig II, it is among the
region's main tourist attractions.
The king aimed to build a huge
palace set in a vast park filled
with statues, fountains and a
canal along its axis. It was to be
the Versailles of Bavaria.

The **Schloss Herren-
chiemsee**, based on Louis
XIV's great Palace of Versailles,
was built to satisfy Ludwig II's
absolutist leanings. Built in
1878–86, it was to outdo all
previous royal palaces, but
it was never finished.

Ludwig II spent a mere nine
days in it, and at the time of his
death only 20 of the 70 rooms
that were planned for the three
wings were ready. They show
an astonishing lavishness and
splendour. Particularly spectacular
are the Große Spiegelgalerie
(Hall of Mirrors), and the

Fountain at Schloss Herrenchiemsee

Chambre de Parade. The
palace also houses a **museum**
dedicated to Ludwig II
There are also the remains
of a church and an Augustinian
monastery on the island.
These are known collectively
as **Altes Schloss**.

🏛️ **Schloss Herrenchiemsee,
König-Ludwig II-Museum and
Altes Schloss**
Tel (08051) 68870. 🕐 Apr–Oct:
9am–5pm daily; Nov–Mar:
9:40am–3:40pm daily. 🅿️

The medieval castle of Höhlenburg, Stein
an der Traun

⑯ Stein an der Traun

Road map E4. 🚌 🚉
ℹ️ Rathausplatz 3, Traunreut, (08669)
85 70. **W** traunreut.de

One of Upper Bavaria's
most distinctive buildings is
Höhlenburg, a castle set 50 m
(160 ft) above the River Traun.
It forms part of a system of
three castles. Torch in hand,
visitors pass through a series
of caves and tunnels. This is
said to be the home of the
fearful Heinz von Stein, a
legendary giant knight who
abducted girls. Casemates
lead between the medieval
upper castle, the lower
castle and the new castle,
which dates from the 15th
century and was rebuilt in
the Neo-Gothic style
in 1885–9.

🏰 **Höhlenburg**
Tel (08621) 25 01. 🕐 Apr–third Sun in
Oct: 2pm Tue–Sun; mid-Jul–mid-Sep:
2 & 4pm Tue–Sun. 🅿️

⓯ Around Chiemsee

Chiemsee, also known as the Bavarian Sea, covers an area of 80 sq km (30 sq miles) and reaches a depth of 73 m (240 ft). Bavaria's largest lake, it is a favourite place for holiday-makers, and its shores are dotted with towns and holiday villages. The Alpine scenery, the watersports facilities and some fascinating buildings are the main attractions here.

⑥ Seebruck
This little town, whose history goes back to Roman times, is today a watersports centre with a large marina.

⑤ Frauenchiemsee
The Benedictine monastery on this island has a Romanesque church with a distinctive onion dome.

④ Herrenchiemsee
This is a favourite destination for visitors, who come to Ludwig II's grand unfinished palace.

0 kilometres 2
0 miles 2

Lambach
Söll •
Ising •
Gollenshausen
Breitbrunn ③
Kailbach
Rimsting
② ⑤
④ *Chiemsee*
⑦
Hirschau
Prien
Harras
①
E52
Bernau-Felden
Bernau

③ Gstadt
From this town there is a pleasant view of Frauenchiemsee, which can be reached by boat from here. An interesting sight is the church "Peter und Paul", decorated in the Baroque style in about 1720.

① Urschalling
The 12th-century Jakobskirche has some fine mural paintings dating from the 13th and 14th centuries.

② Stock
The Bockerl, a steam railway over 100 years old, provides a link between Stock and Prien. There are also boats to the lake's other islands and towns.

⑦ Chieming
Attractions here are the beach, with a 7-km (4-mile) long promenade and houses with *Lüftlmalerei (see p216)* and lavish floral displays.

Tips for Drivers

Tour length: about 65 km (40 miles)
Stopping-off points: There are many cafés and restaurants in all the small towns round Chiemsee.

Key

▬ Suggested route
═ Other route
-- Ferry route

Kloster Seeon, the Benedictine monastery, set on a promontory on Klostersee

⓱ Kloster Seeon

Road map E4. 🚌 🚊 Bad Endorf or Traunstein. ℹ️ Kultur-und Bildungszentrum des Bezirks Oberbayern, Klosterweg 1, (08624) 89 70. 🆆 kloster-seeon.de

On the edge of Klostersee stands **Kloster Seeon**, a monastery that was taken over by Benedictine monks. The original Romanesque **church** was built in stages in the 11th and 12th centuries. Remodelled by Konrad Pürkhel, it acquired its Gothic appearance in 1425–33. The ceiling was decorated by Salzburg painters in 1579.

    St Barbara's Chapel contains the magnificent tomb of Aribo I dating from about 1400 and ascribed to the Salzburg sculptor Hans Heider.

    South of the church is a cloistered courtyard of 1428–33, which has Gothic tombstones.

⓲ Amerang

Road map E4. 🏠 3,600. 🚌 🚊 ℹ️ Wasserburger Straße 11, (08075) 91 9711. 🆆 amerang.de

The Renaissance **palace** in this small town was built by several Italian architects, prominent among whom were members of the Scaligeri family of Verona. Its large cloistered courtyard is a venue for open-air concerts. There is also a museum.

    At the other end of the town is the **Bauernhausmuseum** (open-air museum) with farm-houses, a bakery, a mill and a forge. The **EFA- Automobil-Museum** (Museum of German Automobile History) has 220 cars dating from 1886 to the present.

🏛 **Schloss Amerang**
Open Easter–mid-Oct. **Tel** (08075) 91 920. 📷 on the hour 11am–4pm (except 1pm) Fri–Sun & public hols.

🏛 **Bauernhausmuseum**
Hopfgarten 2. **Tel** (08075) 91 50 90. **Open** mid-Mar–Oct: 9am–6pm Tue–Sun.

🏛 **EFA-Automobil-Museum**
Wasserburger Str. 38. **Tel** (08075) 81 41. **Open** Apr–Oct: 10–6pm Tue–Sun; Jul & Aug: Mon–Sun.

Amerang's Renaissance palace, designed by the Scaligeri family

⓳ Wasserburg am Inn

Road map E4. 🏠 12,300. 🚌 🚊 ℹ️ Marienplatz 2, (08071) 10 522. 🆆 wasserburg.de

Wasserburg is set on a promontory on a bend in the Inn, and is one of the best-preserved historic towns on the river. The best view of it is from the bridge across the Inn.

    The bridge leads to a picturesque Gothic **gate** which in turn leads into Bruckgasse. At No. 25 in this lane is the **Mauthaus**, the ducal customs office, dating from about 1400, with stepped gables and three Renaissance oriel windows, which were added in 1539.

    The street leads to Marienplatz, which is lined with houses. Among them is the **Kernhaus**, which once belonged to the patrician Kern family. The façade features decorative mouldings by Johann Baptist Zimmermann. Opposite stands the Gothic **town hall**, which occupies two buildings with stepped gables. The **Frauenkirche** was built in 1368 and is attached to the watchtower.

    The large **Jakobskirche** was begun in the early 15th century by Jans von Burghausen. The **castle**, with its covered staircase, can be reached from the church. Remaining parts of the castle include the residential wing, which was converted into a granary during the Renaissance, and a 15th-century chapel. The streets of the town are lined with old houses with typical gateways, courtyards, oriel windows and arcades.

The Gothic façade of Wasserburg's town hall

⑳ Rott am Inn

Road map E4. 🏔 3800. 🚌 🚃
ℹ️ Kaiserhof 3. **Tel** (08039) 90 680.
🌐 **rottinn.de**

The former Benedictine church of **Sts Marinus und Anianus** was rebuilt in 1759–63 to plans by Johann Michael Fischer, preserving the 12th-century Romanesque tower. The church has one of the finest Rococo interiors, decorated by the greatest artists of the time: the stuccoist Jakob Rauch, the fresco-painter Matthäus Günther and the sculptor Ignaz Günther. The church has undergone extensive restoration work and is open to the public.

Franz Josef Strauß, the former leader of Bavaria's ruling conservative party, is buried in the cemetery of the church, which is regularly visited by members of his CSU party.

The town square in Rott am Inn

㉑ Bad Aibling

Road map D4. 🏔 17,300. 🚌 🚃
ℹ️ Wilhelm-Leibl-Platz 3, (08061) 90 800. 🌐 **bad-aibling.de**

Bad Aibling is known for its mud baths, which were in use as far back as Roman times. However, it was only in the mid-19th century that it acquired its present status as a spa town.

There is much of architectural interest here. On a hill stands the church of **Mariä Himmelfahrt**, built in the late Gothic style but later remodelled in the Rococo style by Abraham Millauer to plans by Johann Michael Fischer. **Sebastianskirche** was built on the site of a 16th-century votive chapel after the plague epidemic of 1634, which decimated the local population. After a series of fires that destroyed most of the town only a few houses survived. One is the 17th-century house at Kirchzeile 13 (today the **Hotel Ratskeller**), which has painted exterior walls and three oriel windows. The **Heimatmuseum** is also worth a visit.

🏛 **Heimatmuseum**
Wilhelm-Leibl-Platz.
Tel (08061) 46 14. **Open** 3–5pm Fri, 2–5pm Sun.

Environs

Some 6 km (4 miles) southwest of Bad Aibling is **Berbling**, with an authentic Bavarian village atmosphere. The charming Rococo church, the old houses, the barns, the maypole and the fields that stretch right up to the houses are quintessentially Bavarian. The painter Wilhelm Leibl once stayed here, while he was living in Bad Aibling from 1882 to 1889. The Renaissance **Maxlrain Palace**, with its palace brewery, lies on the other side of Bad Aibling, 4 km (2.5 miles) to the north. It was built in 1580–88 and has a steeply pitched roof and four onion-domed towers. At the neighbouring 18th-century inn, beer from the palace brewery is served.

㉒ Neubeuern

Road map E5. 🏔 4,300. 🚌
🚃 Raubling or Rohrdorf. ℹ️
Marktplatz 4. **Tel** (08035) 21 65.
🌐 **kulturdorf-neubeuern.de**

This small town situated in the valley of the River Inn is held to be one of the prettiest in Bavaria, if not the whole of Germany. It owes its present appearance to Gabriel von Seidl, who rebuilt the town and the medieval castle after two devastating fires in 1883 and 1893. Today it is often used by film-makers. With its **town gates, houses** and **church**, all of which are covered with *trompe-l'oeil* paintings, it possesses everything that a director needs to re-create an old-style Bavarian town.

Above the houses, decked with greenery and colourful window boxes, towers the **castle** with its tall keep, built in the local historical style in 1904–08. On fine days there is a good view of the Alps from the castle terraces.

Oriel window in Neubeuern

Environs

Some 4 km (2.5 miles) to the east is **Samerberg**. From its peak there is a panoramic view of the town of Rosenheim, Simssee and the surrounding area. It is worth taking a round-about route via the delightful village of **Rohrdorf** to reach the summit.

The Renaissance Maxlrain Palace near Bad Aibling

UPPER BAVARIA (SOUTH)

Upper Bavaria's southern region looks as if it belongs in the pages of a tourist brochure. It is a region of mountains, lakes and splendid buildings, with plenty to offer holiday-makers, including many opportunities for sporting activities. It borders the River Inn to the east and the Lech to the west. To the south it adjoins the Alps.

The Werdenfelser Land, the southernmost region of the Bavarian Alps, stretches from Murnau to Garmisch-Partenkirchen. Its name comes from that of the now ruined Werden castle, which once defended the surrounding area. The backdrop of this fine sub-Alpine landscape is made up of the imposing Karwendel, Wetterstein and Ammergauer mountain ranges.

The small towns and villages of the region are the essence of Bavaria. The houses are covered with *Lüftlmalerei (see p216),* and have wooden balconies that overflow with geraniums and other flowers.

From the high Alpine pastures you can sometimes hear the *Almschroa* and in the evenings you can join a yodelling concert. The traditional costume of the local Bavarians is widely worn *(see p33),* and not just for show but as everyday wear.

Between the rivers Ammer and Lech, from Wessobrunn to near Steingaden, is the Pfaffenwinkel, or Clerics' Corner, which was named in jest in the 18th century due to the amount of abbeys, churches and chapels here. The finest church is Wieskirche, known as the Lord God's Ballroom.

The largest town in the region is Landsberg, whose historic buildings and inviting small streets, alleys and squares make it an interesting place to explore. The most famous town in the region is Garmisch-Partenkirchen, where the 1936 Winter Olympics and the 2011 Alpine World Ski Championships took place.

Traditional festivals and holidays are celebrated enthusiastically in the towns and villages. The best are the painted carts parade and the St Leonard's Day horseback pilgrimage to Mount Calvary in Bad Tölz.

Satellite receivers outside a historic church in Raisting

◀ Spectacular view of Lake Lautersee, Mittenwald

Exploring Upper Bavaria (South)

This region is Munich's natural recreation ground. The journey south to Garmisch-Partenkirchen, the area's largest winter sports and hiking centre, takes less than an hour and a fast suburban train connects the Bavarian capital with the Starnbergersee and Ammersee. These lakes, together with the Wesslinger See, Wörthsee and Pilsensee, make up the Fünfseenland (Land of Five Lakes) and are also known as Munich's Baths. Rafting expeditions down the Isar start at Wolfratshausen.

Sights at a Glance

1 Landsberg am Lech pp214–15
2 Dießen
3 Andechs
4 Wessobrunn
6 Hohenpeißenberg
7 Schongau
8 Steingaden
9 Wieskirche
10 Murnau
11 Oberammergau
12 Ettal
13 Linderhof
14 Garmisch-Partenkirchen
15 Eibsee
16 Mittenwald
17 Wallgau
18 Walchensee
19 Kochel am See
20 Freilichtmuseum Glentleiten
21 Benediktbeuern
22 Bad Tölz
23 Tegernsee
25 Schliersee
26 Ebersberg

Excursions

5 Around Starnbergersee
24 Alpenstraße

The ornate interior of the Welfenmünster church in Steingaden

Key

▬ Motorway
▬ Main road
▭ Minor road
▬ Scenic route
— Main railway
— Minor railway
▬ International border
△ Summit

Augsburg

Weil · Geltendorf · Türkenfeld

Kaufering

17 · LANDSBERG AM LECH · Windach · Inn

Memmingen · Utting · Seefe

Lengenfeld · Herrsching · Ammersee

ANDECHS

DIESSEN 2

Rott

WESSOBRUNN 4 · Wielenbach

We

HOHENPEISSENBERG 6

SCHONGAU 7 · Peiting · Peissenber

Ammer · Hu

Rottenbuch

23

Schöffau

Staffelsee

8 STEINGADEN · MURNAU

9 WIESKIRCHE

OBERAMMERGAU 11 · Oh

LINDERHOF 13 · ETTAL 12

Ammergebirge · Farchant · Ober

14 GARMISCH-PARTENKIRC

15 EIBSEE

Zugspitze 2963m

Sculpture in the gardens of Ludwig II's palace at Linderhof

Getting Around

The southern region of Upper Bavaria is easily reached. The A8, A95 and A96 motorways from Munich lead to the region. The larger towns all have rail links, and those nearer Munich can be reached on the S-Bahn railway. The smaller towns, particularly those in the foothills of the Alps, are all served by convenient bus routes.

0 kilometres 5
0 miles 5

The sandy promenade at Dießen, on Ammersee

❶ Landsberg am Lech

Landsberg, which rises in terraces up the steep banks of the River Lech, is well worth more than a brief visit. Enclosed by walls set with towers and pierced by gateways, it largely retains its medieval character. The steep narrow streets, the hidden alleys, the market square and the steep-roofed houses create a special atmosphere. Landsberg was also the place where Adolf Hitler was jailed after his abortive putsch, during which time he wrote *Mein Kampf*.

Gothic bas-relief on the church of Mariä Himmelfahrt

The lavishly decorated stuccowork façade of the Historisches Rathaus

Exploring Landsberg

With its many streets, alleyways and squares boasting fine architecture and historic houses, Landsberg is a lovely place to explore on foot. There are delightful little corners, such as the Hexenviertel, Seelberg and Blattergasse. The Hintere Salzgasse is a particularly striking alley with rows of mid-18th-century single-storey cottages with large, steeply pitched roofs.

🏛 Historisches Rathaus

Hauptplatz 152. **Tel** (08191) 12 82 68. **Open** 8am–noon & 2–5pm Mon–Thu, 8am–12:30pm Fri

The Historisches Rathaus, or town hall, stands on the west side of the square. The façade and rooms on the second floor have fine mouldings executed by Dominikus Zimmermann in 1718–20. Outside the Rathaus is the Marienbrunnen, a fountain with a statue of the Madonna, dating from 1783.

🏛 Lechwehr

This weir was built in the 14th century at the point where the Mühlbach stream branches off from the River Lech. Over the centuries, the weir has been repeatedly washed away by floods and rebuilt. The cascades are scenically set against the backdrop of the Old Town.

⛪ Klosterkirche der Dominikanerinnen Hl. Dreifaltigkeit

Peter Dörfler Str. 🖼

The church, with its uniform Rococo decoration, was built in 1764–6. It stands in the same street as the Dominican convent, whose façade was painted with murals in about 1765. This entire group of buildings was the last work that Dominikus Zimmermann executed before his death.

The Bayertor, one of the finest town gates in Bavaria

🏛 Bayertor and Town Walls

Open May–Oct: 10am–noon, 2–5pm daily.

One of the best-known gateways in Bavaria is Landsberg's colourful Bayertor. Built in 1425, it has a 36-m (118-ft) high crenellated tower whose interior contains a stone sculpture of the Crucifixion and armorial cartouches.

The other surviving gates are the Mannerist Sandauertor, dating from 1625–30, the Bäckertor of about 1430, and the Färbertor, built in the later 15th century. The Sandauertor is crowned by the tall, circular Luginsland tower, which functioned as a watchtower during the Middle Ages.

Except for those on the west side, the medieval town walls have been preserved almost in their entirety. The earliest parts, built in the 13th century, can be seen on Vordere Mühlgasse and Hintere Salzgasse. The Schmalzturm, or Schöner Turm, dates from the 13th century. The most recent section of the walls was built in the early 15th century.

⛪ Heilig-Kreuz-Kirche and Neues Stadtmuseum

Von-Helfenstein-Gasse 426. Neues Stadtmuseum: **Tel** (08191) 12 83 60. **Open** 2pm–5pm Tue–Fri, 10am–5pm Sat, Sun & public holidays. 🖼

The Heilig-Kreuz-Kirche was built in 1752–4 to a plan by Ignaz Merani, replacing the previous building of 1580. It was the first Jesuit church in southern Germany. Set high up on a slope overlooking the town, it has a flat façade flanked by belfries with Baroque roofs. The ceiling is decorated with two *trompe-l'oeil* paintings by Thomas Scheffler, a pupil of the Asam brothers. The paintings create the striking illusion of the Holy Cross falling from above. Monastery buildings stand beside the church. Prominent among them are the former Jesuit college's Renaissance cloisters, dating from 1576–1609.

Opposite the church, a little further down the hill, is the former Jesuit college, built in 1688–92 in a refined but pleasingly simple style. Since 1989 the building has housed the local history museum.

The Neues Stadtmuseum and, in the background, Heilig-Kreuz-Kirche

🏠 Mariä Himmelfahrt

Georg-Hellmar-Platz.

The church, built in 1458–88 and retaining its Romanesque tower, was given its present Baroque appearance in about 1700. The windows of the presbytery have late Gothic stained glass, although this is unfortunately obscured by the high altar.

Also in the presbytery, in the Altar of the Rosary made by Dominikus Zimmermann in 1721, is a Gothic figure of the Madonna and Child, an outstanding work executed by Hans Multscher of Ulm in about 1440.

🏠 Johanniskirche

Vorderer Anger.

Built by Dominikus Zimmermann in 1750–52, this church has an oval plan, four semi-circular external corner niches and a separate circular presbytery. Zimmermann, working with Johann Luidl, was also responsible for the decoration of the interior, which features a magnificent high altar.

VISITORS' CHECKLIST

Practical Information
Road map C4. 🔼 28,000.
ℹ️ Hauptplatz 152, (08191)
12 82 46. 🔲 landsberg.de
email: info @landsberg.de
🎭 Ruethenfest (Jul, every four years, the next will be in 2015).

Transport
🚉 Bahnhof-Platz.
🚌 Bahnhof-Platz.

🏛 Mutterturm

Von–Kühlmann-Str. 2. Herkomer Museum: **Tel** (08191) 12 83 60.
Open 2–5pm Tue–Sun.

The Mother Tower, built in 1884–7 on the side of the river opposite the town, was the summer residence and studio of Hubert von Herkomer, the painter and dramatist, who died in 1914. Dedicated to his mother (hence the name), the house was built in the style of a Norman castle keep and stands 30 m (98 ft) high.

The museum in the tower contains objects from the artist's studio as well as a selection of his drawings, etchings and paintings.

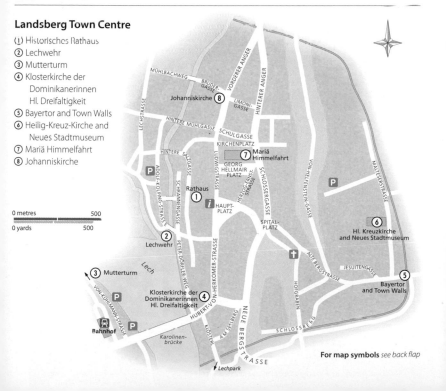

Landsberg Town Centre

1. Historisches Rathaus
2. Lechwehr
3. Mutterturm
4. Klosterkirche der Dominikanerinnen Hl. Dreifaltigkeit
5. Bayertor and Town Walls
6. Heilig-Kreuz-Kirche and Neues Stadtmuseum
7. Mariä Himmelfahrt
8. Johanniskirche

0 metres 500
0 yards 500

For map symbols *see back flap*

Yacht jetty at Dießen on Ammersee

❷ Dießen

Road map C4. 🚹 10,200. 🚌 🚊
🛈 Bahnhofstr. 12, (08807) 10 48.
w tourist-info-diessen.de

This small fishing town is located on Ammersee, Bavaria's third-largest lake. The area is very popular with people from nearby Munich. Although large numbers of tourists come here, their presence is not especially noticeable. It is pleasant to walk along the lakeside promenade, and especially to visit one of the homely restaurants and to sample Ammersee's speciality, the salmon-like *Renken*.

A few old houses survive here, including the oldest wooden **peasant cottage** in Upper Bavaria, dating from 1491. The most exquisite historic building is the early Rococo **Marienmünster**, a church built for the Augustinian monastery in 1732–9 to a design by Johann Michael Fischer. The fine ceiling paintings, executed by Johann Georg Bergmüller in 1736, depict the saints and blessed members of the von Andechs family. The side altars feature depictions of St Sebastian by the Venetian painter Giovanni Battista Tiepolo and of St Stefan by Battista Pittoni.

❸ Andechs

Road map C4. 🚹 3,386. 🚌 🚊
Herrsching. 🛈 Andechser Str. 16, (08152) 93 250. **w gemeinde-andechs.de**

Andechs is home to one of the oldest **churches** in Germany. The main part of the building dates from 1420. The church was remod-elled in the Baroque style in 1669–1751. The stucco-work and painting are the work of Johann Baptist Zimmermann. The church attracts some 200,000 pilgrims every year. Because of its situation almost 180 m (590 ft) above the level of Ammersee, together with the Rococo decoration of its late Gothic church, the Benedictine monastery draws large numbers of visitors.

Another reason for the monastery's popularity with visitors is the strong beer that is brewed here. It is served at the monastery's inn and on the terrace, from which there is a breathtaking view over the lake.

The Rococo interior of the church in Wessobrunn

❹ Wessobrunn

Road map C4. 🚹 2,200. 🚌 🚊
Weilheim. 🛈 Zöpfstr. 1, (08809) 31 300.

The exterior of the former Benedictine abbey here conceals a fine courtyard, lavish stuccowork in the **monastery** and Rococo decoration in the **church**, which was built in 1757–9. Of the original Romanesque buildings, all that remain are the defence tower and the Crucifix in the church. The stuccowork and *trompe-l'oeil* painting in the cloisters and on the monastery staircase were executed by the workshop of Johann Schmuzer in 1680–96.

It was here in 814 that the *Wessobrunner Gebet* was written. It describes the Creation and is the oldest surviving document in the German language. It is today preserved in the Bayerischen Staatsbibliothek in Munich (*see p69*).

Lüftlmalerei

Lüftlmalerei is the style of painting that is widely seen on houses in Upper Bavaria and the Allgäu, particularly in the Alpine and sub-Alpine areas. Dating from the 17th century, it was derived from Italia *trompe l'oeil* painting. A famous exponent of *Lüftlmalerei* was Franz Seraph Zwinck (1748–92), who lived in Oberammergau in a house called Zum Lüftl. It was probably after his house that this style of painting was named.

Lüftlmalerei in Berchtesgaden

❺ Around Starnbergersee

It was in Starnbergesee, near the town of Berg, that Ludwig II, much loved by the Bavarians, drowned in 1886. Like many of Munich's elite, he owned a summer palace on the lake. This scenic region has long enjoyed great popularity. The wealthy citizens of Munich build fine residences here, while those of more modest means come for weekend breaks.

① Starnberg
Linked to Munich by a railway since 1854, Starnberg boasts luxury villas and has a large marina.

⑨ Possenhofen
Royal visitors to this palace have included Elisabeth, future consort of Franz Joseph of Austria, and Sofia, Ludwig II's betrothed.

⑧ Feldafing
From 1855 to 1863 Ludwig II stayed in a romantic palace on nearby Roseninsel with his cousin Elisabeth (known as Sissi), the future empress of Austria.

Fürstenfeldbruck ◀ *München*

② Berg
The spot where Ludwig II met his death is marked by a Neo-Romanesque chapel built on the lakeshore in 1896–1900, and a wooden cross in the shallow water.

③ Assenhausen
In an extensive park stands Bismarck Tower, built in 1896–9 in honour of the German Chancellor.

⑦ Tutzing
A monumental horseshoe-shaped palace surrounded by a landscaped park is currently the home of an

Weilheim

Starnbergersee

⑥ Bernried
The popular Bucheim Museum (north of Bernried) houses a collection of Expressionist and folk art (www.bucheimmuseum.de).

Weilheim

④ Ammerland
The palace here, built in 1683–5, was presented by Ludwig I to the German poet and painter Franz Graf von Pocci in 1841.

Tips for Drivers

Tour length: about 46 km (28 miles).
Stopping-off points: There are many restaurants and cafés in every town on the route. Overnight accommodation is available, although it may be harder to obtain in summer.

Penzberg

⑤ Seeshaupt
This bustling resort, with a marina and elegant lakeside promenade, is very popular with watersports enthusiasts.

0 kilometres	2
0 miles	2

Key

▨ Suggested route
⋯ Other road

❻ Hohen-peißenberg

Road map C5. 🏔 3,700. 🚌
🚉 Peißenberg or Peiting.
ℹ️ Blumenstr. 2, (08805) 12 90.
🌐 **hohenpeissenberg.de**

The mountain known as Hoher Peißenberg rises east of the town of Peißenberg. The summit, at a height of 988 m (3,241 ft) above sea level, is reached by a scenic winding road and offers an extensive panorama of Upper Bavaria, from Ammersee and Starnbergersee to the Alps.

On the summit stands the **Gnadenkapelle**, built in the late Gothic period and remodelled in the Baroque style, the church of **Mariä Himmelfahrt**, built in 1616–19, and a former **chapterhouse** of 1619. The chapel contains a miracle-working image of the Madonna Enthroned dating from 1460–80 and brought here from Schongau in 1514.

❼ Schongau

Road map C5. 🏔 11,700. 🚌 🚉
ℹ️ Münzstr. 1–3, (08861) 21 41 81.
🌐 **schongau.de**

Schongau is picturesquely located on the river Lech and surrounded by idyllic fields and pastures. The town is enclosed by almost completely preserved **town walls** with wooden walkways and towers. They were built

in the 14th century and later reinforced in the 17th century. The main street in Schongau is the wide Münzenstraße, which is lined with shops and restaurants.

One of the town's finest buildings is the church of **Mariae Himmelfahrt**, which was built by Dominikus Zimmermann in 1751–3 on the site of a Gothic church. Also of interest is the former **castle** of the Wittelsbachs, dating from the 15th century and refurbished in 1771–2, and the late Gothic **Ballenhaus**, whose ground floor with open-beamed ceiling houses the town hall. The **Stadtmuseum Schongau**, a local history museum, is to be found in **Erasmuskirche**, a former hospital church, established in the 15th century and rebuilt in the 17th century.

Michaelskirche font, Altenstadt

🏛 **Stadtmuseum Schongau**
Christophstr. 55. **Tel** (08861) 25 46 05. **Open** 2–5pm Wed, Sat, Sun & public hols.

Environs
Some 3 km (2 miles) northwest is **Altenstadt**, which boasts **Michaels-kirche**, the finest surviving monumental Romanesque basilica in Upper Bavaria. Dating from about 1200, it is surrounded by a wall. It is decorated with Gothic frescoes and contains the Great God of Altenstadt, a crucifix 3 m (10 ft) tall, and a carved Romanesque font.

Romanesque cloisters of the abbey in Steingaden

❽ Steingaden

Road map C5. 🏔 2,700. 🚌
🚉 Peiting. ℹ️ Krankenhausstr. 1, (08862) 91 01 13. 🌐 **steingaden.de**

This town has a well-preserved Romanesque **Pfarrkirche St Johannes der Täufer**, built in the second half of the 12th century and partially rebuilt in the 15th century. It is a columned basilica with a triple apse and twin towers above the west front. The interior was decorated with Rococo mouldings and paintings in 1771–4.

In 1147, the Premonstratensians built an **abbey** here, of which the western cloisters, dating from the early 13th century, survive. The architect Dominikus Zimmermann was buried in the Romanesque chapel of St John in 1766.

❾ Wieskirche

Road map C5. 🚌 🚉 Füssen or Peiting. ℹ️ Krankenhausstr. 1, Steingaden, (08862) 91 01 13.
🎵 Abendkonzerte, Festlicher Sommer in der Wies (May–Sep).

The attractive pilgrimage church of **Zum Gegeißelten Heiland**, nestling in the sub-Alpine scenery, is not only the most resplendent example of South German Rococo, but probably the finest Rococo

Green pastures and a country track near Schongau

For hotels and restaurants in this region see p269 and pp281–2

church in the world. UNESCO listed it as a World Heritage Site in 1983.

In 1738, the figure of Christ in a small chapel in the fields southwest of the present church is said to have wept genuine tears, and soon afterwards pilgrims began to flock to the site of the miracle. In 1743–4, the Premonstratensian abbot of Steingaden commissioned Dominikus Zimmermann to design a church here.

Built in 1754 and decorated in 1765, the church represents the work of Dominikus and Johann Baptist Zimmermann at its peak. The nave is built to an oval plan and the ceiling is supported by eight pairs of columns. There is an elongated presbytery. The entire building displays an extraordinary fusion of painting, woodcarving and stuccowork and an almost mesmerising interplay of colour and light. The many windows, in fantastic and varied shapes, enliven the exterior and illuminate the interior. Not surprisingly, the church has been called the Lord God's Ballroom.

Rococo interior of the church in Wies, a World Heritage Site

⑩ Murnau

Road map C5. 🗺 11,300. 🚌 🚉
ℹ️ Kohlgruber Str. 1, (08841) 61 410.
🌐 murnau.de

Murnau is situated on an elevation between two lakes, Staffelsee and Riegsee, north of the marsh known as the Murnauer Moos, on what was once the Roman road to Augsburg. During World War II

an officers' prisoner-of-war camp existed here. Today Murnau is famous for its two breweries.

The **Nikolauskirche** is an interesting building. It was designed by Enrico Zucalli and was completed in 1734, after 17 years' work. The small Baroque **Maria-Hilf-Kirche** stands on Marktstraße, the main street, which commands a view of the Alps to the south.

There are numerous inns and guesthouses, a Neo-Gothic **town hall**, houses with oriel windows and decorative signboards, and narrow, winding alleys which give the town a unique charm. The **monument to Ludwig II**, on Kohlgruber Straße, was erected in 1894 and is the earliest monument to be dedicated to the king.

The finest building in Murnau is the Art Nouveau **Münterhaus**, where the artist Wassily Kandinsky lived from 1909 to

1914 with his student and lifetime companion Gabriele Münter. Today it houses a museum dedicated to the famous painter couple, along with works by other members of the Blaue Reiter group.

🏛 Münterhaus
Kottmüllerallee 6. **Tel** (08841) 62 88 80.
Open 2–5pm Tue–Sun.

Der Blaue Reiter

Cover of the first issue of *Der Blaue Reiter*

Wassily Kandinsky and Franz Marc produced the first issue of *Der Blaue Reiter* in 1911. The journal is now considered one of the most significant manifestos of 20th-century art. The contributors were artists whose aim was to renew art, while retaining their stylistic individuality. They included Paul Klee, Alexej Jawlensky, August Macke and Gabriele Münter. The Blaue Reiter group marked the beginning of lyrical abstract painting.

A colourful flower stall on Untermarkt in Murnau

The Baroque basilica of the Benedictine abbey at Ettal, set in an Alpine valley

⓫ Oberammergau

Road map C5. 🚶 5,100. 🚌 🚃
ⓘ Eugen-Papst-Str. 9a, (08822) 922
740. 🅦 **oberammergau.de**
🎭 Passionspiele (Easter, every ten
years, the next in 2020).

Oberammergau is one of the
best-known towns in Upper
Bavaria. Its renown rests on its
painted houses, and it is the
centre of the colourful style of
trompe-l'oeil house-painting
known as *Lüftlmalerei*, which is
typical of the region *(see p216)*.

The town also has an
international reputation for
its Passion play, which has
been performed here at Easter
ever since 1633, when an
epidemic of the plague finally
passed. Originally an open-
air event, the play has been
performed in a purpose-built
theatre since 1930.

The spectacle, which last
for six hours, is performed by
1,400 amateur actors, all of
whom must be local people
or their family members. The
play attracts an audience from
all over the world.

⓬ Ettal

Road map C5. 🚶 800. 🚌 🚃
Oberammergau. ⓘ Ammergauer Str.
8, (08822) 92 36 34. 🅦 **ettal.de**

Set in a scenic Alpine valley,
this Benedictine **abbey** was
founded by Ludwig IV in 1330.
In 1710, when the church was
remodelled in the Baroque style
to plans by Enrico Zucalli, a
Gothic rotunda was added. The
two-storey façade that Zucalli
intended was not completed
until the early 20th century.

The impressive interior
decoration is in a pure
Rococo style, crowned
by the large dome
that is visible from afar.
The paintings were
executed in 1748–50 by
Johann Jakob Zeiller, and
the stuccowork, one of the
great achievements of
its time, is by Johann
Georg Üblher and
Franz Xaver Schmuzer.
The high altar has a 14th-century
marble statue of the Madonna
made in the workshop of
Giovanni Pisano. The church,

which attracts many pilgrims,
is surrounded by various
monastic buildings.

⓭ Linderhof

Road map C5. 🚌 🚃 Ettal. Palace:
Tel (08822) 92 030. **Open** Apr–15
Oct: 9am–6pm daily; 16 Oct–Mar:
10am–4pm daily. 🎫 🎦 Park:
Open Apr–mid-Oct. 🅦 **linderhof.de**

Of all Ludwig II's many
fairytale residences, the **palace**
at Linderhof best shows his
great fondness for France
and his regard for the
Bourbons and Louis
XIV. The smallest of
Ludwig II's castles
and the one he
visited most often, it
was built by Georg von
Dollmann in 1870–86
and is surrounded by
an extensive **park**.
The extravagant
luxury of the
interior decoration
is based on French Baroque
style. Although it was intended
as a private residence, the
palace still has an ornate
royal audience chamber. The
other rooms in the palace,
including the Tapestry Room
and Hall of Mirrors, are no less
extravagantly decorated.

The palace is surrounded
by French-style formal gardens
and by Italianate terraced
gardens with cascades, which
in turn are surrounded by
landscaped grounds. There is
an artificial **grotto** dating from
1876–7 with a lake, a stage

Vase in the Linderhof
park

The Hotel Alte Post in Oberammergau

For hotels and restaurants in this region see p269 and pp281–2

and a throne with colourful lighting that brings to mind the Venus Grotto in Wagner's opera *Tannhäuser*. Ludwig II would take rides on the lake in a conch-shaped boat.

Another attraction of the park surrounding the palace is the **Moorish kiosk**, made by Karl von Dibitsch in 1850 and purchased by the king in 1876. Inside it is a lavish Peacock Throne. Just as resplendent is the **Moroccan House** of 1878–9, which was installed here in 1989.

Visitors admiring Ludwig II's palace at Linderhof

⓮ Garmisch-Partenkirchen

Road map C5. 🄰 28,000. 🚌 🚊 🛈 Richard-Strauss-Platz 2, (08821) 18 07 00. 🆆 **garmisch-partenkirchen.de**

Two villages, Garmisch and Partenkirchen, separated by the rivers Loisach and Partnach, were conjoined one year before the 1936 Winter Olympics. Thus came into being one of the best-known winter sports centres in Germany, with a convenient motorway link to Munich. The Alpine Ski World Championships were last held here in 2011.

Partenkirchen, the older of the two villages, has its roots in the Roman town of Partanum, while Garmisch is first mentioned in a document from the 9th century. Both parts of the town have many houses with character-istically painted façades, some old and others quite modern.

A house with *Lüftlmalerei* decoration in Garmisch-Partenkirchen

The finest churches here include **St Anton**, in Partenkirchen, a pilgrimage church dating from the first half of the 18th century, with *trompe-l'oeil* painting by Johann Holzer. There are also two **churches** in Garmisch dedicated to St Martin. One is medieval, with Gothic frescoes in the interior, and the other is Baroque, with stuccowork executed by Josef Schmuzer in 1730–33 and paintings by Matthäus Günther of 1733.

The **Olympic stadium** in the south part of Partenkirchen was built in 1934. As well as having ski-jumps, it is decorated with larger-than-life sculptures that are typical of Fascist art.

Environs
A road south of Partenkirchen leads to the scenic **Partnach river gorge** (Partnachklamm). Further along, an uphill walk of several hours leads to Ludwig II's hunting lodge in Schachen, just below the summit of Dreitorspitze. Built in 1870 in imitation of a Swiss chalet, the lodge has an ornate Oriental-style interior. The king celebrated his birthdays in the lodge, and also came here on hunting trips.

⓯ Eibsee

Road map C5. 🚌 🚊 Garmisch-Partenkirchen.

The greenish-blue waters of this lake, surrounded by wooded mountain slopes, lie 974 m (3,195 ft) above sea level. The scenic paths along its shores lead to secluded jetties for yachts and boats.

A regatta, with processions of yachts and great firework displays, takes place here every summer. Above the lake towers **Zugspitze**, which at 2,963 m (9,717 ft) is the highest peak in the German Alps. The summit can be reached by cablecar or an old funicular train, which passes through many tunnels.

Eibsee, the lake at the foot of Zugspitze

Mittenwald, a town on a former trade route at the foot of the Alps

⓰ Mittenwald

Road map C5. 🅜 7,300. 🚌 🚉
ⓘ Dammkarstr. 3, (08823) 33 981.
🆆 mittenwald.de

Situated at the foot of the Karwendel mountain range, this small town stands on what was once the main trade route between Verona and Augsburg. Up until the Thirty Years' War, its wealth was founded on trade but from the 17th century its mainstay was craftsmanship, particularly violin-making.

The beginnings of the local violin-making trade can be traced back to the 17th century and Matthäus Klotz (1653–1743), a pupil of the famous Nicolo Amati. A violin school was founded in 1853, and in 1930 the **Geigenbaumuseum** (Museum of Violin-Making) was established in the house where Klotz was born.

St-Peter-und-Paul-Kirche was built in 1738–40 by Josef Schmuzer. The late Gothic presbytery survives, and the tower was completed in 1746. The *Lüftlmalerei* on the façade is an outstanding example of this type of decoration *(see p216)*. It is by Matthias Günther, who also executed the paintings inside the church. The monument to Matthäus Klotz that stands outside the church was designed by Ferdinand Miller in 1890.

Mittenwald is now widely known as a tourist resort, and is especially popular with winter sports enthusiasts.

🏛 **Geigenbaumuseum**
Ballenhausgasse 3. **Tel** (08823) 25 11.
Open 10am–5pm Tue–Sun (11am–4pm Jan, mid-Mar–mid-May & mid-Oct–Nov).

⓱ Wallgau

Road map C5. 🅜 1,400. 🚌
🚉 Mittenwald. ⓘ Mittenwalderstr. 8, (08825) 92 50 50. 🆆 wallgau.de

This delightful village has small wooden **cottages** built in the 17th and 18th centuries with *Lüftlmalerei (see p216)* by Franz Kainer dating from the 1770s. Most of the cottages have been thoroughly modernized and now function as hotels, spanning a range of categories.

The town is popular with the smart Munich set, who come to play golf on the fine local courses, which are set in breathtaking scenery. The **Gasthaus zur Post** is renowned as the place where Heinrich Heine stayed in 1828 on his journey to Italy.

One of the many fine golf courses around the town of Wallgau

⓲ Walchensee

Road map C5. 🅜 600. 🚌
🚉 Kochel am See. ⓘ Ringstr.1, (08858) 411. 🆆 walchensee.de

This lake, which lies in an attractive green valley, is swept by strong winds, and is therefore very popular with windsurfers.

The small **church** near the lake was built in 1633 and refurbished in 1712–14.

Environs
In the nearby town of **Zwergern** stands the picturesque Margarethen-kirche, which was built in the 14th century and remodelled in the Baroque style in 1670. Beside it stands a monastery known as the Klösterl. Built in 1686–9, it has striking white walls and a tall, steeply pitched roof.

Near **Urfeld**, hidden in the woods, stands a small bust of the great 19th-century German writer Johann Wolfgang von Goethe, who stayed in the town when he set off on his famous Italian travels in 1786.

Walchensee hydroelectric power station on the banks of Kochelsee

⓳ Kochel am See

Road map C5. 🅜 4,000. 🚌 🚉
ⓘ Bahnhofstr. 23, (08851) 338.
🆆 kochel.de

Kochel is a popular resort on Kochelsee. The local church, **Michaelskirche**, was built in 1688–90, probably by Kaspar Feichtmayr. The frescoes and stuccowork were added in about 1730.

Two famous figures are associated with Kochel. One is the blacksmith who became the hero of the Bavarian uprising against Austria in 1705 – a statue of him was erected in 1900. The other is the painter Franz Marc. The house in which he lived is now a museum of his paintings and the works of other artists of the group Der Blaue Reiter (see p219).

🏛 Franz-Marc-Museum
Franz-Marc-Parc 8–10. **Tel** (08851) 924880. **Open** 10am–6pm Tue–Sun & public hols (until 5pm Nov–Mar). **Closed** 24 & 31 Dec.

Environs
On the banks of Kochelsee is **Walchensee hydro-electric power station**. It was built in 1918–24 to a design by Oskar von Miller, who aimed to electrify the Bavarian rail network and to supply electricity to the whole country. Walchensee power station is still one of the largest in Germany today.

⓴ Freilichtmuseum Glentleiten

Road map C5. 🚌 🚉 Kochel am See, Murnau. 🛈 (08851) 18 50. **Open** 19 Mar–11 Nov: 9am–6pm Tue–Sun (Jun–Sep: also on Mon).

The largest Freilichtmuseum (open-air museum) in Upper Bavaria opened near Großweil in 1976. It re-creates the atmosphere of a traditional Bavarian village, with cottages and workshops. The interiors show the way villagers once lived. The surrounding fields and meadows are cultivated in the traditional way. Cows, horses, sheep and goats graze nearby.

The extensive cloisters of the monastery at Benediktbeuern

㉑ Benediktbeuern

Road map C5. 🏔 3,500. 🚌 🚉 🛈 Prälatenstr. 3, (08857) 248. 🌐 benediktbeuern.de

The holiday resort of Benediktbeuern, at the foot of the Bekediktenwand mountains, is known for its former Benedictine **monastery**. Founded in 739 as part of the see established by St Boniface, it was one of the first missionary monasteries that he founded in Bavaria.

Work on the present late Baroque **church**, which stands on the site of a Romanesque church, began in 1682 under the direction of Kaspar Feichtmayr of Wessobrunn. The interior features some fine stucco-work strongly influenced by Italian art. The vaulting over the nave and the side chapels was painted by Hans Georg Asam, father of the renowned Asam brothers, in 1683–7. The monumental altar, built to resemble a triumphal arch, is made out of three different kinds of marble.

By the presbytery, which is fronted by towers, stands the two-storey **Anastasiakapelle**. It was built in 1750–53 by Johann Michael Fischer and has an oval floor plan. The decoration, by Johann Michael Feichtmayr and Johann Jakob Zeiller, is a masterpiece of Bavarian Rococo style.

Also worth visiting are the **monastery buildings**, now owned by Silesians. Dating from 1669–1732, they are arranged around two courtyards. The Alter Festsaal (Old Banqueting Hall), the Kurfürstensaal (Assembly Hall) and the former library, now a refectory, are particularly worth seeing.

Franz Marc 1880–1916

Heavenly Horses, one of Marc's best-known paintings

The Munich-born painter Franz Marc began his artistic career under the influence of the Impressionists and of Wassily Kandinsky, with whom he set up the group Der Blaue Reiter (see p219). Marc adopted Paul Delaunay's pure palette of Symbolist colours and the crystalline forms of the Italian Futurists. His paintings of humans and animals show them in harmony with their surroundings. Marc enjoyed painting from nature outdoors and was often visited in his home by followers of the movement. He was killed in 1916 at the Battle of Verdun at the age of 36.

Wooden figure of a fisherman in the lakeside resort of Kochel am See

② Bad Tölz

Road map D5. 🏔 18,000. 🚉
ℹ️ Max-Höfler-Platz. 1, (08 041) 78
670. 🆆 bad-toelz.de
🎭 Leonhardifahrt (6 Nov).

Until quite recent times, the
inhabitants of Bad Tölz, on
the River Isar, made their living
through a combination of
trade, logging and making and
selling their famous painted
furniture. When iodine-rich
springs were discovered here
in 1846, the village became a
health spa. To exploit the local
mineral water, a water park at
Alpamare, one of the largest

A painted cart used in the festival of St Leonhard

in Germany, was built, and
transport links, saunas and
solariums were installed.
    The character of the old
town has been well preserved
around **Marktstrasse**, which
leads down to the Isar. Many
of the houses, dating from
the 17th to the 19th centuries,
have characteristic *trompe-l'oeil*
wall paintings and striking
stuccowork, and distinctive
overhanging eaves.
    The **church** on Kalvarienberg,
one of the most famous in
Bavaria, was begun in 1726 and
completed at the end of the 19th
century. Particularly impressive
is the **Holy Staircase**
inside the church. At the
festival of St Leonhard,
patron saint of horses
and cattle, a procession
with old-fashioned
painted carts and horses
(Leonhardiritt) ascends
Kalvarienberg and is
then blessed. A small fair
and dancing events are
part of the celebration.

③ Tegernsee

Road map D5. 🏔 3,600. 🚌
🚉 Tegernsee. ℹ️ Hauptstr. 2, (08022)
18 01 40. 🆆 tegernsee.de

For the inhabitants of
Munich, Tegernsee, within
easy reach of the bustling
capital, is an upper-class
recreation ground.
    The first settlement to be
founded in the valley was the
Benedictine **monastery** near
Tegernsee, established in the
8th century. The monastery
became an important centre
of culture, and in the 11th
century the Romanesque
stained-glass windows made
here were renowned. Examples
can be seen in Augsburg
cathedral. In 1823–4 Leo
von Klenze converted the
monastery into a summer
residence for Maximilian I
Joseph. Von Klenze also
designed a new façade for
the monastery church, built
by Enrico Zucalli in the
Baroque style.

④ Alpenstraße

In 1927, plans were made for a panoramic road
that was to pass through the most beautiful parts
of the German Alps. The route alternates between
the High Alps and the foothills lying between
Bodensee and Königssee. It traverses the most
scenic areas, allowing travellers to admire Lower
Bavaria's stunning scenery. Particularly impressive
are the winding sections of the route, such as
those around Hindelang and Bayrischzell, which
offer breathtaking views.

② Jochstraße
The scenic road
that winds round
Hindelang, at
altitudes varying
as much as 300m
(985 ft) along a
7-km (4-mile) long
route, offers views
of Ostrachtal.

Key

▬ Suggested route

⋯ Other road

▬ Scenic route

Augsburg

Marktoberdorf   **Schongau**

Memmingen

E5496

Kempten   12   12

12   19

19   310   309   *Forggensee*

Lindau   1   308   **Füssen**   307

Bodensee   **Sonthofen**   308   2

Feldkirch   E532   187

19

Baad   IMST

① Immenstadt
This picturesque little
town, which has
some fine historic
buildings, is situated
near the lake, Alpsee.

0 kilometres   20
0 miles   20

③ Zugspitze
At 2,963 m (9,721 ft), this peak is
the highest in Germany. It is
topped by a distinctive cross.

The town of Schliersee seen from the lake

㉕ Schliersee

Road map D5. 🅰 6,700. 🚍
ⓘ Perfallstr. 4, (08026) 60 650.
🆆 **schliersee.de**

Situated east of Tegernsee and known as its "younger brother", Schliersee offers visitors much peace and quiet and makes for a popular escape in the summer. The houses on the northern lakeshore all have balconies laden with window boxes.

The local **church of St Sixtus** has frescoes and stuccowork executed by Johann Baptist Zimmermann in 1714. The church also has a distinctive figure of God the Father with Christ ascribed to Erasmus Grasser, and a Madonna ascribed to Jan Polack. The interesting **Heimatmuseum** (local history museum) is housed in an 18th-century hut.

🏛 **Heimatmuseum**
Lautererstr. 6. **Tel** (08026) 23 29.
Open May–Oct: 2–5pm Tue–Sat.

㉖ Ebersberg

Road map D4. 🅰 11,400. 🚍
ⓘ Marienplatz 1, (08092) 82 55 92.
🆆 **ebersberg.de**

This little town lies at the southern end of Germany's largest expanse of forest. Of the Augustinian monastery that was founded here in A.D. 934 all that remains is the **Sebastianskirche**, built in 1217–31 and remodelled in 1472–1504 in the Gothic style. Notable among the tombs, which span the 14th to the 16th centuries, is that of the couple who founded the church. It features a model of the church made by Wolfgang Leb in 1501. On Marienplatz, along with Baroque and Neo-Classical houses, is the **monastery inn**, now the town hall.

Doorway of Sebastianskirche in Ebersberg, with gilded figures

---

④ Bayrischzell
In this famous health resort beneath the Wendelstein mountains, the first Alpine folklore association was founded, in 1883. Traditional Bavarian dress is still worn here today.

⑥ Berchtesgaden
This architecturally rich town, at the foot of Watzmann, is the hub of the tourist area known as Berchtesgadener Land.

Tips for Drivers

Tour length: About 450 km (280 miles).
Stopping-off points: The route takes in Bavaria's best-known places, where restaurants and accommodation are plentiful.

⑤ Hintersee
The forest covering the foothills around this lake east of Ramsau – one of the many lakes in Berchtesgadener Land – is known as the Zauberwald (Magic Forest).

For hotels and restaurants in this region see p269 and pp281–2

THE ALLGÄU

The Allgäu is the part of Swabian Bavaria lying between the Landsberg-Memmingen motorway and the Allgäu Alps. In the east it borders the Lech valley, and in the west Baden-Württemberg, into which it protrudes as far as Bodensee (Lake Constance). The Allgäu is one of the least industrialized regions of Bavaria. Its main sources of wealth are cattle farming, dairy processing and tourism.

This verdant, hilly region, set against the backdrop of the sheer, craggy peaks of the Alps, attracts holidaymakers from Europe all year round. The gentle climate, the unspoiled scenery, the villages and towns with their historic buildings, and the excellent terrain for various sports makes this a suitable area for the developing tourist trade. The lush meadows and pastures are grazed by the characteristic brown Allgäu cows. The region's dairy produce is famous throughout the country and Germany's largest dairy processing plant is located in Kimratshofen, near Kempten.

Traditions and customs are still very much alive in the region. Local folk costumes, which vary from one district or village to another, are donned not exclusively for special occasions but are worn as everyday clothing. After World War II, the influx of migrants (many from Sudetenland) considerably altered the structure of the population. The former inhabitants of Gablonz (Jablonec), in the Czech Republic, settled near Kaufbeuren in Neugablonz, bringing with them their traditional trade of jewellery-making.

In the Allgäu Alps, world-class sports are practised. In Oberstdorf, which is famous for its huge ski-jump, there is also a figure-skating school for young men and women from all over the country. The Alpine rockfaces are suitable for both amateur and professional mountaineers, while the cliff-tops are ideal starting-places for colourful paragliders and hang gliders. Neuschwanstein, the most extravagant of Ludwig II's castles, attracts visitors from all over the world.

Rolling green countryside around Immenstadt

◄ The magnificent setting of Neuschwanstein Castle

Exploring the Allgäu

The capital of the Allgäu is Kempten, a town with Roman origins. Memmingen also has many historic monuments, but these are not the region's main attraction. Tourists are drawn to the castles of Hohenschwangau and Neuschwanstein at the foot of the Alps, which are reached by the Romantische Straße (Romantic Road). Equally splendid are the Renaissance castles of the Fuggers in Babenhausen and Kirchheim, and Ottobeuren Abbey. The south of the Allgäu has breathtaking Alpine scenery, including the Breitach gorge and Sturmannshöhle, a cave with stalactites, near Oberstdorf. This town is renowned for the Four Ski Jumps Tournament.

The church in Wasserburg on Bodensee (Lake Constance)

0 kilometres 10
0 miles 10

Sights at a Glance

1 *Memmingen pp230–31*
2 Ottobeuren
3 Babenhausen
4 Kirchheim
5 Mindelheim
6 Bad Wörishofen
7 Kaufbeuren
8 Neuschwanstein
9 Schloss Hohenschwangau
10 Füssen

12 Bad Hindelang
13 Oberstdorf
14 Immenstadt
15 *Lindau pp238–9*
16 Wasserburg
17 *Kempten pp240–41*
18 Maria Steinbach

Excursions
11 Around Neuschwanstein

For map symbols *see back flap*

Cows grazing in pastures at the foot of the Allgäu Alps

Getting Around

All the region's major towns have rail links, while the smaller towns are served by buses. The Allgäu can be reached by motorway A96. Lindau is the starting point of the Deutsche Alpenstraße, one of the finest scenic roads in Germany. Motorway A7 runs from north to south via Memmingen and Kempten. The Allgäu has convenient links with Munich and Stuttgart airports.

Key

- Motorway
- Main road
- Minor road
- Scenic route
- Major railway
- Minor railway
- International border
- Regional border

Schloss Hohenschwangau, in a stunning location

● Memmingen

Memmingen, a town known as the gateway to the Allgäu, was founded in the 12th century. It stands on the site of an Alemani settlement, on the course of an old Roman road. In 1438 Memmingen became a Free Imperial City, in 1522 it accepted the Reformation, and in 1803 it became part of Bavaria.

Memmingen has retained all the characteristics of a large trading centre. Various residential and artisans' districts have developed both within and outside the town walls. The wide streets often functioned as cargo-handling areas. The mainly timber-framed houses that line them have preserved their Gothic character.

The rich Gothic carvings on the stalls in Martinskirche

The façade of the town hall, with decorative Rococo stuccowork

🏛 Rathaus
Marktplatz 1.

Originally built in 1488, the Gothic town hall was remodelled and enlarged in the 16th century. Its current appearance dates from 1589, the Rococo stucco-work was added later to the façade in 1765. This elegant Renaissance building has a projecting central axis with oriel windows on the lower storeys culminating in a polygonal tower, and the wings are flanked by side towers.

🏛 Steuerhaus
Marktplatz 16.

The former customs house was built in 1495 to an elongated rectangular plan. It opens on to Marktplatz with an arcade of 20 arches. The second floor and the shaped gables were added in 1708. The painting on the façade dates from 1906–09. The building currently houses various municipal offices.

🏛 Hermansbau
Zangmeisterstr. 8. Stadtmuseum und Heimatmuseum Freudenthal: **Tel** (08331) 85 01 34. **Open** May–Oct: 10am–noon and 2–4pm Tue–Sat, 10am–4pm Sun & public holidays.

This late Baroque patrician palace with an arcaded courtyard was built in 1766 for Benedikt Freiherr von Herman. The façade is lavishly decorated with stuccowork, and the central section has a gable with an armorial cartouche.

🏛 Martinskirche
Zangmeisterstr. 13. **Tel** (08331) 85 69 20. **Open** Easter Sun–Apr & Oct: 10am–4pm daily (till 5pm May–Sep).

The Protestant Martinskirche was built in the 15th century, replacing a Romanesque basilica. This late Gothic church has a quadrilateral tower with a later steeple.

The interior has notable wall paintings dating from the 15th and 16th centuries. The most interesting feature of the interior, however, is the presbytery stalls, made by craftsmen from Memmingen in 1501–07. The decorative carvings, with lifelike portraits of the founders, are among the most outstanding examples of late Gothic Swabian art.

🏛 Westertor and Town Walls
The walls of the old town were completed before 1181. The outer walls were added in the 13th–15th centuries. In the 19th century they were partially demolished, but significant fragments with bastions and walkways have been preserved.

The most noteworthy gate is Westertor, which was rebuilt in 1648, and Kemptentor, built in 1383 and topped by a tall brick tower.

🏛 Antonierhaus
Martin-Luther-Platz 1. Strigel- and Antoniter-Museum: **Tel** (08331) 85 02 45. **Open** 10am–noon and 2pm–4pm Tue–Sat, 10am–4pm Sun & public holidays.

This former Antonine monastery and hospital, the oldest established by the order, was built in 1383. It stands on the site of an earlier castle.

The four-winged building has internal cloisters with external staircases. Painstakingly rebuilt, since 1996 they have housed a library as well as a café and cultural institutions.

Decorative armorial cartouche on the façade of the Steuerhaus

🏠 Fuggerbau

Schweizerberg 8.
The house of the Fugger family *(see p256)* was built in 1581–91 for Jakob Fugger. It is a monumental four-winged building with two square stairwells rising from the corners of the courtyards.

🏠 Frauenkirche

Frauenkirchplatz 4. **Tel** (08331) 22 53.
This three-nave basilica was originally a Romanesque building. It was enlarged at the end of the 14th century, and was remodelled in 1456. From 1565 to 1806 the church was shared by Catholics and Protestants.

The late Gothic paintings on the walls and ceiling were uncovered in 1893. Their state of preservation and wide thematic range make them among the most significant in southern Germany.

🏠 Siebendächerhaus

Gerberplatz 7.
The "House with Seven Roofs", built in 1601, was specially designed for drying hides.

Destroyed in April 1945 and painstakingly rebuilt, it is one of the town's most distinctive buildings.

Theater

Theaterplatz 2. **Tel** (08331) 94 59 16.
The building on what is now Theaterplatz was originally a monastery's barn. Built in 1680, it became an arsenal and then a theatre in 1803, when the Neo-Classical façade was added.

The distinctive Siebendächerhaus, the "House with Seven Roofs"

🏠 Kreuzherrenkirche

Hallhof 5. **Open** Apr–Oct: 2–5pm Tue–Fri & Sun; 10am–12:30pm, 2–5pm Sat.
This two-nave church with a tall onion-domed clock tower was built in 1480–84 in the Gothic style. In 1709 the interior was decorated with lavish Baroque stuccowork by Matthias Stiller and paintings in the style of Johann Baptist Zimmermann.

When the church was deconsecrated in 1803, the interior was horizonally divided to make two storeys. After World War II it was restored and has since served as a gallery and concert hall.

Memmingen Town Centre

① Rathaus
② Steuerhaus
③ Hermansbau
④ Martinskirche
⑤ Westertor and Town Walls
⑥ Antonierhaus
⑦ Fuggerbau
⑧ Frauenkirche
⑨ Siebendächerhaus
⑩ Theater
⑪ Kreuzherrenkirche

For map symbols *see back flap*

The lavishly decorated interior of the abbey church at Ottobeuren

❷ Ottobeuren

Road map B4. 🚠 8,000. 🚌 🚉
ℹ️ Marktplatz 14, (08332) 92 19 50.
🌐 **ottobeuren.de**

The Benedictine abbey in Ottobeuren, whose beginnings go back to the 8th century, is one of the finest Baroque monasteries in Germany. The abbey **Church of St Theodore and St Alexander**, rebuilt and refurbished on numerous occasions, received its present appearance in 1748–66, when it was remodelled by Johann Michael Fischer.

Nestling in wooded slopes overlooking the River Günz, this fine monumental building is a breathtaking sight. The lavish interior, in a uniform Rococo style, features four domes, the largest of which is 25 m (82 ft) high. The decoration and furnishings are by various artists, including Johann Michael Feichtmayr and Johann Jakob and Franz Anton Zeiller.

The **abbey**, to the west of the church, is known as "the Escorial of Swabia". Built to plans by Christoph Vogt in 1711–31, it is an imposing quadrilateral edifice with four cloisters.

Ottobeuren Abbey has been in the hands of Benedictine monks since its foundation. Today the Library, the Abbot's Chapel, the Theatre Hall and the Knights' Hall are open to visitors.

The **Klostermuseum** contains exhibits that include sculpture dating from the 12th to the 18th centuries, the works of artists who worked in Ottobeuren (on the church murals, for example), clocks and other artifacts.

The abbey's Kaisersaal is occupied by the **Staatsgalerie**, an interesting art gallery devoted to the works, mostly on religious themes, of Swabian Gothic painters. The gallery forms part of the Bayerische Staatsgemäldesammlungen.

🏛️ **Klostermuseum Abtei Ottobeuren and Staatsgalerie Ottobeuren, Kaisersaal**

Abbey. **Tel** (08332) 79 80. **Open** Palm Sunday–end-Oct: 10am–noon & 2–5pm daily; Nov–Mar: 2–5pm daily.

❸ Babenhausen

Road map B4. 🚠 5,300. 🚌 🚉
ℹ️ Auf des Wies 4, (08333) 92 36 23.
🌐 **babenhausen-schwaben.de**

The most prominent landmarks in this town are the castle and the parish church.

The **castle**, which is mentioned as early as 1237, became the property of the von Rechberg family after 1378. It was probably they who were responsible for the steep-roofed two-storey edifice built here in the 15th century and incorporated into the castle. In 1539 the castle passed into the hands of the Fuggers *(see p257)*, who refurbished it in 1541, adding the west and south wings. In 1955 the **Fuggermuseum** was founded, with the family retaining ownership of the park surrounding the castle.

The **church**, which is con-nected to the castle, was rebuilt in the Baroque style in 1715–30. The interior contains Baroque altars and a pulpit, as well as the tombs of the Rechbergs and Fuggers.

🏛️ **Fuggermuseum**
Tel (08333) 29 31. **Open** Apr–Nov: 10am–noon & 2–5pm Tue–Sat, 10am–noon & 1–6pm Sun. ♿

The castle and church in Babenhausen

❹ Kirchheim

Road map B4. 🚣 2,500. 🚌 🚉
Mindelheim. *i* Marktplatz 6, (08266)
86 080. **W** kirchheim-schwaben.de

The main attraction of this small
town is the Renaissance **castle**,
owned by the Fugger family
since the mid-16th century.
The famous Cedar Hall is
decorated with wood-
carvings on its ceiling
and door, and on its
window surrounds and
chimneypieces.

The altar of **St-Peter-
und-Paul-Kirche** features
a painting of the Holy
Family ascribed to
Domenichino and of the
Assumption ascribed
to Rubens. Also worth
seeing is the tomb of
Hans Fugger, who died
in 1598. Made of white
limestone, it was the work
of Alexander Colin.

Part of the inlaid ceiling of the Cedar Hall
at Kirchheim Castle

❺ Mindelheim

Road map B4. 🚣 14,200. 🚌 🚉
i Maximilianstr. 26, (08261) 99
15 20. **W** mindelheim.de 🎭
Frundsbergfest (every three years
in Jun–Jul, the next in 2015).

During the 15th and 16th
centuries **Mindelburg**,
built by Heinrich der Löwe
in 1160, belonged to the
Frundsberg family, as did the
whole town. The castle was
rebuilt in the late 15th to early
16th centuries and again
in the late 19th century.

The town's two main
streets, Maximilianstraße and
Kornstraße, are lined with fine
town houses. The former Jesuit
Maria-Verkündigungs-Kirche,

built in 1625–6 and refurbished
in 1721, has fine stuccowork
and altars.

Stephanskirche, built in
the early 18th century and
rebuilt in the early 20th
century, contains the tomb
of Duke Ulrich von Teck
and his two brides. In
the former of St Sylvester
is the **Schwäbisches
Turmuhrenmuseum**,
displaying belfry clocks.

Knight statue,
Kirchheim Castle

**🏛 Schwäbisches
Turmuhrenmuseum**
Hungerbachgasse 9.
Tel (08261) 90 97 60.
Open 2–5pm Wed & the
last Sun in the month.

❻ Bad Wörishofen

Road map B4. 🚣 14,400. 🚌 🚉
i Hauptstr. 16, (08247) 99 33 55/56.
W bad-woerishofen.de

This spa resort owes its
existence to the priest Sebastian
Kneipp. Among the 19th-cen-
tury guest houses here are the
Sebastianeum at Kneippstraße
8 and the **Kneipplanum** at
Alfred-Baumgartenstraße 6. The
Justinakirche and **Klosterkirche**
both have decoration by
Dominik and Johann Baptist
Zimmermann.

🏛 Sebastian-Kneipp-Museum
Schulstr. **Tel** (08247) 39 56 13.
Open Feb–mid-Nov: 3–6pm Tue–
Sun; 26 Dec–6 Jan: 3–5pm Sun.

❼ Kaufbeuren

Road map D4. 🚣 41,600. 🚌
🚉 *i* Kaiser-Max-Str. 3a, (08341)
437 850. **W** kaufbeuren.de
🎭 Tänzelfest (Jul).

With steep, winding narrow
streets lined with colourful
houses, the hilltop town of
Kaufbeuren retains much of
its medieval character.

The old town still has its
fortifications, complete with
walls and defensive towers, one
of which is the Fünfknopfturm,
which was built in about 1420.
After World War II, Neugablonz,
a settlement for refugees from
Sudetenland, now part of the
Czech Republic, was built here.

The Gothic Fünfknopfturm, part of
Kaufbeuren's fortifications

Sebastian Kneipp (1821–1897)

Sebastian Kneipp, a parish priest from St Justina's
Church in Bad Wörishofen, introduced a
method of therapy involving five factors –
water, movement, herbal treatment, diet
and inner harmony – but above all cold
baths, showers and exercise. In 1903 a
monument to Duke Kneipp was erected
in the street bearing his name. Portraits
of the clergyman (painted in 1936) can
be seen on the ceiling of Justinakirche,
and the town's former Dominican monastery
contains a museum dedicated to him.
The local rose-gardens also grew a new
variety of rose, the Kneipp Rose.

The Kneipp Monument in Bad Wörishofen

Schloss Neuschwanstein seen against its woodland backdrop

❽ Neuschwanstein

Road map B5. 🛈 Neuschwansteinstr. 20, Hohenschwangau, (08362) 93 08 30. 🌐 neuschwanstein.com

Schloss Neuschwanstein, one of Ludwig II's most renowned castles, was built at enormous expense from 1868 to 1892. It received its present name after the king's death in 1886.

The monumental castle was built to plans by the theatre designer Christian Jank, who expressed the king's vision inspired by Wagner's operas *Lohengrin and Tannhäuser*. The interior decoration was executed by Julius Hoffmann in 1880.

The castle has a breathtaking situation on an outcrop of rock towering over a gorge in the River Pöllat. There is a particularly memorable view from Marienbrücke, which giddily spans the rushing waters in the ravine below.

🏰 **Schloss Neuschwanstein**
Open Apr–15 Oct: 9am–6pm daily; 16 Oct–Mar: 10am–4 pm daily. **Closed** 1 Jan, 24, 25, 31 Dec. 🈲 🎞️

❾ Schloss Hohenschwangau

Road map B5. 🛈 Alpseestr. 12, (08362) 93 08 30. 🌐 hohenschwangau.de

This 14th-century castle, which was destroyed during the Napoleonic Wars, was acquired by Maximilian II, the king of Bavaria, in 1832. The restoration and rebuilding work executed up to 1837

was primarily the work of Domenico Quaglio.

A bulky building, set with towers and painted yellow, it is situated over a lake against a picturesque backdrop of Alpine scenery.

🏰 **Schloss Hohenschwangau**
Open Apr–15 Oct: 8am–5:30pm daily; 16 Oct–Mar: 9am–3:30 pm daily. 🈲

Statue of the Madonna and Child in St Mang-Kirche at Füssen

❿ Füssen

Road map B5. 🚹 14,500. 🛈 Kaiser-Maximilian-Platz 1, (08362) 93 850. 🌐 stadt-fuessen.de

The town's location in the foothills of the Alps, surrounded by lakes and overlooking the River Lech, together with its proximity to Schloss Neuschwanstein and Schloss Hohenschwangau, ensure that it is always full of tourists.

In Roman times Füssen stood on the road connecting northern Italy with Augsburg. In 1313 it passed into the hands of the bishops of Augsburg, who made it their summer residence.

The town's rapid growth was interrupted by the Thirty Years' War and a fire in 1713. After the secularization of the state and its incorporation into Bavaria in 1803, Füssen again enjoyed a period of prosperity, thanks to the interest that the Bavarian kings took in the region.

Füssen has many fine old buildings. The medieval **castle** has an arcaded façade decorated with *trompe-l'oeil* paintings executed in 1499. Its halls now house the **Filialgalerie der Bayerischen Staatsgemäldesammlungen** (art gallery).

The **Benedictine monastery**, founded in the 9th century, houses the **Museum der Stadt Füssen**, a local history museum, where a collection of locally made lutes and violins is displayed. Beside it is **St Mang-Kirche**, built in 1720-21. The façade of **Heilig-Geist-Spitalkirche**, painted by Joseph Anton Walch in 1749, is also of note.

🏛️ **Museum der Stadt Füssen**
Lechhalde 3. **Tel** (08362) 90 31 46. **Open** Apr–Oct: 11am–5pm Tue–Sun; Nov–Mar: 1–4pm Fri–Sun. 🈲

🏛️ **Filialgalerie der Bayerischen Staatsgemäldesammlungen**
Magnusplatz 10. **Tel** (08362) 90 31 46. **Open** Apr–Oct: 11am–5pm Tue–Sun; Nov–Mar: 1–4pm Fri–Sun. 🈲

The painted façade of Heilig-Geist-Spitalkirche in Füssen

⊕ Around Neuschwanstein

This tour, probably the most scenic in the whole of Bavaria, takes about a day, as it inevitably involves queueing for tickets at both the castles. They are reached from car parks at the foot of Schloss Hohenschwangau. An effortless way of reaching the giddy heights of Schloss Neuschwanstein is by horse-drawn chaise. Another memorable experience is a boat trip on Alpsee.

① Kolomanskirche
This small, distinctive Baroque church of 1673–82 stands in isolation at the foot of Schwangauer Berge.

② Tegelbergbahn
Recently discovered remains of Roman buildings can be seen from the lower station of this cable car, which runs to the summit of Tegelberg.

Schongau

Schwangau

Fussen

Fussen

Lussbach

Rautbach

Hohenschwangau

0 metres 500
0 yards 500

Alpsee

⑤ Marienbrücke
The cast-iron bridge that spans the Pöllat gorge is constantly occupied by people fascinated by staring 90 m (300 ft) down into the giddy depths.

③ Schloss Hohenschwangau
Part of the richly furnished interior of this castle is open to visitors.

④ Neuschwanstein
The white silhouette of Ludwig II's castle, set with numerous turrets, has an almost surreal appearance when it is seen against the woodland backdrop, which changes colour through the seasons.

Key
▬ Suggested route
▬ ▬ Suggested walk
═ ═ Other road
▬ ▬ Railway line

Tips for Drivers

Tour length: about 15 km (9 miles).
Stopping-off points: Meals and refreshments are available near Schloss Hohenschwangau and Schloss Neuschwanstein.

The Oberstdorf ski jumps, where the Four Ski Jumps Tournament is held

⑫ Bad Hindelang

Road map B5. 🔺 4,900. 🚌
🚉 Sonthofen. ℹ️ Am Bauernmarkt 1,
(08324) 89 20. 🌐 **badhindelang.net**

This health resort is set in beautiful woodland scenery in the Ostrach river valley. The town is best explored by walking down Marktstraße, starting from the Neo-Gothic **church**. The 17th-century **bishop's palace** opposite now houses the town hall. The beautifully restored houses are covered in colourful flowers in summer.

Environs
About 1 km (0.6 mile) south of Hindelang is the spa resort of **Bad Oberdorf. Hinterstein**, 6 km (4 miles) further on, is popular with mountaineers. The road to **Oberjoch**, 6.5 km (4.5 miles) northeast, known as the Jochstraße, is the most tortuous section of the **Deutsche Alpenstraße**.

⑬ Oberstdorf

Road map B6. 🔺 9,600. 🚌 🚉
ℹ️ Prinzregenten-Platz 1, (08322)
700 700. 🌐 **markt-oberstdorf.de**

The best-known health resort and holiday centre in the Allgäu, Oberstdorf, situated in the Iller river valley, is also renowned for its **ski jumps** on the slope of Schattenberg. One event in the Four Ski Jumps Tournament is

held here every year. The best-known ski jump in Oberstdorf is in the Stillach valley. It was the first large-scale ski jump *(Skiflugschanze)* in the world, and competitors can achieve distances of more than 170 m (550 ft). It was built in 1949–50 by the ski jumper and architect Heini Klopfer. The town itself, with its narrow streets and old houses, is extremely attractive. The **Heimatmuseum** has exhibits relating to local history, and includes the world's largest shoe.

Lüftlmalerei on a hotel in Hindelang

🏛️ **Heimatmuseum**
Oststr. 13. **Tel** (08322) 54
70. **Open** 10am–noon, 2–
5:30pm Tue–Sun & public hols. **Closed**
3 weeks in Apr & May; Nov–Christmas.

Environs
The **Breitach river gorge**, 6 km (4 miles) west of Oberstdorf, is a major attraction. A vertiginous track winds for 2 km (1.25 mile) above the water that rushes between sheer cliffs rising to heights of 100 m (325 ft). For the walk, a waterproof

overgarment and sturdy hiking boots will be needed.
At the **Sturmannshöhle** cave outside **Fischen**, some 200 steps lead to a large cavern with impressive stalactites and stalagmites. The cave's galleries are connected by rushing underground streams that can be heard from the cave mouth.

⑭ Immenstadt

Road map B5. 🔺 14,000. 🚌 🚉
ℹ️ Marienplatz 12, (08323) 91 41 76.
🌐 **immenstadt.de** 📷
Klausentreiben (5–6 Dec).

It is best to approach Immenstadt from the north, as this route provides a fine view of Alpsee. The town has much to offer to watersports enthusiasts and mountaineers. It also contains many historic buildings. **Nikolauskirche** has been rebuilt several times since the Middle Ages. In 1602–20 a **palace** was built on the market square. One of its apartments has a stuccowork ceiling of about 1720 with hunting scenes and views of castles. The **town hall** was built in 1649 and the local history museum is in a **mill** dating from about 1451.

Environs
2 km (1.25 mile) north is **Bühl**, where Stephanskirche contains a chapel that was built as a replica of the Holy Sepulchre in Jerusalem. The nearby Maria Loretto Chapel of Our Lady of Loretto is made up of the Baroque choir of St Annakapelle.

⑮ Lindau

See pp238–9.

Sarcophagus in Nikolauskirche in Immenstadt

16 Wasserburg

Road map A5. 🗺 3,600. 🚌 🚉
ℹ️ Lindenplatz 1, (08382) 88 74 74.
🌐 **wasserburg-bodensee.de**

With a stunningly beautiful location on the tip of a promontory on Bodensee (Lake Constance), Wasserburg is a charming village of flower-filled streets with views of the lake and its backdrop of hills. Its location makes it a popular place for sailing and other watersports.

The village's history dates from the 8th century, then in the 10th century a **castle** was built here to resist Hungarian invaders. The castle was modernized in the 13th century and rebuilt after a fire in 1358. It is a three-winged building with an irregular plan. The east wing is a vestige of the medieval structure, while the south wing dates from the 16th century and the west wing from the 18th century. It is now a hotel.

Georgskirche is equally historic. It was founded in the 8th century but was later converted and together with the cemetery wall was incorporated into the town's fortifications. Remnants of these defences reach down to the shores of the lake. The present building is a late Gothic fortified hall dating from the second half of the 15th century.

The square tower, built in 1396–1403, was given its onion dome in 1656. The church is connected to a two-storey presbytery.

The **Malhaus** (1597), once a residence of the Fuggers *(see p256)*, now houses a **museum** illustrating the culture of the region and also the fishing industry, formerly Wasserburg's main source of livelihood.

🏛 Museum im Malhaus
Halbinselstr. 77. **Tel** (08382) 89 369 or (08382) 75 04 57. **Open** mid-Apr–Oct: 10:30am–12:30pm Tue–Sun, 2:30–5pm Wed, Sat & Sun.

Georgskirche beside Bodensee (Lake Constance) in Wasserburg

17 Kempten

See pp240–41.

18 Maria Steinbach

Road map A4. 🚌 🚉 Leutkirch.
ℹ️ Markt Legau, Marktplatz 1, (08330) 94 010. 🌐 **legau.de**

Maria Steinbach is famed for its pilgrimage church, **Mariä Schmerzen**, which is a masterpiece of Rococo architecture. Situated on a hill in the idyllic rolling landscape of the Iller river valley, the church was built in

The Rococo church in Maria Steinbach

1746–54 on the site of earlier Romanesque and Gothic shrines. The building was inspired by the works of Dominik Zimmermann. The undulating façades, with *trompe-l'oeil* painting, conceal a dazzling interior. The outstanding mouldings and painting by Franz Georg Hermann, the stuccowork of the altars, pulpit, stalls, confessionals and organ loft combine to produce a unified whole.

The figure of the Grieving Madonna, which since 1730 has been renowned for its miracle-working powers, was an object of pilgrimage in southern Germany during the 18th century.

The group of **presbytery buildings** set around a courtyard west of the church dates from the mid-18th century. The **Wallfahrtsmuseum** contains a large collection of votive gifts made to the Madonna by pilgrims.

🏛 Wallfahrtsmuseum
Kirchhof 4. **Tel** (08394) 92 40.
Open by appointment.

Bodensee (Lake Constance) and the Alps seen from Wasserburg

⑮ Lindau

Lindau is one of the three towns on Bodensee (Lake Constance) that is officially in Bavaria. The old part of the town, which stands on an island in the lake, is connected to the mainland by a railway and road bridge. Founded as a fishing settlement in Roman times, Lindau is an extremely pleasant town. It was granted the status of a city in the 13th century. It still retains its medieval plan, which is based around three long parallel streets.

Maximipanstraße, the main street in Lindau

🏠 Maximilianstraße

The town's main street, Maximilianstraße, is also its widest. Like the parallel streets of In der Grub and Ludwigstraße, it contains houses dating from the 15th to 19th centuries.

The small, compact houses with gables facing the street have windows that are often divided by columns, while the façades are broken up by oriels. The arcades and the old hoisting devices of the warehouses in the garrets bear witness to the town's character as a centre of trade.

🏠 Altes Rathaus

Bismarckplatz 4.

The old town hall, built in 1422–36, was remodelled several times during the 16th century, and again in 1724 and 1865. The programme of rebuilding that took place in 1885–7 was undertaken by Friedrich von Thiersch, who restored the stepped gable that had been removed in 1865 and re-constructed the exterior staircase. The façade was also painted by Joseph Widmann.

🏠 Neues Rathaus

Bismarckplatz 3.

The new town hall, built in 1706–17, was also remodelled by Friedrich von Thiersch in 1885. A two-storey building crowned by a tall shaped gable decorated with vases and obelisks, it now houses a cloth shop.

🏠 Haus zum Cavazzen

Marktplatz 6. Städtisches Museum: **Tel** (08382) 94 40 73. **Open** Easter–Oct: 11am–5pm Tue–Fri, Sun, 2–5pm Sat. 📷

This elegant patrician building is named after the de Cavazzo family, in whose ownership it was from 1540 to 1617.

The present Baroque house was built for the von Seutter family in 1729–30. It has a tall mansard roof and the façade is covered with paintings of herms, atlantes, sphinxes and garlands of fruit. The house now accommodates the **Städtisches Museum** (local history museum), which contains an interesting collection of artisans' tools.

🏠 Stephanskirche

Marktplatz 8. **Tel** (08382) 33 44.

Originally a Catholic church, it became a Protestant church in 1528. The original 12th-century Romanesque building was refurbished several times during the 14th, 15th and 16th centuries. Its present-day form – a three-nave, barrel-vaulted basilica – dates from 1781–3, when it was remodelled.

🏠 Münster "Unserer Lieben Frau"

Stiftsplatz 1. **Tel** (08382) 58 50.

The church originally belonged to the Benedictine monks who settled here in about 800. Vestiges of the pre-Romanesque church, which was built after 948, are preserved in the west wall. In about 1100 a Romanesque basilica with a transept and a west tower was built.

After the fire that devastated the town in 1728, the church was rebuilt to its Romanesque plan. The present airy Baroque church, lavishly decorated with mouldings and wall paintings, resulted from work carried out in 1748–55 under the direction of Johann Caspar Bagnato.

Baroque epitaph in the Haus zum Cavazzen

A lion and a lighthouse framing the harbour entrance against the Alps

VISITORS' CHECKLIST

Practical Information
Road map A5. 24,500.
Alfred-Nobel-Platz 1, (08382)
26 00 30. Lindau.de
lindau-tourismus.de
email: info@prolindau.de

Transport
Tel (08382) 94 44 16.

The Harbour

The harbour that was built at the southern end of the island in 1811 was modernized in 1856. A marble Lion of Bavaria set on a pedestal 6 m (20 ft) high was added to the tip of the mole at the harbour entrance. A new lighthouse, 33 m (108 ft) high was built on the tip of the opposite mole. These two structures came to symbolize Lindau.

The promenade beside the harbour, where the former lighthouse, known as the **Mangturm**, stands, is popular with tourists. Built in about 1200, the old lighthouse has a projecting upper storey with a pointed steeple covered in 19th century glazed tiles. It was originally part of the city's fortifications.

Peterskirche

Oberer Schrannenplatz 5/7.
This is one of the oldest churches in the entire Bodensee region. The presbytery and eastern section date from about 1180. The western part was added in the late 15th century. The five-storey tower that stands near the apse, and that was originally in the Romanesque style, was rebuilt in 1425. The interior walls are decorated with frescoes dating from the 13th to 16th centuries. They include works ascribed to Hans Holbein the Elder. Since 1928 the church has functioned as a memorial to war heroes.

Beside the church stands the **Diebsturm** (Thieves' Tower), a circular watchtower built in 1370–80, which was used in conjunction with the Pulverturm (Powder Tower), Ludwigsbastion and Maximilianschanze (Maximilian's Redoubt).

The Mangturm, formerly a lighthouse and watchtower

Lindau City Centre

1. Maximilianstraße
2. Altes Rathaus
3. Neues Rathaus
4. Haus zum Cavazzen
5. Stephanskirche
6. Münster
7. Harbour
8. Peterskirche

For map symbols see back flap

ⓗ Kempten

Originally a Roman town, Kempten was divided into a monastic and a secular district in the Middle Ages. The monastic district was centred around a Benedictine abbey, and in 1712 the monks were granted city rights. The secular district of Burghalde, which grew at the foot of the hill, was a Free City of the Empire from 1289 and accepted the Reformation in 1527. In 1802 the two districts were combined into a single entity and incorporated into Bavaria. Today Kempten is the Allgäu's thriving capital.

Façade of the town hall, featuring Kempten's coats of arms

🏛 Rathaus

Rathausplatz.
The late Gothic town hall, built in 1474, has a stepped gable crowned by a small tower. The wooden ceilings of the interior date from about 1460 and originally came from the house of the weavers' guild. Before the town hall stands a copy of a Mannerist fountain of 1601.

🏛 Rathausplatz

The square on which the town hall stands is lined with patrician palaces and merchants' and guildsmens' houses, which were either remodelled or newly built in the Baroque and Neo-Classical periods. The three-storey Londonerhof at No. 2 has a Rococo façade lavishly covered with stuccowork and featuring a Neo-Baroque doorway of 1899. The Hotel Fürstenhof at No. 8 was built in about 1600. The Ponickauhaus at Nos. 10 and 12 was created in 1740 when two 16th-century houses were knocked together, the first floor being converted into a lavishly decorated Festsaal.

🏛 St-Mang-Kirche

St-Mang-Platz 6.
The original church dedicated to St Mang was built in 869. The present church dates from 1426–28, when it was built as the parish church of the Free Imperial City. In 1525 it became a Protestant church, and was remodelled as a three-nave basilica with a tall tower. It was last rebuilt in 1767–8, when the vaulting and late Rococo mouldings were added.

🏛 The Residence

Residenzplatz. Prunkräume der Residenz: **Tel** (0831) 25 62 51.
Open Jan–Mar (& Nov): 10am–4pm Sat; Apr–Sep: 9am–4pm Tue–Sun; Oct: 10am–4pm Tue–Sun. 📷

In 1651–74 a group of 11th-century buildings, which were destroyed in 1632, was replaced by a new Baroque monastery. It was also a residence. The monastery consists of buildings grouped around two courtyards. The elegant apartments on the second floor, which were decorated in 1732–42, echo those of the Residenz in

The late Gothic façade of St-Mang-Kirche, with its tall tower

Munich (see pp78–81). The mouldings were executed by stuccoists from Wessobrunn, while the vaulting is by Franz Georg Hermann. The Throne Hall is one of the finest examples of Bavarian and Swabian Rococo interiors.

🏛 The Orangery

The garden once adjoined the Residence on its southern side. The orangery that was built here in 1780 now houses the municipal library.

🏛 Alpinmuseum and Alpenländische Galerie

Landwehrstr. 4. **Tel** (0831) 25 25 740.
Open 10am–4pm Tue–Sun.
Closed mid-Nov–1 Mar. 📷
The Alpine Museum, in the Residence's former stables, is dedicated primarily to skiing and mountaineering, but also encompasses topography and the natural environment, and poetry and painting relating to the mountains. There is also a gallery of regional art.

One of the fine apartments in the Residence

⌂ Lorenzkirche
Landwehrstr. 3.

The church is a three-nave basilica with two pairs of domed side chapels and an octagonal presbytery that is also crowned by a dome. This arrangement created two separate areas: one for the faithful and one for the friars. The interior is breathtaking. The stuccowork in the nave, aisles and presbytery was executed by Giovanni Zuccalli in 1660–70, and the ceilings were painted by Andreas Asper. A comparatively modest twin-towered façade is fronted by a grand staircase. To the east of the presbytery stands the Residence.

▦ Kornhaus
Großer Kornhausplatz 1. Allgäu-Museum: **Tel** (0831) 54 02 120. **Open** 10am–4pm Tue–Sun.

The prominent towers and dome of the Lorenzkirche

This former grain warehouse was built in 1700. Today it houses a museum dedicated to the history, culture and art of the town and the region.

⌂ Burghalde
Burgstr.

In 1488 a castle was built on a hill beside the River Iller, where

a Roman fort once stood. The castle was incorporated into the town's fortifications and was then demolished in 1705. Part of the town walls, together with the northern tower and its wooden gatehouse of 1883 survive. Today, Burghalde is an open-air theatre with concerts and cinema. You can also walk round the town walls.

⌂ Archäologischer Park Cambodunum
Cambodunumweg 3. **Tel** (0831) 79 731. **Open** Mar–Apr & Nov: 10am–4:30pm Tue–Sun; May–Oct: 10am–5pm Tue–Sun. **Closed** Dec–Feb. 🅿

Kempten was once the Roman settlement of Cambodunum. Excavations have uncovered a forum, a basilica and baths. The most impressive building was the basilica, which was as large as the present St Lorenz-Basilica.

Remains of Roman baths in the settlement of Cambodunum

Kempten Town Centre

① Rathaus
② Rathausplatz
③ St-Mang-Kirche
④ Residence
⑤ Orangery
⑥ Alpinmuseum & Alpenländische Galerie
⑦ Lorenzkirche

0 metres 200
0 yards 200

For map symbols see back flap

NORTHERN SWABIA

Northern Swabia constitutes that part of historical Swabia that now belongs to Bavaria, hence its name – Bayerisches Schwaben (Bavarian Swabia). In terms of its politics and its culture as well as its scenery, it is the most diverse region of southern Bavaria. Its main attractions for tourists are its historic towns, notably Augsburg, the great Ries Basin and its scenic river valleys.

Throughout the course of history, this region was divided into numerous ducal and monastic possessions and Imperial Cities (Reichsstädte). This served to promote the development of art, which can be seen in the region's castles and palaces and particularly in its churches and monasteries. From 1803 Swabia formed part of Bavaria, and was subjected to integration. However, in this transitional area between the German states of Bavaria and Baden-Württemberg, significant differences in attitude, language and customs survive to this day among Swabians.

The historical need for differentiation, self-definition and individuality has made Swabia a country of small towns each with their own character and history. This is particularly apparent during local festivals. The scenery is equally diverse and varied.

The north consists of the rolling wooded hills of the western Schwäbische Alb massif. Beside them lies the Nördlinger Ries. This area, renowned for its micro-climate and its rich soil, has been inhabited since Palaeolithic times.

The Danube cuts through the northern part of Swabian Bavaria. The extensive moors of the Donauried (the Danube valley) bear witness to frequent river flooding in the past. Lying almost parallel from south to north are the great moraine valleys of the Iller, the Günz and the Lech.

Augsburg, almost in the centre of the region and founded in Roman times, was an early centre of the Reformation and of goldsmiths. West of Augsburg is the Westliche Wälder, a vast forest reserve whose unspoiled scenery makes it popular with hikers.

A flower shop in Augsburg, with its displays spilling onto the pavement

◀ Panoramic view from Burgfelsen castle rock in Wallerstein

Exploring Northern Swabia

Northern Swabia's principal city is Augsburg. The third-largest city in Bavaria after Munich and Nuremberg, Augsburg demands several days' exploration, as it has much to offer of architectural interest. The city is also a useful starting point for various excursions. Within easy reach to the north are the Ries Basin, a huge crater nestling the town of Nördlingen, and the impressive Harburg Castle, as well as towns on the Danube such as Donauwörth, Dillingen and Günzburg. In the southwest are the castles belonging to the Fugger family. With their varied architecture and scenic settings, all of the region's towns have much to interest visitors.

Christ on a donkey, from the former Augustinian monastery at Wettenhausen

Sights at a Glance

- **9** *Augsburg pp252–6*
- **16** Dillingen
- **8** Donauwörth
- **11** Friedberg
- **15** Günzburg
- **5** Harburg
- **18** Höchstädt
- **6** Kaisheim
- **17** Lauingen
- **7** Leitheim
- **1** *Nördlingen pp246–7*
- **3** Oettingen
- **12** Roggenburg
- **10** Sielenbach
- **2** Wallerstein
- **13** Weißenhorn
- **4** Wemding
- **14** Wettenhausen

Getting Around

Two motorways run through Swabia. The A8, running along an east–west axis, connects Munich and Stuttgart via Augsburg and Günzburg. The A7 runs in a north–south direction, following the course of the River Iller. Parallel to it is the Romantische Straße (Romantic Route), which passes through towns such as Nördlingen, Harburg, Donauwörth and Augsburg. The good road network makes the other towns of the region easily accessible by car or by bus. The larger cities also have rail links. Situated near to Munich, Augsburg has its own airport.

Gundelfinge

Heidenheim

Stuttgart

Leipheim

15 GÜNZB

Bur

Ulm
Neu-Ulm
Nersingen

WETTENHAUSEN

Pfaffenhofen   Ichenh

Senden

13 WEISSENHORN

Vöhringen   **12** ROGGENBURG

Krumbach

Illertissen

Babenhausen

Mindelheim

Memmingen

Harburg Castle overlooking the Wörmitz river valley

For map symbols *see back flap*

Key

- ▬▬ Motorway
- ▬▬ Major road
- ▭▭▭ Minor road
- ▬▬ Main railway
- ▬▬ Minor railway
- ▬▬ Regional border

The Mannerist Stadtmetzg in Augsburg, designed by Elias Holl

ndingen

Nürnberg

3 OETTINGEN

466

'ALLERSTEIN

R i e s

1 NÖRDLINGEN

4 WEMDING

Nürnberg

Monheim

Möttingen

Wörnitz

25

5 HARBURG

2

6 KAISHEIM

7 LEITHEIM

DONAUWÖRTH **8**

s w ä b i s c h e   A l b

Bissingen

Burgheim

16

Asbach-Bäumenheim

Neuburg an der Donau

Tapfheim

Rain

ingen

HÖCHSTÄDT **18**

Mertingen

Donau

Buttenwiesen

Pöttmes

NGEN **16**

AUINGEN

D o n a u r i e d

Wertingen

Thierhaupten

Langweid

Ingolstadt

Affing

Aichach

300

N a t u r p a r k

A u g s b u r g -

Gersthofen

W e s t l i c h e

10 SIELENBACH

eppach

W ä l d e r

Neusäss

8

10

Dinkelscherben

AUGSBURG **9**

11 ▯▥▤▯

FRIEDBERG

Stadtbergen

300

München

Thannhausen

Königsbrunn

Kissing

Bobingen

Mering

Wertach

Kirchheim in Schwaben

17

Lech

Schwabmünchen

Landsberg am Lech

0 kilometres   10

0 miles   10

● Nördlingen

Nördlingen, encircled by defensive walls, is the "capital" of the Ries Basin and one of the most picturesque towns in Swabia. Several hours can be spent wandering along its streets and alleys, where the Gothic and the Renaissance periods have left their mark. In the 14th century the town almost doubled in size and was surrounded by walls. The streets that run from the five town gates merge on Marktplatz, at the heart of the town. A good time to visit is in July, when the Scharlachrennen, a horse race and parade dating back to the 15th century, is held.

Exploring Nördlingen

The most attractive aspect of Nördlingen is its houses, most of which are half-timbered, with colourful, cascading window boxes. Many of the houses are several storeys high, with attic store-rooms. In the Gerberviertel, the tanners' quarter, the houses on the River Eger are well preserved. Two of the town's most interesting houses are that at Paradiesstraße 4, dating from 1350 and the town's oldest half-timbered house, and the 1678 Wintersches Haus at Braugasse 2, the best-preserved private house in Nördlingen.

Bas-relief of a fool on the town hall

🏛 Rathaus

Marktplatz 1.
The town hall was built in the 13th century and rebuilt after 1500, acquiring its present form at the beginning of the 17th century. Its most noteworthy feature is the external stone stairway, built by Wolfgang Waldberger. Beside the doors beneath the stairway is a bas-relief depicting a fool, with the ironic inscription "*Nun sind unser zwey*" ("Now it is the two of us") addressing the reader. The wall of the grand Federal Room on the second floor has a painting of the heroic feats of the biblical Judith by Hans Schäufelein.

⛪ Georgskirche

Am Obstmarkt.
Georgskirche, built in 1427–1505, stands in the centre of the town. Like many other buildings in the region, it was built with suevite from the Ries Basin (*see p248*). The interior features finely carved late Gothic stalls and a pulpit, a sacrarium of 1522–5 and numerous epitaphs and tombs. The tower, 90 m (295 ft) high, known as the Daniel Tower, can be seen from far away. A flight of 331 stairs leads to the top. The effort of climbing them is rewarded by a panoramic view of the Ries Basin. For 300 years a night watchman has called from the top of the tower,

Organ loft in the Gothic Georgskirche

sometimes every half hour. Today this occurs only between 10pm and midnight.

🏛 Tanzhaus

Marktplatz 15.
This Gothic half-timbered hall dating from 1442–4 was built for official dances and receptions. The ground floor con-tained bakers' shops, which is why the building was also known as the Brothaus (Bread House). On a console on the eastern façade stands a Gothic statue of 1513. Known as *The Last Knight*, it depicts Maximilian I as a knight in armour. Max-imilian was a frequent visitor to Nördlingen, which he greatly admired.

The richly decorated Mannerist doorway of the Klösterle

⛪ Klösterle

Beim Klösterle 1.
The monastery church known as the Barfüßerkirche, built in 1422, was converted into a Renaissance-style grain ware-house by Wolfgang Waldberger in 1584–6. The southern façade has a fine doorway dating from 1586, crowned with the town's coat of arms and decorated with figures of tradesmen. Today the Klösterle houses a hotel.

🏛 Hohes Haus

Marktplatz 16.
This tall, nine-storey house, next to the Tanzhaus, is the oldest brick building in Nördlingen. It is mentioned as early as 1304 and was used as a warehouse.

🏛 Spital

Vordere Gerbergasse 1. Stadtmuseum:
Tel (09081) 27 38 23 0. **Open** mid-
Mar–4 Nov: 1:30–4:30pm Tue–Sun.
🖼 Eugene-Shoemaker-Platz 1.
Rieskrater-Museum: **Tel** (09081) 84
710. **Open** Nov–Apr: 10am–noon, 1:30–
4:30pm; May–Oct: 10am–4:30pm. 🖼

The town's former hospital
complex is the largest in
Germany. The buildings
of the Spitalkrankenhaus
and Holzhofstadel that
form part of it have been
converted into museums.

The **Stadtmuseum**, founded
in 1960, has a collection of
paintings on panel by late
Gothic and Renaissance artists
including Friedrich Herlin,
Hans Schäufelein and Sebastian
Daig, and a model of the
Battle of Nördlingen of 1634
with 6,000 tin soldiers. The
Rieskrater-Museum features
among its exhibits Moon rocks
donated by NASA.

🏛 Hallgebäude

Weinmarkt 1.
On the south side of the Wine
Market stands a fine building
of 1543 with four attic storeys.
A corner has polygonal oriels,
one of them decorated with a
cartouche containing the civic
coat of arms. The building was

The domed Löpsinger Tor, one of
Nördlingen's five town gates

once used for storing wine and
salt, for currency offices and the
town weights.

🏛 Alte Schranne

Schrannenplatz.
This storehouse, built in 1602,
has a total of five storeys, three
of which are in the attic area.
The southern façade features a
sundial and an Art Nouveau
fountain is in the square before
the building.

VISITORS' CHECKLIST

Practical Information
Road map B2. 🚏 19,300.
ℹ️ Marktplatz 2, (09081) 84 116.
🎉 Stabenfest (second Mon in
May); Scharlachrennen (Jul).
🌐 noerdlingen.de
email: tourist-information@
noerdlingen.de

Transport
🚉

🏛 Löpsinger Tor and Town Walls

Stadtmauermuseum: **Tel** (09081) 91
80. **Open** Apr–Oct: 10am–4:30pm
Tue–Sun.

Construction of the walls
encircling Nördlingen was
begun in 1327. The walkway
around the fortifications
provides a variety of views
over the town. The walls are
pierced by five gates, 12
towers and a bastion. All the
gates except the Baldinger
Tor have towers. They are the
Reimlinger Tor, the oldest and
largest gate, on the road from
Augsburg; the Berger Tor; the
Löpsinger Tor, which houses
the **Stadtmauermuseum**, whose
domed circular tower dates
from 1593–4, and the taller
and narrower Deininger Tor.

Nördlingen Town Centre

1. Rathaus
2. Georgskirche
3. Tanzhaus
4. Hohes Haus
5. Klösterle
6. Spital
7. Hallgebäude
8. Alte Schranne
9. Löpsinger Tor and
   Town Walls

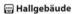

| 0 metres | 150 |
| 0 yards | 150 |

For map symbols see back flap

❷ Wallerstein

Road map B2. 🚠 3,200. 🚌 🚉
ℹ️ Weinstr. 19, (09081) 27 600.
🌐 **markt-wallerstein.de**

Wallerstein is a small town at the foot of a hill on which stands a castle that commands a fine view of the Ries Basin. On the hilltop are the remains of 12th-century fortifications, which were destroyed in 1648, as well as a restaurant and a ducal brewery. **Fürst Wallerstein Brauhaus** is a traditional brewery that has been brewing beer since 1598, using locally sourced Spalter hops.

Albanskirche was built in 1242 in the Gothic style. The **plague column** commemorates the Marseilles plague of 1722–25, has figures of saints and is crowned with figures of St Mary and the Holy Trinity.

Plague column in Wallerstein

🏭 **Fürst Wallerstein Brauhaus**
Berg 78. **Tel** (09081) 78 21 21.
🎫 guided tours only.

❸ Oettingen

Road map B2. 🚠 5,200. 🚌 🚉
ℹ️ Schlossstr. 36, (09082) 70 952.
🌐 **oettingen.de**

This town, with an oval outline, was surrounded by a wall in the late 13th century. The town gates on the south side – the **Unteres Tor** and the **Königsturm**, which was built in the 16th century – still stands. Schlossstraße, the main street, is lined with half-timbered town houses built between the 15th and 18th centuries. The 15th-century Gothic **town hall** contains the local history museum.

Despite their elegance, the **town houses** pale in comparison to **Residenzschloss**, the resplendent Baroque residence of the Dukes of Oettingen-Spielberg, built in 1679–83. To the west the palace looks out over landscaped gardens, which are peopled with statues of dwarfs and a Hercules of 1678 based on the statue on the fountain in Augsburg by Adriaen de Vries. The palace, whose interior is decorated with stuccowork and mural paintings, is now the **Staatliches Museum für Völkerkunde**. Visitors can see the apartments and reception rooms and admire the collections of 18th-century pewter, porcelain and faience. The palace courtyard is surrounded by outbuildings and has a fountain dating from 1720–28 in the centre.

The **Jakobskirche** which stands nearby was remodelled in the Baroque style after 1680 and decorated with stuccowork by Matthias Schmuzer the Younger. Inside is an interesting pulpit and baptismal font from the last quarter of the 17th century, and numerous tombstones as well as plaques from the 15th to 18th centuries.

❹ Wemding

Road map B2. 🚠 5,600. 🚌 🚉
ℹ️ Mangoldstr. 5, (09092) 96 90 35.
🌐 **wemding.info**

Set on the rim of the Ries Basin, this charming little town retains its medieval character. The main square, lined with Renaissance and Baroque houses with typically Bavarian decorated gables, has often been used as a location by filmmakers.

Prominent among these houses is the Renaissance **town hall** of 1551–2. On Wallfahrtstraße, near the gate tower, is a typical mid-16th-century house with a corner oriel, now the **Gasthaus zum Weißen Hahn** inn. The tower of **Emmeramskirche** dominates the skyline. The church dates from the 11th century, but its current Baroque form is the result of rebuilding carried out in the 17th century.

Renaissance tombstone in Jakobskirche, Oettingen

Ries Basin

This crater, 25 km (15 miles) across, was made when a meteorite hit the Earth 15 million years ago. The impact melted the rocks, creating suevite, or Swabian rock, which the local people used as a building material. NASA carried out scientific studies on the crater and used it for astronauts who were to be sent to the Moon. They later found rock identical to suevite on the Moon. A suevite moon rock donated by NASA can be seen in the Rieskrater-Museum (see p247).

Suevite on the edge of the Ries Basin

It is worth taking a walk along the **defensive walls**, built in the first half of the 14th century and particularly well preserved on the north side of the town.

On the road leading out towards Oettingen the small pilgrimage chapel of **Maria Brünnlein** can be seen in the distance. The interior is decorated with Rococo mouldings and frescoes by Johann Baptist Zimmermann.

The Baroque palace and palace chapel at Leitheim

One of the courtyards in Harburg Castle

❺ Harburg

Road map B2. ▨ 5,500. 🚌 🚉
ℹ️ Schlossstr. 1, (09080) 96 99 24.
🌐 stadt-harburg-schwaben.de

The large **castle** was built by the Hohenstaufens before 1150. It was later acquired by the counts of Oettingen, and since 1731 has been in the possession of the Oettingen-Wallerstein family. It is one of the oldest, largest and best-preserved castles in southern Germany.

Dramatically situated on a high rocky hill overlooking the Wörnitz river valley, Harburg castle dominates the entire area. In the 14th and 15th centuries it was surrounded by walls set with towers. It has an outer and an inner gate on the west side, with a picturesque gatehouse dating from 1703. Within the walls stands **Michaelskirche**, the castle church. At the bottom of the castle hill nestles the small

town of Harburg. It is worth a visit for a walk around the charming and diminutive market square and along the winding streets, which have picturesque old houses.

❻ Kaisheim

Road map C2. ▨ 3,800. 🚌 🚉
ℹ️ Münsterplatz 5, (09099) 96 600.
🌐 kaisheim.de

The extensive complex of the former Cistercian monastery consists of the 14th-century Gothic **Mariae Himmelfahrtskirche** as well as the monastery itself, which has two cloisters dating from 1716–21. The monastery was converted into a prison in the 19th century. The exquisite Kaisersaal (Imperial Hall), with ornate stuccowork, was completed in about 1720.

Notable features of the church include the Baroque organ loft of 1677, whose carvings are ascribed to Andreas Thamasch. In the nave is a sarcophagus of 1434 with a statue of the founder of the original Romanesque church, who died in 1142, showing him holding a model of the church in his hands.

Crest in the Kaisersaal, Kaisheim

❼ Leitheim

Road map C2. 🚌 🚉 Kaisheim.
ℹ️ Münsterplatz 5, Kaisheim, (09099) 96 600.

Set high on a bank of the Danube, **Schloss Leitheim and a chapel** were built in 1685 to designs by Wölfl as a summer residence for Cistercian monks from the monastery at Kaisheim. For centuries the monks tended vineyards on the sunny slopes around the residence. Indeed, Leitheim was one of the centres of wine-making in the Danube region, and the quality of the wine produced here rivalled that of the Rhine wines.

The chapel was decorated in the late 17th century by artists from Wessobrunn. In the mid-18th century an additional storey and a mansard roof were added to the palace. The stucco-work and painting in the state rooms on the second floor are among the finest examples of Bavarian-Swabian Rococo. After 1835 the palace passed into the hands of the Tucher von Simmeldorf family. The owners organize highly popular chamber concerts here.

🏰 **Schloss Leitheim**
Schlossstr. 1. **Tel** (09097) 10 16.
Open May–Sep: by prior arrangement only.

... 91 51.

... ...dertag (first
ever... ...fest (Jul,
... xt in 2015),
Donauwo... ...tage (Oct).

Donauwörth is one of the largest
towns in Swabian Bavaria. It is
located at the confluence of
the Wörnitz and the Danube,
and its development was
shaped largely by its position
at the point where major trade
routes crossed the Danube.

Reichsstraße, the main street,
is lined with colourful gabled
houses and is one of the finest
streets in southern Germany.
It stretches from **Zu Unserer
Lieben Frau**, the church built
in 1444–67 and decorated with
15th- and 16th-century frescoes,
to the **town hall**, remodelled
in the Neo-Gothic style in 1854.

The west end of the town
is dominated by a former
Benedictine monastery, of
which the **Kreuzkirche**, built
by Josef Schmuzer in 1717–20,
formed a part.

Romantische Strasse

Information signpost at
Neuschwanstein

The Romantic Route follows
the course of the Roman
Via Claudia. Beginning in
Franconian Würzburg, it
passes through the towns
of Nördlingen, Donauwörth,
Augsburg, Landsberg,
Schongau, Steingaden
and Füssen, in southern
Bavaria, and ends at
Neuschwanstein, Ludwig
II's famous castle. The
best known and most
frequented of the tourist
routes in Germany, it is
particularly popular with
American and Japanese
tourists. Directions are
even given in Japanese.

The picturesque Reichsstraße in
Donauwörth

Not to be missed is a walk
along the **town walls**, which
run parallel to an arm of the
Wörnitz. The **Rieder Tor**, one
of the two town gates, houses
a museum dedicated to the
town's history. Also worth
visiting are the **Heimatmuseum** of local history and
the **Käthe-Kruse-Puppen-
Museum**, with a collection
of dolls made by Käthe Kruse.

Käthe-Kruse-Puppen-Museum
Pflegstr. 21a. **Tel** (0906) 78 91 70.
Open Apr and Oct: 2–5pm Tue–Sun;
May–Sep: 11am–5pm Tue–Sun; Nov–
Mar: 2–5pm Wed, Sat–Sun & public
hols; 25 Dec–6 Jan: 2–5pm daily.

Heimatmuseum
Insel Ried, Museumsplatz 2. **Tel** (0906)
78 91 70. **Open** May–Oct: 2pm–5pm
Tue–Sun; Nov–Apr: 2pm–5pm Wed,
Sat & Sun.

❾ Augsburg

See pp252–7.

❿ Sielenbach

Road map C3. 1,500.
Weissenhorn. Schwaigstr. 16,
(08258) 91 40. **sielenbach.de**

The pilgrimage church of
**Unserer Lieben Frau im
Birnbaum** (Mary in the Pear
Tree) is located at the southern
end of the town, which it
dominates. It is an exceptional
work of 17th-century Bavarian
architecture. It was built in

1661–8 by Konstantin Bader
to a design by Jakob von
Kaltenthal, a Commander of
the Teutonic Knights. It consists
of five circular, semi-circular
and oval rooms. In particular
the towers and onion domes
are unique, and are reminiscent
of an Eastern church.

The interior, which is lit by
large windows in the shape
of upright ovals and decorated
with stuccowork by Matthias
Schmuzer the Younger, is far
more unified.

The object of worship is a
late Gothic Pietà dating from
the early 16th century, to
which miraculous powers are
ascribed. It stands on the high
altar in a pear tree. The tree
and the name of the church
commemorate the miraculous
survival of the figure in 1632,
during the Thirty Years' War
when in the course of the
Swedish invasion the figure
survived thanks to its being
hidden in a pear tree.

Unserer Lieben Frau im Birnbaum, an
Eastern-style church in Sielenbach

⓫ Friedberg

Road map C3. 27,000.
Marienplatz 5, (0821) 60 02 611.
friedberg.de Friedberger
Zeit (every three years in Jul, the
next in 2016).

During the Middle Ages this
town was a fortress, its purpose
being to protect the region
from attacks by the inhabitants
of Augsburg. In about 1490
defensive walls set with
semicircular towers were added.

The Baroque town hall in Friedberg's main square

The medieval **castle** in the north of the town was destroyed during the Thirty Years' War and rebuilt in 1559. It now houses a local history museum, the **Museum Wittelsbacher Schloss**.

The streets are lined with outstanding houses dating from the 17th and 18th centuries. In the centre of the main square stands the **town hall**, built in 1673 and decorated in the style of Elias Holl. **Jakobskirche**, which has an unusual design, was built in 1871 in imitation of the Romanesque cathedral of St Zeno in Verona.

The finest building in Friedberg is **Herrgottsruh**, a pilgrimage church located in the east of the town. In the Middle Ages it was built as a rotunda resembling the Church of the Holy Sepulchre in Jerusalem. Fragments of the building were uncovered beneath the presbytery of the present church.

The latter, built in 1731–51 by Johann Benedikt Ettl, has a tall tower and imposing domed rotunda. The paintings in the presbytery and the dome are by Cosmas Damian Asam, while those in the nave are by Matthäus Günther. The Rococo mouldings are

by Franz Xaver Feichtmayer and Johann Michael Feichtmayr. The silver antependium of the high altar was made by Johann Georg Herkomer of Augsburg. The altar in the south aisle contains a 15th-century group of figures of the Sorrowing Christ to which miraculous powers are ascribed. Votive images fill the aisles.

🏛 **Museum Wittelsbacher Schloss**
Schlossstr. 21. **Tel** (0821) 600 21 48. **Open** 2–6pm Tue–Fri, 11am–5pm Sat–Sun and public holidays.

⑫ Roggenburg

Road map B3. 🚹 2,700. 🚌 🚊
🚹 Vohringen. Prälatenhof 2. **Tel** (07300) 96 960. 🌐 roggenburg.de

The towers of the town's former Premonstratensian monastery can be seen from a distance and rightly suggest that this is an exceptional building. Despite its monumentality, the cavernous interior of **Mariä-Himmelfahrt-Kirche**, which was built in the late 18th century, produces an impression of levity, and it is light even though the windows, which are concealed behind the columns, cannot be seen. The organ loft is one of the finest in Germany. However, the real rarities here are the two reliquaries with

Interior of the church in Roggenburg

painted images of the bodies of St Severinus and St Laurentius, in fine costume of the period. The monastery, built from 1732 to 1766, houses local government offices, although parts are open to the public.

Painting from Oberes Tor, one of Weißenhorn's town gates

⑬ Weißenhorn

Road map A3. 🚹 13,200. 🚌 🚊
🚹 Memmingerstr. 59. **Tel** (07309) 840. 🌐 weissenhorn.de

Neat, quaint and tidy, Weißenhorn is a quintessential small Swabian town. Its historic character is pre-served virtually intact. The main thoroughfare is the Hauptstraße, running from a large, irregular square where the church and palace stand, to the **Unteres Tor** (Lower Gate). The 15th-century **Oberes Tor** (Upper Gate), flanked by circular towers, opens on to the square. Adjoining the gate is the former **weigh-house**, dating from the 16th century, and the **Neues Rathaus**, built in the 18th century, which together form a harmonious group.

The **Altes Schloss**, dating from 1460–70, and **Neues Schloss**, built by the Fuggers (*see p257*) in the 16th century, are interconnected. The dominant building in the town is **Mariä-Himmelfahrt-Kirche**, built in 1864–71, one of the finest examples of the revivalist trend in Swabia's religious architecture.

❾ Street-by-Street: Augsburg

Bavaria's third-largest city, Augsburg has a population of just over a quarter of a million and is the main university town of Bavarian Swabia. Founded by the Emperor Augustus on the final stretch of the trans-Alpine Via Claudia, it was a bridgehead for Italian culture. It stands at the confluence of the rivers Lech and Wertach, and because of its system of canals it has been called the Venice of the North. Tourists are drawn by the city's history and magic. It is the city of the Protestant Confession of Augsburg and a centre of the goldsmith's art. It is also the birthplace of Bertolt Brecht, Rudolf Diesel and the ancestors of Mozart.

Period houses
on Steingasse were destroyed by World War II air raids in 1941, but were rebuilt in the 1960s.

STEINGASSE

Dom

RATHA
PLA

PHILIPPINE-WELSER-STR.

Augustusbrunnen
This statue of the Emperor Augustus on the fountain on Rathausplatz is a copy. The original, cast in bronze in 1588, is in Augsburg's Town Hall.

★ Annakirche
The chapel of the Fugger family (1509–12) is an architectural jewel. It is the earliest Renaissance building in Germany.

ANNA STR.

BGM.-FISCHER-

★ Maximilianmuseum
The museum, currently being renovated, is located in two of the city's finest patrician palaces, built in 1543–6. Exhibits include artifacts by local goldsmiths.

Zeughaus
The old arsenal, which was begun in 1607 by Elias Holl, features a beautiful frontage built in the Mannerist style by Josef Heintz.

KÖNIGS–
PLATZ

ZEUGGA

| 0 metres | 50 |
| 0 yards | 50 |

Key

— Suggested route

The Perlachturm is a tower 70 m (230 ft) on the west front of Peterskirche. Its height was increased through the centuries, and in 1616 Elias Holl added the steeple.

VISITORS' CHECKLIST

Practical Information
Map C3.
Tel 012 345 6789.
273,000. Schiessgrabenstr. 14, (0821) 50 20 70.
Frühjahrsplärrer (week after Easter), Herbstplärrer (Aug/Sep), Friedensfest (8 Aug), Mozartsommer (Aug), Christkindlmarkt (Dec).
w augsburg-tourismus.de email: **tourismus@regio-augsburg.de**

Transport
5 km (3 miles) north.

★ Rathaus
Built in 1615–20 by Elias Holl, Augsburg's town hall is the finest secular Mannerist building in Europe. The famous Golden Hall is on the second floor.

Merkurbrunnen fountain has a sculpture cast by Wolfgang Neidhart in 1599 after a model by Adriaen de Vries. It is crowned by a statue of Mercury, god of trade.

Moritzkirche, a Gothic-Baroque church, was modernized several times over the centuries. Destroyed by bombing in 1944, it was rebuilt in 1946–51.

Maximilianstraße
Augsburg's main street, with its two fountains, Mercury and Herkules, by Adriaen de Vries, is one of the finest in southern Germany.

St-Ulrich-und-St-Afra-Kirche

Fuggerhäuser
The two adjacent palaces at Maximilianstraße 36 each have elegant, airy Renaissance courtyards.

Exploring Augsburg

Augsburg is known for its secular buildings. Although many of them were destroyed by air raids in 1944, they were rebuilt after World War II. The city's appearance was largely defined in the early 17th century by Elias Holl, the architect of many of the buildings here, most notably the Mannerist town hall. The surrounding countryside, with its forests and the Kuhsee, provides the inhabitants with ideal places for weekend outings.

The entrance to the Baroque Fürstbischöfliche Residenz

The Gothic Dom Unserer Lieben Frau

🔼 Dom Unserer Lieben Frau
Frauentorstr. 1.

The cathedral, whose origins go back to the 9th century, retains the twin towers on the west front that were built in 1150, and two Romanesque crypts. It was remodelled in the Gothic style in the 14th and 15th centuries.

Among the cathedral's many notable features is the world's oldest Romanesque stained-glass window, dating from 1140 and depicting figures of the Prophets. Its 11th-century Romanesque bronze doors, with scenes from the Old Testament, are now on display in the Diocesan Museum.

🔲 Fürstbischöfliche Residenz
Fronhof 10.

The former bishop's residence was given its present appearance in 1743–52. Since 1817 it has housed the government offices of Bavarian Swabia.

It was in the ornate Festsaal in the west wing that the Emperor Karl V received the historic Confession of Augsburg in 1530. The Hofgarten adjoining the residence contains a fountain and 8th-century gnomes.

🔲 Stadtmetzg
Metzgplatz 1.

This Mannerist building was built by Elias Holl in 1606–09 for the butchers' guild. A technological innovation of the time was routing one of the town's canals beneath the cellars of the Stadtmetzg so that they would be kept cool for the effective storage of perishable food.

🔲 Fountains

Augsburg is renowned for its beautiful fountains, of which there are more than 30. The most famous are the Mannerist Augustus, Mercury and Hercules fountains, made in the late 16th century to mark the city's 1,600th anniversary. The two latter, located on Maximilianstraße, were designed by Adriaen de Vries (although they are copies, the originals now being in the Maximilianmuseum). Also noteworthy are the Neptunbrunnen of 1536, the Georgsbrunnen of 1565, and the Art Nouveau Gold-schmiedebrunnen of 1913.

🔲 Schaezlerpalais
Maximilianstr. 46. **Tel** (0821) 32 44 102. **Open** 10am–5pm Tue–Sun. Staatsgalerie: **Open** 10am–5pm Tue–Sun. 🖼

The palace, the finest Rococo building in Augsburg, was built in 1765–70. The famous Festsaal features fine stucco-work, paintings, carvings, chandeliers and candelabras.

The palace's art galleries – the **Staatsgalerie** and the Deutsche Barockgalerie – contain works by such masters as Dürer, Hans Holbein the Elder, van Dyck and Tiepolo.

Town Hall

This, Europe's largest and finest Mannerist town hall, was built by Elias Holl in 1615–20. The building's showpiece is the Golden Hall. Its exquisite ornate ceiling is attached to the roof beams by means of 27 chains.

Destroyed during air raids in 1944, the town hall was meticulously restored, and the ceiling of the Golden Hall was reconstructed in 1985 to commemorate the 2,000th anniversary of the foundation of the city in 15 BC.

Onion-domed flanking towers

Gable with painted coat of arms

Windows of the Golden Hall on the second floor

For hotels and restaurants in this region see p269 and p283

🏠 Fuggerhäuser
Maximilianstr. 36/38.

These two neighbouring early 16th-century Renaissance palaces of the Fugger family were rebuilt after being destroyed in 1944. The splendour of the original buildings with their inner courtyards can be seen in the arcaded marble Damenhof. The palace was inhabited by the family of Jakob II der Reiche Fugger and his descendant Anton.

🏛 Zeughaus
Zeugplatz 6.

The arsenal, Elias Holl's first project and also one of his finest works, was built in 1607. The façade is decorated with a bronze sculpture by Hans Reichle depicting St Michael overcoming Satan.

🏠 Annakirche
Im Annahof 2.

The former Carmelite church of St Anne, now Protestant, was built in the 14th century, at the same time as the monastery. It was rebuilt in the 15th century and the tower, designed by Elias Holl, was added in 1607. In the mid-18th century the interior was remodelled in the Rococo style. It contains one of the earliest organ lofts in Europe, dating from 1512.

An exceptional example of Renaissance art is the burial chapel of the Fuggers (1509–12), with epitaphs by Albrecht Dürer, a sculpted *Lamentation* by Hans Daucher, and figures of putti on the balustrade.

Putto in the burial chapel in Annakirche

🏛 Römisches Museum
Dominikanergasse 15. **Tel** (0821) 32 44 131. **Open** 10am–8pm Tue, 10am–5pm Wed–Sun.

The Roman Museum is housed in the former Domini-can mon-astery, built in 1513–15. The two-naved hall, which is divided by a row of columns, was rebuilt in the Baroque style in 1716–24. The ceiling, which dates from that time, is decorated with religious stuccowork and paintings. The museum has

---

Augsburger Puppenkiste

The celebrated Augsburg Puppet Shows take place in the central part of the Heilig-Geist-Spital, built in 1623–31 by Elias Holl. These outstanding shows are always played to a packed auditorium. It is not only the colourful marionettes themselves but the skilled artistry with which they are manipulated that inspires wonder. Such is their reputation that the shows are also broadcast on German television.

Scene from a puppet show

---

interesting exhibits from the Roman and as well as the early Medieval periods, including a gilded horse's head that once formed part of a Roman equestrian statue.

🏠 St-Ulrich-und-St-Afra-Kirche
Ulrichplatz 23.

This late Gothic triple-nave basilica is the most recent in a succession of churches built for the Benedictine monastery that has stood here since about 1000, but that was dissolved in the early 19th century. Work on the basilica began in 1474 and continued for almost 140 years. Although two towers were planned, only the northern one was built, in 1594. Rising a height of 93 m (305 ft) high, it is visible from a great distance.

Baroque grille, St-Ulrich-und-St-Afra-Kirche

The Mannerist furnishings were added in 1604–08. The exquisitely designed and crafted altar, pulpit, organ loft and stalls harmonize well with the late Gothic architecture of the interior. The nave and aisles are separated by a delicate grille of 1/12.

🏛 Rotes Tor and City Walls
The Rotes Tor (Red Gate) was built by Elias Holl in 1622, replacing the medieval gate. Leading in from the road that followed the old Roman Via Claudia, it was the main gate into the city. The Rotes Tor, together with the Wallanlage and the Heilig-Geist-Spital, are the finest group of buildings designed by Elias Holl.

Large sections of the city walls still stand to the north and east, as do the walls surrounding the Jakobervorstadt, with two bastions of about 1540, and the Gothic Jakobertor. There is a landing stage for canoes at the tower of the Oblatterwall bastion.

✡ Synagogue
Halderstr. 8. Jüdisches Kulturmuseum: **Tel** (0821) 51 36 58. **Open** 9am–6pm Tue–Thu (to 8pm every 1st Wed of month), 9am–4pm Fri, 10am–5pm Sun. 📷

Built in 1913–17, the synagogue is one of the finest to be built in Europe at the time. The exquisite interior is crowned by a tall dome decorated in the Byzantine style. The **Jüdisches Kulturmuseum** (Jewish Culture Museum) is laid out in one of the wings of the synagogue.

The Fuggerei of Augsburg

Among Augsburg's main tourist attractions is one of the world's oldest public housing projects. It was established by Jakob II Fugger, "the Rich", together with his brothers, for the people of Augsburg who had fallen on hard times. Built by Thomas Krebs in 1514–23, it was called the Fuggerei in honour of its founder. Situated east of Rathausplatz, in the Jakobervorstadt, this walled "town within a town" has retained its medieval atmosphere. This can best be savoured outside the tourist season, when it is less crowded. The Fuggerei is entered through gates that bear the original dedication, the date 1519 and the Fuggers' armorials.

★ **Fuggereimuseum**
On view here is an apartment (bedroom and kitchen) furnished in the style of the period.

★ **Markuskirche**
The church was built in 1581 by Johannes Holl, father of the renowned Elias Holl. Destroyed in 1944, it was subsequently rebuilt.

0 metres 20
0 yards 20

Fountain
At the point where Herrengasse and Mittlere Gasse meet, forming a small square, stands a modest fountain. The focal point of the Fuggerei, it is also the favourite meeting place both of the local residents and of tourists.

Key

— Suggested route

For hotels and restaurants in this region see p269 and p283

Gardens at the rear of the houses in the Fuggerei

Exploring the Fuggerei

The estate originally comprised 53 buildings designed to house 106 families. Partly forming a continuous, symmetrical ensemble, they stand on an uneven plot of land and are surrounded by a wall with five gates.

The houses have modest façades and steep roofs with stepped gables. Each front door still has its bell-pull and iron handle, and the exterior walls still have sandstone plaques with the old house numbers inscribed on them.

The Fuggerei was badly damaged by the air raids of 1944. During the painstaking process of reconstruction, which was carried out in 1947–55 and was financed by the Fugger estate, 14 additional houses were built.

Today about 200 people live in the Fuggerei. All the houses have been modernized and have electricity, heating and other modern conveniences. The estate of the Fugger family decides who can live in the Fuggerei. Designated for needy people, this welfare housing project houses Catholics who must have lived in Augsburg for at least two years. Residents pay a nominal annual rent equal to 1 Rhenish guilder (88 cents), in return for which they undertake to say three daily prayers for the founders. There is also supplement of €46 per month

Herrengasse, the main street in the Fuggerei

to finance communal services. An interesting feature of the Fuggerei is the fine late Gothic oriel of 1504–07 on the corner of the Seigniory House by the gate on Jakoberstraße. It was transferred from the bombed ruins of a house belonging to the Höchstetter family, contemporaries of the Fuggers. The **Seigniory House,** which was rebuilt after 1954, contains on its ground floor a Gothic chapel that was trans-ferred here in 1962 from the ruined house of the Welsers.

Markuskirche, in Herrengasse, is decorated with a tall shaped gable and has an Angelus bell. It is furnished with items from various other churches. A *Crucifixion* by Jacopo Palma the Younger of about 1600 can be seen on the Mannerist high altar. Ulrich Fugger's epitaph, depicting the deceased wrapped in a shroud, was designed by Albrecht Dürer and made by Adolf Daucher in 1512–15.

The resident of the house at Mittlere Gasse 14 was Franz Mozart, great-grandfather of the composer Wolfgang Amadeus. He made himself unpopular with his clients by carrying out burials for the executioner, which was considered to be a disgraceful deed. As a result he lost business and became so impoverished that he had to go and live in the Fuggerei.

Memorial plaque to Franz Mozart, one-time resident of the Fuggerei

The Fuggers

The career of the Fuggers began in 1367, when Hans Fugger, a native of Graben, came to Augsburg. Jakob I (who died in 1459) founded the family of merchants and bankers that still exists today. His sons Ulrich, Georg and particularly Jakob II, "the Rich", acquired unheard-of wealth, ensuring a life of opulence for the entire family. Jakob II was banker to emperors, kings and popes. He funded the election of Karl V as German Emperor. He was also known as a patron of the arts, and thanks partly to him Renaissance art took root in Germany. He also founded social institutions. Once the owners of 100 villages, the Fuggers still own several castles in Bavaria.

Monument to Hans Jakob Fugger, Augsburg

The Imperial Hall of the former Augustine monastery in Wettenhausen

⑭ Wettenhausen

Road map B3. 🚌 🚉 Günzburg.
Abbey: Kammeltal, Dossenberger-str. 46. **Tel** (08223) 40 040.

Standing like a fortress, the old Augustinian monastery in Wettenhausen dominates the surrounding landscape. **Mariä-Himmelfahrt-Kirche**, originally a Romanesque church, was rebuilt in the late Gothic style in the early 16th century and remodelled in the Baroque style in 1670. The frescoes, of about 1685, and the highly decorative altars and pulpit, dating from the same period, create a unified interior. The altar in the south chapel features a fine late Gothic Coronation of the Virgin carved in 1524.

Part of the **abbey**, including the Imperial Hall and the cloistered courtyard, are open to the public. The rooms in the cloister are visible through a decorative wrought-iron grille. One of them contains a figure of Christ seated on a donkey made in 1456, probably in the workshop of Hans Multscher of Ulm.

⑮ Günzburg

Road map B3. 🚌 20,000. 🚌 🚉
ℹ️ Schloßplatz 1, (08221) 200 444.
🌐 guenzburg.de

The origins of this sizeable town at the confluence of the rivers Günz and Danube go back to Roman times. Much of it has been pedestrianized, and it invites leisurely strolls through its attractive streets.

Münzgasse, lined with 17th- and 18th-century houses with projecting upper storeys, is especially picturesque.

The main square, closed off by the 14th-century **Unteres Tor** (Lower Gate), is surrounded by Baroque houses with typically Swabian gables. These houses recall the days when the town was at its height. Notable is **Brentanohaus** at No. 8, built in 1747 with a tiled mansard roof and Rococo mouldings on its elegant façade.

Beside the old Franciscan monastery stands the **Frauenkirche**, built in 1736–41 by Dominikus Zimmermann. Substantial fragments of the 15th-century town walls, defensive towers and gateways survive.

Houses in Münzgasse, one of Günzburg's picturesque streets

⑯ Dillingen

Road map B3. 🚌 18,000. 🚌 🚉
ℹ️ Königstr. 37, (09071) 54 208, 54 209. 🌐 dillingen-donau.de

For centuries Dillingen, the spiritual capital of Swabia and a town dubbed the "Rome of Swabia", was the seat of the bishops of Augsburg and a major university town. The main street, Königstraße, lined with patrician town houses, defines the town's character. Königstraße leads into Kardinal von Waldburgstraße, on which the elongated Baroque façade of the **Jesuit University** rises. It was built in 1688–9 to a design by Michael Thumb and visitors can admire the Rococo Golden Hall within. The former **college** beside the university has a fine Baroque library, which occupies two floors and has furnishings carved by Johann Georg Bschorer. The highlight of the town is the formerly Jesuit **Mariä-Himmelfahrt-Kirche**, built in the early 17th century by Johann Alberthal. The early Baroque architecture of the building and its

Lion outside the castle in Dillingen

Rococo stuccowork, painting and furnishings combine to produce a splendid ensemble. The high altar still has its *Theatrum Sacrum*, where the tradition of performing Passion plays at Easter was recently revived.

The early Rococo **Franciscan monastery** and **church** were designed by Johann Georg Fischer. The stately 13th-century **castle**, which before the secularization of the state was the seat of the capital and of the bishops of Augsburg, has preserved its defensive character despite rebuilding on numerous occasions over the centuries. Fragments of the town walls, set with towers and pierced by the **Mitteltor** (Middle Gate), can still be seen today.

Roman ruins in Faimingen, a suburb of Lauingen

⑰ Lauingen

Road map B3. 🚊 10,500. 🚌 🚉
ℹ️ Herzog-Georg-Str. 17, (09072) 99 80. 🔼 **lauingen**.de

Set on a high bank overlooking the Danube, this town has largely preserved its medieval char-acter. It has an oval outline and was once surrounded by walls, the surviving parts of which are a **gate** and two bastions.

The slender outlines of two tall towers that dominate the town can be seen from a distance. The more distinctive of the two is the former watchtower that stands in the main square. Exceptionally tall and narrow, it was built in 1457–78 together with the adjacent arcades containing market stalls, and was extended in 1571. It is known as the **Schimmelturm** (Grey Mare Tower) because of the image of the horse near the bottom, which has been renewed and repainted several times.

The **town hall**, built in 1782 to a Neo-Classical design by Lorenz J Quaglio, was erected on the orders of the Elector Karl Theodor despite strong opposition from the townspeople.

Martinskirche, the parish church built in 1515, is one of the last Gothic hall-churches to have been built in southern Germany. Its triple-nave interior with web vaulting is unparalleled in height and the walls and ceilings are decorated with frescoes painted in 1521.

Among the many tombs and epitaphs is a fine cenotaph that is the symbolic tomb of Elisabeth, wife of the Palatine, who died in 1563. The tomb is surrounded by a wrought-iron grille and on it lies a white marble figure of the deceased supported by four lions. The tall free-standing **belfry** is, with the Schimmelturm, a defining feature of the town's skyline.

Environs
In the suburb of Faimingen, on the road to Günzburg, the remains of Roman buildings can be seen. The partially reconstructed **Temple of Apollo Grannus**, the Roman deity who also came to be worshipped by the Celts, bears witness to Lauingen's long history.

The Schimmelturm, the tallest tower in Lauingen

⑱ Höchstädt

Road map B3. 🚊 6,500. 🚌 🚉
ℹ️ Herzog Philipp-Ludwig-Str. 10, (09074) 44 12. 🔼 **hoechstaedt**.de

This little town on the banks of the Danube is flanked by its church and its castle. On the west side are the church and the town hall, on a square located between two streets that lead to the castle.

The late Gothic **Mariä-Himmelfahrt-Kirche**, which was completed in about 1520, is decorated with frescoes in the same style, painted in 1520–30 and also with Mannerist frescoes in a contrastingly florid style dating from about 1600. The town's finest historic building is the turret-shaped Gothic sacristy, built in attractive sandstone in 1480–90. The Baroque altar was added in 1695.

The polygonal **chapel** beside the church was built in 1664. It features a deep niche containing a Pietà dating from the first quarter of the 18th century. Above the statue is a theatrical scene depicting Christ and the Apostles on the Mount of Olives. The scene, consisting of figures set against a painted background, was created by Johann Michael Fischer in 1760.

The **Heimatmuseum** has numerous collections of objects relating to local history, including a display of 9,000 tin soldiers re-creating the Battle of Höchstädt that took place in 1760.

On a hill overlooking the town stands the Renaissance **castle**, built in about 1589 to replace the medieval seat of Duke Philip Ludwig, the Palatine of Neuburg. Well restored, it is now used as the museum's headquarters. The castle complex has an almost square plan with a central courtyard, four circular corner towers and a chapel in the west wing. The main entrance is a doorway flanked by pairs of columns, with coats of arms in the tympanum and a barrel-vaulted archway with coffered ceiling.

🏛️ **Heimatmuseum**
Marktplatz 7. **Tel** (09074) 44 12.
Open Apr–Sep: 9am–6pm every Sun.

The doorway of the castle in Höchstädt

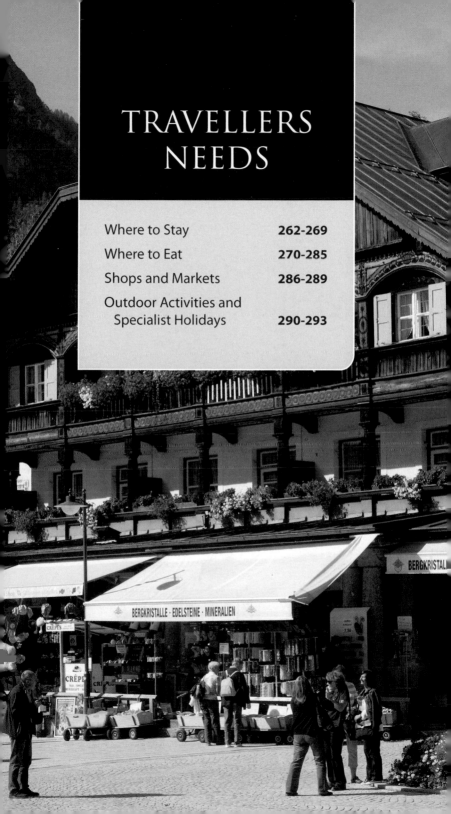

TRAVELLERS NEEDS

Where to Stay   **262-269**

Where to Eat   **270-285**

Shops and Markets   **286-289**

Outdoor Activities and Specialist Holidays   **290-293**

WHERE TO STAY

The Bavarian Alps are Germany's most popular tourist destination. The region offers a wide variety of hotels with different levels of service. Finding somewhere to stay, either in Munich itself or throughout the Bavarian Alps, is rarely a problem, whatever the requirements. As well as luxury hotels, which are often converted stately palaces or romantic castles, and international chains such as the Marriott, Hilton or Sheraton, travellers to the Bavarian Alps have a choice of many small hotels and guesthouses. However, accommodation of any sort can be harder to find in Munich during the Oktoberfest and when trade fairs take place in the city, and during festivals and public holidays, when tourist resorts become more crowded.

The Vier Jahreszeithen Kempinski hotel in Munich *(see p266)*

Finding Accommodation

In towns and cities hotels are usually in or near the historic centre or close to tourist attractions. When choosing somewhere to stay, try to ensure that it is not near a noisy street, a night-spot, or a church, as the ringing of church bells can awaken the deepest sleeper.

If you decide on a hotel in central Munich, you may need to enquire about parking. If you choose a hotel further from the centre, make sure that it is near public transport links. Most hotels, including luxury hotels, are on the periphery of the Old Town and in Schwabing. There are also hotels around Munich's main railway station, although these are not high standard. Hotels belonging to major groups such as the Marriott and Sheraton are located near main highways.

The Range of Hotels

Many hotels are marked with stars indicating their quality (and cost). Top-class hotels usually have their own high-quality restaurants, as well as swimming pool, gyms, saunas and laundry facilities. Those outside cities may also have tennis courts and golf links.

There is also a network of modern bed-and-breakfast hotels with far fewer amenities. On motorways and major roads, you can find motels or *Rasthäuser*, which are basically restaurants with single-night accommodation.

In tourist towns a common type of accommodation is *Halbpension* (half-board lodgings), where a hot meal is offered in addition to breakfast, or *Vollpension*, (lodging with full board).

All hotels and other types of accommodation are extremely clean. Toilet and bathroom facilities, even when shared, are of a high standard. Regardless of the category of the establishment, guests are often offered many extras.

Hotel Prices

Hotel prices vary greatly. A single room can range from €40–75 in a tourist-class hotel to €150, in a top-class hotel, and over €300 in a luxury

Guests checking into a small hotel

◄ Hotel Schiffmeister with the Alps in the background, Berchtesgaden

Quirky dining area at Hotel Hirsch *(see p269)* in Füssen

establishment. Prices in Munich are naturally higher than elsewhere, and highest during the Oktoberfest.

At holiday and spa resorts a three-tier price system operates – high season, mid-season and low season. Prices at high season can be double those of low season.

Many hotels offer reductions at weekends and even if you turn up without a reservation, you may be able to negotiate a discount. If you are planning a longer stay, you may also be able to negotiate a discount, especially during those times of the year when business is slack.

How to Book

Hotel accommodation can be booked direct by telephone, as well as by e-mail or through the Internet. Travellers already in Bavaria can obtain brochures and lists of addresses at tourist offices.

When making a reservation, you will need to confirm the method of payment. An advance payment or credit card details will sometimes be requested.

On arrival guests are asked to complete a registration form and may be requested to show their passport. Full payment is made when checking out and, especially

in the case of small provincial hotels, it is always worth making sure in advance what means of payment are accepted. In health spas an additional charge known as a *Kurtaxe* is payable. In top-class and luxury hotels, tips are expected for additional services. It is also customary, even in modest hotels, to leave a few Euros for the chambermaid.

Disabled Travellers

An increasing number of hotels and hostels cater for disabled travellers. Most

The ornate courtyard of the Opera hotel in Munich *(see p267)*

have ramp access and a few rooms with bathrooms and toilets adapted for wheelchair users. Facilities are, however, most likely to be better in hotels of a higher standard than in budget hotels.

Handicapped-Reisen Deutschland is a guide that lists hotels in Germany with facilities for disabled people. Information can also be obtained from BAGH and CBF *(see p261)*.

Travelling with Children

Travelling with children in the Bavarian Alps should not present any special problems. Most hotels will provide an additional bed or cot, often at no extra charge.

Many hotels have children's corners – play areas equipped with children's furniture as well as games and toys – and some have babysitting facilities. If a child is sick, the hotel's reception will call for a doctor or paediatrician.

A high chair for toddlers is standard equipment in many restaurants, while menus often include the option of smaller portions for children.

Tourist resorts offer special programmes of supervised activities for children.

Rooms in Private Houses

Visitors should note that bed and breakfast accommodation is not widespread in cities. However, in popular tourist areas and most smaller towns, you will often come across houses with a sign that says *"Zimmer"* (rooms). The sign will be accompanied by another, saying either *"frei"* (vacancies) or *"belegt"* (no vacancies).

Prices for such rooms are relatively low – often as reasonable as €15 per person. Other benefits are a homely atmosphere and a lavish breakfast. Toilets and bathrooms are usually shared, but rooms have washbasins and telephones.

Stunning view of the Mandarin Oriental

Holiday Apartments

For visitors spending their holiday in one particular place, holiday apartments *(Ferienwohnung)* are the best and cheapest type of accommodation. They are available in all holiday resorts, with brochures at tourist information centres.

The size, standard and price of apartments vary. Most have a kitchen, TV, vacuum cleaner, iron, bookshelves, and cupboard with glasses and tablecloths.

Holiday apartments are found mainly in private houses and apartment blocks, and in some larger hotels. They are rented for at least a week. An additional charge for final cleaning *(Endreinigung)* is often levied.

Farm Stays

Staying on a farm *(Bauernhof)* is a popular and inexpensive way of spending a holiday. It is particularly suitable for families with children. Rooms in large farmhouses or separate apartments are provided, and range from modest to luxurious. Among other activities, guests have the opportunity to help with the daily farm work, and children can feed the animals. A popular attraction is the delicious food, particularly the fresh dairy produce.

Another type of getaway is a riding holiday. Guests stay on horse or pony farms *(Reiterhöfe* and *Ponyhöfe)*, and go horse-riding or pony-trekking.

Youth Hostels

Almost every sizeable Bavarian town has a youth hostel *(Jugendherberge)*. These divide into four categories according to their location and standard. Many are relatively comfortable, although often the only available beds will be in a dormitory. Toilets and bathrooms are usually communal. Almost all youth hostels have dining rooms where breakfast and hot meals are served. Many hostels have their own sports facilities. The cost of accommodation is about €13 per night, and about €22 per night in Munich. In popular tourist resorts early booking is recommended.

Bavarian youth hostels are open to anyone, though discounts are available for members and priority given to those under the age of 27.

Mountain Shelters

Mountain shelters offering food, rest and sometimes accommodation to skiers and hikers are found in many places in the Bavarian Alps. The German Alpine Association (Deutscher Alpenverein - DAV) alone has some 100 shelters. Members can use them at a discount and have priority in

Logo of the German Youth Hostel Association

booking. Along with individual rooms, the shelters have bunk beds in communal rooms.

Shelters are usually open during the summer months, from May or June to September or October. Shelters near skiing pistes and along the most popular hiking trails are also open in winter.

Camping

Southern Bavaria's many campgrounds are usually in picturesque locations and ideal for peaceful holidays. Although they vary in size and standard, most have good toilet and washing facilities, and may also have a shop and café. Many also offer activity programmes. Most campgrounds are open April to October, although some are open year-round.

Gasthöfe

For travellers looking for unpretentious accommodation, roadside inns known as *Gasthöfe*, and found throughout Bavaria, are attractive and convenient. The sign *"Gasthof"* will probably be accompanied by another saying *"Zimmer"* (rooms). Prices are very affordable – usually between €25 and €40 for a double room. Drinking beer and eating simple homemade fare is one of the great pleasures of staying in a *Gasthof*.

A mountain shelter for hikers and skiers near Zugspitze

Spa Resorts

The bracing mountain air, and the many mineral springs and curative muds in the Bavarian Alps, have led to a large number of spa resorts. Most have the word *"Bad"* (bath) before the name of the town. In these resorts, a spa tax *(Kurtaxe)* is added to the room rate. This small additional charge allows for a reduction on the entry charge to many cultural and sporting facilities, and various kinds of therapy on offer.

Bavarian spas specialize mostly in respiratory and circulatory disorders and rheumatic ailments. Visitors to the spas have excellent rest and recuperation facilities at their disposal, with doctors and convalescence specialists to monitor their health.

Recommended Hotels

The hotel recommendations on the following pages have been allocated one of several categories. *Pensions* and *Guesthouses*

A well-kept *Gasthof*, one of the many roadside inns in Bavaria

cover smaller, family-run and usually less expensive places. *Mid-range, Budget* and *Modern* hotels are chain hotels or similar good-value standbys. *Historic* hotels are set in older buildings with a palpable sense of the past, whereas *Boutique* and *Minimalist* hotels offer stylish

accommodation, often with a modern feel. The final fifth category, *Luxury*, covers all the world-class places where you can spoil yourself. Places highlighted as DK Choice are especially recommended and guarantee a memorable night's stay.

DIRECTORY

Information on Accommodation & Reservations

Bayern Tourismus Marketing Gmbh
Leopoldstr. 146, Munich.
Tel (089) 21 23 97 0.
W **bayern.by**

Tourismusamt München
Neues Rathaus,
Marienplatz. **Tel** (089) 23 39 65 00. **Open** 10am–8pm Mon–Fri, 10am–5pm Sat, 10am–4pm Sun. Hauptbahnhof, Bahnhofplatz 2.
Open 9am–8pm Mon–Sat, 10am–6pm Sun.
W **muenchen-tourist.de**

Bed & Breakfast

Bed & Breakfast Mitwohnzentrale
Schulstr. 31, Munich.
Tel (089) 16 88 781.
W **bedandbreakfast.de**

City Mitwohnzentrale
Lämmerstr. 6, Munich.
Tel (089) 19 430.

Farm Stays

AG Urlaub & Freizeit auf dem Lande
Lindhooper Str. 63 27283 Verden.
Tel (04231) 96650.
W **bauernhofferien.de**

Zentrale für den Landurlaub Landschriften–Verlag GmbH
Maarstr. 96, 53227 Bonn.
Tel (0228) 96 30 20.
W **bauernhofurlaub. com**

Youth Hostels

DJH München Park
Miesingstr. 4, Munich.
Tel (089) 78 57 67 70.

DJH München City
Wendl-Dietrich-Str. 20, Munich.
Tel (089) 20 24 44 90.

Haus International
Elisabethstr. 87, Munich.
Map 1 A1.
Tel (089) 12 00 60.
W **haus-international.de**

Landesverband Bayern des DJH
Mauerkircherstr. 5, Munich.
Tel (089) 92 20 980.
W **djh.de**

Mountain Shelters

DAV Summit Club
Am Perlacher Forst 186, 81545 Munich.
Tel (089) 64 24 00.
W **dav-summit-club.de**

Verband Deutscher Gebirgs- und Wandervereine e.V
Wilhelmshöher Allee 157–159, 34121 Kassel.
Tel (0561) 93 87 30.
W **wanderverband.de**

Camping Sites

Deutscher Camping Club
Mandlstr. 28, Munich.
Map2 F2.
Tel (089) 38 01 420.W **camping-club.de**

Langwieder See
Eschenrieder Str. 119, Munich. **Tel** (089) 86 41 566.

München-Obermenzing
Lochhausener Str. 59.
Tel (089) 81 12 235.

München-Tahlkirchen
Zentralländstraße 49.
Tel (089) 72 31 707.

Disabled Travellers

Bundesarbeits gemeinschaft Selbsthilfe e.V
Kirchfeldstr. 149, 40215 Düsseldorf
Tel (0211) 31 00 60.
W **bag-selbsthilfe.de**

Bundesverband 'Selbsthilfe' Körperbehinderter e.V. (BSK)
Altkrautheimerstr. 20, 74238 Krautheim.
Tel (06 294) 428 10.
W **bsk-ev.org**

Club Behinderter und ihrer Freunde (CBF)
Pallaswiesenstr. 123a, 64293 Darmstadt
Tel (06151) 81 220.
W **cbf-da.de**

Where to Stay

Munich

Old Town (South)

Daniel €
Mid-range **Map** 3 A2
Sonnenstraße 5, 80331
Tel *(089) 548240*
Ⓦ hotel-daniel.de
Modern hotel with corporate-style decor. Friendly staff.

Deutsche Eiche €
Boutique **Map** 3 C3
Reichenbachstraße 13, 80469
Tel *(089) 231166*
Ⓦ deutsche-eiche.com
This stylish hotel is popular with young, trendy guests. Well-located, and complete with a bar and sauna.

DK Choice

**Motel One München
Sendlinger Tor** €
Modern **Map** 3 A3
Herzog-Wilhelm-Str. 28, 80331
Tel *(089) 51777250*
Ⓦ motel-one.com
This fantastic budget chain has taken off in Germany over the last decade. The rooms, with turquoise decor, have a certain minimalist elegance. There is a 24-hour lounge and café-bar as well.

Pension Seibel €
Pension **Map** 3 C3
Reichenbachstraße 8, 80469
Tel *(089) 2319180*
Ⓦ seibel-hotels-munich.de
Family-run, with traditional Bavarian furnishings.

Asam Hotel €€
Modern **Map** 3 A2
Josephspitalstraße 3, 80331
Tel *(089) 2309700*
Ⓦ hotel-asam.de
This hip hotel with its 1980s ambience offers bright rooms.

Concorde €€
Minimalist **Map** 4 D2
Herrnstraße 38–40, 80539
Tel *(089) 224515*
Ⓦ concorde-muenchen.de
Spartan rooms with a friendly vibe. Wi-Fi available at a charge.

Hotel am Viktualienmarkt €€
Mid-range **Map** 3 B3
Utzschneiderstraße 14, 80469
Tel *(089) 2311090*
Ⓦ hotel-am-viktualienmarkt.de
Comfortable hotel that serves a great breakfast buffet with home-made jams and local meats.

Hotel Torbräu €€
Historic **Map** 3 C3
Tal 41, 80331
Tel *(089) 242340*
Ⓦ torbraeu.de
Housed in a historic building dating to 1490, this hotel offers classically furnished rooms.

Louis Hotel €€
Modern **Map** 3 C3
Viktualienmarkt 6, 80331
Tel *(089) 41119080*
Ⓦ louis-hotel.com
Lovely, airy rooms furnished with Italian fabrics, wooden floors and natural stone tiles.

Schlicker €€
Modern **Map** 3 C2
Tal 8, 80331
Tel *(089) 2428870*
Ⓦ hotel-schlicker.de
A choice of quiet courtyard bedrooms or those with street views.

Cortiina €€
Boutique **Map** 3 C2
Ledererstraße 8, 80331
Tel *(089) 2422490*
Ⓦ designhotels.com
Individually-decorated rooms with Sky TV. Swanky cocktail bar.

Platzl €€–€€€
Modern **Map** 3 C2
Sparkassenstraße 10, 80331
Tel *(089) 237030*
Ⓦ platzl.de
Dine in a 16th-century restaurant, and enjoy the classy spa facilities.

Old Town (North)

Bayerischer Hof €€€
Luxury **Map** 3 B2
Promenadeplatz 2–6, 80333
Tel *(089) 21200*
Ⓦ bayerischerhof.de
With five gourmet restaurants, six bars, a spa and a rooftop pool, this hotel attracts celebrities regularly.

Boutique interiors of a bedroom in the Mandarin Oriental

Mandarin Oriental €€€
Luxury **Map** 3 C2
Neuturmstraße 1, 80331
Tel *(089) 290980*
Ⓦ mandarinoriental.com
City views from the rooftop pool, and a Michelin-starred restaurant.

Vier Jahreszeithen Kempinski €€€
Luxury **Map** 3 C2
Maximilianstr. 17, 80539
Tel *(089) 21252799*
Ⓦ kempinski.com
Boutique-style rooms and a swathe of five-star facilities.

Around the Isar

Admiral €€
Mid-range **Map** 3 C3/4
Kohlstraße 9, 80469
Tel *(089) 216350*
Ⓦ hotel-admiral.de
Traditional in style, with classic rooms with a lush garden for guests.

Adria €€
Boutique **Map** 4 D1
Liebigstraße 8a, 80538
Tel *(089) 2421170*
Ⓦ adria-muenchen.de
Arty decor and spacious bathrooms. Fabulous breakfast buffet.

Domus €€
Modern **Map** 4 D1
St.-Anna-Straße 31, 80538
Tel *(089) 2177730*
Ⓦ domus-hotel.de
Beautiful rooms with balconies. The hotel has a superb Italian restaurant.

Hilton Munich City €€
Business **Map** 4 E4
Rosenheimer Straße 15, 81667
Tel *(089) 48040*
Ⓦ hilton.de
Four-star hotel with a 24-hour gym, and bike and car hire.

Hotel Ritzi €€
Boutique **Map** 4 F1/2
Maria-Theresia-Straße 2A, 81675
Tel *(089) 41424089*
Ⓦ hotel-ritzi.de
Posh hotel with an Art Deco bar and an Italian-Asian restaurant.

H'Otello €€
Boutique **Map** 3 C3
Baaderstraße 1, 80469
Tel *(089) 45831200*

W hotello.de
This urban hotel has immaculate rooms and a lovely terrace.

Splendid-Dollmann €€
Historic **Map** 4 D3
Thierschstraße 49, 80538
Tel *(089) 238080*
W hotel-splendid-dollmann.de
Elegant 19th-century town house with a *fin-de-siècle* touch to the rooms.

Opera €€€
Guesthouse **Map** 4 D1
St.-Anna-Straße 10, 80538
Tel *(089) 2104940*
W hotel-opera.de
Upmarket townhouse with a beautiful façade and a stunning Italian Renaissance courtyard.

University District

Carolin €
Pension **Map** 2 E4
Kaulbachstraße 42, 80539
Tel *(089) 345757*
W pension-carolin.com
Smart, modern rooms on the first floor of an apartment building.

Am Siegestor €
Historic **Map** 2 D/E4
Akademiestraße 5, 80799
Tel *(089) 399550*
W siegestor.com
Bright rooms, and an antique lift dating back to the late 1800s.

Cosmopolitan Hotel €€
Boutique **Map** 1 B2
Hohenzollernstraße 5, 80801
Tel *(089) 383810*
W cosmopolitanhotel.de
Elegant rooms and vogue interiors. The hotel reflects a passion for design.

Hauser €€
Modern **Map** 2 D4
Schellingstraße 11, 80799
Tel *(089) 2866750*
W hotel-hauser.de
Complete with a spa, sauna and wonderful breakfast buffet.

Museums District

Leonardo Boutique €
Boutique **Map** 2 D5
Amalienstraße 25, 80333
Tel *(089) 287870*
W leonardo-hotels.com
A historic building with modern furnishings and classy rooms.

Dorint Novotel €€
Modern **Map** 4 E4
Hochstraße 11, 81669
Tel *(089) 661070*
W novotel.com
Family-friendly four-star chain with a playroom and a spa centre.

Simple yet elegant façade of the Hotel Kriemhild

Charles Hotel €€€
Luxury **Map** 5 A1
Sophienstr. 28, 80333
Tel *(089) 5445550*
W charleshotel.de
Top-class hotel with dreamy views of the neighbouring botanic gardens.

Further Afield

Amalienburg €
Boutique
Amalienburgstraße 24-26, 81247
Tel *(089) 8911550*
W amalienburg.de
Found in a tranquil corner of Munich with attractive, contemporary rooms.

Carat Hotel €
Modern **Map** 3 A3
Lindwurmstraße 13, 80337
Tel *(089) 230380*
W carat-hotel-muenchen.de
Enjoy the superb breakfast buffet at this centrally-located hotel.

Hotel Laimer Hof €
Historic
Laimer Straße 40, 80639
Tel *(089) 1780380*
W laimerhof.de
Peaceful Neo-Renaissance villa which offers bikes to explore the area.

Ibis München City West €
Modern
Westendstraße 181, 80686
Tel *(089) 5794970*
W ibishotel.com
Great lodgings with a 24-hour bar, restaurant and fitness centre.

Hotel Bavaria €€
Mid-range
Gollierstr. 9, 80339
Tel *(089) 5080790*
W hotel-bavaria.com
Long-standing hotel with lovely rooms, breakfast buffets and a bar.

Hotel Kriemhild €€
Mid-range
Guntherstraße 16, 80639
Tel *(089) 1711170*
W kriemhild.com
Family-run hotel with lovely spacious rooms.

Upper Bavaria (North)

DACHAU: Fischer €
Mid-range **Map** D4
Bahnhofstraße 4, 85221
Tel *(08131) 612200*
W hotelfischer-dachau.de
No-frills hotel with a good Bavarian restaurant and lively bar.

DK Choice

DACHAU: Zieglerbräu €
Guesthouse **Map** D4
Konrad-Adenauer-Straße 8, 85221
Tel *(08131) 454396*
W restaurant-hotel-dachau.de
This cheerful place in the old town has large, sleek rooms – including a romantic four-poster suite – and a fantastic Bavarian restaurant with its own brewery.

EICHSTÄTT: Adler Hotel €
Modern **Map** C2
Marktplatz 22, 85072
Tel *(08421) 6767*
W adler-eichstaett.de
The Baroque exterior gives way to a contemporary, chic decor.

FREISING: Bayerischer Hof €
Mid-range **Map** D3
Untere Hauptstraße 3, 85354
Tel *(08161) 538300*
W bayerischerhof-freising.de
Includes a converted brewery, bar, sauna and Asian restaurant.

INGOLSTADT: Hotel Ammerland Garni €€
Boutique **Map** D2
Hermann-Paul-Müller-Straße 15, 85055
Tel *(0841) 953450*
W hotel-ammerland.de
Arty rooms, two saunas and a bar. Located outside the town centre.

For more information on types of hotels *see page 265*

Brightly coloured exterior of Neuwirt in Neuburg

NEUBURG: Neuwirt €
Mid-range Map C2
Färberstraße 88, 86633
Tel *(08431) 2078*
Ⓦ neuwirt-neuburg.de
This is a typical Bavarian hotel
with a tavern and beer garden.

Lower Bavaria

DEGGENDORF NH: Parkhotel €
Modern Map F2
Färberstraße 88, 86633
Tel *(08431) 2078*
Ⓦ nh-hotels.de
This trendy hotel has large, airy
rooms. Bike hire and steam room.

**LANDSHUT: Romantik
Hotel Fürstenhof** €€
Boutique Map E3
Stethaimerstraße 3, 84034
Tel *(0871) 92550*
Ⓦ fuerstenhof.la
Family-run, three-star hotel with
a pretty garden and sauna.

DK Choice

PASSAU: Wilder Mann €
Historic Map G3
Rathausplatz,94032
Tel *(0851) 35071*
Ⓦ wilder-mann.com
This hotel has attracted the likes
of US Astronaut Neil Armstrong
and the Austrian empress
Elizabeth II. The rooms have a
sense of history and sport heavy
antique furniture – one even
features Bavarian King Ludwig II's
wedding bed. The hotel is
located in the shadows of
Passau's town hall clock tower.

PASSAU: Hotel Schloss Ort €€
Mid-range Map G3
Im Ort 11, 94032
Tel *(0851) 34072*
Ⓦ schlosshotel-passau.de
Pleasant hotel located at the
confluence of the Ilz and
Danube rivers.

PASSAU: Hotel Weisser Hase €€
Historic Map G3
Heiliggeistgasse 1, 94032
Tel *(0851) 92110*
Ⓦ weisser-hase.de
With its 16th-century charm,
the hotel offers a sauna and
solarium.

STRAUBING: Asam €€
Boutique Map E2
Wittelsbacher Höhe 1, 94315
Tel *(09421) 788680*
Ⓦ hotelasam.de
Enjoy modern luxury and
excellent spa treatments here.

STRAUBING: Römerhof Hotel €€
Mid-range Map E2
Ittlinger Straße 136, 94315
Tel *(09421) 99820*
Ⓦ roemerhof-straubing.de
Three-star hotel with a good
regional restaurant.

Upper Bavaria (East)

ALTÖTTING: Zur Post €
Historic Map F4
Kapellplatz 2, 84503
Tel *(08671) 5040*
Ⓦ hotelpostaltoetting.de
Kings, archdukes and bishops
have stayed here.

DK Choice

**BAD REICHENHALL:
Axelmannstein** €€
Luxury Map F5
Salzburger Straße 2-6, 83435
Tel *(08651) 7770*
Ⓦ axelmannsteinresort.de
Pamper yourself in this
Alpine spa hotel, whose
many excellent facilities
include a spa complex,
with an array of massages
and beauty treatments, a
putting green and tennis.
There is a lovely restaurant,
and the hotel is set in a
beautiful park.

**BERCHTESGADEN: Berghotel
Edelweiß** €
Pension Map F5
Renothenweg 2, 83471
Tel *(08652) 5559*
Ⓦ berghotel-edelweiss.de
Traditional Bavarian hotel
with rooms that have attached
balconies. Facilities include
sauna and table tennis.

**BERCHTESGADEN: Vier
Jahreszeiten** €
Mid-range Map F5
Maximilianstr. 20, 83471
Tel *(08652) 9520*
Ⓦ hotel-vierjahreszeiten-
berchtesgaden.de
Family-run hotel with Bavarian
decor and wooden furnishings.
Alpine views from many of
the rooms.

DK Choice

**BERCHTESGADEN:
InterContinental
Berchtesgaden Resort** €€€
Luxury Map F5
Hintereck 1, 83471
Tel *(08652) 97550*
Ⓦ intercontinental.com
This exclusive five-star offers
pristine views of the Bavarian
Alps. It has posh bedrooms, a
splendid spa, indoor and
outdoor pools and gourmet
restaurants that use a variety
of interesting local ingredients
in their dishes.

REIT IM WINKL: Unterwirt €€
Mid-range Map E5
Kirchplatz 2, 83242
Tel *(08640) 8010*
Ⓦ unterwirt.de
A vibrant chalet with a frescoed
façade, spa facilities, Alpine
furniture and a games room.

**WASSERBURG AM INN:
Paulanerstuben** €
Guesthouse Map E4
Marienplatz 9, 83512
Tel *(08071) 3903*
Ⓦ paulanerstuben-wasserburg.de
This 16th-century house has
simple, contemporary rooms
that lie above a great old tavern.

Upper Bavaria (South)

**BAD TÖLZ: Jodquellenhof
Alpamare** €€
Luxury Map D5
Ludwigstraße 14, 83646
Tel *(08041) 5090*
Ⓦ jodquellenhof.com
Elegant, rural hotel with free use
of the adjacent waterpark.

DIESSEN: Strandhotel €
Guesthouse Map C4
Jahnstraße 10, 86911
Tel *(08807) 92220*
🆆 strandhotel-diessen.de
Rooms with balconies, and
a private beach. Superb
home-made cakes.

DK Choice

GARMISCH-PARTENKIRCHEN:
Gasthof Frandorfer €
Guesthouse Map C5
Ludwigstr. 24, 82467
Tel *(08821) 9270*
🆆 gasthof-fraundorfer.de
A guesthouse that celebrates
Bavarian culture. Murals decorate
the house, the rooms have
regional themes, and there is
nightly Bavarian dancing and
yodelling in the restaurant and bar.

GARMISCH-PARTENKIRCHEN:
Hotel Edelweiss €
Guesthouse Map C5
Martinswinkelstr. 15–17, 82467
Tel *(08821) 2454*
🆆 hoteledelweiss.de
Romantic guesthouse with country-
style rooms. Short walk from a spa.

KOCHEL AM SEE: Grauer Bär €
Pension Map C5
Mittenwalder Straße 82–86, 82431
Tel *(08851) 92500*
🆆 grauer-baer.de
Lakeside lodging with pleasant
rooms and terrific spa facilities.

LANDSBERG AM LECH: Goggl Garni €
Historic Map C4
Hubert von Herkomer Str. 19/20, 86899
Tel *(08191) 3240*
🆆 hotelgoggl.de
Built in 1667, the rooms of this
house have handpainted furniture.

OBERAMMERGAU: Hotel
Maximilian €€
Guesthouse Map C5
Ettaler Str. 5, 82487
Tel *(08822) 948740*
🆆 maximilian-oberammergau.de
Gorgeous boutique rooms, a spa
and a beer garden.

The Allgäu

DK Choice

FÜSSEN: Hotel Hirsch €€
Modern Map B5
Kaiser-Maximilian-Platz 7, 87629
Tel *(08362) 93980*
🆆 hotelfuessen.de
Enjoy live music in the beer
garden, or soak in the stunning
Alpine view from the sun terrace.
The rooms are individually
furnished, according to local and
historical themes, and the restau-
rant serves top-notch local food.

FÜSSEN: Hotel Luitpoldpark €€
Modern Map B5
Bahnhofstraße 1–3, 87629
Tel *(08362) 9040*
🆆 luitpoldpark-hotel.de
Majestic hotel with extensive spa
facilities and several restaurants.

KEMPTEN: Bayerischer Hof €€
Boutique Map B5
Füssener Straße 96, 87437
Tel *(0831) 57180*
🆆 bayerischerhof-kempten.de
Riverside hotel with themed
rooms. Facilities include sauna
and solarium.

LINDAU: Spiegel-Garni €
Pension Map A5
In der Grub 1, 88131
Tel *(08382) 94930*
🆆 hotel-spiegel-garni.de
The rooms range from
simple to extravagantly Alpine.

LINDAU: Reutemann €€
Modern Map A5
Ludwigstr. 23, 88131
Tel *(08382) 9150*
🆆 reutemann-lindau.de
Extraordinary harbour-side
location, and a great restaurant.

LINDAU: Bayerischer Hof €€€
Luxury Map A5
Bahnhofplatz 2, 88131
Tel *(08382) 9150*
🆆 bayerischerhof-lindau.de

Neo-Classical hotel in a prime
lakefront location.

OBERSTDORF: Saschas
Kachelofen €
Pension Map B6
Kirchstraße 3, 87561
Tel *(08322) 97750*
🆆 saschas-kachelofen.de
Traitional inn with rooms that are
located above a rustic restaurant.

Northern Swabia

AUGSBURG: Dom Hotel €€
Modern Map C3
Frauenstorstr. 8, 86152
Tel *(0821) 343930*
🆆 domhotel-augsburg.de
Serene cathedral-district hotel
with a spa. Free minibar and coffee.

AUGSBURG: Steinberger Drei
Mohren €€
Boutique Map C3
Maximilianstraße 40, 86150
Tel *(0821) 50360*
🆆 steigenberger.com
Antiques, oil paintings and
modern flat-screen TVs.

DILLINGEN: Dillinger Hof €
Boutique Map B3
Rudolf-Diesel-Straße 8, 89407
Tel *(09071) 58740*
🆆 dillingerhof.de
Artistically done hotel with a tree
in the dining room.

DONAUWÖRTH: Posthotel
Traube €
Modern Map C2
Kapellstraße 16, 86609
Tel *(0906) 706440*
🆆 posthoteltraube.de
Indulge in the café-bar, beer
garden and massage parlour.

NEU-ULM: Römer Villa €€
Historic Map A3
Parkstraße 1, 89231
Tel *(0731) 80004*
🆆 roemer-villa.de
Turreted hotel at the edge of a
park, with a quality wine bar.

DK Choice

NÖRDLINGEN: Klösterle €
Historic Map B2
Beim Klösterle 1, 86720
Tel *(09081) 87080*
🆆 nh-hotels.de
Housed in a venerable, old
Franciscan monastery with a
stepped gabled roof, this hotel
has stunning, angular rooms. The
facilities include a sauna, gym and
bike rentals. The breakfast buffet
is also exemplary.

Spacious room with fantastic Alpine views at Hotel Hirsch, Füssen

For more information on types of hotels *see page 265*

WHERE TO EAT AND DRINK

Although the food normally served in the Bavarian Alps is rather basic traditional fare, it is always tasty and satisfying. Grilled knuckle of pork, sausage, dumplings and the ubiquitous litre beer mugs are enjoyed everywhere from village inns to renowned Munich pubs. Consumed against a background of conversation, laughter and singing, they are part of a much larger culinary experience. The beer garden (Biergarten), in particular, is one of Bavaria's trademarks. The best-known, often attached to breweries, are popular gathering places for both locals and tourists. However, those looking for more sophistication will find variety in most towns and holiday resorts, with Italian, Turkish and Greek restaurants the most popular.

Dallmayr restaurant and coffee house, Munich Old Town (see p277)

Types of Restaurants

The variety of restaurants found in the Bavarian Alps reflects the fact that the region is orientated towards tourism. Genuine Bavarian meals are served primarily in Gasthaus-type establishments. In central Munich and in tourist resorts, restaurants tend towards the kitsch, and the quality can be poor. It is better to eat in an inn frequented by locals, where prices are lower and where dishes, although served with less ceremony, usually taste much better. Be prepared for a little local colour: local inns can be noisy with over-indulgent drinkers.

A good bet is usually the Ratskeller, a pub in the cellar of the town hall, serving regional specialities. There are also traditional wine bars (Weinstuben), which serve good, if pricier, food.

Other options for good regional food and local beer are Bierstuben and Bierkeller:

pubs usually belonging to a local brewery. They are often noisy, and seating is on long benches where you soon fall into conversation with other diners and drinkers.

Attractive features of Bavarian beer-drinking rituals are the gigantic beer tents (Bierzelte) put up during local holidays, as well as the charming little beer gardens (Biergärten), where customers order their drinks from the bar. You can even bring your own food to some of them.

There are also Italian pizzerias, Greek tavernas, steak houses, and Chinese, Turkish and Balkan restaurants as well as fast-food outlets and snack bars. At the other end of the scale, particularly in Munich, there are elegant, discerning restaurants with elevated standards of service, decor and cuisine, with high prices to match.

Smoking is banned in all public places, including restaurants, bars and clubs.

Exotic murals covering the walls of one of Munich's dining rooms

What and When to Eat

Breakfast is usually hearty, with various types of bread accompanied by cheese, sausages and marmalade. On Sunday a brunch buffet is served in many places until 2pm. During the lunch period (noon to 2pm) most establishments serve excellent salads or bowls of filling soup, while many restaurants offer a fixed-price menu. Restaurants

A sunny beer garden near the Viktualienmarkt, Munich

Stylish restaurant with artistic interiors, Yum *(see p276)* in Munich

start to fill up in the evenings between 6 and 7pm, although dinner is ofen eaten after 8pm.

Opening Hours

Cafeterias and fast-food chains open at 9am, but most other establishments open at noon and usually close after the lunchtime period until about 6pm. Many restaurants close on one day of the week, known as a *Ruhetag*. Beer gardens in towns usually close at 11pm. Many restaurants stay open right up until midnight or 1am.

Menu

Most restaurants post their menu, together with their prices, at the door, with daily or seasonal additions attached on a separate sheet. Desserts and soft and alcoholic drinks are usually listed on a separate menu.

In many restaurants the menu is written in German and English, and sometimes also in French. In cafés and less expensive restaurants, the menu may be handwritten, in which case staff may be able to help with a translation.

Reservations

Reservations are essential at the best restaurants and advisable in most medium-standard restaurants on a Friday or Saturday night or on public holidays. Without a reservation, you may be asked to wait or to return later.

Many inns and restaurants in Bavaria have a *Stammtisch*, a table set aside for regular local people and groups at certain times on certain days.

Prices and Tips

Prices charged in Bavarian restaurants are diverse, those in Munich's top restaurants being the highest. A meal consisting of roast meat with dumplings and salad served in a country inn can be almost half the price.

The cost of a main course in an inn or restaurant ranges from €7–8 in the cheapest places to €14–19 in superior establishments. The average cost of a three-course meal including salad and beer is about €26. This includes tax and service, but it is customary to leave a 10 per cent tip. If paying by card, this can be added to the bill.

Vegetarian Food

Vegetarian food is now a common choice in Germany.

The number of vegetarian restaurants has increased, and snack bars offering vegetarian meals are popular. More inns and restaurants all over Germany now include meat-free meals on their main menus, while vegetarian pizzas are a standard item in Italian restaurants.

Disabled Visitors

Many inns and restaurants sadly lack wheelchair access. Doorways are often too narrow and tables too closely placed, and adapted toilets absent. Be sure to enquire what the situation is when making a reservation.

Recommended Restaurants

The recommended restaurants on the following pages have been chosen to provide a taste of the cuisines of the region. As a result places serving good quality German and regional cuisine have been favoured. Where possible, alternatives have also been suggested – which will likely prove particularly useful to vegetarians or those wanting lighter fare.

In all cases we have picked restaurants where the quality of the food or the experience marks them out somehow. Places recommended for DK Choice are our top recommendations, chosen for offering something special or simply for being the best of their type.

The main room of the Munich Ratskeller

The Flavours of Munich and Bavaria

Bavarian cooking has a reputation for huge portions of hearty food, best enjoyed along with a beer. Sausages of all kinds, superb pork and beef, regional fish, and freshly baked breads and cakes are the standard fare for locals and visitors alike. But many restaurants now also prepare local and other German dishes with a lighter touch – indeed, Munich once spearheaded German *nouvelle cuisine*. While the city has lost its gourmet crown to the likes of Hamburg, Düsseldorf, and Berlin, the general standard of cooking in the Bavarian capital is still superb.

Harzer Roller and Emmentaler cheeses

Giant pretzels, best eaten warm and soft from the oven

Hearty Bavarian Cooking

Bavarian cooking developed in the countryside, where hard-working farmers needed high-carbohydrate food made using local, fresh produce – homemade bread, noodles and dumplings along with things like home-reared meat, farm-produced cheeses, and river fish such as trouts. In Munich,

during its centuries as the seat of the Wittelsbach dynasty, these country influences were refined into a solidly bourgeois cuisine. To this day, the hearty, no-nonsense dishes of Bavaria are what the world considers to be German cuisine. *Weißwürstchen* (white veal sausages with a beer pretzel) are enjoyed in the morning, often with a beer. Dinner might be soup with liver

dumplings, roast pork, *sauerkraut* and a pile of potato dumplings or noodles. Local produce is still held in high regard. Delicatessens abound in Munich, and markets are found throughout the region. Pride of place goes to the Viktualienmarkt, in the historic heart of town *(see p68)*, where you can shop for, sample and eat authentic Bavarian cooking at the many food stalls.

Mehrkornsemmel (mixed grain roll)

Laugensemmel (salty sourdough rolls)

Berliner Landbrot (mild rye bread)

Grau- oder Mischbrot (wholewheat)

Milchbrötchen (milk-dough roll)

Selection of typical German loaves and bread rolls

Bavarian Dishes and Specialities

Bavarian cooking is a great blend of filling dishes and tasty snacks or *brotzeit* ("bread time") between main meals. A typical *brotzeit* consists of any cold meat, such as smoked bacon or sausage, slices of roast pork or liver sausage, freshly sliced *radi* (radish) and some cheese, preferably Obatza, a creamy Camembert mousse. Main courses focus on pork, with the famous Schweinshaxe and Schweinsbraten (with beer gravy) leading the field. The Schweinshaxe in particular is a must-have in Munich. Both are eaten with potato dumplings – the famous Bavarian *knödel* – to absorb the rich gravy. Of course, none of these dishes would be complete without a nice, cold beer.

Pork salamis

Leberknödelsuppe is a rich, clear beef broth in which little liver dumplings are lightly poached.

Fresh vegetables on display at Munich's historic Viktualienmarkt

Munich's Gourmet Revolution

It may seem strange that a city of hearty and hefty cooking instigated a trend for low-fat gourmet German cuisine. At the forefront was Eckart Witzigmann (still Germany's most popular chef) who, inspired by French *nouvelle cuisine*, began to reinvent Bavarian and German dishes using unusual combinations of exquisite ingredients. Witzigmann's legendary Munich-based Aubergine was the first German restaurant to gain three Michelin stars. Munich's top restaurants still retain a reputation for innovative cooking. Certain chic venues have also attracted the *bussi-bussi* (air kissing) crowd with Italian, Asian and Fusion cuisine, served in a stylish setting.

Bavarian Beer

Of the more than 1,250 breweries in Germany, many of the largest and most famous are in Munich, among them Löwenbräu, Augustiner, Paulaner and Hofbräu. Beer is still brewed in strict accordance

Beer served in a traditional Munich *Biergarten* (beer garden)

to the "Reinheitsgebot", a Bavarian decree of 1516 ordering that only malted barley, hops and water should be used. Today there many different kinds of beer available, from dark, strong Bock beer to lighter (in colour and alcohol) beers such as the famous Weizen or *Weißbier* (white beer).

Most beers on tap in Munich are served in a *mass*, a special 1-litre (2 pint) glass mug. For the more faint-hearted, there is also a *halbe*, a half-litre mug.

The exuberant annual highlight of Munich's proud beer culture is the famous Oktoberfest *(see p33)*.

WEISSWÜRSTE

There is no other dish from Bavaria as classic as a pair of Weisswürste. These delicious veal sausages are steamed and served hot with sweet, grainy mustard and a *Brezen* (beer pretzel). Traditionally, they should be eaten in the morning, as a second breakfast or a snack before lunch, but never at other times of the day; hence the old Munich saying that "the sausage should not hear the clocks sound noon". But even if it's early, a beer is the right accompaniment for Weisswürste. Some locals don't eat the sausages with a knife and fork, but simply suck out the meat from the Weisswürste's thin skin, an art called *auszuzeln* in Munich.

Tafelspitz, poached beef brisket with vegetables, is usually served with red cabbage and horseradish.

Schweinshaxe, or roast pork knuckle, is a Bavarian classic. It is eaten with potato dumplings and krautsalat.

Rohrnudeln is a Bavarian yeasted dumpling cake that is soaked in a delicious vanilla-caramel sauce.

Beer in Bavaria

Bavaria is famous the world over for its excellent beer, which is exported to over 140 countries. As part of their cultural tradition, Bavarians scrupulously observe the *Reinheitsgebot*, a law of 1516 according to which the only ingredients brewers may use are barley, hops and water. The Bavarians even made accession to the Weimar Republic in 1919 conditional on the acknowledgment of this law. The Starkbieranstich, at the beginning of Lent, is the high point of Bavaria's brewing tradition.

The Oktoberfest – a folk festival that is cheerfully celebrated by the Bavarians

Logo of one of Bavaria's best-known breweries

The famous Löwenbräu beer

A beer mat

Bavarian Breweries

In 1040 the monks of Weihenstephan monastery, which is now on the outskirts of modern Freising, were granted a licence to brew beer by the city's bishop. The brewery, which still produces beer to this day, is the oldest in the world. Fifty percent of all breweries in the European Union are located in Bavaria. Many Bavarian breweries have centuries of tradition behind them. The best-known are the main Munich breweries – Löwenbräu, Hofbräu, Paulanerbräu, Augustinerbräu, Spatenbräu and Hacker-Pschorrbräu.

Many smaller breweries can also be found throughout the region, usually with their own inns (*Wirtschaften*) or pubs with beer gardens. Many of them are the object of special "pilgrimages" made both by Bavarians and by tourists. The most highly esteemed of these inns include the Klosterbrauerei Andechs, the Weltenburg and Irsee breweries, which continue the time-honoured tradition of monastic brewing, and Schlossbrauerei Kaltenberg, which belongs to Duke Luitpold of Bavaria. The long-standing debate over who brews the best beer will, quite obviously, never be resolved.

Traditional Dark and Light Beers

Until the 19th century, the only beer drunk in Bavaria was the sweeter dark beer (*Dunkel*). Some breweries continue to specialize in *Dunkel* today; the best known of these are the Weltenburg monastery brewery (which makes Barock Dunkel) and the Schlossbrauerei Kaltenberg (König Ludwig Dunkel).

In the 20th century dark beer was replaced by lighter lager-type beer (*Helles*), which is clear, a little more potent and with a less bitter taste. *Naturtrüb*, an unfiltered beer with an excellent taste, is slightly cloudy because of its yeast content.

Good beer is served cold and should have a thick head that does not settle quickly. It is served in a litre (2-pint) mug (*eine Maß*), as a half litre (1 pint) (*eine Halbe*) and more rarely as a quarter litre (half a pint) (*ein Kleines*). It tastes best when served from the barrel (as *Fassbier*). Beer served from a keg under pressure is sacrilege to a Bavarian. On hot days, people may drink *Radler*, which is *Helles* mixed with lemonade.

Berchtesgaden lager

König Ludwig dark beer

Paulanerbräu lager

Märzenbier

Before the invention of refrigeration systems, beer was brewed in winter, when the heat would not disrupt the fermentation process. The last brewing was in March and the beer had a higher alcohol content, which helped to prevent it going off. If the brewers' stocks lasted until autumn, before the new season's beer was brewed the cellars were opened and a beer festival was held. The brewing of *Märzenbier* (March beer) continues to this day, even though modern technology has rendered the process obsolete.

At the big autumn beer festivals millions of litres of this strong-tasting light-brown beer are consumed. Beer brewed by the major Munich brewers specially for the Oktoberfest is called *Oktoberfestbier* or *Wiesenbier*. In the autumn it is on offer in many pubs and is sold bottled in shops.

The most widely used type of beer mug

Oktoberfestbier from the Paulanerbräu

Bock And Doppelbock

This famous beer gets its name from the town of Einbeck in Lower Saxony. The word "Einbeck" was transmuted by the Bavarian brogue into "Oanbock", which was abbreviated to "Bock". *Bockbier* was first brewed by the court brewery *(Hofbräu)*, founded in 1589. The Pauline monks were later renowned for making this type of beer. A more potent variety called *Doppelbock* was produced under the name Salvator. This beer, which the monks used to help them through the rigours of Lent, was brewed to celebrate 19 March, the feast day of St Joseph, the order's patron saint. To this day Josefitag marks the beginning of Munich's *Starkbierfest* (strong beer festival), which takes place in the Paulaner brewery's pub. Salvator inaugurated the production of several other *Doppelbock* beers. The beer is an amber colour and has a strong, slightly bitter taste and a 7 per cent alcohol content.

Salvator
Doppelbock

Pretzels – a perfect snack to enjoy with beer

Weizenbier

This type of beer is extremely popular in southern Germany, particularly in summer as it is a very refreshing drink. During the brewing process, twice the amount of malted wheat is added to the malted barley, which is why it is known as *Weizenbier* (wheat beer).

Weizenbier has a 5 per cent alcohol content and is a *Vollbier* (full beer). To enhance the flavour it is often drunk with a sliver of lemon. There are many kinds of wheat beer: the light and dark *Weizen-Bockbier* and the yeasty *Hefeweizen* beer. The frothy *Weizen* is slowly poured into a glass which broadens at the top. Mixed with lemonade, it is called *Russn*.

Franziskaner
Hefe-Weißbier

Paulanerbräu
wheat beer

Chinesischer Turm, a popular beer garden *(see p284)*

Where To Drink

Beer, the Bavarian national drink, is also called "liquid nourishment". It is drunk anywhere and everywhere throughout the region – from the most exclusive restaurants down to the smallest food stalls. However, beer is best enjoyed in beer gardens or at the inns of breweries.

Almost every town in Bavaria holds a folk festival at least once a year that involves a lot of beer-drinking. .

Where to Eat and Drink

Munich

Old Town (South)

Bratwurstherzl €
Regional Map 3 C3
Dreifaltigkeitsplatz 1, 80331
Tel *(089) 295113* **Closed** *Sun*
Traditional tavern that serves
marvellous Bratwurst sausages,
especially those from Nürnberg.

Milagros €
Mexican Map 3 C3
Frauenstraße 9, 80469
Tel *(089) 2323872929*
Zesty food, with a menu that
includes great *tamales* and a
wonderfully rich chocolate
Kahlua dessert flan.

**Nürnberger Bratwurst Glöckl
am Dom** €
Regional Map 3 B2
Frauenplatz 9, 80331
Tel *(089) 2919450*
This traditional eatery specializes
in Nürnberger sausages. Great
for hearty noodle soups and
delicious ox filet.

Prinz Myshkin €
Vegetarian Map 3 B2
Hackenstraße 2, 80331
Tel *(089) 265596*
This arty restaurant is great for
a break from the otherwise
meaty Bavarian fare.

Ratskeller €
Regional Map 3 B/C2
Marienplatz 8, 80331
Tel *(089) 2199890*
Charming townhall cellar where
top-quality food is served.
Popular among tourists.

Riva Tal €
Italian Map 3 C3
Tal 44, 80331
Tel *(089) 220240*

Pizzeria and espresso bar with
cheerful service an appetizing
variety of dishes.

Sababa €
Middle Eastern Map 3 C3
Westenriederstraße 9, 80331
Tel *(089) 23237881* **Closed** *Sun*
This simple yet renowned Persian
eatery serves wonderful falafel
and caters with a smile.

Sushi Sano €
Japanese Map 3 A2
Josephspitalstraße 4, 80331
Tel *(089) 267490*
Authentic noodle dishes and
delicious sushi. Available in
takeaway boxes for picnickers.

Viktus €
German Map 3 C3
Frauenstraße 2, 80331
Tel *(089) 23077645*
This bistro serves healthy fast food.
Splendid salads and soups, includ-
ing a tasty Asian chicken soup.

Weisses Bräuhaus €
German Map 3 C2
Tal 7, 80331
Tel *(089) 2901380*
Popular beer hall, whose liver
dumplings with *sauerkraut* are
absolutely divine.

Yum €
Asian Map 3 B3
Utzschneiderstraße 6, 80469
Tel *(089) 23230660*
Trendy eatery with pretty
orchids, gilded Buddhas and an
artistic Thai food bar that draws
glamorous celebrities often.

Café Glockenspiel €€
International Map 3 B2
Marienplatz 28, 80331
Tel *(089) 264256*
This café-cum-restaurant has a
lovely terrace with expansive views.

Try the seafood glass noodles, or
the salmon on saffron spinach.

Fisch Poseidon €€
Seafood Map 3 C3
Westenriederstraße 13, 80331
Tel *(089) 299296* **Closed** *Sun*
With its self-service and
established decor, this eatery
serves phenomenal Bouillabaisse
and superb seafood spaghetti.

Niederlassung €€
International Map 3 C3
Buttermelcherstraße 6, 80469
Tel *(089) 32600307* **Closed** *Mon*
A bar and lounge that is also a
hip nightspot. More than 80
varieties of gin available.

Stadtkantine €€
Mediterranean Map 3 B2
Neuhauser Straße 15a, 80331
Tel *(089) 24293699* **Closed** *Sun*
Slick, modern bistro tucked into
an alleyway. A creative antipasta
platter, outstanding spare ribs
and a good wine selection.

The Victorian House €€
International Map 3 C3
Frauenstraße 14, 80469
Tel *(089) 25546947*
Local chain of English-themed
cafés, which serve great break-
fasts, delicious sandwich lunches
and Earl Grey tea with scones.

Weinhaus Neuner €€€
International Map 3 A2
Herzogspitalstraße 8, 80331
Tel *(089) 2603954* **Closed** *Sun*
This splendid wine bar serves
food strongly influenced by the
Mediterranean. Don't miss the
roasted vegetables and the
biting Bavarian mustard sauces.

Old Town (North)

Due Passi €
Italian Map 3 C2
Ledererstraße 11, 80331
Tel *(089) 224271* **Closed** *Sat & Sun*
This is a simple pasta bistro
that uses authentic recipes.
The service is always wonderful.

Tavernetta €
Italian Map 4 D2
Hildegardstraße 9, 80539
Tel *(089) 21269424* **Closed** *Sun*

Antique-furnished dining area at The Victorian House

Simple and understated decor at Bar München

Fantastic food, with tasty antipastas such as the courgette and wild mushroom carpaccio. Complete the meal with a mean tiramisu.

Zum Franciskaner €
Regional Map 3 C1
Residenzstraße 9, 80333
Tel *(089) 2318120*
Venerable brewery and restaurant that serves superb meatloaf and a fine selection of beer. Famous for its white sausages, a local speciality.

Ederer €€
Seafood Map 3 B1
Kardinal-Faulhaber-Straße 10, 80333
Tel *(089) 24231310* **Closed** *Sun*
Try the terrine of sardines with sweet peppers, or the pea soup and prawns. Extensive wine list.

Eisbach €€
International Map 3 C1
Marstallstraße 3, 80539
Tel *(089) 22801680*
Perfect for long lunches or pre-theatre dining. Soups, salads and other light fare are served in a summer courtyard setting.

Garden Restaurant €€
International Map 3 B2
Promenadeplatz 2–6, 80333
Tel *(089) 2120993*
Fine dining in this roof-garden restaurant at the luxury hotel, Bayerischer Hof. Mediterranean and South German dishes.

Kulisse €€
International Map 4 D2
Maximilianstraße 26, 80539
Tel *(089) 294728*
This Kammerspiele theatre restaurant offers a wide choice of Asian and Bavarian dishes.

Le Stollberg €€
French Map 4 D2
Stollbergstraße 2, 80539
Tel *(089) 24243450* **Closed** *Sun*

Bright and airy restaurant, where top-quality ingredients are used to prepare an array of fantastic dishes.

Spatenhaus an der Oper €€
Regional Map 3 C3
Residenzstraße 12, 80331
Tel *(089) 2907060*
A prominent Bavarian food bastion. The lower floor is less formal with heartier food, while the upper floor is reserved for opera house views.

Austernkeller €€€
French Map 4 D2
Stollbergstraße 11, 80539
Tel *(089) 298787*
Long-established seafood eatery with expertise in cooking oysters. The dishes are inspired by what's best in the market.

Bar München €€€
International Map 4 D2
Maximilianstraße 36, 80539
Tel *(089) 229090*
This contemporary eatery offers good seafood, cocktails and an oft-changing menu.

Beautiful interiors at Mark's, a classy fine-dining restaurant

Dallmayr €€€
International Map 3 C2
Dienerstraße 14, 80331
Tel *(089) 2135* **Closed** *Mon & Sun*
A Munich institution, famous for its coffee-house and patisserie, Dallmayr is attached to an elegant restaurant. Don't miss the zucchini ratatouille with lobster.

DK Choice

Mark's Restaurant €€€
International Map 3 C2
Neuturmstraße 1, 80331
Tel *(089) 29098875*
Mark's offers fine-dining in beautiful surroundings. With a Michelin-starred chef, the lavish French and Mediterranean menu includes white halibut in wild garlic and artichoke sauce, and medallion of beef with green asparagus and morel risotto.

Restaurant Pfistermühle €€€
International Map 3 C3
Pfisterstraße 4, 80331
Tel *(089) 23703865* **Closed** *Sun*
Small regionally-inspired menu that changes often. The dishes are served under 16th-century arches. Reservations are essential.

Trader Vic's €€€
Polynesian Map 3 B1
Promenadenplatz 2–6, 80333
Tel *(089) 2120995*
Michael Jackson and Tina Turner ate here. Creative food and superb cocktails.

Around the Isar

Königsquelle €
Regional Map 3 C3
Baaderplatz 2, 80469
Tel *(089) 220071*
The whiskey bar here is a big draw for many, but the schnitzels are also highly-recommended. Friendly ambience.

DK Choice

Wirtshaus in der Au €
Regional Map 4 D4
Lilienstraße 51, 81669
Tel *(089) 4481400*
This lovely old Bavarian inn is a master in experimental dumplings – spinach and beetroot anyone? Come late September, it runs a dumpling restaurant – the Münchner Knödelei – on the Oktoberfest grounds. It also hosts cookery courses, and has published a dumpling cookbook.

For more information on types of restaurants *see page 271*

Lavish interiors of the well-reviewed Königshof

Dukatz €€
Mediterranean **Map** 3 B1
St.-Anna-Straße 11, 80538
Tel *(089) 23032444*
This splendid café serves delicious French tartes, cakes, cookies and fine coffee.

Gandl €€
International **Map** 4 D1
St.-Anna-Straße 1, 80538
Tel *(089) 29162525*
Part of the Opera Hotel *(see p267)*, Gandl serves Italian food during the day and French dishes at night.

Goa €€
Indian **Map** 4 D2
Thierschstraße 8, 80538
Tel *(089) 21111789*
This popular eatery offers a variety of chicken and lamb curries, kormas and koftas.

Nektar €€
International **Map** 4 E3
Stubenvollstraße 1, 81667
Tel *(089) 45911311*
Contemporary dining in a futuristic setting. There are performances between courses.

Nero €€
Italian **Map** 3 C3
Rumfordstraße 34, 80469
Tel *(089) 21019060*
Hip pizzeria with incredible thin-crust creations, as well as fresh antipasti, pasta and steaks.

Käfer Schänke €€€
International **Map** 4 F1
Prinzregentenstraße 73, 81675
Tel *(089) 4168247* **Closed** *Sun*
This is an eminent gourmet destination for politicians and business high-flyers. The intimate dining room has a contemporary decor with a feel of traditional Bavaria.

University District

Cohen's €
Jewish **Map** 1 B4
Theresienstraße 31, 80333
Tel *(089) 2809545* **Closed** *Sun*
Stews and German dishes served with a Jewish twist at this hip eatery. Attracts students and artists alike.

Kytaro €
Greek **Map** 2 F4
Franz-Josef-Strauß-Ring 4, 80539
Tel *(089) 21268230*
Classic dishes such as kebabs, stuffed aubergines, roast lamb and mezes. Party atmosphere in the evenings.

Sangeet €
Indian **Map** 3 C1
Brienner Straße 10, 80333
Tel *(089) 28674557*
A large restaurant with stylish interiors and hospitable service. Sangeet is renowned for its fresh, top-quality spices and its tandoori oven.

Huckebein Essen & Trinken €€
Regional **Map** 2 D4
Amalienstraße 89, 80799
Tel *(089) 281780*
Both young and old can be found revelling in the laidback atmosphere of this stylish restaurant. Huckebein Essen & Trinken also offers a selection of excellent wines.

Reitschule €€
Mediterranean **Map** 2 F4
Königinstrasse 34, 80802
Tel *(089) 3888760*
Long-standing, chic bistro, named after its views of a riding school. Reitschule serves a small selection of well-priced daily specials.

Vanilla Lounge €€
International **Map** 4 F1
Leopoldstraße 65, 80802
Tel *(089) 38666836*
This breakfast café becomes a cocktail bar and club by night. Apart from the colourful lights and glassy decor, Vanilla Lounge offers a small Italian menu.

Museums District

Rilano No. 6 €€
International **Map** 3 A1
Ottostraße 6, 80333
Tel *(089) 5491300* **Closed** *Sun*
Well-crafted gourmet food and expert wine pairings. The restaurant is housed in a Renaissance building.

Königshof €€€
Gourmet **Map** 3 A2
Karlsplatz 25, 80335
Tel *(089) 551360* **Closed** *Sun*
An elegant 19th-century parlour ambience. The seasonal dishes are created by a Michelin-starred chef.

Further Afield

Augustiner Bräustuben €
Regional
Landsberger Straße 19, 80339
Tel *(089) 507047*
This jovial beer hall serves great dumplings with duck, pork knuckle or mushroom sauce, on benches.

Leonrod €
Middle Eastern
Leonrodstraße 45, 80636
Tel *(089) 1235661*
Share a large mezze platter for a taste of different items, or try the Sunday brunch buffet, at this outstanding Lebanese joint.

Acetaia €€
International
Nymphenburger Straße 215, 80639
Tel *(089) 13929077*
This discreet yet stylish restaurant offers a menu based entirely on balsamic vinegar. Great soup and ravioli.

Al Pino €€
Italian
Frans-Hals-Straße 3, 81479
Tel *(089) 799885*
Classical decor and superb quality food. Don't miss the red mullet on fennel, or the courgette ravioli.

Broeding €€
International
Schulstraße 9, 80634
Tel *(089) 164238* **Closed** *Sun*
The fine-dining creation of an Austrian wine importer. Offers a five-course menu with pairings.

Jasmin Asia Cuisine €€
Asian **Map** 4 E4
Lindwurmstraße 167, 80337
Tel *(089) 76775712*
Amazing pan-Asian and Vietnamese food. Spicy, with fresh ingredients and herbs.

Ruffini €€
Italian
Orffstraße 22–24, 80637
Tel *(089) 16116* **Closed** *Mon*
Café and patisserie serving regional Italian since 1978. The menu changes daily.

Acquarello €€€
International
Mühlbaurstraße 36, 81677
Tel *(089) 4704848*
Savour Michelin-starred Italian food with fresh ingredients at this kitsch restaurant. Think fig-and-foie gras tortellini.

Smart, subtle decor at Tantris, a Munich institution for over 30 years

Vibrant dining area at Acquarello, known for its flavourful Italian food

Tantris €€€
Gourmet
Johann-Fichte-Straße 7, 80805
Tel *(089) 3619590* **Closed** *Mon & Sun*
From the 1970s, Tantris offers delicious contemporary food. The restaurant boasts two Michelin stars. Booking is essential.

Upper Bavaria (North)

DACHAU: Aurora €€
Gourmet **Map** D4
Roßwachtstraße 1, 85221
Tel *(08131) 515328*
Fine regional food with a fixed-price menu and excellent meat dishes, such as steak, lamb and venison.

DK Choice

EICHSTÄTT: Gasthof Krone €
Regional **Map** C2
Domplatz 3, 85072
Tel *(08421) 4406*
Bavarian food is served with panache at this family-run guesthouse. The meals here are award-winning: the schnitzel in creamy mushroom sauce is remarkable, and the lamb is divine. A peaceful beer garden offers an alternative to the 1670s dining room in summer.

EICHSTÄTT: Pizzeria Piccola €
Italian **Map** C2
Luitpoldstr. 32, 85072
Tel *(08421) 6149* **Closed** *Sun*
Pizza-by-the-slice available at this small joint. The terrific pizzas are of top-rate quality.

ERDING: Gaststätte Kreuzeder €
Regional **Map** D3
Münchener Straße 56, 85435
Tel *(08122) 5377*
Traditional inn with quick, helpful service. Portions are large, and the dumplings are to die for.

FREISING: Zur Alten Schiessstätte €
Regional **Map** D3
Dr.-von-Daller-Straße 1–3, 85356
Tel *(08161) 532441*
This restaurant has a 16th-century vaulted beer cellar and garden. Part of the Dorint hotel, it serves top-notch food.

HAINDLFING (NEAR FREISING):
Gasthaus Landbrecht €€
Regional **Map** D3
Freisinger Straße 1, 85354
Tel *(08167) 8926* **Closed** *Mon & Tue*
Regional gourmet specials and seasonal dishes are served here. The classic tiled stoves and wood panelling adds to the rustic ambience.

INGOLSTADT: Taj Mahal €
Indian **Map** D2
Beckerstraße 11, 85049
Tel *(0841) 9814618*
Delicious, quality north Indian food. The restaurant is known for its bargain lunch buffets.

INGOLSTADT: Daniel €€
German **Map** D2
Roseneckstraße 1, 85049
Tel *(0841) 35272* **Closed** *Mon*
For unbeatably good traditional food, visit this modestly done cult pub.

INGOLSTADT: Hummel €€
International **Map** D2
Feldkirchener Straße 69, 85055
Tel *(0841) 954530* **Closed** *Sun*
A friendly restaurant with a contemporary decor. Lovely potato soup and tasty smoked trout.

INGOLSTADT: Restaurant
im Stadttheater €€
International **Map** D2
Schloßlände 1, 85049
Tel *(0841) 935150* **Closed** *Mon*
Impressive city views and a seasonal menu, which includes an array of interesting dishes.

**NEUBURG AN DER DONAU:
Elisenlounge** €
International **Map** C2
Elisenplatz 16, 86633
Tel *(08431) 6497099*
Fancy cocktails and a good
range of simple dishes, with
delicious steaks. Elisenlounge
is a fun place to unwind in
the evenings.

**NEUBURG AN DER DONAU:
Zum Klosterbräu** €€
Regional **Map** C2
Kirchplatz 1, 86633
Tel *(08431) 67750*
Perfect Sunday roasts. The
restaurant offers a choice of
dining rooms for a more
intimate feel.

Lower Bavaria

DEGGENDORF: Grauer Hase €€
International **Map** F2
Untere Vorstadt 12, 94469
Tel *(0991) 371270* **Closed** *Sun*
Excellent fish and meats. The
chef here remakes the old
favourites using fruits and
exotic ingredients.

GRAFENAU: Säumerhof €€
Regional **Map** G2
Steinberg 32, 94481
Tel *(08552) 408990* **Closed** *Mon*
Pleasant restaurant that is part
of a country hotel. The menu
includes hearty local specialties.
The ingredients come from
surrounding farms, rivers
and forests.

**LANDSHUT: L&D
Suppenkultur** €
Vietnamese **Map** E3
Ländgasse 135a, 84028
Tel *(0871) 4303836* **Closed** *Sun*
Hidden down a quiet Old Town
street, this place serves authentic
dishes and great sandwiches.

DK Choice

**LANDSHUT: Schloss
Schönbrunn** €€
Regional **Map** E3
Schönbrunn 1, 84036
Tel *(0871) 95220*
Now a bastion of old-fashioned
cooking, this magnificent 17th-
century Bavarian castle is a must-
visit. Specialities include grilled
fish, crunchy pork knuckle, roast
chicken and spare ribs.

LANDSHUT: Taverna Delphi €€
Greek **Map** E3
Isargestade 742, 84028
Tel *(0871) 21159* **Closed** *Mon*
Modern bistro that serves
delicious feta salads, gyros and
fish. Crisp, fresh flavours.

PASSAU: Heilig Geist €
Regional **Map** G3
Heiliggeistgasse 4, 94032
Tel *(0851) 2607* **Closed** *Wed*
This rustic winebar specializes in
Bavarian food. Good local fish,
pork and beef.

PASSAU: Christophorus Stüberl €€
International **Map** G3
Pfaffengasse 7, 94032
Tel *(0851) 7568090*

Off a narrow Old Town street,
this tavern offers a variety of fish
and meat. The eel and bison
are superb.

PASSAU: Loungerie €€
Regional **Map** G3
Heuwinkel 10, 94032
Tel *(0851) 37211* **Closed** *Sun*
Pedestrian district bistro with
a small Bavarian and Austrian
menu. The dumpling desserts
are absolutely delectable.

PASSAU: Pizzeria Gallo Nero €€
Italian **Map** G3
Schmiedgasse 5, 94032
Tel *(0851) 36315* **Closed** *Tue*
Pizzas and pastas, but also
amazing grilled fish. The mussels
in white wine are delicious.

STRAUBING: Seethaler €
German **Map** E2
Theresienplatz 9, 94315
Tel *(09421) 93950* **Closed** *Sun*
Traditional inn that dates back to
1462. It serves excellent regional
food, beer and wine.

STRAUBING: Unterm Rain €
Regional **Map** E2
Unterm Rain 15, 94315
Tel *(09421) 22772*
Cheerful, modest restaurant and
beer garden. Generous portions
of pan-German specialties such
as schnitzel and sausages,
are served.

STRAUBING: Bella Vista €€
Italian **Map** E2
Krankenhausgasse 19, 94315
Tel *(09421) 89154* **Closed** *Mon & Sun*
Wonderful food and outstanding
wines since 1996. The Sicilian
swordfish is the house special.

Upper Bavaria (East)

**ALTÖTTING: Graminger
Weissbräu** €
Regional **Map** F4
Graming 79, 84503
Tel *(08671) 96140* **Closed** *Thu*
This old brewery has a lovely
beer garden in the shade of
chestnut trees. Delightful
Bavarian cooking.

**ASCHAU IM CHIEMGAU: Heinz
Winkler** €€€
Gourmet **Map** E5
Kirchplatz 13, 83229
Tel *(08052) 17990*
A splendid Baroque restaurant,
Heinz Winkler is named after
the chef who took over in 1989.
It has since become a fabulous
gourmet pilgrimage destination,
and is a must-visit.

Beautiful outdoor seating with mountain views at Heinz Winkler, Aschau Im Chiemgau

Elegant seating at Herrenhaus, popular for its classic Bavarian dishes

BAD REICHENHALL:
St Aegidi-Keller €€
Italian Map F5
Poststr. 20, 83435
Tel *(08651) 65333*
This 12th-century wine cellar and
restaurant is replete with Gothic,
wooden furniture.

BERCHTESGADEN: Café
Restaurant Am Luitpoldpark €€
International Map F5
Külbersteinstr. 2, 83471
Tel *(08652) 964555* **Closed** *Mon*
Enjoy beautiful mountain views
and feast on the tapas, pastas
and burgers.

DK Choice

BERCHTESGADEN:
Restaurant 3'60° €€€
International Map F5
Hintereck 1, 83471
Tel *(08652) 97550*
As the name suggests, this
restaurant offers spectacular
views of the mountains. Part
of the InterContinental Resort
Berchtesgaden, Restaurant
3'60° has a gorgeous open
kitchen where local ingredients
come together to become
exquisite dishes. The menu
includes a range of rich, meaty
dishes, but there are several
excellent healthy options as
well. This is one of the finest
eateries among the resort
dining options.

BURGHAUSEN:
Bayerische Alm €
Mediterranean Map F4
Robert-Koch-Straße 211, 84489
Tel *(08677) 9820*
An appetizing variety of duck,
lamb, venison and trout can
be found at Bayerische Alm.

Dine to stunning alpine and
castle views.

BURGHAUSEN: Chillis €
International Map F4
Marktler Str. 5, 84489
Tel *(08677) 877550*
Chillis offers a broad selection
of dishes: Asian, Indian, steaks,
fresh fish, baked potatoes and
much more. Bargain lunches are
also available.

CHIEMSEE:
Fritzi's Biergarten €
Regional Map E4
Frauenchiemsee 39, 83256
Tel *(08054) 902936*
With its stunning lakeside
beer garden, this eatery is
blessed with lovely sunset
views. The menu includes fresh
Chiemsee fish and interesting
local specialities.

SEEON: Rauchhaus €€
Regional Map E4
Altenmarkter Str. 6, 83370
Tel *(08624) 829922* **Closed** *Tue*
Opened in 1679, this
atmospheric place, with its
aged interior, serves high-end
Bavarian food. Must try the
steak, ox and zander.

TITTMONING: Florianstube €
Regional Map F4
Stadtplatz 44, 84529
Tel *(08683) 1032* **Closed** *Thu*
Modest country restaurant
with a range of local dishes.
Cheerful, relaxed service and
great value meals at this low-
key eatery.

WAGING AM SEE:
Strandkurhaus €
Regional Map F4
Am See 1, 83329
Tel *(08681) 47900*

This charming lakeside
restaurant has a traditional
Bavarian decor. It offers a menu
of fish and local specialities.
Strandkurhaus only uses organic
ingredients in the dishes.

WASSERBURG AM INN:
Herrenhaus €€
Regional Map E4
Herrengasse 17, 83512
Tel *(08071) 5971170* **Closed** *Mon*
& Sun
Daily Bavarian seasonal
menu, with some great
French specials. The fresh
pike in mushroom sauce
and the salmon in Riesling
are remarkably good.

Upper Bavaria
(South)

ANDECHS: Kloserhof
Andechs €
German Map C4
Bergstraße 9, 82346
Tel *(08152) 93090*
A local monastery provides
the ingredients at this traditional
restaurant. Beautiful valley
views and fantastic beer. Cash
accepted only.

BAD TÖLZ:
Altes Fährhaus €€
Regional Map D5
An der Isarlust 1, 83646
Tel *(08041) 6030* **Closed** *Mon*
& Tue
Located in a picturesque
setting, this old ferry house
sits on the banks of the River
Isar. The menu includes dishes
made using fresh local fish and
game. Don't miss out on the
venison in sloe gin.

For more information on types of restaurants *see page 271*

Tasteful and colourful interiors of Restaurant Vaun, Garmisch-Partenkirchen

**BAYRISCHZELL: Der
Alpenhof** €€€
International **Map** D5
Osterhofen 1, 83735
Tel *(08023) 90650*
Michelin-starred restaurant
with gorgeous alpine views.
Der Alpenhof serves interna-
tional gourmet with a hint of
the Bavarian.

**GARMISCH-PARTENKIRCHEN:
Restaurant Vaun** €€
German **Map** C5
Zugspitzstr. 2, 82467
Tel *(08821) 7308187* **Closed** *Sun*
Try the delicious lime and sweet
potato soup, or the smoked cod
with radish. Evening reservations
are recommended.

**GARMISCH-PARTENKIRCHEN:
Colosseo** €€
Italian **Map** C5
Klammstr. 7, 82467
Tel *(088) 2152809*
The well-sized pizzas and
delicious pasta choices ensure
that this regular Italian place is
always busy. It is located right
above a supermarket.

DK Choice

**GARMISCH-PARTENKIRCHEN:
Caspar B** €€€
International **Map** C5
Burgstr. 97, 82467
Tel *(08821) 7020*
This charming restaurant is part
of the Grand Hotel Sonnenbichl,
a venerable Art Nouveau hotel.
It has an inventive menu that
allows guests to choose from
delicious renditions of Bavarian
favourites. The menu is regional.

**GARMISCH-PARTENKIRCHEN:
Best Western Hotel** €
International **Map** C5
Mühlstraße 22, 82467
Tel *(08821) 7040*
Magnificent alpine vistas and
assorted dishes. A less formal bar
serves rustic Bavarian specials.

**GARMISCH-PARTENKIRCHEN:
Reindl's** €€
French **Map** C5
Bahnhofstraße 15, 82467
Tel *(08821) 943870*
The gourmet options include
marinated wild salmon, veal
kidneys, rack of lamb and venison.

MITTENWALD: Arnspitze €€
Regional **Map** C5
Innsbrucker Str. 68, 82481
Tel *(08823) 2425* **Closed** *Tue & Wed*
The freshest local ingredients are
used here. Try the duck liver pâté
with apple jelly.

**OBERAMMERGAU:
Zauberstub'n** €
German **Map** C5
Ettaler Str. 58, 82487
Tel *(08822) 4683* **Closed** *Tue*
Traditional food, and the magic
show, makes Zauberstub'n a must-
visit when travelling with kids.

OBERAMMERGAU: Böld €€
Regional **Map** C5
König-Ludwig-Straße 10, 82487
Tel *(08822) 9120*
This restaurant is in a classic
chalet-style hotel with a rustic
decor. Regional recipes.

TEGERNSEE: Lieberhof €
Regional **Map** D5
Neureuthstraße 52, 83684
Tel *(08022) 4163* **Closed** *Mon & Tue*

Chalet-style restaurant with
several alpine dining rooms.
Hearty Bavarian food.

The Allgäu

FÜSSEN: Michelangelo €
Italian **Map** B5
Lechhalde 1, 87629
Tel *(08362) 924924* **Closed** *Mon*
Find giant pizzas and home-
made pasta in this bright
restaurant. Lovely terrace.

DK Choice

**FÜSSEN: Hotel
Luitpoldpark** €€
Gourmet **Map** B5
Bahnhofstraße 1–3, 87629
Tel *(08362) 9040*
Relish the many dining
options at this magnificent
hotel: from classic Bavarian
to Mexican and international
cuisines. There is also a lovely
Viennese café.

**FÜSSEN-HOPFEN AM SEE: Hotel
am Hopfensee** €
Regional **Map** B5
Uferstraße 10, 87629
Tel *(08362) 50570*
The fish from the Hopfen lake is a
speciality here. Stunning views of
the Alps.

KEMPTEN: Peterhof €
Italian **Map** B5
Salzstraße 1, 87435
Tel *(0831) 52440*
This contemporary Italian
restaurant in the Peterhof Hotel
serves all the local favourites.

DK Choice

KEMPTEN: Rendez-vous à Quiberon €€
French Map B5
Rathausstr. 2, 87435
Tel *(0831) 5208116*
One of the best French restaurants in Bavaria, this eatery is well-priced and serves light bites. Don't miss the smoked salmon and radish *galette* (a type of crepe) - the perfect summer meal.

LINDAU: Alte Post €€
German Map A5
Fischergasse 3, 88131
Tel *(08382) 93460*
This inn serves schnitzels, boiled beef and home-made maultaschen. The cobbled terrace is a gorgeous summer venue.

LINDAU: Bayerischer Hof €€
International Map A5
Bahnhofplatz 2, 88131
Tel *(08382) 9150*
Grande dame-style dining room, swathed in rich fabrics: a formal setting for gourmet dining.

LINDAU: Zum Sünfzen €€
Regional Map A5
Maximilianstr. 1, 88131
Tel *(08382) 5865*
Charming 14th-century place. Fresh Bodensee fish is the speciality, and the venison is also excellent.

LINDAU: Villino €€€
Regional Map A5
Hoyerbergstraße 34, 88131
Tel *(08382) 93450*
This is an exquisite family-run hotel and restaurant with an idyllic garden and terrace. The gourmet dishes have their roots in Asia and Italy.

MEMMINGEN: Da Enzo €
Italian Map B4
Rennweg 14, 87700
Tel *(08331) 2585*
Modest Italian eatery that offers a few Balkan dishes as well. Friendly service and good prices.

OBERSTDORF: Restaurant-Café-Allgäu €
Regional Map B6
Pfarrstrasse 10, 87561
Tel *(08322) 809657* **Closed** *Mon*
Typical Bavarian food and hospitality. The schnitzel with seasoned spinach and cheese is wonderful.

OBERSTDORF: Exquisit €€
Regional Map B6
Lorettostraße 20, 87561
Tel *(08322) 96330*
Country-style restaurant with a range of choices: gourmet to low-calorie. Splendid lawns and views.

Northern Swabia

AUGSBURG: Drei Königinnen €
Regional Map C3
Meister-Veits-Gäßchen 32, 86152
Tel *(0821) 158405*
Highly recommended for its bustling beer garden. Good variety of spätzle and pasta dishes.

AUGSBURG: Berghof €€
German Map C3
Bergstr. 12, 86199
Tel *(0821) 9984322*
Simple German food, such as grilled chicken with roasted potatoes, done to perfection.

DK Choice

AUGSBURG: Manyo €€
Japanese Map C3
Schertlinstraße 12a, 86159
Tel *(0821) 571119* **Closed** *Tue*
Thanks to eateries like this, Japanese food is now an integral part of the urban gastronomic landscape. Much showmanship accompanies the teppanyaki, prepared at your table. The food is first-class and this lovely place is deservedly popular.

AUGSBURG: Ratskeller €€
Regional Map C3
Rathausplatz 2, 86150
Tel *(0821) 31988238*
This vaulted cellar restaurant serves hearty Bavarian dishes. Live jazz music on Monday nights.

AUGSBURG: August €€€
International Map C3
Frauentorstraße 27, 86152
Tel *(0821) 35279* **Closed** *Sun–Tue*
Seasonal cooking with an emphasis on light flavours. The delicate preparation is atypical of Bavaria.

AUGSBURG: Die Ecke €€€
Regional Map C3
Elias-Holl-Platz 2, 86150
Tel *(0821) 510600*
Swabian-Bavarian specialist in catfish. Choices include catfish baked with horseradish and rice with Riesling sauce.

AUGSBURG: Magnolia Restaurant im Glaspalast €€€
International Map C3
Beim Glaspalast 1, 86153
Tel *(0821) 3199999*
Part of a wave of creative gourmet places in Germany, this eatery is a strong Michelin contender.

DILLINGEN: Storchennest €€
Regional Map B3
Demleitnerstraße 6, 89407
Tel *(09071) 4569* **Closed** *Mon & Tue*
Here, the dining room centres around an attractive tiled stove. The restaurant offers daily specials, a six-course menu and great wines.

FRIEDBERG: Conte Luigi €
Italian Map C3
Bauernbräustraße 15, 86316
Tel *(0821) 607127* **Closed** *Mon*
An interesting variety of Italian dishes and a fantastic antipasti buffet. Lovely courtyard seating in summer.

NEU-ULM: Kon-Ya Sushi €€
Japanese Map A3
Ludwigstraße 11, 89231
Tel *(0731) 40361511*
With its Japanese minimalist decor and light dishes, Kon-Ya Sushi is a treat. Outstanding sushi.

NEU-ULM: Landhof Meini €€
Regional Map A3
Marbacher Straße 4, 89233
Tel *(0731) 70520*
This pleasant restaurant serves Swabian food, fresh fish and chicken salads. Traditional rustic decor meets modern elegance.

NÖRDLINGEN: Meyers Keller €€€
International Map B2
Marienhöhe 8, 86720
Tel *(09081) 4493* **Closed** *Mon & Tue*
An elegant restaurant, where quality ingredients are used to produce creative dishes. A choice of interesting seasonal specials are on offer, with seating at lovely garden tables.

Typical Japanese seating area at Kon-Ya Sushi, Neu-Ulm

For more information on types of restaurants *see page 271*

Pubs, Cafés and Bars in Munich

Munich abounds with bars, cafés, clubs and, of course, hugely popular pubs and beer gardens. There is something for every taste. Places where people go to drink coffee or beer, to have a snack or simply to socialize informally are mostly concentrated in the city centre and in Schwabing. Even in the more outlying districts an abundance of pleasant cafés and bars can be found. Many food shops also set aside a corner for eaters and drinkers.

Pubs and Beer Gardens

The features most typical of Munich, and seen everywhere in the city, are spacious pubs often fronted by gardens shaded by chestnut or linden trees. These pubs serve beer from the local breweries as well as generous helpings of good Bavarian food. Waitresses dressed in the traditional *Dirndl* wind their way among the tables and sometimes there is an oompah band playing a repertoire of folk melodies.

Munich's most famous pub is the **Hofbräuhaus**, which today is filled with more American and Japanese tourists than local drinkers. Seated on wooden benches at large tables arranged in spacious rooms, garrulous crowds of guests enjoy their favourite drink as they sing along with and sway in time to the Bavarian music.

Almost equally renowned is the **Augustiner Gaststätte**, which also has a restaurant. The interior is decorated in late 19th-century style, and has a very pleasant courtyard surrounded by arcades, which induce the desire to linger for as long as possible.

Munich's next most famous pubs are the **Löwenbräukeller** and the **Donisl**. In the latter, with its old-style furnishings, authentic Bavarian folk music is also played. It is currently closed for renovation until 2015. The city's finest beer garden is the **Chinesischer Turm** in the Englischer Garten, where there are a total of 6,000 seats for its international clientele.

Many beer gardens allow drinkers to bring their own food.

Beer is best served straight from the barrel. A popular type of beer is *Helles*, a light lager beer. Also widely drunk is *Radler*, beer to which lemonade is added *(see p274)*.

Cafés, Bars and Bistros

A great variety of different establishments come under the name of "café". They include traditional coffee shops, where people go for *Kaffee und Kuchen* (coffee and cake), the coffee helping to wash down a large pastry or slice of cake. Two such coffee shops are the old-world **Café Kreutzkamm**, which moved here from Dresden after World War II (it is known for its chocolates, **Dresdner Stollen** and pyramidal cakes), and the **Café Luitpold**, which tempts with its equally excellent cakes and chocolates.

A real oasis of peace – a commodity highly valued by the citizens of Munich – is the **Café am Beethovenplatz**. Time passes more slowly here, and the gentle classical music seems to make the coffee smell and taste better than elsewhere. The atmosphere of the **Kaffeehaus Altschwabing** takes you back to the turn of the 19th and 20th centuries. Thomas Mann and other writers once enjoyed the strong coffee that is served here.

Another type of café is a place offering hot and cold food and a range of soft and alcoholic drinks. The atmosphere is more like that of a bar or bistro. These bar-type cafés are the centre of the social life of Munich. They range from somewhere to

go to grab a sandwich or drop in for a coffee or beer, to pretentious places where high society meets. There are also gay and lesbian bars, such as **Café Glück** and **Café Nil**, and bars for businessmen, as well as bars for connoisseurs of wine or whisky and for pool players.

Many bars serve large and delicious breakfasts and lunches. Others specialize in ice cream. Many, including the **Roxy**, are open until late at night.

A feature once unique to Munich was Kunstpark Ost, an extensive leisure park near the Eastern Station. Some of its famous clubs, discos (such as the hugely popular Babylon) restaurants and bars (such as the much-frequented Bongo Bar) still exist or have moved to the Optimol Area.

Take-aways (take-outs)

Numerous booths and stalls selling takeaway food are to be seen in the streets of Munich, particularly in the main shopping areas of the Old Town and Schwabing, as well as in pedestrian subways and at railway stations.

The traditional takeaways are those of the well-known international fast-food chains. There are also many take-away pizza, sausage, baguette and kebab houses. The **Nordsee** restaurant offers delicious freshly made sandwiches with herring, fried fish or crab salad, and the **Wienerwald** restaurants sell chicken cooked in every possible way.

There are also takeaway stands in almost all butcher's shops, where pre-packaged lunch dishes in aluminium trays are sold. The food sold in Munich's most renowned delicatessens, the **Dallmayr** and **Käfer**, is excellent, although the prices can seem a little high *(see p287)*. A good alternative is the hot food stalls to be found in **Viktualienmarkt** *(see p68)*.

DIRECTORY

Pubs

Andechser am Dom
Weinstr. 7A. **Map** 3 B2, 6
D3. **Tel** 29 84 81.

**Augustiner
Gaststätte**
Neuhauser Str. 27. **Map** 3
A2, 5 B3. **Tel** 23 18 32 57.

Augustiner-Keller
Arnulfstr. 52. **Tel** 59 43 93.

Chinesischer Turm
Englischer Garten 3.
Map 2 F4. **Tel** 38 38 730.

Donisl
Weinstr. 1. (Closed for
renovation until 2015.)
Map 3 B2, 6 D3.
Tel 22 01 84.

Franziskaner Garten
Friedenspromenade 45.
Tel 43 00 996.

Hofbräuhaus
Am Platzl 9. **Map** 3 C2, 6
E3. **Tel** 29 01 36 100.

Hofbräukeller
Innere Wiener Strasse 19.
Tel 45 99 250.

Kaisergarten
Kaiserstr. 34.
Tel 34 02 02 03.

Löwenbräukeller
Nymphenburger Str. 2.
Tel 54 72 66 90.

Paulaner Bräuhaus
Kapuzinerplatz 5.
Tel 54 46 110.

Seehaus
Kleinhesselohe 3.
Tel 38 16 130.

Tassilogarten
Auerfeldstr. 18.
Tel 44 80 022.

Wintergarten
Elisabethplatz 4B. **Map** 2
D3. **Tel** 27 37 31 34.

Cafés and Bars

Atzinger
Schellingstr. 9. **Map** 2 D4.
Tel 28 28 80.

Holy Home
Reichenbachstr. 21.
Map 3 C3. **Tel** 20 14 546

Café Altschwabing
Schellingstr. 56.
Map 1 C4. **Tel** 27 31 022.

**Café am
Beethovenplatz**
Goethestr. 51.
Tel 54 40 43 48.

Café Glück
Palmstr. 4. **Map** 3 A5.
Tel 20 11 673.

Café Glyptothek
Königsplatz 3. **Map** 1 B5.
Tel 28 80 83 80.

ELLA im Lenbachhaus
Luisenstr. 33.
Map 1 B5.
Tel 700 88 177.

Café Kreutzkamm
Maffeistr. 4. **Map** 3 B2.
Tel 99 35 570.

Café Luitpold
Brienner Str. 11.
Map 6 D1. **Tel** 24 28 750.

Café Puck
Türkenstr. 33. **Map** 2 D4.
Tel 28 02 280.

Café Reitschule
Königinstr. 34.
Tel 38 88 760.

Café Schwabing
Belgradstr. 1. **Map** 2 D2.
Tel 30 88 856.

Café Wienerplatz
Innere Wienerstr. 48.
Map 4 E3. **Tel** 44 89 494.

Charivari
Türkenstr. 92. **Map** 2 D4.
Tel 28 28 32.

Café Nil
Han-Sachs-Straße 2.
Map 3 B4. **Tel** 23 88 95 95.

Cyclo Restaurant Bar
Theresienstr. 70. **Map** 1
C5. **Tel** 28 80 83 90.

Jazzbar Vogler
Rumfordstr. 17. **Map** 3 C3,
6 D5. **Tel** 29 46 62.

Kaffee Giesing
Tegernseer Landstr. 96.
Tel 62 00 03 57.

Königsquelle
Baaderplatz 2. **Map** 3 C3,
6 E5. **Tel** 22 00 71.

Kao Kao
Tulbeckstr. 9. **Tel** 50 54 00.

Le Bouchon
Thierschstr. 65. **Tel** 23 70
83 55. **Map** 4 E2.

Mauz
Leopoldstr. 20. **Map** 2 E3.
Tel 38 32 99 47.

Müller & Söhne
Kazmairstr. 28.
Tel 45 23 78 67.

**Westend Café
and Restaurant**
Anglerstraße 32.
Tel 50 83 41.

Niederlassung
Buttermelcherstr. 6
Map 3 C3, 6 D5.
Tel 32 60 03 07.

Pacific Times
Baaderstr. 28. **Map** 3 C3, 6
E5. **Tel** 20 23 94 70.

Pusser's
Falkenturmstr. 9.
Tel 22 05 00.

Roxy
Leopoldstr. 48
Map 2 E3.
Tel 34 92 92.

Schumann's
Odeonsplatz 6.
Map 4 D2, 6 F3.
Tel 22 90 60.

**Spatenhaus an
der Oper**
Residenzstr. 12.
Map 3 C2, 6 D2.
Tel 29 07 060.

**Stadtcafé im
Stadtmuseum**
St-Jakobs-Platz 1.
Map 3 B2, 5 C4.
Tel 26 69 49.

Tambosi
Odeonsplatz 18.
Map 3 C1, 6 D1.
Tel 29 83 22.

Tresznjewski
Theresienstr. 72.
Map 1 C5. **Tel** 28 23 49.

Wiener's Kaffeebar
Neuturmstr. 2.
Map 3 C2. **Tel** 29 25 69.

Take-aways

Der Kleine Chinese
Tal 28. **Map** 3 C2, 6 D3.
Tel 29 16 35 36.

Nordsee
Viktualienmarkt 10.
Map 3 B3.
Leopolstr. 82.
Map 2 E3.

Thai Magie
Blumenstr. 1.
Map 3 B3, 5 B5.

Wienerwald
Leonrodstraße 91.
Tel 20 20 94 71.

SHOPS AND MARKETS

Retailers in the Bavarian Alps who cater both to the tourist trade and to the more affluent Bavarians offer for sale virtually everything from the finest luxury goods to local arts and crafts. A particularly ubiquitous Bavarian speciality is sports, hiking and mountaineering equipment, which is displayed for sale in many outlets. There

is also a large market for anything in traditional Bavarian style, from beer steins to *Lederhosen* to fine glass and porcelain. An enjoyable way of spending a few hours is to stroll among the stalls in the spa towns selling locally made items. In complete contrast, Munich, one of the most sophisticated European cities, has some very exclusive shops.

The greengrocer's counter in one of Munich's elegant delicatessens

Where to Shop

Shops ranging from department stores to boutiques to souvenir shops can be found in Munich. All larger towns in the Bavarian Alps have a shopping district, usually pedestrianized.

Also popular are the out-of-town superstores, which attract large numbers of shoppers because of their competitive prices and ease of parking for drivers.

Shopping in Munich

Munich's main shopping district is the pedestrianized area of the Old Town around Neuhauser Straße, Kaufinger Straße and the Marienplatz area, where stores and shops of major European retailers are located. This whole area probably has the largest daily turnover in the whole of Germany, and one of the best stores is Ludwig Beck am Rathauseck on Marienplatz.

Around Theatinerstraße, Maximilianstraße and Brienner Straße are exclusive clothes shops such as Versace, Gucci, Escada and Donna Karan, whose prices are out of the reach of most tourists.

Maximilianstraße is also the home of the eccentric Munich couturier Rudolph Moshammer.

In the famous Schwabing district, particularly in the area between Amalienstraße, Schellingstraße and Türkenstraße, exclusive boutiques and tasteful second-hand shops can be found, as well as many bookshops (selling both new and second-hand books) and antique shops.

Opening Hours

Shops are legally permitted to open from 6am to 8pm from Monday to Saturday. In practice, most food shops open between 7am and

9am (bakeries opening the earliest), and close at 8pm. Other shops, including supermarkets, are usually open from 9am to 8pm.

Small shops, particularly in more out-of-the-way places, often close for lunch then stay open until 6pm. At railway stations in large towns it is possible to buy food and beverages until 11pm, even on Sunday. Petrol (gas) stations that also sell food and drink are often open until late at night; some open 24 hours.

Paying

Travellers' cheques and credit cards are accepted in department stores and in larger shops. In Germany the most widely accepted credit card is Eurocard. Most boutiques and bigger shops will accept Mastercard and VISA. In smaller shops cash is preferred.

Food and Drink

As elsewhere in Europe, food shops have largely been taken over by retail chains. The exceptions are small butcher's shops, bakeries and confectioners. Fruit and vegetables are

The showroom of a shop specializing in Nymphenburg porcelain

Advertisement for an exclusive designer fashion shop in Ruhpolding

still sold in markets, with the most famous being the Viktualienmarkt *(see p68)*. A visit to the delicatessens **Dallmayr** and **Käfer** will be memorable.

The decorative entrance to one of Munich's delicatessens

Gifts and Souvenirs

It is virtually impossible to leave the Bavarian Alps without a souvenir beer mug or a decorative bottle of beer. Particularly suitable as presents are bottles of the local spirits and drinks presented in stoneware bottles, often bearing the portrait of the legendary king Ludwig II.

Tourist resorts are full of souvenir shops. Besides the folksy kitsch there is some good-quality woodcarving, pottery, painted glass and porcelain. Stylized Bavarian costume and accessories made of natural materials are ubiquitous. Conforming to the latest fashion, they are

often quite attractive. The best place in Munich for gifts of this type are the **Trachten Angermaier** and **Lodenfrey**.

Specialist Shops

Munich boasts several specialist shops of renown. **SportScheck** is an outstanding sports shop. The best bookshops include **Geobuch**, which specializes in maps and guidebooks, **Hugendubel** and **Werner**, which sell books on art, architecture and design. **Hieber Lindberg** specializes in musical instruments and literature, while **Zauberflöte** sells classical music and opera CDs. Lovers of fine antique furniture and paintings should visit the famous antique shop **Bernheimer Fine Old Masters**.

A shop in Augsburg selling pottery and basketware

What to Buy in the Bavarian Alps

Besides a vast range of German and European goods, the visitor to the Bavarian Alps can also purchase local products that make perfect gifts and souvenirs. They are usually inspired by folk traditions, and their artistic merit varies greatly. The sheer quantity of gift-shop kitsch is quite overwhelming, particularly items related to beer-drinking ceremonies and devotional art. However, it is also perfecly possible to find good-quality, tasteful and authentic examples of the arts and crafts of the Bavarian Alps.

Porcelain
Dolls dressed in Bavarian costume make good presents for girls or collectors.

Folk Art

Many shops selling folk art can be found in the Bavarian Alps. As well as wood carvings, for which Oberammergau is particularly renowned, good-quality paintings and antique items of often striking simplicity are available.

S HUBERTUS

Painting on Glass
Painting on glass is a widespread craft in the region, with the main centre being Murnau. Subjects are usually images of saints or religious scenes depicted in a naïve style.

Copy of a
Baroque statue

A 19th-century
votive painting

Flat tin figure painted
in enamels

Glass and Ceramics

Workshops in the Bavarian Forest region are famous for their glassware (Waldglas). They produce both classic functional items, as well as modern art glass in a range of novel shapes and colours. Folk ceramics include painted pottery and stoneware that characteristically has the colour of grey granite. One of the most prominent centres of ceramic production is Dießen.

Stoneware snuff box

Plate with the Bavarian coat of arms

Bavarian Waldglas

Nymphenburg Porcelain
Usually of a high artistic quality and relatively expensive, hand-painted figurines like this are produced by the famous Nymphenburg porcelain factory.

Regional Costume

Bavarian folk costume is attractive and practical in its modern-day form. Usually made of high-quality wool, linen or leather, it gives protection from cold or heat. Recommended for children are the famous Bavarian Lederhosen, which are practically dirt-proof but also machine washable should the need arise.

The famous Bavarian *Lederhosen*

A decorated leather belt

A soft woollen *Janker*

Leather Goods

Bavaria is renowned for its high-quality leather goods. The material is surprisingly soft, and the items often have a crude but deliberate old-worldliness about them.

Knitted woollen socks

Decorated hunter's bag

Leather shoes in Bavarian folk style

Silver necklace with colourful pendants

Embroidered tasselled shawl

Drinking Accessories

Among the articles most widely produced by the souvenir industry are beer mugs of all descriptions, ranging from simple stoneware vessels to highly colourful mugs decorated with paintings or reliefs and fitted with pewter lids. They are characteristic of Bavaria and make good gifts.

A finely decorated beer bottle

Beer mug with the coat of arms of Bavaria

Collectors' Items

Both beer-related artifacts as well as antique beer mugs and lids are valued items that are bought and sold by international antiques collectors.

Antique beer mug lids

OUTDOOR ACTIVITIES AND SPECIALIST HOLIDAYS

Munich and Bavaria offer an amazing variety of sporting and leisure activities. Throughout the year active holiday makers head to the region's hills, forests, mountains, rivers and lakes. Various national organisations can provide details on a particular sport and have regional contacts. Cycling, running and Nordic walking rank highest among the area's most popular sports, while snow sports in the easily accessible Alps keep visitors active during the winter months. During the summer this nation of outdoor lovers flock to the lakes and rivers to swim and sail.

Hiking amongst the spectacular scenery of the Mittenwald Alps

Walking and Hiking

Walking and hiking is a popular activity for both young and old. Numerous paths are well preserved and marked along rivers, through forests and up mountains. Every town has its own rambling or hiking club. The foothills of the Alps provide some easy terrain for gentle hikes but the higher you go the more demanding it becomes. Family-friendly trails on higher terrain involve taking a cable car up the mountain. Lenggries near Bad Tölz *(see p224)* is good for family trails and the **Deutscher Wanderverband** (German hiking Club) and **Deutscher Volkssportverband e.V.** (German Sports Federation) can provide further details. For information on guided walking tours contact the local tourist office in each area, or the **Verband Deutscher Gebirgs/und Wandervereine e.V.** (German Mountaineering and Hiking Club) who will direct you to smaller regional

clubs. The **Kneipp-Verein München** or **DAV Summit Club** also have regional clubs who organise hikes and tours.

Cycling

Because cycling is such a popular sport the cycling paths here are excellent. Bikes can be hired in towns and cities throughout the region and there are plenty of bike stands available. Munich is Germany's most bike-friendly city with some 700km (435 miles) of cycle paths. Cycling is one of the best ways to take in the beautiful scenery between Lake Constance and Bad Tölz, and to see the towns and villages of Dachau, Passau, Wasserburg and Bayerischzell. Contact the **Allgemeiner Deutscher Fahrrad Club** (German Cycling Federation) in Munich for details and tips before planning a trip. They provide tour plans, maps, route suggestions and tips for all over Bavaria. They also give advice on the latest regulations for transporting bikes on trains, which is possible with prior booking and a nominal fee.

Water Sports

If you are in this part of Germany in the warmer months, you simply have to take a dip in one of the lakes or rivers. The water is very clean, safe and totally refreshing. The Strandbad, indicating the beach area, is visible in every lakeside town and denotes free public bathing. Excellent sailing conditions can be found on Starnbergersee, Ammersee, Chiemsee and Bodensee, and the area near Lindau is famous for its yacht building wharves and sailing clubs. Contact the **Deutscher Segler-Verband** (German Sailing Club) for information on locations, regulations and possibilities of sailing or hiring a boat. To hire or sail a yacht, you will need a current licence showing your sailing abilities and competence. Sailing on Bodensee requires a special Bodensee license. Canoeing is also popular on the Bavarian

Cyclists touring the beautiful Bavarian countryside

rivers, especially on the Altmühl between Gunzenhausen and Kelheim or at Loisach near Garmisch, where the World Wild Water Championships have been held. For further details contact the **Deutscher Kanu-Verband e.V.** (German Canoe Federation) or the **Bayerischer Kanu-Verband** (Bavarian Club).

Skiing in one of the many resorts in the Bavarian Alps

Skiing and Mountain Sports

Garmisch Partenkirchen (see p221) is Germany's best ski area, others include Reit im Winkl (see p205). There are plenty of hotels and ski hire companies in these areas and the relevant tourist office can provide further details as well as maps of ski lifts and runs. Skiing is also possible at other Alpine peaks in Lenggries or near Berchtesgaden. Langlauf (cross-country skiing) can be pursued on many well-kept routes, marked clearly in towns at the foothills of the Alps. Other enquiries can be directed to the **Deutscher Skiverband e.V.** (German Ski Association) who can give tips and suggestions for planned visits or tours. **Sporthaus Schuster** or **SportScheck**, two large sports department stores in Munich centre, have travel offices that organise skiing trips and can advise on the hiring of equipment and on ski packages available. Climbing is also big in the mountainous areas. Whichever level you are you can find your match here, especially in the

Canoeing on the popular Altmühl River in Bavaria

Allgäu. If you want to hire a guide contact the **Verband Deutscher Berg-und Skiführer** (Association of German Mountain and Ski Guides). Climbing walls such as **High-East Kletterhalle** in Munich offer an indoor alternative, or a chance to practice. Further information regarding climbing, or rock formations for example, can be obtained from the German Alpine Association, **Deutscher Alpenverein** (DAV).

Golf and Tennis

Both golf and tennis are increasing in popularity and several towns have excellent clubs, golf courses and tennis courts. To be allowed on a golf course, you will need to prove proficiency and pre-book, so plan well ahead. Contact the **Deutscher Golf Verband e.V.** for information on courses and rules. Many Bavarian golf enthusiasts head out to the course at Wallgau (see p222) where the conditions are good and the scenery beautiful. Tegernsee and the Bayerischer Wald have a few golf-oriented hotels with special packages.

The **Deutscher Tennis Bund e.V.** has information on local tennis clubs and the procedure for booking a court. Some hotels are geared towards tennis, such as the Tannenhof in Allgäu, the Espacio in Garmisch or the Ödhof Sporthotel in the Bayerischer Wald.

National Parks

The Bayerischer Wald is Germany's oldest National Park (see p191). Lying in the area behind Grafenau, it has a wealth of unusual wildlife, forests and rivers. Tours operate within the protected area of the park, but the surrounding forest area has camping sites and hiking routes where you will find people mountain biking and Nordic walking. An all-round outdoor fitness sport that involves walking at a brisk pace with the support of sticks, Nordic walking has increased in popularity over the past few years. For further details contact the **Nordic Walking Association**.

Summer is a good time to visit the park when you can see more of the wildlife and fauna indigenous to the woods and waterways. Be sure to stick to the marked paths and to observe the safety and conservation regulations.

Nordic walking in a peaceful park in Lower Bavaria

Camping and Caravanning

A great number of Germans head south in the summer months from June to August to the sites at lakesides, forests and riversides throughout Bavaria. The Germans love the great outdoors and for this nation of campers, sites are plentiful and well organised. The majority of families who camp are in caravans, while tents are favoured by the younger generation and foreign tourists. Pitching a tent is highly regulated and allowed only at official camping grounds. The majority of camping sites are privately owned, friendly and offer plenty of extras. Washing facilities are always available, and some sites have shops, a bar and restaurants. Well established and more expensive sites tend to offer group activities, especially for children, and electricity. Campfires are popular and sites have designated areas for them. For details and advice on camping and caravanning, contact the **Deutscher Camping Club e.V.** and also the **Backpacker Network Germany.**

Historic and Scenic Routes

Travelling along the Alpenstrasse, the German Alpine Road, is a great way to experience the best of the scenery in the Bavarian Alps. The road was built in 1927 and connects Lake Constance with Berchtesgaden. At its highest point the road

The fairy-tale Linderhof Palace, one of many of Ludwig II's residences

reaches 1735m (5690 ft) and is ranked among the world's best scenic routes. Travel between Lindau, Füssen, Oberammergau, Garmisch, Kochel, Chiemsee, Tegernsee, Bad Reichenhall and on to Berchtesgaden. On route take in Linderhof Palace and Neuschwannstein Castle, the Zugspitze mountain in Garmisch and the salt mines at Berchtesgaden. For more information visit **www. alpenstrasse.de**

The Romantischestrasse, Romantic Road, also runs through Bavaria between Würzburg and Füssen, with old medieval town centres, churches and the rivers Lech and Danube on route. The Alpine foothills form part of the scenery, as does the Ammersee lake, moors and the Allgäu mountains. There is plenty to enjoy from thermal baths, to tobbogan runs, nature conservation areas and hiking paths. Visit **www.romantis chestrasse.de** for further details.

Steingaden is the point where these two routes intersect and has a health resort as well as a famous pilgrimage and ecclesiastical treasures.

Specialist Holidays

For the best information on German language courses in Bavaria, contact the Goethe Institut in London or Munich. The institute runs its own courses for various lengths of time and from beginner to

advanced levels. There are many additional language schools in Munich, which can be found using the internet. Augsburg also has a small but good language school. To find out more contact **Augsburger Deutschkurse.**

Cooking holidays are increasing in popularity and Bavaria has a few to offer. The holidays give you the opportunity to learn the basics of gourmet cuisine from masterchefs in their own restaurants. Students stay in the hotel itself and partake in cookery lessons on site. Two great places to visit in Bavaria are Heinz Winkler's Residenz hotel and restaurant at Aschau near Chiemsee *(see p280)* and André Greul's Fürstenhof in Landshut.

Although Bavaria is famous for its beer rather than its wines, cookery courses also teach you about great German wines. The stretch of Lake Constance behind Lindau produces several varieties of white wine. The best way to experience the country's offerings is to visit a wine festival, held in many towns towards the end of the summer. For more information visit **Deutsches Weininstitut.**

Another popular holiday activity is horse-riding and a weekend of riding can be arranged with one of several private equestrian centres. The **Deutsche Reiterliche Vereinigung e.V.** can provide information on centres throughout the region.

Family fun at one of Germany's well-equipped camp sites

Spa Vacations

"Wellness" is a term cropping up in many hotels in the countryside. This denotes a spa area for health and wellbeing. It is now possible to take a weekend, or longer stay, to enjoy a variety of spa treatments including water therapy, swimming, steam rooms, massages, exercise routines and walks in the healthy, fresh air. **Deutscher Heilbäderverband e.V.,** the German spa association of spas, has information on hotel spas and packages throughout the region. Towns with the word "Bad" preceding the name signifies a spa town. Here you are guaranteed a longstanding tradition of health regimes, rest and relaxation as well as thermal baths. The **Therme Erding** is a paradise of thermal baths, just outside Munich. For more of a family fun holiday, stay at the water park at Alpamare *(see p224),* a spa village rich in mineral water. The park is one of the largest in Germany.

DIRECTORY

General Sporting Information

Deutscher Olympischer Sportbund
Otto-Fleck-Schneise 12, 60528, Frankfurt am Main.
Tel 069 67000. W **dosb.de**

Walking and Hiking

DAV Summit Club
Am Perlacher Forst 186, 81545, München.
Tel 089 64240194.
W **dav-summit-club.de**

Deutscher Volks-sportverband e.V.
Fabrikstraße 8, 84053, Altötting. **Tel** 08671 96310.
W **dvv-wandern.de**

Deutscher Wanderverband and Verband Deutscher Gebirgs/und Wandervereine e.V.
Wilhelmshöher Allee 157–159, 34121, Kassel.
Tel 0561 938730.
W **wanderverband.de**

Kneipp-Verein München
Prinz-Ludwig-Straße 6, 80333, München. **Tel** 089 283780. W **kneipp verein-muenchen.de**

Cycling

Allgemeiner Deutscher Fahrrad Club (ADFC)
Platenstraße 4.
Tel 089 773429.
W **adfc-muenchen.de**

Water Sports

Bayerischer Kanu-Verband
Georg-Brauchle-Ring 93, 80992, München.
Tel 089 15702418.
W **kanu-bayern.org**

Deutscher Kanu-Verband e.V.
W **kanu.de**

Deutscher Segler-Verband
Gründgensstr. 18, 22309, Hamburg. **Tel** 040 6320090. W **dsv.org**

Golf and Tennis

Deutscher Golf Verband e.V.
Postfach 2106, 65189, Wiesbaden. **Tel** 0611 990200. W **golf.de/dgv**

Deutscher Tennis Bund e.V.
Hallerstraße 89, 20149, Hamburg. **Tel** 040 411780.
W **dtb-tennis.de**

Skiing and Mountain Sports

Deutscher Alpenverein (DAV)
Von Kahr Straße 2–4, 80997, München.
Tel 089 140030.
W **alpenverein.de**

Deutscher Skiverband e.V.
Am Erwin-Himmelseherplatz, Hubertusstraße 1, 82152, Planegg. **Tel** 089 857900.
W **ski-online.de**

High-East Kletterhalle
Sonnenallee 2, 85551, Kirchheim/Heimstetten.
Tel 089 92794796.

Sporthaus Schuster
W **sportschuster.de**

SportScheck
W **sportscheck.com**

Verband Deutscher Berg-und Skiführer (VDBS)
Fraunhoferstr. 4, 82377, Penzberg.
Tel 08856 9360913.
W **bergfuehrer-verband.de**

National Parks

Naturpark Bayerischer Wald
Infozentrum 3, 94227, Zwiesel.
Tel 09922 802480.
W **naturpark-bayer-wald.de**

Nordic Walking Association
W **nordicportal.net**

Camping and Caravanning

ADAC Camping Referat
Am Westpark 8, Munich.
Tel 089 76760.

Backpacker Network Germany
Turnerstr. 3, 20357, Hamburg. **Tel** (040) 18055757. W **backpacker network.de**

Deutscher Camping Club e.V.
Mandlstraße 28, 80802, München.
Tel 089 3801420.
W **camping-club.de**

Specialist Holidays

Augsburger Deutschkurse
W **adk-german courses.com**

Goethe Institut
Dachauer Straße 122, 80637, München.
Tel 089 159210.
W **goethe.de**
(UK) 50 Princes Gate, Exhibition Road, London, SW7 2PH.
Tel 020 7596 4000.

Deutsche Reiterliche Vereinigung e.V.
Freiherr von Langen Straße 13, 48231, Warendorf.
Tel 02581 63620.

Deutsches Weininstitut
Gutenbergplatz 3–5, 55116, Mainz.
Tel 06131 28290.

Spa Vacations

Deutscher Heilbäderverband e.V.
Reinhardstraße 46, 10117, Berlin.
Tel 030 2463 6920.

Therme Erding
Thermenallee 1, 85435, Erding.
Tel 08122 2270100.
W **therme-erding.de**

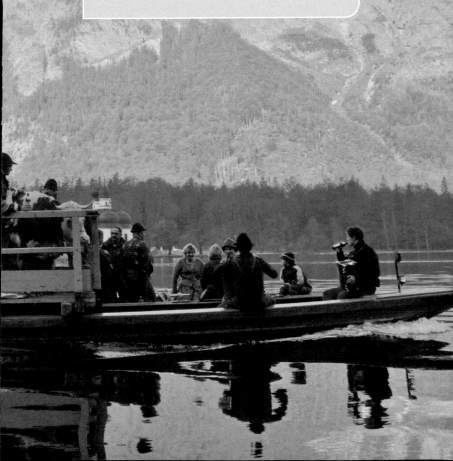

SURVIVAL GUIDE

Practical Information   296–305

Travel Information   306–315

PRACTICAL INFORMATION

Famous for breathtaking scenery and historic monuments, the Bavarian Alps are the most popular destination for visitors to Germany. Like Munich, the regional capital, the mountains are well equipped to receive tourists. Hotels and catering facilities, as well as excellent road, rail and urban transport, make travelling in the area a pleasure. The Bavarians are generally friendly and hospitable, although communication may be difficult in smaller towns and villages unless you speak German. This, however, is not a problem in cosmopolitan Munich.

When to Go

Bavaria is a year-round destination, but the weather there is finest from June to September. This is the season for sports such as hiking, cycling, para-gliding and kayaking, and the beer gardens are thrown open to happy drinkers. Prices tend to be lower in the spring (March to May) and early autumn (October), and the crowds smaller. Ski resorts operate from late November to sometime in March, depending on the snow. The Bavarian calendar is packed with cultural and sporting events, religious celebrations and festivals (see pp34–5). Entertainment listings can be found in the local press, including free newspapers.

Visas and Passports

The border between Bavaria and Austria is practically non-existent. However, travellers crossing the border need to carry their passport.

Citizens of countries in the European Union, the US, Canada, Australia and New Zealand do not require a visa to visit Germany, as long as their stay does not exceed three months. Visitors from India and South Africa will need a visa. While citizens of most EU countries do not require a passport to enter Germany, a national ID card with photograph is necessary. Visa requirements may change so it is advisable to check details before you travel.

Customs

German regulations totally prohibit the import of firearms, drugs, animals and exotic plants that are under special protection.

Customs limits for travellers from outside the EU are 200 cigarettes, or 250g (9oz) of tobacco or 50 cigars, one litre of spirits or two litres of wine. Items for personal use, provided they are not in quantities intended for trade, are not subject to customs duty.

Tourist Information

Tourist information bureaux are generally found in town centres, in main squares and near railway stations. In Munich, the best source of information is **Tourismusamt München**, with big offices in the main train station and on Marienplatz, and an excellent source of detail online. In small towns, the town hall (Rathaus) or civic centre (Gemeindever-Waltung) does the job, while in spa resorts try the Resort Administration Kurverwaltung. In addition to free town maps, tourist offices provide a range of brochures on local attractions, guided tours, shows and cultural events. They also assist tourists who are seeking accommodation, sometimes for a fee.

CityTourCard

Admission Prices

Many museums and historic monuments offer reductions on admission prices. Information on these can be obtained at tourist offices or hotel reception desks.

A good discount option is the CityTourCard, valid for one or three days for one person or for groups of up to five people (prices range from €9.80 to €48). You can buy a card covering just Munich's city centre or for the suburbs as well. The CityTourCard gives price reductions of up to 50 per cent to more than 30 attractions including museums, theatres and sightseeing tours, plus free use of public transport throughout the city. The card is sold at all suburban railway stations (S-Bahn), underground stations (U-Bahn), tram and bus stations, and selected hotels – look for the CityTourCard logo.

Tourists in the formal gardens at Schloss Nymphenburg in Munich

◀ Cattle-drive celebration on Konigssee lake, Berchtesgadener Land, Upper Bavaria

Opening Hours

Most museums are open from 10am to 5pm or 6pm, Tuesday to Sunday. Bavarian state-run museums, exhibition halls and castles are usually free on Sundays. In Munich, major museums such as the three Pinakothekes and the Bayerisches Nationalmuseum charge just €1 on Sundays. Churches are generally open to visitors from 8am until evening worship, but visitors should note that sightseeing is not allowed during services.

Large department stores are generally open from 9am or 9:30am to 8pm, Monday to Saturday. Large supermarkets operate from 8am to 8 pm or 9pm, Monday to Saturday. Smaller retailers tend to keep shorter hours, opening from 10am to 6pm or 7pm.

Etiquette and Smoking

Bavarians tend to dress conservatively. For business or social events such as the opera or theatre, and to get into Munich's upmarket nightclubs, smart dress is recommended.

A firm handshake is the standard greeting among both men and women, but also be prepared for a hug or kiss on the cheek. On the telephone, start by giving your last name both when calling and picking up. In smaller shops, it is good form to greet the owner with *"Grüss Gott"* and bid *"Auf Wiedersehen"* when you leave.

Try to be on time for both formal and informal occasions; arriving late is considered impolite. At large parties, things may be more relaxed.

In Bavaria, smoking is prohibited in all public buildings as well as restaurants, bars, cafés and beer tents. Individuals can be fined if they flout the law. In supermarkets and bars, the minimum age is 16 for purchasing cigarettes and alcohol (beer and wine), and 18 for stronger drinks such as whiskey and spirits.

Public Conveniences

In Bavaria's larger towns and cities, public conveniences can be found without much difficulty and are usually clean. Look for the familiar male and female silhouettes, or the letter D *(Damen)* for Ladies and H *(Herren)* for Gentlemen. Department stores are equipped with restrooms, although a small payment of €0.20 to €0.50 should be given to the on-site attendant. Toilets are also provided in restaurants and cafés, but if you are not a customer you should ask permission to use the facilities. Other options in town include shopping centres, public institutions and hotels, and coin-operated, self-cleaning cubicles. On the road, seek out car parks and petrol (gas) stations.

Taxes and Tipping

Most goods sold in Germany are subject to 19 per cent value-added tax *(Mehrwertsteuer)*. Books, foodstuffs, artworks and concert tickets are taxed at 7 per cent VAT. Visitors from countries outside the EU are entitled to a tax refund on the price of any non-edible goods. Shops with the Tax Free sign will issue a certificate or Tax-Free cheque when the value of the items purchased exceeds a specified total, which is usually around €50. You will need to show your passport before a certificate or cheque can be issued. When going through Customs on leaving Germany, the certificate must be stamped. Visitors may be asked to show the goods, which must be in their original packaging, unopened and unused. The tax is either refunded at the border or mailed to you.

By law, sales tax and a service charge are included in restaurant bills. However, it is customary to add a small tip

TAX FREE SHOPPING

Tax-free shopping

of 5 to 10 per cent if you are happy with the service. Give the tip directly to your waiter, rather than leaving it on the table, and state the total amount including the tip. If you do not expect change back, say *"es stimmt so".* For taxi drivers, add 5 percent or round up to the nearest euro on small transactions. Porters are usually given €1 per bag.

Tourist enjoying the sights in bustling Marienplatz

Travellers with Special Needs

Almost all modern public buildings have ramps and other access facilities for disabled visitors, and designated parking spaces are common. Seats on public transport near doors are to be vacated on demand for mobility-impaired, pregnant or senior travellers.

For the sight-impaired, pavements are equipped with a grooved guidance system, and speakers at pedestrian crossings beep at a higher frequency when it is safe to cross. Train timetables are published in Braille.

The Munich tourist office has a useful guide, in print or for download, with details on public transport, hotels and restaurants with facilities for disabled visitors. Munich's Association for the Disabled (**Sozialverband VDK**) offers a series of guides, but only in German.

Travelling with Children

Munich has plenty to charm younger visitors – a large zoo and aquarium, playgrounds and sprawling parks, child-friendly museums and even a regular circus. Bavaria-Filmstadt is as much a theme park as a working film studio (see p147). Cycling the city on safe, dedicated paths is always an adventure (see pp312–13). A wide range of discounts are available for children so be sure to ask about them.

Public attitudes towards children are fairly tolerant, but parents are expected to keep their children in line. A few hotels have a no-children policy, so check before you book. Many restaurants have high chairs and children's menus. Hotels should have a list of babysitters on hand. Facilities for changing nappies are generally limited to department stores, major museums and train stations. Breast-feeding in public is accepted if done discreetly.

When driving children must be restrained in suitable car seats, which car rental firms will provide for a small fee.

Children enjoying the Olympiapark in Munich

Senior Travellers

Older travellers (usually from age 65) are entitled to many discounts on public transport, admission to museums and other attractions. Proof of age is sometimes needed at ticket counters, and a passport or ID card is sufficient.

Munich's public transport system offers monthly passes to travellers aged 60 and older (€43.90 for the city centre). Another great deal is the *BahnCard 50* from German rail service **Deutsche Bahn**, giving 50 per cent off of tickets and available to seniors at half-price.

Diversity flags flying in the New Town Hall, Munich

Gay and Lesbian Travellers

While homosexuality is legal in Germany, Bavaria's community of gays (*Schwule*) and lesbians (*Lesben*) keep a low profile. The exception is Munich, where the scene is vibrant. Held every July, the city's Christopher Street Day parade and celebrations are nearly as lively as those held in Berlin and Cologne. Nuremberg and Regensburg have modest communities of their own. In rural areas, some hotels may turn away openly gay couples.

Travelling on a Budget

While Bavaria is not a bargain destination, travellers under 18 years, and in some cases under 20, can benefit from many reductions to tourist attractions, exhibitions and cultural events – just ask at the ticket counter. Holders of an International Student Identity Card (ISIC) are entitled to reductions at many cultural institutions.

The growing ranks of youth hostel-hotels offer a surprisingly high level of comfort and facilities for a bargain price (see p264). Europe-wide train passes InterRail (for EU citizens only) and Eurail (for non-EU) offer significant savings for a month's travel, while the German national *BahnCard* gives reductions of 25 or 50 per cent for a full year (see p308). Lift services from a carpool company like **Citynetz Mitfahrzentrale** are a good-value travel option.

Time

Germany is on Central European Time (GMT plus one hour). Clocks move forward one hour on the last Sunday in March and back on the last Sunday in October.

Electricity

The electrical system in Germany provides 230-volt, 50 Hz AC. Electric plugs are of the two-pin European type. UK 230-volt appliances can be plugged into German sockets with an adaptor. US 110-volt appliances will have to be used with a transformer. All hotels in Germany have 230-volt sockets for razors and hair-dryers. Certain appliances run on both 110-volt and 230-volt current.

Responsible Tourism

In Germany, Bavaria has long been at the forefront of green travel and environmental trends. Recycling of rubbish is highly organized and most households have access to bins for sorting packaging, paper and glass. Larger communal recycling banks for various colours of glass bottles and jars, paper and card, and tin cans are dotted around town centres. Packages marked with the green triangle (*Grüner Punkt*) are recyclable.

Woman depositing bottles in communal recylcing bins

In larger towns there are organic (bio) supermarkets and farmers' markets, and organic produce features on many restaurant menus.

Eco-friendly tours are readily available; leading operators include **Viabono** and **Forum Anders Reisen**, who promote responsible travel to protected nature areas. Package tours feature outdoor activities, organic meals and spa treatments with a view to minimizing their environmental impact. Accommodation often includes like-minded hotels, guesthouses, B&Bs and holiday rentals. Hike-and-sleep holidays can be booked through **Deutscher Alpenverein**, where overnight stops range from sparse mountain huts to plush lodges.

Since 2003, certified EU eco-hotels must meet strict standards for the use of renewable energy, lower energy and water consumption, and waste reduction. Bavaria's regional tourist offices (see p296) carry an up-to-date list.

DIRECTORY

Tourist Information

Bayern Tourismus Marketing Gmbh
Arabellastraße 17,
Munich. **Tel** (089) 21 23
970. W bayern.by
W bavarian-alps.travel

Tourismusamt München, Rathaus
Marienplatz 8, Munich.
Map 3 B2, 6 D3.
Tel (089) 23 39 65 00.
W muenchen.de

Tourismusverband Allgäu/Bayerisch Schwaben
Schießgrabenstr. 14,
Augsburg. **Tel** (0821) 45
04 010. W allgaeu.info

Tourismusverband München-Oberbayern
Radolfzellerstr. 15,
Munich. **Tel** (089) 82 92
180. W oberbayern.de

Tourismusverband Ostbayern
Im Gewerbepark D 02/
D 04, Regensburg.
Tel (0941) 58 53 90.
W ostbayern-tourismus.de
(in German)

Travellers with Special Needs

Club Behinderter und ihrer Freunde
Johann-Fichte-Str. 12,
Munich.
Tel (089) 35 68 808.
W cbf-muenchen.de

Sozialverband Vdk
Schellingstr. 31, Munich.
Map 2 D4.
Tel (089) 21 170.
W vdk.de

Travelling with Children

Bavaria Tourism
Arabellastraße 17,
Munich. **Tel** (089) 21 23
970. W bavaria.by

Senior Travellers

Deutsche Bahn
Tel 0180 6 99 66 33.
W bahn.de

Skan-Club 60 plus
(Travel club for senior travellers)
Gehrenkamp 1,
Isenbüttel.
Tel (05374) 9191 1111.
W senior enreisen.de
(in German)

Gay and Lesbian Travellers

International Gay & Lesbian Travel Association
1201 NE 26th St, Fort
Lauderdale, USA.
Tel (01) 954 630 1637.
W iglta.org

Travelling on a Budget

Citynetz Mitfahrzentrale
Adalbertstr. 6, Munich.
Map 2, D4–E4.
Tel (089) 19 444.
W citynetz mitfahrzentrale.de

Euraide, Hauptbahnhof
Bahnhofplatz 2, Munich.
Tel (089) 59 38 89.
W euraide.de

Railway passes
W bahn.de/bahncard
W interrail.net
W eurail.com

Responsible Tourism

Deutscher Alpenverein
W alpenverein.de
(in German)

Forum Anders Reisen
Wippertstr. 2, Freiburg.
Tel (0761) 40 12 69 90.
W forumanders reisen.de

Viabono
Hauptstr. 230, Rösrath
Tel (02205) 91 98 353.
W viabono.de

Embassies

Australia
Wallstr. 76–79,
10179 Berlin.
Tel (030) 880 08 80.

Canada
Embassy
Leipziger Platz 17,
10117 Berlin.
Tel (030) 20 31 20.
Consulate
Tal 29, Munich.
Tel (089) 21 99 570.

New Zealand
Friedrichstr. 60,
10117 Berlin.
Tel (030) 20 62 10.

Republic of Ireland
Jägerstr. 51, 10117 Berlin.
Tel (030) 22 07 20.

South Africa

Embassy
Tiergartenstr. 18,
10785 Berlin.
Tel (030) 22 07 30.
Consulate
Sendlinger Tor Platz
5, Munich.
Tel (089) 23 11 630

United Kingdom

Embassy
Wilhelmstr. 70,
10117 Berlin.
Tel (030) 20 45 70.
Consulate
Möhlstraße 5, Munich.
Tel (089) 21 10 90.

USA

Embassy
Pariser Platz 2,
10117 Berlin.
Tel (030) 83 050.
Consulate
Königinstr. 5, 80539
Munich.
Map 2 E5.
Tel (089) 28 880.

Security and Health

Like the rest of Germany, Munich and the Bavarian Alps benefit from a rigorous public safety policy, and are exceptionally safe for travellers. The police presence is discreet yet the state has one of the lowest crime rates inthe country, a tribute to Bavaria's buoyant economy and a deep respect for law and order amongst its fairly conservative constituents. Stations and trains are patrolled by officers of the Border Police (Bundesgrenzschutz). Munich is safer than other large German cities, although, as in all large urban areas, you have to watch for pickpockets. Tourists who experience crime of any kind should go to the police for help.

Police

German federal police (Bundespolizei) wear blue uniforms and drive blue-and-white vehicles. For municipal and state police in Bavaria the primary colour is currently green, but a switch to blue is partly carried out. Traffic police (Verkehrspolizei) take care of safety on the streets, roads and motorways, and are distinguished by their white caps. Parking inspectors in navy-blue uniforms are responsible for catching motorists who have parked illegally or who have failed to pay the correct parking fee. Criminal investigation officers (Kriminalpolizei) are usually dressed in plain clothes, but will produce their identification and insignia as necessary.

What to be aware of

Although theft is not a major problem in Munich, special care should be taken in crowded trains and U-Bahn and S-Bahn stations, in and around the central railway station and around large beer-halls, all of them places where pickpockets operate. Keep your wits about you at Oktoberfest, a gold mine for light-fingered thieves. At any time of year, the station is not somewhere to linger, as it is frequented by drug addicts and a few harmless albeit annoying drunks and tramps.

Tourists should take basic safety precautions, such as not carrying large sums of money and keeping cameras safe. Most hotels have secure lockers or safes to store documents and valuable items. For owners of expensive cars, the extra cost of a guarded car park is worth the peace of mind. Never leave valuables in view in a parked car, and it is wise to lock or remove your stereo and GPS unit.

It is advisable to take out comprehensive insurance cover before travelling. Victims of theft should immediately report the crime to the police, who will issue a certificate enabling you to make an insurance claim.

In an Emergency

For assistance in an emergency, dial 112 (toll-free) for any emergency service (police, ambulance and fire brigade), 110 can also be called for the police only. The fire brigade can also be notified by operating special alarms. You will be asked to provide your name, the reason for the call and your location. Once you have explained what has happened, the relevant emergency vehicle should arrive quickly. You may be asked to visit a police station to file a report on the incident. Bring a passport or ID card for any possible paperwork.

Lost and Stolen Property

If property has been lost, it is worth asking at the local police station or lost property office (Städtisches Fundbüro). Lost property offices in smaller towns and spa resorts are generally located within the town hall or spa administration building.

For items lost on trains in Munich, contact the Deutsche Bahn Fundbüro there. For things that go missing on city rail, buses or trams, contact the MVG Fundstelle. The regional transport network, Regionalverkehr Oberbayern, deals with lost property found on buses. The central post office has a lost property office for any items left in its branches.

Ambulance

Fire engine

Police van

Pharmacies dispense both medicines and simple medical advice

Safety in the Mountains

One of the greatest attractions of the Bavarian Alps is the scope that they offer for hiking, skiing and snow-boarding. However, personal safety depends on awareness and preparation. Hikers can easily be misled by fine weather. For hiking in the mountains, it is essential to take proper hiking-boots, a rucksack with warm clothes and something to eat and drink. Be sure to carry a detailed map, a first-aid kit and a form of identity. A mobile phone has become a vital asset because rescue teams can sometimes use GPS signals to locate them. Reception is variable in remote areas.

Hikers should plan their route in advance, match its level of difficulty with their own physical condition, and keep to marked routes. Skiers and snowboarders should beware of avalanches, and never go off-piste or use closed runs. For more difficult routes, it is advisable to hire a guide or consult the local **Deutscher Alpenverein** office or tourist information bureau.

In an emergency, summon help by repeating a sound or light signal six times a minute, with one-minute breaks. Respond to a call for help with a signal three times a minute.

Hospitals and Pharmacies

Germany has some of the world's best healthcare services. When called, ambulances arrive promptly. People able to reach a hospital by themselves should enter by the entrance marked *Notaufnahme* (Accident and Emergency). Less serious cases can be dealt with in the many private clinics or simple medical advice can also be obtained in a pharmacy *(Apotheke)*. Most pharmacies are open until 6pm, some until 8pm. Every district is assigned one all-night pharmacy, the location of which changes according to schedule. You will find the address of the nearest all-night pharmacy posted on the door of each pharmacy.

Travel and Health Insurance

All EU members can receive medical and dental treatment in Germany at a reduced rate. Before travelling, British visitors should obtain a European Health Insurance Card (EHIC) – the form is available from Post Offices – and seek a refund on their return home. It is still a good idea to take out some form of health insurance, and visitors from other countries should do the same. If your plans include hiking, skiing or other sporting activities, make sure that the policy covers the costs of rescue services. Insurance against loss of luggage and holiday cancellation is also advisable.

Pharmacy logo

DIRECTORY

Emergency Services

Ambulance
Tel 112.

Duty Doctor and Pharmacy Information
Tel 116/117.

Emergency dentist
Tel (089) 69 39 53 63.
🔳 notdienst-zahn.de

Fire brigade
Tel 112.

Police
Tel 110/112.

Lost Property

Deutsche Bahn Fundbüro
Hauptbahnhof, Munich.
Tel (089) 13 08 66 64.
Open 7am–8pm Mon–Fri,
8am–6pm Sat–Sun.

MVG Fundstelle
Hauptbahnhof, Munich.
Tel (089) 21 91 32 40.
Open 8am–noon &
12:30–4pm Mon–Fri;
9am–12:30pm & 1–5pm
Sat & Sun.

Regionalverkehr Oberbayern (RVO)
Hirtenstr. 24, Munich.
Tel (089) 55 16 40.

Open 7:30am–3:30pm
Mon–Fri.
🔳 rvo-bus.de

Städtisches Fundbüro
Oetztaler Str. 17, Munich.
Tel (089) 23 39 60 45.
Open 7:30am–noon Mon,
Wed & Fri, 8:30am–noon
& 2–6pm Tue, 8:30am–
3pm Thu.

Hospitals and Pharmacies

Bavarian Pharmacists Association
🔳 lak-bayern.
notdienst-portal.de
(all-night online branch
locator, in German)

Städtisches Klinikum München
Englschalkinger Str.
77, Munich.
Tel (089) 92 700.
🔳 klinikum-
muenchen.de

Mountain Safety

Deutscher Alpenverein (DAV)
Von-Kahr-Str. 2, Munich
Tel (089) 29 07 090.
🔳 alpenverein.de

Banks and Currency

Although there is no limit to the amount of currency that can be taken in or out of Germany, for large amounts of cash a statement of import (or export) may be required by the customs department. Credit cards are widely accepted in large shops and restaurants. You will be expected to pay for small purchases in cash, although in many cases a European bank debit card will be accepted. Foreign currency can be exchanged in larger banks, at exchange bureaux and at currency exchange machines. Travellers' cheques are still accepted but their use is in decline.

Banks and Bureaux de Change

Banks in Germany are open from at least 9am to 4pm Monday to Thursday, and until 2pm on Friday. Branches in urban centres tend to stay open until 6pm one or two days a week. Currency can be changed at branches of major banks and bureaux de change *(Wechselstuben)* located throughout Munich and in larger towns in the Bavarian Alps. Generally, a flat fee of €3 is charged for amounts under €100, or one per cent with a minimum charge of €5 for amounts above €100. Some of the most competitive rates are offered by **Reisebank**, which has branches in large train stations. Another reliable option is the **American Express** foreign exchange service.

Commissions for credit card withdrawals are usually more expensive. Currency can also be exchanged at automatic exchange machines.

A typical *Geldautomat* or automatic cash machine (ATM)

ATMs

The cheapest and fastest way to obtain cash is by using a withdrawal card at a *Geldautomat*, or automatic cash machine (ATM). Cards with a Cirrus, Delta, Maestro, Plus or Star logo can be used to withdraw cash and pay for goods and services all over the country. Machines are usually located in bank lobbies, in all large shopping centres and in many post office branches.

Debit and Credit Cards

Credit cards are accepted in most hotels and restaurants, all department stores and many shops. Smaller shops, restaurants, bars and cafés may not accept them. European bank debit cards equipped with the EC logo or international payment networks such as Maestro are happily accepted. A minimum transaction of €5 in supermarkets and grocery stores and €15–20 in restaurants is expected. When using a debit card, you will be asked either to provide a four-digit PIN code or a signature.

DIRECTORY

Banks in Munich

American Express
Promenadeplatz 6. **Map** 3 B1.
Tel (089) 22 80 14 65.
w americanexpress.com

Bayerische Landesbank
Brienner Str. 18. **Map** 3 B1.
Tel (089) 21 71 01.
w bayernlb.de

Commerzbank
Leopoldstr. 230. **Map** 2 F1.
Tel (089) 35 640.
w commerzbank.de

Deutsche Bank
Promenadeplatz 15.
Map 3 B2, 5 C2. **Tel** (089) 23 900.
w deutschebank.de

HypoVereinsbank
Kardinal-Faulhaber-Str. 12. **Map** 3 B1, B2, 5 C2. **Tel** (089) 37 80.
w hypovereinsbank.de

Reisebank
Hauptbahnhof. **Tel** (089) 54 50 60 97. Franz-Josef-Strauß Airport.
Tel (089) 97 01 721.
w reisebank.de

Sparda-Bank
Oskar-von-Miller-Ring 35.
Map 2 5D. **Tel** (089) 55 14 24 00.
w spardabank.de

Wiring Money

w moneygram.com
w westernunion.com

Head office of HypoVereinsbank, in Munich

Wiring Money

If you have funds wired from home, you can expect commissions as high as 12 per cent. **Moneygram** and **Western Union** can arrange an instant cash transfer to virtually any large bank and post office in Bavaria.

Currency

The euro (€) is the common currency of the European Union. It went into general circulation on 1 January 2002, initially for 12 participating countries. Germany was one of those 12 countries, with the original currency phased out the same year.

Euro notes are identical throughout the Eurozone, each bearing designs of fictional architectural structures. Notes and coins are exchangeable in each of the participating euro countries.

Euro Bank Notes

Euro bank notes have seven denominations. The €5 note (grey in colour) is the smallest, followed by the €10 note (pink), €20 note (blue), €50 note (orange), €100 note (green), €200 note (yellow) and €500 note (purple). All notes show the stars of the European Union.

5 euros

10 euros

20 euros

50 euros

100 euros

200 euros

500 euros

2 euros

1 euro

50 cents

20 cents

10 cents

Coins

The euro has eight coin denominations: €1 and €2; 50 cents, 20 cents, 10 cents, 5 cents, 2 cents and 1 cent. The €2 and €1 coins are both silver and gold in colour. The 50-, 20- and 10-cent coins are gold. The 5-, 2- and 1-cent coins are bronze.

5 cents

2 cents

1 cent

Communications and Media

The postal and telecommunications services in Germany are very efficient. Although it may be necessary to queue for a while in the post office, letters and postcards are usually delivered within the country in 24 hours. Telephone boxes can still be found on street corners and in train stations, but in dwindling numbers as users rely on mobile phones. Wireless Internet has become a common feature in hotels, cafés and some public areas. Mail boxes (yellow with a postal horn logo) are found everywhere, even in the most out-of-the-way corners of the Bavarian Alps.

A typical public telephone booth in Munich

International and Local Telephone Calls

Germany's public telephone network is fast and efficient. Public telephones run by national provider Deutsche Telekom are located in U-Bahn and S-Bahn stations, post offices, restaurants and cafés, and on some street corners. Phone boxes (booths) are magenta and grey in colour, although you may still find some older ones in yellow.

The number of payphones taking either cards (*Telefonkarten*) or sometimes coins is constantly shrinking. Telephone cards (costing €5 to €25) can be bought at post offices and most newsagents. Public telephones operated by credit card can be found in busy areas.

Avoid making calls on the phone in your hotel room, as this can be much more costly than using a payphone.

Mobile Phones

Visitors are relying increasingly on mobile phone services. The most popular providers are T-Mobile and Vodafone. Before you leave home, you can sign up with your regular provider for an international roaming plan, which allows you to change countries while keeping rates down. Your handset will need to be compatible with the GSM network used in much of Europe. Visitors from North America need to take a tri-band handset. Be sure to take a plug adapter for your phone charger.

Buying a local SIM card with a German telephone number and a chip can give you access to local rates. Your handset will need to be unlocked to accept a different SIM card. The phone manufacturer should do this for you if requested. Alternatively, many small electronics shops can unlock your phone on the spot for a small fee.

Another option is to purchase an inexpensive phone from a German electronics warehouse such as **Saturn** or **MediaMarkt**. Companies like **Telestial** or **Planet Omni** sell mobile phone packages from around €30 including airtime.

Internet and Wi-Fi

Most hotels now offer Internet access, either from dedicated terminals in the lobby or via wireless Internet (WLAN or Wi-Fi). Many bars, cafés and some public places are equipped for wireless surfing, although you may need to buy a drink or time on the local network to use the service. Internet cafés charge around €1 to €2 per half-hour. For owners of app-enabled devices such as the iPhone, Blackberry or Android, there are numerous free Wi-Fi apps to guide you to the next hotspot. Reliable access points include **Internetcafé München** in the basement of the Hauptbahnhof and **Cyberice Café** at Sendlinger Tor.

Postal Services

Post offices are run by **Deutsche Post** which has a bright yellow logo. In large towns post offices are usually open from 8am to 6pm on weekdays and from 8am until noon on Saturdays. At airports and in large railway stations, branches are open longer hours and open on Sundays.

Stamps (*Briefmarken*) for letters and postcards can be bought at post offices and from vending machines. Some newsstands and souvenir shops also sell stamps.

Mailboxes usually have two slots – for local post and for all other destinations. Collections times are also displayed. Delivery services are quick, with letters to German destinations usually arriving the following day and within three or four days to most of Europe. Letters sent to North America, Australia or Asia take about a week.

Useful Telephone Numbers

- National directory enquiries in English: 11 837.
- International directory enquiries: 11 834.
- To make an international call: dial 00, wait for the dialling tone, then dial country code, area code + number, omitting the first 0.
- Country codes: UK 44; Eire 353; Canada and USA 1; Australia 61; South Africa 27; New Zealand 64.
- Country and area code for Munich: 49 89.

Deutsche Post also operates an international courier and parcel service, **DHL**. You can send packages from all postal outlets or arrange a pick-up from your address. Prices are competitive and delivery can be tracked online.

Slot for local letters   Collection times   Slot for long-distance mail

The most typical style of mail-box seen in Germany

Newspapers and Magazines

International newspapers such as the *International Herald Tribune, The Guardian, Le Monde, El País, Neue Zürcher Zeitung* and *Corriere della Sera* are available at kiosks on the day they are published, while others appear a little later. *The Economist, Newsweek* and *Time* are also found on newsstands at major train stations.

The serious German press is led by the centre-right newspaper **Frankfurter Allgemeine Zeitung**, the centre-left **Süddeutsche Zeitung** and the more conservative **Die Welt**. The weekly newspaper **Die Zeit** covers intellectual and literary topics. Published in Munich, the *Süddeutsche Zeitung* is issued with a large local supplement. Weekly magazines **Focus** and the legendary **Der Spiegel** set the standard for investigative journalism. All these publications have online editions.

Also widely read in Munich is the sensationalist **Bild**, as well as the regional tabloids **Abendzeitung** and **tz**. In the evenings, papers are sold by vendors doing the rounds in bars and restaurants.

The magazines **Prinz**, the free **InMünchen**, and **Munich Found** in English carry good entertainment listings, as does **The Local** online. Throughout the Bavarian Alps you will find local magazines such as *Allgäu* and *Journal Kempten*.

A newspaper kiosk in Munich

Television and Radio

The main public television networks ARD and ZDF, and regional channel BR, face stiff competition from a host of cable and satellite broadcasters. These include the sophisticated cultural and news channel Arte (a French-German joint venture), plus popular entertainment options on RTL, Pro Sieben, SAT1 and VOX.

German radio offers a familiar mix of mainstream pop, chat, classics and oldies. Bavarian radio stations are Antenne Bayern (101.3 FM), with modern music and news and Bayerischer Rundfunk (91.3, 88.4 and 97.3 FM), with music and local news. Traffic news (with reports of delays on motorways) is broad-cast mainly on Bayern 3 (97.3 FM).

DIRECTORY

Mobile Phones

MediaMarkt
W mediamarkt.de

Planet Omni
W planetomni.com

Saturn
Neuhauser Str. 39.
Map 3 A2.
Tel (089) 23 687.

Telestial
W telestial.com

Internet Access

Cyberice Café
Sendlinger Tor Platz 5.
Map 3 A3.
Tel (089) 18 91 22 20.
W cyberice.de

Internetcafé München
Hauptbahnhof, basement level. **Tel** (089) 51 61 79 95.
W internetcafe muenchen.de

Postal Services

Deutsche Post
Tel 0228 43 33 111.
W deutschepost.de

DHL
Tel (0180) 63 45 30 01 (national delivery),
(0180) 63 45 30 03 (international delivery).
W dhl.com

Post Office Branches
Alter Hof 6–7.
Map 3 C2, 6 D2. **Open** 9am–6:30pm Mon–Fri, 9:30am–12:30pm Sat.

Bahnhofsplatz 1
Open 8am–8pm Mon–Fri, 9am–4pm Sat.

Franz-Josef-Strauß Airport (3rd floor)
Open 7:30am–9pm daily.

Newspapers and Magazines

Abendzeitung
W abendzeitung-muenchen.de

Bild
W bild.de

Der Spiegel
W spiegel.de

Die Welt
W welt.de

Die Zeit
W zeit.de

Focus
W focus.de

Frankfurter Allgemeine Zeitung
W faz.net

InMünchen
W in-meunchen.de

Munich Found
W munichfound.de

Prinz
W prinz.de

Süddeutsche Zeitung
W sueddeutsche.de

The Local
W thelocal.de

TZ
W tz-online.de

TRAVEL INFORMATION

Thanks to Bavaria's excellent road and rail network, and to Munich's large, modern international airport, reaching the Bavarian Alps is easy from anywhere in Europe. Buses are comfortable and efficient and are particularly useful in rural areas not served by rail. In Munich, public transport is a swift and convenient way of moving around the city. The Bavarian Alps are also a gateway on the route into Italy, and roads heading south can be congested at peak holiday times.

Green Travel

Bavaria is a long-time leader in environmental trends. The state prides itself on the high quality of its air and water in its pristine lakes and rivers. The famous Bavarian car manufacturer, BMW, has been developing zero-emission, hydrogen-powered cars.

The state's excellent train and bus networks mean you can easily plan holidays without a car, reducing your carbon footprint. Only in remoter Alpine regions will you need your own car, as bus services can be infrequent there.

The train is the cleanest, most viable alternative to carbon-heavy air and road travel. The national railways run by **Deutsche Bahn** (DB) are modern and efficient and many trains run on electric power. DB also offers special CO_2-neutral trips to nature reserves near Berchtesgaden and in the Allgäu.

In Munich, there are park-and-ride options from the suburbs, which is not only a green scheme, but also solves the problem of parking in the city centre. Other great ways to go green are through

cycle hire and walking and bicycle tours; perfect for exploring the city (see pp312–13). Bicycles are allowed on the U-Bahn and there are especially designated spaces for bicycles on trains and the S-Bahn.

Arriving by Air

Munich's Franz-Josef-Strauß International Airport is Germany's second-busiest airport after Frankfurt am Main. Main airlines with links between the UK and Bavaria include **British Airways** and **Lufthansa**, Germany's national airline. Both operate regular flights from London direct to Munich. Low cost airlines **easyJet** and **BMI Regional** also offer regular flights from several airports in the UK.

For domestic flights, **German Wings** and Air Berlin run services to Munich from many German destinations. However, it is worth noting that unless you are coming from Berlin in northern Germany, flights are hardly faster than the train once you take into account time for waiting and travel to the airport.

Direct flights to Germany are available from major US cities, including New York (JFK),

Airplanes outside the control tower at Munich airport

Washington DC, Boston, Chicago, San Francisco and Los Angeles. Most arrive at Munich or Frankfurt. Airlines from North America with regular services to Munich include **Air Canada**, **Delta Air Lines**, **United Airlines** and **US Airways**. Many connections to Munich are routed through the large international hub of Frankfurt am Main.

On international flights, visitors from countries outside the European Union will be given a landing card to fill out before arrival. It should be presented with a passport to the border guards. For customs regulations, see p296.

Air Fares

Scheduled air fares can vary considerably, with possible reductions for children, students, people under the age of 26, senior travellers, and groups. The cheapest fares tend to be offered by the low-cost airlines, and you can make big savings by booking early, travelling mid-week (Tuesday

Inside Terminal 1 at Munich's Franz-Josef-Strauß International Airport

to Thursday), or by staying over a Saturday. Apart from the popular Christmas period, some of the cheapest fares are available from November to March, coinciding with the best Alpine skiing conditions.

Big international websites such as **Expedia**, **Orbitz** or **Yapta**, and German sites such as **Billig Flieger.de** enable users to personalize searches of many or all flights to a destination and to find good prices. Also check the airlines' own websites for deals.

Since 2011, a departure tax of €8 for short flights and €25 to €45 for medium and long-haul flights is included in the price of a ticket.

Munich Airport

Many airlines such as British Airways and Lufthansa have self-service check-in stations to speed boarding. Passengers waiting for their flights have a wide variety of shops, bars, fast-food outlets and restaurants to choose from. Travellers wishing to shop can buy Bavarian delicacies, as well as clothes, toys and souvenirs. Terminal 1 has dozens of retail and restaurant outlets, including a pharmacy, a hairdresser and a post office, as well as bookshops and newsagents. The larger] Terminal 2 offers even more.

For travellers needing to stay near the airport there are several hotels nearby.

Arriving by bus or train, two ways of getting to Munich airport

Getting to the City Centre

Franz-Josef-Strauß International Airport is one of Europe's most modern air hubs. It is located 28 km (17 miles) outside Munich, but you can reach the city centre by public transport in about 45 minutes. The motorway can take longer, especially during the rush hour.

The quickest and most reliable way of getting to and from the airport is by the S-Bahn – lines S1 and S8 run from about 4am to 1am (with a service every 20 minutes after 5am). Travellers taking the S1 to the airport should board one of the rear carriages marked "*Flughafen*" (airport), as the train's front carriages are uncoupled at Neufahrn and continue to Freising.

The station for commuter rail service **MVV** is situated beneath the airport, and all directions are clearly signposted. Before boarding, buy a ticket at the automated ticket machines with cash, EC debit cards or credit cards. The fare between Munich and the airport costs €10.40 but a *Streifenkarte* for €12.50 works out cheaper, as you need to stamp only eight of the 10 sections *(see p311)*. Children aged 6–14 pay €1.25 for one red section of a child *Streifenkarte*. A group ticket *(Partner-Tageskarte)* costs €21.30 for up to five people.

Taxi fares between Munich and the airport are high – around €50–60. An *Airport-Bus* runs between Munich's Central Station and the airport every 20 minutes: the fare is €10.50 for adults and €5.50 for children. The first bus leaves Central Station at 5:15am and the last at 7:55pm. There are also bus links to other towns and cities in Bavaria.

DIRECTORY

Airlines

Air Canada
Tel (069) 27 11 52 30.
W aircanada.ca

BMI Regional (UK)
Tel (069) 770 673 016.
W bmiregional.com

British Airways
Tel (01805) 26 65 22.
W britishairways.com

Delta Air Lines
Tel (01803) 33 78 80.
W delta.com

Easyjet
Tel 01806 060 606.
W easyJet.com

GermanWings
Tel (0900) 19 19 100.
W germanwings.de

Lufthansa
Tel (069) 86 79 97 99.
W lufthansa.com

Qantas
Tel 0421 69641 100.
W qantas.com.au

United Airlines
Tel (069) 50 98 50 51.
W united.com

Transport

Deutsche Bahn
Tel 0810 6 99 66 33.
W bahn.de

Franz-Josef-Strauß Airport
Tel (089) 97 500.
W munich-airport.de

Lufthansa Airport Bus
Tel (089) 82 30 40.
W airportbus-muenchen.de

MVV
Tel (089) 41 42 43 44.
W mvv-muenchen.de

Flight Websites

W billigflieger.de
W expedia.com
W orbitz.com
W yapta.com

Hauptbahnhof, Munich's central railway station

Arriving by Train

Bavaria has a vast railway network. Trains are frequent and delays are a rarity. You can buy tickets and plan your journey on the website of **Deutsche Bahn**, the national railway service. Munich has direct connections with most major European cities. The most popular route is to travel to Brussels by Eurostar and pick up an onward connection to Germany from there. Ferry connections still operate from the UK, but cheap flights have all but eclipsed them.

German Rail

Deutsche Bahn's trains have a reputation for being swift, comfortable and efficient. Services are generally on-time but trains are sometimes crowded, especially during the peak holiday season. The fastest trains, the high-speed InterCity Express (ICE), have air-conditioning and airline-style seats, a bistro and restaurant, card-operated payphones, and newspapers and earphones on sale. Somewhat slower and less costly are the InterCity (IC) trains and EuroCity (EC), on which a small supplement is payable regardless of the distance travelled. The network also runs short-distance links between towns: Regional-Express (RE), Regionalbahn (RB) and suburban S-Bahn trains.

Munich's busy main station, Hauptbahnhof, serves 300,000 passengers daily. It is a 20-minute walk from Marienplatz or a short ride by U-Bahn, S-Bahn or bus.

Train Tickets

Train tickets can be bought at railway stations, from ticket machines and the ticket office, or online. You can buy them in advance and reserve seats. Tickets are €2 cheaper from the machines than at the counter, but it is wise to allow 10–15 minutes extra time (staff are on hand to help at the complicated vending machines). Tickets bought for high-speed ICE trains are valid only for a specific journey, meaning you will need to exchange tickets if you need a later connection. Tickets for IC journeys are valid for a month. Short journeys up to 100 km (62 miles) are valid only on the day of purchase.

Train fares in Germany are expensive. However, a wide range of discounts is available. One way to travel more cheaply is to buy a *BahnCard,* which gives a 25 or 50 per cent discount, costing €61 and €249 respectively. The InterRail pass, available to all EU citizens, and the Eurail pass for non-EU citizens, are both valid for a month's train travel.

In Bavaria, the *Bayern-Ticket* offers good value. A one-day ticket for one person costs €22 from machines and €24 from counters. Each additonal

passenger (up to four persons) costs an additional €4. These tickets are valid only on RE, RB and S-Bahn trains and most regional public buses and time restrictions apply. The *Schönes Wochenend-Ticket* (€42 for up to five people) can be used only on RE, RB, IRE and S-Bahn trains, but is valid all day and most of the night on either a Saturday or a Sunday. Both tickets also give free travel on urban transport in Munich.

Arriving by Coach

Munich and other cities in the Bavarian Alps can be reached by coach (long-distance bus). Coaches from Vienna, Zurich or Bozen (Bolzano) terminate at Munich's central bus terminal at Hackerbrücke. Routes from the UK are operated by **Eurolines**, while **Berlinlinienbus** runs a useful connection to and from Berlin. **Busabout** is a hop-on, hop-off network offering passes of varied duration to 33 destinations in Europe, including Munich.

Travelling by Bus

Almost all Bavarian towns and villages are connected by a local bus network, particularly in places where there is no railway station. Bus time-tables are designed to suit commuters, so that the service is frequent at peak hours and sparse at weekends and on public holidays.

Most towns have a *Zentraler Omnibus Bahnhof* (ZOB) close to the train station. It is here that most bus services originate and where tickets can be purchased, and service timetables and other information can be obtained.

Stops are frequent in rural areas, sometimes by request in the middle of nowhere. A

Comfortable, long-distance, double-decker coach

timetable is posted at every stop, and the driver sells tickets on board.

Boat Trips

Bavaria's many rivers and lakes make boat trips a great attraction. The most scenic of these trips are on the region's largest lakes – the Starnbergersee, Ammersee, Tegernsee, Chiemsee and Königssee – and on rivers such as the Danube.

To the north of Munich, kayaking and canoeing are popular activites in the Altmühl Naturpark *(see p187).* On the Königssee, you can take an electric-powered boat to the picturesque church

of St Bartholomä, which is framed on all sides by vertiginous Alpine slopes *(see p204).*

On the smaller lakes you can hire boats with or without a captain. Rafting is popular on the River Salzach near Burghausen *(see p203),* and on the River Isar from Wolfratshausen to Thalkirchen, a southern district of Munich. **Flößerei Josef Seitner** offers trips on traditional wooden rafts. Tours are 5–7 hours long, depending on the water level

Longer cruises are available on the Danube from Passau to Vienna, and can be combined with a tour of the historic sights along the Danube valley.

Boats moored at the jetty at Stock am Chiemsee

DIREC

Train Travel

Deutsche Bahn
Information and reservation.
Tel 01806 99 66 33.
🆆 bahn.de

Arriving by Coach

Berlinlinienbus
Tel (030) 33 84 480.
🆆 berlinlinienbus.de

Busabout
Tel 08450 267 514 (UK).
🆆 busabout.com

Eurolines
Hackerbrücke 4.
Tel (089) 88 98 95 13.
🆆 eurolines.com

Rafting on The Isar

Flößerei Josef Seitner
Lindenweg 1, 82515
Wolfratshausen.
Tel (08171) 78 518.
🆆 flossfahrt.de

Train Routes in Southern Bavaria

Southern Bavaria has an extensive rail network providing convenient links between all larger towns and cities in the region.

Key
— Railway line
— S-Bahn

1 München-Pasing
2 München Donnersbergerbrücke
3 München Hauptbahnhof
4 München Ost

n's Buses, Trams,
n and S-Bahn

ing in its detail, coordination and efficiency, Munich's
transport will get you where you want to go quickly.
t from eight underground (U-Bahn) lines, the city has an
ensive network of bus and tram routes. The environs are
connected to the core by fast suburban (S-Bahn) trains, mostly
overground lines which link into the city centre and ongoing
transport. In short, the whole of greater Munich is blanketed
by public transport, making the car superfluous for many
travellers. All four networks are part of Munich's municipal
transport services, MVV and MVG, so with one ticket you can
switch effortlessly from bus or tram to the local Bahn.

Travelling by Bus

With over 60 bus routes, Munich
is easily visited without a car.
For tourists in particular, buses
and trams *(see below)*
are an attractive
alternative to the
U-Bahn and S-Bahn
networks, and go
to places the railway
lines do not. They
are also less crowded
and allow passen-
gers to see the city
as they travel.

Buses run generally
at 10-minute intervals
during the day and
every 20 minutes in late
evening. Three lines of
Night Buses *(Nachtbusse)*
run hourly between 12:30
or 1am and 4:30 or 5am,
to make up for the reduced
U-Bahn and S-Bahn services.

Each bus stop has a
route map giving details
of timetables and con-
nections. Tickets can
be purchased at vending
machines at stops, as well
as on the buses. To buy a
ticket, press a button to

select your fare (usually an
option near the top), insert
coins or notes into the slot,
and retrieve your ticket with
any change. When boarding,
you must validate the ticket
by inserting it into a franking
machine located just inside
the doors. Stops are either
announced by a recorded
voice (or the driver) or
displayed on a screen. If
in doubt, ask fellow passengers or the driver.

Typical bus stop, Munich

Travelling by Tram

Munich is well-served by
10 tram services, which
merge seamlessly into the
bus, U-Bahn and S-Bahn
networks. Trams run
generally at 10-minute
intervals during the day
and every 20 minutes in
late evening. Tickets can
be purchased from
the onboard machine
– the driver (in his
separate compartment) won't
sell tickets. Many trams stop at
raised platforms for mobility-
impaired passengers.

Travelling by U-Bahn and S-Bahn

Munich's underground rail
network – the U-Bahn – first
opened in 1971 and is constantly
being expanded. The S-Bahn,
the fast suburban train network,
coincides in some places with
the U-Bahn, which emerges
above ground outside the city
centre. All, except one – S20,
S-Bahn lines run through the
centre of the Old Town, linking
the Hauptbahnhof (main
station) to Karlsplatz and a
main tourist hub at Marienplatz.

The fare system on the
U-Bahn and S-Bahn is the
same as on Munich's buses
and trams. You can buy tickets
at vending machines or counters in most stations. Before
boarding the train, be sure
to frank your ticket in a time-
stamping machine, which is
often located at the top of
the stairs leading down to
the platform.

Tickets for events such as
concerts or football matches
often include the price of the
fare to the venue on the U-Bahn
or S-Bahn. This is stated on the
ticket for the event.

U-Bahn and S-Bahn trains
are frequent and reliable,
although they are likely to become quite crowded during
the morning and evening rush
hours. Before boarding an
S-Bahn train, check the destination given on the electronic
information boards. On the
U-Bahn, trains travelling in
opposite directions come in
on either side of the platform,
so boarding the wrong train
can easily happen. Check the
direction *(Richtung)* panel
as well as the destination
to ensure that you board
the correct train.

A Munich bus, serving one of many bus routes in the city

Useful Bus and Tram Routes
This map shows the best bus and tram routes for sightseeing in Munich. The locations of any sights are marked, as well as the nearest useful bus stop.

Key

▪ Major sight

▬ Tram routes

▬ Bus routes

O Stop (selected stops only)

Nearly all U-Bahn and S-Bahn stations are fitted with special ramps, lifts or travelators to assist mobility-impaired passengers.

Many U-Bahn and S-Bahn stations are decorated with local motifs. For example, the U-Bahn station at Königsplatz reflects exhibits displayed in the museums on the square.

One of the U-Bahn's blue trains at an underground station

Tickets

Munich and its environs are divided into four zones, each indicated on maps by a different colour. For tourists, Zone 1 (white zone) is the most important because it covers the city centre. Single tickets cost €2.60 for travel within Zone 1, €5.20 for Zone 2, €7.80 for Zone 3 and €10.40 for Zone 4. If you intend to make several journeys, it is cheaper to buy a *Streifenkarte* (strip card), which costs €12.50. The card is divided into ten sections; you will need two sections for each zone you enter. The ticket should be folded at the appropriate place and inserted into the franking machine. The last stamp made cancels all previous ones.

For short journeys of up to four bus and tram stops, or two U-Bahn and S-Bahn stops, you can buy a *Kurzstrecke* ticket costing €1.30. Alternatively, you can frank just one section of a *Streifenkarte*. If you forget to validate your ticket, you could be fined €40 for fare-jumping by roving plain-clothed officers.

For tourists, one of the most useful tickets is the one-day *Tageskarte*, or the three-day *3-Tageskarte*. Both are available for a single person (*Single*) or for groups of up to five people (*Partner*). Two children aged 6–14 count as one person. A *Tageskarte* costs €6, while a *3-Tageskarte* costs €15 (both only for Zone Innenraum or the city centre). These tickets are available at all ticket vending machines. Once stamped they are valid until 6am the next day.

For visitors staying in Munich for a longer period, a weekly, monthly or even annual *IsarCard* may be the best option. This card allows unlimited travel on public transport. Single tickets for travellers aged 6–20 cost €1.30, or one strip.

Business travellers participating in trade fairs and conferences should check to see if they are eligible for a MVV Congress Ticket, which allows travel within a selected area. Many events often include the price of public transport in the ticket, such as those held at the Staatstheater am Gärtnerplatz (see p146.

If you are confused about which ticket to buy, ask staff or use the MVV's online ticket navigator, which works out the cheapest fare and highlights possible price reductions. In addition, the online journey planner of the MVV and the **MVG**, its inner-city sister organization, will guide you to your destination with a timetable and the most appropriate mix of public transport.

Franking Machine

1 The letter E denotes a franking machine found outside the entrance to a U-Bahn station

2 Slot for inserting a ticket for it to be stamped

DIRECTORY

Mobile phone MVV journey planner
[w] efa.mobi

Münchner Verkehrs- und Tarifverbund MVV
Tel (089) 41 42 43 44.
[w] mvv-muenchen.de

Münchner Verkehrsgesellschaft MVG
Tel (089) 21 91 0.
[w] mvg-mobil.de

etting around Munich on oot, Bicycle, Taxi and Car

Most of Munich's tourist attractions and historic monuments are located in the city centre and distances between them are not far, making it easy to enjoy many sights on foot. Numerous cafés, squares and parks provide ample opportunity to relax in pleasant surroundings. Due to traffic congestion and a perennial shortage of parking, driving in Munich is less inviting. By contrast, cycling is very popular and bicycles are widely available for hire.

Neuhauser Str.

A typical Munich street sign

Around Munich on Foot

Exploring Munich on foot is a rewarding experience. Much of the Old Town has been closed to traffic, and only in the main shopping streets do you have to struggle through crowds.

Most of the tourist attractions in the Old Town are within less than 20 minutes' walk of each other. Further afield, strolling through the city's outlying districts can be a pleasant experience in itself.

Drivers are courteous to pedestrians, especially when it comes to stopping at pedestrian crossings. Almost no-one crosses against the light even if the road is clear, in part to set an example for children. Keep an eye out for the many cyclists, who can pose a hazard to tourists who unwittingly stray into the cycle lanes.

Locating a particular address in Munich is straightforward. Street names are posted at junctions and buildings are clearly numbered, with odd and even numbers on opposite sides of the street.

Munich's many parks make walking in the city a delight. To escape the urban bustle, seek out the Englischer Garten or the green spaces of Maximiliansanlagen on the river bank, or take a trip to Nymphenburg Park or the Botanical Gardens. In summer, paths along the Isar River lead

Pedestrian zone

you through lush greenery to beaches filled with sun-worshippers. A cold brew in a beer garden is an excellent reward.

For an overview of the city, the steeples of the Frauenkirche (see pp64–5) and Peterskirche (see p66) provide views over the Old Town, Marienplatz and Viktualienmarkt. From its 190-m (623-ft) high observational platform, the Olympic Tower (see p139) affords breath-taking vistas as far as the Alps, and has a restaurant.

Guided Tours

Munich has a wide variety of guided walking and cycle tours, usually with hired bikes provided. You may be able to just show up and join a scheduled tour, but it is advisable to reserve ahead. Some of the best trips are given by **Radius Tours**, located within a bike-rental shop in the Hauptbahnhof. Daily themed tours (in English)

last around 2 hours and cover the major historical sights, Third Reich and Bavarian beer. Excursion tours take in Neuschwanstein Castle (see p234) and Dachau Concentration Camp (see p175).

Other reliable operators include **Mike's Bike Tours**, which conduct a popular beerhall-and-gardens tour, and **Spurwechsel**, focusing on cultural and historic tours for groups by advance booking.

Tours in open-topped, double-decker buses run by **Münchner Stadtrundfahrten** require less energy.

For a more personalized experience, **Taxi Guide München** offers themed tours of the city's main sights in several languages, famous palaces, Olympiapark (see pp138–9) and places as far afield as Salzburg. Prices range from €80 for a 1-hour tour for up to eight passengers to €440 for a full day's outing.

By Bicycle

Munich is tailor-made for cyclists. The city centre is largely flat and easy to navigate, with cycle lanes marked on pave-ments (sidewalks) and on the edges of roads. Bicycle stands are situated throughout the city, including large facilities at railway and S-Bahn stations. Bicycles should always be locked to an immovable object.

Bicycles can be taken on the U-Bahn and S-Bahn in the last carriage marked with a cycle logo, except at rush hour from

Cycling – a quick and popular way of getting around Munich

6am to 9am and 4pm to 6pm. In addition to a regular passenger ticket, you will need to buy a one-day *Farrad-Tageskarte* for €2.50.

You can find bicycle hire points *(Fahrradverleih)* in the city centre, at MVV stations and major tourist spots. In addition, **DB Call-a-Bike** bikes are scattered throughout the city for immediate use. Look for a blinking green light, which means the silver-and-red bike is ready to be activated. Provide a credit card number by phone and you will receive a code to unlock the bike. After a modest sign-up fee, rates are €0.08 per minute and €15 per day. After use, lock the bike to a fixed object and call the bike return number. Bikes can also be hired from **Aktiv-Rad**.

Tourist offices provide cycle maps of Munich with routes of the best cycling tours. MVV's guide entitled *Radeln mit dem MVV* (Cycling with MVV), shows 52 scenic cycle routes around the city. You can order it online before you arrive.

By Taxi

As elsewhere in Germany, taxis in Munich are large cream-coloured cars with a "TAXI" sign on the roof; this is illuminated when the taxi is available. Taxis can be hailed on the street, booked by telephone or picked up at a taxi rank. If the rank is empty, a cab can be called from the telephone at the rank. The standard starting fare is €3.30, plus a per-kilometre fee of €1.40–1.70. A tip of 5–10 per cent is customary – or just round up the bill. A leisurely alternative is the pedicab rickshaw. The covered three-wheelers of **Riksha-Mobil** depart from Marienplatz with fares starting at €3. A 20-minute trip for two people to the Chinesischer Turm, English Garden, will cost around €17.

A taxi in Munich, identifiable by its cream colour and "Taxi" sign

Parking sign

Driving in Munich

Munich is the hub of a motorway network radiating in many directions. To the south are motorways A8 to Salzburg and A95 to Garmisch Partenkirchen, to the southwest is motorway A96 to Lindau, to the west is motorway A8 to Stuttgart, to the north motorway A9 to Nuremberg, and to the east motorway A95 to Passau.

There is a ring road (Autobahnring) around the city, although this is often congested. Munich also has two smaller ring roads, the Mittlerer Ring and the Altstadtring, which relieve some congestion but are also often full of traffic. Only vehicles with low-emissions are allowed to drive in the central green zone. Be sure to buy an environmental badge (Umweltplakette) before entering the city centre or you could be fined. Motorway signs direct drivers to automobile testing centres where badges cost €8 to €12, or you can buy one online from the **Environmental Badge Climate Company**.

One of the biggest challenges is finding a parking space. Although there are many multi-storey car parks (Parkhäuser), they are expensive and often full. ("Frei" indicates that spaces are available.) Most on-street parking must be paid for, either by inserting coins into a meter or by buying a pay-and-display ticket. Another issue is the time limit, 1 hour often being the maximum in the centre. Parking attendants issue fines when cars are illegally parked or parking is unpaid.

DIRECTORY

Guided Tours

Mike's Bike Tours
Bräuhausstr. 10. **Map** 3 C2.
Tel (089) 25 54 39 87.
W mikesbiketours.com

Münchner Stadtrundfahrten
Tel (089) 55 02 89 95.
W stadtrundfahrten-muenchen.de

Radius Tours
Arnulfstr. 3, Hauptbahnhof.
Tel (089) 4 34 8777-40.
W radiustours.com

Riksha-Mobil
Müllerstraße 6. **Map** 3 B3, 5 C5.
Tel (089) 24 21 68 80.
W pedalhelden.de

Spurwechsel
Ohlmüllerstrasse 5.
Map 3 C5.
Tel (089) 69 24 699.
W spurwechsel-muenchen.de

Taxi Guide München
Tel 0175 48 12 848.
W taxi-guide-muenchen.de

Bicycle Hire

Aktiv-Rad
Hans-Sachs-Str. 7. **Map** 3 B4.
Tel (089) 26 65 06.
W aktiv-rad.de

DB Call-a-Bike
Tel 069 427277-22.
W callabike-interaktiv.de

Taxis

Taxi München
Tel (089) 21 610 or 1 94 10.

Driving in Munich

Environmental Badge Climate Company
Helmholtzstraße 2–9,
10587 Berlin.
Tel (030) 39 88 72 140.
W green-zones.eu

Travelling by Car

By far the swiftest and most comfortable way to tour Bavaria is by *Autobahn*, or national motorway. Secondary roads are usually of excellent quality too. However, during the holiday season, roads in the Bavarian Alps swell with motorists from northern Europe travelling to Austria and Italy. To avoid a tiresome *stau* (traffic jam), check the holiday calendar in advance or avoid the motorways altogether. Although slower, travelling off the main motorways gives you a more intimate view of the countryside.

One of the many picturesque roads with a view of the Alps

Getting to the Bavarian Alps

Visiting the area by car is quite easy. However, in the summer months and over public holidays, considerable queues can build up at border crossings into Germany, especially from the Czech Republic. During Okt-berfest *(see p33)*, routes to and from Italy through Switzerland are also congested. At other times, drivers can expect few delays or border formalities.

Non-EU citizens do not need to declare goods for customs on arrival, but limits do apply to the amount of duty-free goods that can be brought into the country *(see p296)*.

What to Take

Drivers must carry a valid driving licence, their vehicle's registration document and their insurance policy. Before leaving home, check with your insurer whether you are covered in Germany. If you plan on driving in the city entre and your vehicle is a low-emission vehicle,

you must obtain an environmental badge *(Umweltplakette)*. You can pre-order a badge through the **Environmental Badge Climate Company** or buy one from automobile testing centres TÜV or Dekra in Bavaria.These are signposted on motorways.

Cars must bear a sticker or plate indicating country of origin. A first-aid kit, a fluorescent yellow or orange safety jacket and a red warning triangle, for use in case of breakdown, are also required.

Roads and Motorways

National motorways *(Autobahnen)* in Germany are toll-free and have petrol stations and facilities with toilets, restaurants and motels spaced at regular intervals. An *Autobahn* is indicated by the letter "A" followed by a number. Some motorway signs also have the letter "E" and a number, indicating that the road crosses the German border. A *Bundesstraße* (main road) is indicated by the letter "B" and a number.

Car Rental

Major international car rental companies such as **Hertz** and **Avis** have offices in the Bavarian Alps, particularly near railway stations and at airports. They are rivalled by Munich-based **Sixt** and up-and-coming firms such as **Buchbinder**.

Rates for car rental vary greatly so shop around before booking. Be sure to look at combined tickets offered by airlines and travel agencies. These include car rental and often turn out cheaper than booking each separately.

For holidaymakers another option is to rent a camper van *(Wohnmobile)*, which outside the holiday season can be rented for the price of a mid-sized car, but offers a great deal more freedom.

Parking

Towns and cities in the Bavarian Alps are crowded during normal business hours, making parking a problem. Weekends are more relaxed, and parking tends to be free from midday Saturday. As elsewhere in Germany, parking attendants will issue a ticket even if you are only a few minutes over the limit.

Roadside Assistance

Germany's system of roadside assistance is superb. On motorways, emergency telephones *(Notrufsäulen)* are situated at intervals of 1 km (0.62 mile). The main port of call is **ADAC** (Allgemeiner Deutscher Automobil-Club), the German motoring association. If you break down, call from any roadside telephone and help will arrive quickly. ADAC repairmen will tow the stricken vehicle to a garage, but be prepared to pay extra if you are not an ADAC member. In the event of a road accident, the police, ambulance, fire brigade and air ambulance (helicopter) will attend as necessary.

Motorway telephone

An Aral petrol (gas) station, one of the most widely seen in Bavaria

Petrol (Gas) Stations

On motorways, petrol and diesel stations are most often located at junctions or at *Rasthöfe* – rest areas. Their facilities include car parks, restaurants, bars, shops and toilets with showers.

The price of fuel by the main providers (Shell, BP, Aral and DEA) is fairly uniform. Petrol stations in shopping centres are often a cheaper option, and Jet is always cheap.

Many petrol stations stay open late at night or even 24 hours, and also sell food, refreshments, newspapers and motor oil. In rural areas, petrol stations are few and far between, so it is always a good idea to fill up when you do see one.

Rules of the Road

Speed limits in Germany are 50 km/h (30 mph) in built-up areas and 100 km/h (62 mph) elsewhere. They are clearly marked when you enter the speed zone. Although Germany's famous *Autobahnen* were designed without speed limits, many sections actually have them. Limits of 100–130 km/h (62–80 mph) apply in curvy or built-up areas, and may be slower along construction sites.

When travelling with a caravan or camping trailer, the basic limit is 70 km/h (44 mph) and on motorways 100 km/h (62 mph). Speed traps are frequent and fines stiff. The maximum blood limit for alcohol is 0.5 per cent. Seat belts must be worn at all times, with children under 12 in the back seats and infants secured in child seats. For drivers, mobile phones can be used only with hands-free sets.

Scenic Routes

An hour's drive southeast of Munich, some jaw-dropping Alpine scenery beckons. From the A8 near Bernau, exit onto the E52 to explore the *Deutsche Alpenstrasse*, a 322-km (200-mile) scenic route dating from the 1930s. Stops include an 11th-century castle at Marquartstein, where Richard Strauss composed *Salome;* Reit im Winkl, a mecca for skiers with Tyrolean-style houses; and Ruhpolding, home to a Madonna carved in around 1230. The route meanders through forests and pastureland into a vast national park around Berchtesgaden *(see p204)*. Here, the church at Ramsau enjoys a setting framed by snow-capped Alps (route: 90 km/56 miles total).

Bavaria's crystalline lakes are legendary. About 30 km (19 miles) southwest of Munich, the Starnbergersee *(see p217)* is rimmed with upmarket villas and restaurants serving freshly-caught char *(Saibling)*. From the motor-way E533, take the Starnberg exit and the St2063 down the western shore. Continue on the St2063 until you rejoin the motorway, and drive 15 km (9 miles) south to the Zell exit, where the St2062

Signs to the motorway

travels through peaceful farmland towards the beautiful Kochelsee. At Kochel am See *(see p223)*, turn right on the B11. Here the road is at its most scenic, climbing higher through a dense forest of firs, beech and spruce. Gradually you descend towards the pristine blue Walchensee *(see p222)*, where the Nazis were said to have deposited gold – but none was ever found. Today the lake is better known for its windsurfing championships (route: 70 km/43 miles total).

DIRECTORY

Emergency Numbers

Ambulance
Tel 112.

Fire Brigade
Tel 112.

Police
Tel 110 & 112.

What to Take

Environmental Badge
Climate Company
Tel (030) 39 88 72 140.
W green-zones.eu

Roadside Assistance

ACE (Auto Club Europa)
Tel 0711 530 33 66 77; 0711 530 34 35 36 (24 hour emergency call).
W ace-online.de

ADAC
Tel 0180 22 22 222.
W adac.de

Car Rental Companies

Avis
Tel (0180) 217702.
W avis.com

Buchbinder
Tel (089) 9789 18820.
W buchbinder.de

Europcar
Tel 040 520 187 654.
W europcar.de

Hertz
Tel 01806 333 535.
W hertz.de

Sixt
Tel 01806 25 25 25.
W sixt.com

eneral Index

ge numbers in **bold** refer to
ain entries

A

Abbeys **28–9**
 Ettal **220**
 Fürstenzell **1\90**
 Höglwörth 203
 Kloster Indersdorf **175**
 Kloster Niedernburg
  (Passau) **194**
 Metten 179, **186**
 Ottobeuren **28–9**, **232**
 Rohr **186**
 Wessobrunn **216**
 see also Monasteries
The Abduction of the
 Daughters of Leukippos (Rubens)
 124
Abendzeitung Schalterhalle
 (Munich) 147
Accidents 314
ACE 315
ADAC 315
ADAC Camping Referat
 293
Adoration of the Magi
 (Holbein) 122
Adoration of the Magi
 (Tiepolo) 117
Adoration of the Magi
 (Weyden) 124
Afra, St 40
Agilolfing dynasty 41
Agnes Bernauer Festspiele
 (Straubing) 35
Agrotourism **264**, 265
Air Canada 307
Air travel **306–7**
Akademie der Bildenden Künstte
 (Munich) **108**
Aktiv-Rad (Munich) 313
Alamanni 40, 41
Alberthal, Hans 166
Alberthal, Johann **258**
Albrecht III the Pious, Duke of
 Bavaria 35, 46, 143, 188
Albrecht IV the Wise, Duke of
 Bavaria 46
Albrecht V, Duke of Bavaria
 47
 Bayerische Staatsbibliothek
  (Munich) 107
 Bayerisches
  Nationalmuseum (Munich) 112
 Hofgarten (Munich) 89
 Münzhof (Munich) 87
 Residenz (Munich) 80, 81
 Staatliches Museum Ägyptischer
  Kunst (Munich) 81
Aldersbach **196**
Allerheiligenkirche am Kreuz
 (Munich) **73**

Allgäu 11, **229–41**
 hotels 269
 map 228–9
 restaurants 282–3
Allgäuer Festwoche
 (Kempten) 35
Allgemeiner Deutscher
 Fahrrad Club (ADFC) 293
Allianz Arena (Munich) 147
Alpamare (Bad Tölz) 224
Alpenländische Galerie (Kempten)
 240–1
Alpenstraße tour 11, **224–5**
Alpines Museum (Munich) **95**
 Street-by-Street map 93
Alpinmuseum (Kempten) **240–1**
Alps see Bavarian Alps
Altdorfer, Albrecht
 The Battle of Issus 122, 124
 Susanna and the Elders 56
Alte Anatomie (Ingolstadt) **170**
Alte Pinakothek (Munich) 56,
 122–25
 Street-by-Street map 117
Alte Residenz (Passau) **193**
Alte Schranne (Nördlingen)
 247
Altenstadt 26, 218
Alter Botanischer Garten
 (Munich) **131**
Alter Hof (Munich) **87**
Altes Rathaus (Ingolstadt) **171**
Altes Rathaus (Lindau) **238**
Altes Rathaus (Munich) **67**
 Street-by-Street map 61
Altes Rathaus (Passau) **194–5**
Altheim culture 39
Altmühl, River 161, 163, 179,
 180
Altmühl Valley **187**
Altötting 199, **202**
 hotels 268
 restaurants 280
Amalienburg (Nymphenburg) 134
Amalienstraße (Neuburg an
 der Donau) **172**
Amati, Nicolo 222
Amberger, Christoph 30, 31
 Portrait of Felicitas Welser 31
Ambulances 301, 315
Amerang **208**
American Embassy 299
American Express 303
Ammergauer 211
Ammerland
 Starnbergersee tour 217
Ammersee 211, 213, 216
Andechs **216**
 restaurants 281
Andechs family 216
Andechser am Dom (Munich) 285
Anger **203**
Annakirche (Augsburg) **255**
 Street-by-Street map 252

AntikPalast (Munich) **145**
Antonello da Messina
 The Annunciation 125
Antonierhaus (Memmingen) **230**
Antonílez, Claudio José 125
Apartments, holiday 264
Appiani, Pietro Francesco 175
Archäologische Staatsammlung
 (Munich) **111**
Archäologischer Park
 Cambodunum (Kempten) **241**
Architecture
 Bavarian Alps **26–7**
 Castles of Ludwig II **50–1**
Aribo I 208
Arnulf of Carinthia 41, 81
Art
 Bavarian Alps 30–1
 Lüftlmalerei 11, 31, **216**
Art Nouveau architecture 15
 Art Nouveau house in
  Ainmillerstraße (Munich)
  108, 109
 Münchner Kammerspiele im
  Schauspielhaus (Munich) **88**
 Neue Pinakothek (Munich) 129
 Schwabing (Munich) 109
Art Nouveau house in
 Ainmillerstraße (Munich) 108, 109
Asam, Cosmas Damian 27, 31,
 72
 Asam-Schlössl (Munich) 142
 Asambasilika (Osterhofen)
  197
 Asamkirche (Munich) **70–1**
 Bürgersaal St Maria de
  Victoria (Ingolstadt) 170
 Damenstift St Anna (Munich) 73
 Dreifaltigkeitskirche (Munich) 86
 Freising cathedral 169
 Fürstenfeldbruck 175
 Georgs- und Martinskirche
  (Weltenburg) 186
 Heilig-Geist-Kirche (Munich) 67
 Herrgottsruh (Friedberg) 251
 Jakobs- und Tiburtiuskirche
  (Straubing) 189
 Klosterkirche St Anna (Munich) 94
 Mariä Himmelfahrt (Aldersbach)
  196
 Michaelskirche (Metten) 186
 portrait of 31
 Schleißheim Palace 176
 Ursulinenkirche (Straubing) 188
Asam, Egid Quirin 27, 31, **72**
 Asam-Schlössl (Munich) 142
 Asambasilika (Osterhofen) 197
 Asamhaus (Munich) **72**
 Asamkirche (Munich) **70–1**
 Bürgersaal St Maria de Victoria
  (Ingolstadt) 170
 Damenstift St Anna (Munich) 73
 Freising cathedral 169
 Fürstenfeldbruck 175

Asam, Egid Quirin (cont.)
Georgs-und Martinskirche
(Weltenburg) 186
Heilig-Geist-Kirche (Munich) 67
Jakobs- und Tiburtiuskirche
(Straubing) 189
Klosterkirche St Anna (Munich) 94
Mariä Himmelfahrt (Aldersbach)
196
Mariä Himmelfahrt (Rohr) 186
Peterskirche (Munich) 61, 66
portrait of 72
Ursulinenkirche (Straubing) 188
Asam, Hans Georg 72, 169, 223
Asam-Schlössl (Munich) **142**
Asamhaus (Munich) **72**
Asamkirche (Munich) 14, 56,
70–1
Asamkirche Maria de Victoria
(Ingolstadt) 10, 170
Aschau **206**
restaurants 280
Asper, Andreas 241
Assenhausen
Starnbergersee tour 217
Atzinger (Munich) 285
Au (Munich) **140**
Audi 19, 53, 170
Auer Dult (Munich) 34, 35, 36
Augsburg 11, 160, 243, 244,
252–57
architecture 26
art 30, 31
festivals 34
Fuggerei 11, **256–7**
history 39
hotels 269
restaurants 283
Street-by-Street map 252–3
Augsburger Deutschkurse 293
Augsburger Plärrer (Augsburg) 34
Augsburger Puppenkiste **255**
Augustiner Gaststätten (Munich)
285
Augustiner-Keller (Munich)
285
Augustinerbräu (Munich) **62**
Street-by-Street map 60
Augustus, Emperor 39, 252
Augustusbrunnen (Augsburg)
Street-by-Street map 252
Aurelius, Marcus, Emperor 40
Australian Embassy 299
Automatic cash machines (ATMs)
302
Autumn **36**
Avis 315

B

Babenhausen **232**
Backpacker Network Germany 293
Bad Aibling **209**
Bad Hindelang 22, **236**
Bad Oberdorf 236

Bad Reichenhall 199, **203**
hotels 268
restaurants 281
Bad Tölz 31, 211, **224**
festivals 36
hotels 268
restaurants 281
Bad Wörishofen **233**
Bader, Isaak the Elder 196
Bader, Joseph Georg 62
Bader, Konstantin 250
Bagnato, Johann Caspar 238
Baiovarii 40
Baldung Grien, Hans 124
Banking **302**
Banknotes 303
Barelli, Antonio 83
Baroque architecture 27
Baroque art 31
Bars, Munich **284**, 285
Basic Bio (Munich) 145
Basilika St Bonifaz (Munich) **118**
Street-by-Street map 116
Baths
Müllersches Volksbad
(Munich) **97**
The Battle of Issus (Altdorfer) 122,
124
Bavaria-Filmstadt (Munich) **142**
Bavarian Alps
Allgäu **229–41**
Alpenstraße tour **224–5**
architecture **26–7**
art **30–1**
festivals **34-7**
history **39–53**
landscape 22, **24–5**
Lower Bavaria **179–97**
map 160–1
monasteries and abbeys **28–9**
mountain safety 300–1
Northern Swabia **243–59**
plants and animals **25**
traditions **32–3**
travel **306–15**
Upper Bavaria (East)
199–209
Upper Bavaria (North)
163–77
Upper Bavaria (South)
211–25
Bavarian Army Museum (Ingolstadt)
171
Bavarian Film Studios
(Munich) 147
Bavarian Forest *see*
Bayerischer Wald
Bavarian People's Party 49
Bavarian Sea *see* Chiemsee
Bayerische Landesbank (Munich)
302
Bayerische Staatsbibliothek
(Munich) **107**
Street-by-Street map 105

Bayerische Staatskanzlei **89**
Bayerischer Kanu-Verband 293
Bayerischer Wald 179, **197**, 293
tour by car **191**
Bayerisches Nationalmuseum
(Munich) 57, **112–13**
Bayerisches Schwaben *see*
Northern Swabia
Bayern Tourismus Marketing
Gmbh 265, 299
Bayertor and Town Walls (Landsberg
am Lech) **214**
Bayrischzell
Alpenstraße tour 225
restaurants 282
Beaker culture 39
Becker, Karl Peter 170
Beckmann, Max 120
Bed-and-breakfast
accommodation **264**, 265
Bed & Breakfast Mitwohnzentrale
265
Beduzzi, Antonio 192
Beer 23, **274–5**
Augustinerbräu (Munich) **62**
beer gardens 284
festivals 34
Hofbräuhaus (Munich) **88**
Löwenbräukeller (Munich)
131
Oktoberfest 21, **33**, 36, 143,
147
Behnisch, Günter 138
Beilngries 163, **168**
Bellony 85
Benedictines 28, 169, 232
Benedikt, Freiherr von
Herman 230
Benediktbeuern 40, **221**
festivals 36
Berbling 209
Berchtesgaden **204**
Alpenstraße tour 225
hotels 268
restaurants 281
Berchtesgaden National Park 199
Berg
Starnbergersee tour 217
Berg am Laim (Munich) 27, **140**
Bergmüller, Johann Georg 216
Bernau 201
Bernauer, Agnes 35, 46, 188, 189
Bernheimer Fine Old Masters
(Munich) 287
Bernheimerhaus (Munich) 130
Bernini, Gianlorenzo 84
Bernried
Starnbergesee tour 217
Betz, Walter and Bea 139
Beuys, Joseph 119
Bicycles 312, 313
Bieber, Oswald 131
Biennais, Martin Guillaume 79
Biennale (Munich) 34

Bier-und Oktoberfestmuseum (Munich) **68**
Bille, Otto 140
Bismarck, Otto von 48, 217
Bistros, Munich 284
Der Blaue Reiter 109, 119; **219**, 222
Blutenburg (Munich) 26, **143**
BMW 23, 53, 133, 179
  BMW Museum (Munich) **138–9**
  BMW Welt (Munich) **138–9**
Boat trips **309**
Bock 275
Bockberger, Hans 173
Böcklin, Arnold 111
  Play of the Waves 127, 129
Bodensee 228, 237, 238
Bogenberg **186**
Boniface, St 40, 41, 223
Bonnard, Pierre 129
Bormann, Martin 205
Bosch, Hieronymus 124
Botanischer Garten (Munich) **138**
  see also Alter Botanischer Garten
Botticelli, Sandro
  Pietà 122
Boucher, François
  Portrait of the Marquise de Pompadour 123, 125
Boys on the Beach (Liebermann) 129
Bradl, Jakob 193
Brancas, Alexander von 126, 168
Braque, Georges 120
Braun 101
Braunfels, Stephan 121
Breakfast in the Studio (Manet) 127
Brecht, Bertolt 252
Breitach river gorge 236
Breweries *see* Beer
Bridges
  Ludwigsbrücke (Munich) **97**
  Marienbrücke 235
  Maximiliansbrücke (Munich) 93
British Airways 307
Bronze Age 39
Brouwer, Adriaen
  Peasants Playing Cards 123, 124
Brueghel, Pieter
  Land of Cockaigne 123, 124
Bschorer, Georg **258**
Buchbinder 315
Bühl 236
Bundesarbeitsgemeinschaft Hilfe für Behinderte (BAGH) 265
Bureaux de change 302
Burg Trausnitz 10, **185**
Bürgersaal (Munich) 31, **62**
  Street-by-Street map 60
Burghalde (Kempten) **241**
Burghausen 200, **202**
  restaurants 281

Burghausen, Hans von 184, 202, 208
Burgkmair, Hans 30, 31
Bürklein, Friedrich
  Maximilianeum (Munich) 95
  Maximilianstraße (Munich) 88, 92
  Regierung von Oberbayern (Munich) 94
Buses 307, **308–9**, **310–11**
Bustelli, Franz Anton 134
Bystrup, Bregenhoj & Partners 143

C

Cable cars 235
Café Altschwabing (Munich) 285
Café am Beethovenplatz (Munich) 285
Café Glück (Munich) 285
Café Glyptothek (Munich) 285
Café Kreutzkamn (Munich) 285
Café Luitpold (Munich) 285
Café Nil (Munich) 284, 285
Café Puck (Munich) 285
Café Reitschule (Munich) 285
Café Schwabing (Munich) 285
Café Wienerplatz (Munich) 285
Cafés, Munich **284**, 285
Campendonk, Heinrich 109
Camping 265, **292**, 293
Camuzzi, Giovanni Petro 197
Canadian Embassy 299
Canaletto 125
Candid, Peter 30, 80, 176, 185
Canova, Antonio 80, 128
Capuchin monks 167
Caravanning **292**, 293
Carlone, Giovanni Battista 192
Carlone family 193
Cars 313, **314–15**
  BMW Museum (Munich) **138–9**
  car rental 315
  driving in Munich **313**
  getting from Munich Airport 307
  MEFA-Automobil-Museum (Amerang) 208
  see also Tours by car
Carus, Carl Gustav 128
Casimir Jagiellon, King of Poland 32, 43
Castles
  Burg Trausnitz **185**
  Castles of Ludwig II **50–1**
  Harburg 244, **249**
  Herzogskasten (Ingolstadt) **171**
  Herzogschloss (Straubing) **188**
  Höhlenburg 206
  Neuburg an der Donau **173**
  Neues Schloss (Ingolstadt) **171**
  Neuschwanstein 11, **50–1**, 160, 229, **234**, 235

Castles (cont.)
  Schloss Hohenschwangau **235**, 235
  Willibaldsburg (Eichstätt) **168**
  see also Palaces
Cathedrals
  Dom Unserer Lieban Frau (Augsburg) 30, **254**
  Dom St Stephan (Passau) 27, **192**
  Eichstätt **166**
Catholic Church 22–23
Cavazzo family 238
Caves
  Sturmannshöhle 236
  Tropfsteinhöhle 187
Celts 39, 40
Centre for New Technology (Munich) 101
Cephisodotus 56
Ceramics shops 288
Cézanne, Paul 129
Charivari (Munich) 285
Charlemagne, Emperor 41
Chieming
  Chiemsee tour **207**
Chiemsee 24, 199
  Tour by car 207
  restaurants 281
Children
  bus and tram travel 310–11
  entertainment in Munich 147
  in hotels 263
  shopping in Munich **148**, 145
Chinesischer Turm (Munich) 285
Chirico, Giorgio de 108, 120
Christian Democratic Union (CDU) 53
Christian Social Union (CSU) 53
Christianity, history 40
Christkindlmarkt 37
Christmas 37
Christmas fairs **33**, 37
  Munich 145
Church Ruins in the Forest (Friedrich) 128
Churches
  opening hours 296
  Allerheiligenkirche am Kreuz (Munich) **73**
  Annakirche (Augsburg) 252, **255**
  Asamkirche (Munich) 14, 56, **70–1**
  Basilika St Bonifaz (Munich) 116, **118**
  Bürgersaal (Munich) 60, **62**
  Damenstift St Anna (Munich) **73**
  Dominikanerkirche (Landshut) **184**
  Dreifaltigkeitskirche (Munich) **86**
  Frauenkirche (Memmingen) **231**

Churches (cont.)
Frauenkirche (Munich) 61, **64–5**
Georgskirche (Nördlingen) **246**
Heilig-Geist-Kirche (Munich) **67**
Heilig-Kreuz-Kirche (Landsberg am Lech) **214–15**
Hofkirche (Ingolstadt) **172**
Jakobs- und Tiburtiuskirche (Straubing) **189**
Jesuitenkirche (Landshut) **184**
Jodokkirche (Landshut) **184**
Johanniskirche (Landsberg am Lech) **215**
Kapuzinerkirche Kreuz und zum Heiligen Grabkirche (Eichstätt) 10, **167**
Karmelitenkirche (Straubing) **188**
Kirche St Peter (Straubing) **189**
Klosterkirche der Dominikanerinnen Hl. Dreifaltigkeit (Landsberg am Lech) **214**
Klosterkirche St Anna (Munich) 92, **94**
Klosterkirche St Walburg (Eichstätt) **168**
Klösterle (Nördlingen) **246**
Kreuzherrenkirche (Memmingen) **231**
Liebfrauenmünster (Ingolstadt) **170**
Lorenzkirche (Kempten) **241**
Ludwigskirche (Munich) 105, **107**
Maria Gern **204**
Mariä Himmelfahrt (Landsberg am Lech) **215**
Maria Steinbach **237**
Martinskirche (Landshut) 183, **184**
Martinskirche (Memmingen) **230**
Michaelskirche (Munich) 26, 60, **62–63**
Michaelskirche (Passau) **193**
Moritzkirche (Ingolstadt) **171**
Münster "zur Lieben Frau" (Lindau) **238**
Paulskirche (Passau) **195**
Peterskirche (Lindau) **239**
Peterskirche (Munich) 61, **66**
Peterskirche (Neuburg an der Donau) **172**
Pfarrkirche St Anna (Munich) 93, **94**
Pfarrkirche St Sebastian (Ramsau) **205**
St-Mang-Kirche (Kempten) **240**
St-Nikolai-Kirche (Munich) **96**
St-Ulrich-und-St-Afra-Kirche (Augsburg) 26, **255**
Salvatorkirche (Munich) 76, **84**
Salvatorkirche (Passau) **194**
Sankt Hermann **190**
Schutzengelkirche (Eichstätt) **166–7**

Churches (cont.)
Spitalkirche (Landshut) **184**
Stephanskirche (Lindau) **238**
Theatinerkirche (Munich) 56, 75, 76, **83**
Ursulinenkirche (Straubing) **188**
Wallfahrtskirche Mariahilf (Passau) **195**
Wieskirche **218–19**
see also Abbeys; Cathedrals; Convents; Monasteries
Cinema see Film
Circus Krone Bau (Munich) 147
Cistercians 190, 249
City Mitwohnzentrale 265
Claude Lorrain 125
Clemens August, Bishop of Cologne 140
Clemens Joseph, Bishop of Cologne 140
Clothing
Bavarian folk costume 23, **33**
shops in Munich **144**, 145
Club Behinderter und ihrer Freunde (CBF) 265
Coach travel **308–9**
Coins 303
Colin, Alexander 233
Cologne School 124
Commerzbank (Munich) 302
Communications **304–5**
Concentration camps
Dachau 163, **175**
Constance, Lake see Bodensee
Consulates 299
Convents
Kloster Notre Dame du Sacré Coeur (Eichstätt) **167**
Corinth, Lovis 119, 129
Cornelius, Peter 89, 107
Corot, Camille 128
Corpus Christi 34
Counter-Reformation 170
Courbet, Gustave 128
Cranach, Lucas the Elder 124, 195
Credit cards 302
public telephones 304
shopping 286
Crime 300
Crisis Hotline 301
Crystals Museum (Riedenburg) 10, 187
CSU 23
Currency **302–3**
Customs and visa regulations 298
Cuvilliés, François 31
Amalienburg (Nymphenburg) 134
Benediktuskirche (Freising) 169
Cuvilliés-Theater (Munich) 81

Cuvilliés, François (cont.)
Erzbischöfliches Palais (Munich) 84
Palais Porcia (Munich) 84
Residenz (Munich) 80
Theatinerkirche (Munich) 84
tomb of 84
Cuvilliés-Theater (Munich) 77, 79, **81**
Cycling **290**, 293, 312, 313

D

Dachau 163, **175**
hotels 267
restaurants 279
Daguerre, Louis 100
Dahl, Johan Christian 128
Daig, Sebastian 247
Dallmayr (Munich) 10, 145, 287
Damenstift St Anna (Munich) **73**
Dance, Munich **146**, 147
D'Angeli, Domenico 192
Danube, River 10, 179, 243
boat trips 186, 309
Danube School 124
Daucher, Adolf 257
Daucher, Hans 255
Daumier, Honoré
Don Quijote 128
DAV Summit Club 293
David, Jacques-Louis 128
DB Call-a-Bike (Munich) 313
Degas, Edgar 129
Deggendorf
hotels 268
restaurants 280
Degler, Johann 86
Delacroix, Eugène 128
Delaunay, Paul 222
Delta Air Lines 307
Denis, Maurice 129
Department stores
Munich **144**, 145
The Deposition (Rembrandt) 123
Der Kleine Chinese (Munich) 285
Desmarées, George 31
Portrait of Karl Albrecht as Emperor Karl VII 136
Deutsche Alpenstraße 236
Deutsche Alpenverein (DAV) 293
Deutsche Bahn 309
Deutsche Bahn Fundbüro 301
Deutsche Bank (Munich) 302
Deutsche Reiterliche Vereinigung e.V. 293
Deutscher Camping Club 265, 293
Deutscher Golf Verband e.V. 293
Deutscher Heilbäderverband 293
Deutscher Segler-Verband 293

eutscher Skiverband e.V. 293
Deutscher Sportbund 293
Deutscher Tennis Bund e.V.
    290
Deutscher Volkssportverband e.V.
    293
Deutscher Wanderverband 293
Deutsches Jagd- und
    Fischereimuseum (Munich)
    63
    Street-by-Street map 61
Deutsches Medizinhistorisches
    Museum (Ingolstadt) 170
Deutsches Museum (Munich) 12,
    98–101
Deutsches Museum
    Verkehrszentrum (Munich)
    142
Deutsches Reisebüro (DER) 309
Deutsches Theater (Munich)
    147
Deutsches Weininstitut 293
Deutschmann, Joseph 190, 196
Dialling codes 304
Dibitsch, Karl von 221
Dießen 213, **216**
    hotels 269
Diebsturm (Lindau) 239
Dientzenhofer, Wolfgang 188
Diesel, Rudolf 252
Dillingen **258**
    hotels 269
    restaurants 283
Dingolfing 179, 181
Disabled visitors 297, 299
    in hotels 263
    in restaurants 271
Disrobing of Christ (El Greco)
    125
DJH München City 265
DJH München Park 265
Doctors 301
Döllgast, Hans 124
Dollmann, Georg von 220
Dom Unserer Lieben Frau
    (Augsburg) 30, **254**
Dom St Salvator und St
    Willibald (Eichstätt) **166**
Dom St Stephan (Passau) 27,
    192
Domenichino 233
Dominikanerkirche (Landshut)
    184
Domplatz (Passau) 192
Donauried 243
Donauwörth 250
    festivals 35
    hotels 269
Donisl (Munich) 285
Doppelbock 275
Dreiburgenland 190
Dreifaltigkeitskirche (Munich)
    86
Drinking accessories 289
Drusus 39
Düll, Heinrich 96

Dürckheim-Montmartin, Count
    Georg Friedrich von 130
Dürer, Albrecht 254
    Alte Pinakothek (Munich) 124
    Annakirche (Augsburg) 255
    Four Apostles 124
    Markuskirche (Augsburg) 257
Dürrenmatt, Friedrich 190, 195

E

E-mail 305
"Eagle's Nest" 199, 204, **205**
easyJet 307
Eberhard, Duke of Bavaria 41
Ebersberg **221**
Eck, Johannes 170
Effner, Joseph
    Nymphenburg 134, 136
    Preysing-Palais (Munich) 77,
    82
    Schleißheim Palace 176
Egkl, Wilhelm 87
Ehem. Stadtschreiberei
    ("Former City Writers'
    Guild") **66–7**
Eibsee **221**
Eichstätt 10, 163, **166–68**
    hotels 267
    map 167
    restaurants 279
Eilleshof (Munich) **82**
    Street-by-Street map 76
Eisner, Kurt 86
Electricity 298
Elisabeth, Empress of Austria
    68, 217
ELLA im Lenbachhaus (Munich) 285
Elsheimer, Adam 124
Embassies 299
Emergencies 300, 301, 315
Emmeram, St, Bishop of Ratisbon
    40, 41
Englburg 190
Englischer Garten (Munich)
    10, **110**
Enlightenment 28
Ensor, James 129
Entertainment
    Munich **146–7**
Environmental Badge Climate
    Company 313, 315
Erding **174**
    restaurants 279,
Ernest, Duke of Bavaria 46,
    189
Erzbischöfliches Palais
    (Munich) **84**
    Street-by-Street map 76
Essing
    Altmühl Valley tour 187
Ettal 28, **220**
Ettenhofer, Johann Georg 86
Ettl, Johann Benedikt 251
Europcar 315
Europe, map 13

F

Fabritius, Carel 125
Fairs, Christmas 33, 37
The Falling Man (Lehmbruck)
    120
Fashion shops **144**, 145
Fauser, Werner 195
FC Bayern Shop (Munich) 147
Feichtmayr, Franz Xavier the
    Elder 175
Feichtmayr, Johann Michael
    223, 232, 251
Feichtmayr, Kaspar 217, 223
Feistenberger, Andreas 62
Feldafing
    Starnbergersee tour 221
Feldherrnhalle (Munich) **82–3**
    Street-by-Street map 77
Ferdinand, Elector 67, 83
Ferdinand Maria, Elector 47, 134
Festivals **34–7**, 297
    Munich **146**, 147
    traditions of the Bavarian
    Alps **32–3**
Feuerbach, Anselm 111, 129
Fichtl, Joseph 86
Film
    Bavaria-Filmstadt (Munich)
    142
    Filmfest München (Munich)
    35
    Munich **146**, 147
Finsterau
    Nationalpark Bayerischer
    Wald tour 191
Fire brigade 300, 301, 315
Firstalm
    festivals 37
Fischen 236
Fischer, Johann Georg 258
Fischer, Johann Michael
    Anastasiakapelle
    (Benediktbeuern) 223
    Asambasilika (Osterhofen)
    197
    Dießen 216
    Höchstädt 259
    Klosterkirche St Anna
    (Munich) 94
    Mariä Himmelfahrt (Bad
    Aibling) 209
    Mariä Himmelfahrtskirche
    (Fürstenzell) 190
    Michaelskirche (Berg am
    Laim) 140
    Ottobeuren 232
    Sts Marinus und Anianus
    (Rott am Inn) 209
Fischer, Karl von
    Karolinenplatz (Munich) 118
    Max-Joseph-Platz (Munich) 82
    Museums District (Munich)
    115
    Prinz Karl Palais (Munich)
    27

Fish Fountain (Munich) 59, 66
Flea markets 145
Flohmarkt Riem (Munich) 145
Flößerci Josef Seitner 309
Folk art 288
Folk costume 23, **33**, 289
Food and drink
    beer **274–5**
    cafés, bars and bistros **284**, 285
    The Flavours of Munich and Bavaria **272–3**
    pubs and beer gardens **284**, 285
    shops 145, 287
    take-away food 284, 285
    Viktualienmarkt (Munich) **68**
    see also Restaurants
Fossils 163, **168**
Fountains
    Augsburg **254**, 256
    Fish Fountain (Munich) 59, 66
    Wittelsbacher Brunnen (Munich) 130
Four Apostles (Dürer) 124
Four Ski-Jump Tournament (Oberstdorf) 37
Fragonard, Jean-Honoré 125
Franks 40, 41
Franz, Michael 168
Franz Josef-Strauß Airport 306–7
Franz Joseph, Emperor 217
Franziskaner Garten (Munich) 285
Fraueninsel
    Chiemsee tour 207
Frauenkirche (Memmingen) **231**
Frauenkirche (Munich) **64–5**
    Street-by-Street map 61
Frederick III, Emperor 182
Free State of Bavaria 49
Freilichtmuseum Glentleiten **223**
Freising **169**
    hotels 267
    restaurants 279
Freyung
    Nationalpark Bayerischer Wald tour 191
Friedberg **250–1**
    restaurants 283
Friedensengel (Munich) 57, **96**
Friedrich, Caspar David
    Church Ruins in the Forest 128
Friedrich Barbarossa, Emperor 42
Friedrich Maria, Elector 107
Fronleichnam 34
Frundsberg family 233
Fugel, Gebhard 202
Fugger, Anton 255
Fugger, Georg 257
Fugger, Hans 233, 257
Fugger, Jakob I 257

Fugger, Jakob II 255, 256, 257
Fugger, Ulrich 257
Fugger family 26, **257**
    Annakirche (Augsburg) 252, 255
    Babenhausen 232
    Fuggerbau (Memmingen) **231**
    Fuggerei (Augsburg) **256–7**
    Fuggerhäuser (Augsburg) **255**
    Kirchheim 233
    Malhaus (Wasserburg) 237
    Palais Porcia (Munich) 84
    Weißenhorn 251
Fuggerbau (Memmingen) **231**
Fuggerei (Augsburg) 11, **256–7**
Fuggerhäuser (Augsburg) **255**
    Street-by-Street map 253
Fünf Höfe (Munich) 145
Fünfseenland 212
Funk, Johann Georg 190
Fürstbischöfliche Residenz (Augsburg) 257
Fürstbischöfliche Residenz (Eichstätt) **166**
Fürstbischöfliche Sommer Residenz (Eichstätt) **167**
Fürstenfeldbrück 163, **175**
Fürstenstein 190
Fürstenzell **190**
Füssen **234**
    hotels 269
    restaurants 282
Füssen-Hopfen am See
    restaurants 282

G

Gabriel, Franz 166
Gabrieli, Gabriel de 166, 167, 172
Galeria Kaufhof (Munich) 145
Galerie im Lenbachhaus (Munich) **119**
    Street-by-Street map 116
Galileo 98
Galleries *see* Museums and galleries
Gardens *see* Parks and gardens
Garibald I, Duke of Bavaria 40, 41
Garmisch-Partenkirchen 22, 211, **221**
    hotels 269
    restaurants 282
Gärtner, Friedrich von 130
    Bayerische Staatsbibliothek (Munich) 107
    Feldherrnhalle (Munich) 82
    Gärtnerplatz (Munich) 68
    Independence Hall (Kelheim) 187
    Ludwigskirche (Munich) 107
    Ludwigstraße (Munich) 106
    Siegestor (Munich) 108

Gärtnerplatz (Munich) 10, **68**
Gärtnerplatztheater (Munich) 68
Gasteig (Munich) **97**
Gasteig Culture Center (Munich) 147
Gasthöfe 265
Gäubodenfest (Straubing) 35
Gäubodenmuseum (Straubing) **188–9**
Gauguin, Paul 129
Gedon, Lorenz 171
Gemmingen, Konrad von, Bishop of Eichstätt 168
Geobuch (Munich) 287
Georg (son of Ludwig the Rich) 32, 35, 182
Georg, Johann 169
Georgskirche (Nördlingen) **246**
Gerhard, Hubert 30
    Hofgarten (Munich) 89
    Marienplatz (Munich) 66
    Michaelskirche (Munich) 63
    Residenz (Munich) 80
Géricault, Théodore
    Heroic Landscape with Fishermen 126, 128
German Theatre Museum (Munich) 89
Germany, map 12–13
Ghirlandaio, Dominico 125
Gift shops 287
Giotto 125
Girl with Straw Hat (Von Amerling) 126
Gisela, St 194
Glassware
    Passauer Glasmuseum (Passau) **195**
    shopping 288
Glyptothek (Munich) 27, 56, **119**
    Street-by-Street map 116
Goethe, Johann Wolfgang von 131, 223
Goethe-Institut 293, 299
Golf **291**, 293
Gorham, Christian the Younger 192
Gothic architecture 26
Gothic art 30
Götz, Matthias 196
Goyen, Han van 125
Graf, Oskar Maria 85
Grafenau
    restaurants 280
Grasbergerhaus (Landshut)
    Street-by-Street map 183
Grasser, Erasmus 30
    Altes Rathaus (Munich) 67
    Bad Reichenhall 203
    Frauenkirche (Munich) 65
    Freising cathedral 169
    Maria Himmelfahrt (Ramersdorf) 140
    Peterskirche (Munich) 61, 66
    St Sixtus (Schliersee) 225
    Stadtmuseum (Munich) 69

El Greco
  Disrobing of Christ 125
Green Travel 306
Greiff, Johann Georg 67
Greuze, Jean-Baptiste 125
Grossaert, Jan 124
Grünewald, Matthias 124
Grünwald (Munich) **142**
Gstadt
  Chiemsee tour 207
Guardi, Francesco 125
Guided tours 312, 313
Gumpp, Anton von 62
Gunetzrhainer, Johann Baptist
  84, 86, 174
Gunetzrhainer brothers 73
Günther, Ignaz 31
  Asamkirche (Munich) 70
  Bürgersaal (Munich) 62
  Frauenkirche (Munich) 61,61
  Ignaz-Günther-Haus
  (Munich) 68–9
  Michaelskirche (Berg am Laim)
  140
  Sts Marinus und Anianus
  (Rott am Inn) 209
  Schleißheim Palace 176
  Theatinerkirche (Munich) 76
Günther, Matthäus 175, 209, 221,
  222, 251
Günz, River 232, 243, 258
Günzburg 258

H

Hackert, Jacob Philipp 128
Haidhof 180
Haiger, Ernst 108
Haindlfing near Freising
  restaurants 279
Hallertau 24, 161, 163
Hallgebäude (Nördlingen) 247
Hallstatt period 39
Hals, Frans
  Portrait of Willem van Heythuysen
  125
Halsbach, Jörg von
  Allerheiligenkirche am
  Kreuz (Munich) 73
  Altes Rathaus (Munich) 67
  Frauenkirche (Munich) 64
Hans-Eisenmann-Haus
  Nationalpark Bayerischer Wald
  tour 191
Hans Goltz (Munich) 287
Hans von Aachen 124
Harbour (Lindau) 239
Harburg 244, 249
Hartmann, Thomas von 109
Haßler, Benedikt 140
Hauptbahnhof (Munich) 308
Hauptbahnhof, Radius-Tours
  (Munich) 313
Haus zum Cavazzen (Lindau) 238
Haus International 261
Haus der Kunst (Munich) 111
Health 300–301

Heavenly Horses (Marc) 222
Hefele, Melchior 192
Heider, Hans 208
Heilige Kreuzkirche
  (Landsberg am Lech)
  214–15
Heilig-Geist-Kirche (Munich) 67
Heilmeier, Max 96
Heine, Heinrich 222
Heinrich der Löwe (Henry the Lion)
  42
  Ludwigsbrücke (Munich) 97
  Marienplatz (Munich) 66
  Mindelburg Castle 233
Heintz, Josef 26, 252
Heinz von Stein 206
Helbig, Henry 108
Hellabrunn (Munich) see Tierpark
  Hellabrunn
Helmschrot, Heinrich 174
Hemsch, Jean Henri 113
Henriette Adelaide, Princess
  143
  Damenstift St Anna (Munich) 73
  Theatinerkirche (Munich) 83
  tomb of 83
Henry II, Emperor 194
Henry XIII, Duke of
  Bavaria 46
Herbst Dult (Munich) 36
Herigoyen, Joseph Emanuel
  von 86, 131
Herkomer, Hubert von 215
Herkomer, Johann Georg 251
Herlin, Friedrich 247
Herman, St 190
Hermann, Franz Georg 237, 240
Hermansbau (Memmingen)
  230
Heroic Landscape with Fishermen
  (Géricault) 126, 128
Herrenchiemsee 11, 51, 161, 199,
  206
  Chiemsee tour 207
Hertz 315
Herzogskasten (Ingolstadt) 171
Herzogsschloss (Straubing) 188
Hesperides II (Marées) 129
Hieber Lindberg (Munich) 287
High-East Kletterhalle 293
Hiking 290, 293
  safety 300–1
Hildebrand, Adolf von 97, 130
Hintersee
  Alpenstraße tour 225
Hinterstein 236
Historic routes 292
History 39–53
Hitler, Adolf 49, 52, 107
  assassination attempts 97
  "Eagle's Nest" 199, 204, 205
  Haus der Kunst (Munich) 111
  Hitler-Putsch (1923) 83
  Mein Kampf 214
  Schwabing (Munich) 109
Hocheder, Carl 97

Höchstädt 259
Höchstetter family 257
Hofbräuhaus (Munich) 10, 88, 285
Hofbräukeller (Munich) 285
Hoffmann, Julius 234
Hofgarten (Munich) 89
Hofkirche (Ingolstadt) 172
Höglwörth 203
Hohenpeißenberg 218
Hohenschwangau see Schloss
  Hohenschwangau
Hohenstaufen family 249
Hohes Haus (Nördlingen) 246
Höhlenburg 206
Holbein, Hans the Elder 30,
  31, 254
  Adoration of the Magi 122
  Jakobs- und Tiburtiuskirche
  (Straubing) 189, 196
  Peterskirche (Lindau) 239
Holiday apartments 264
Holidays, public 37
Holl, Elias 26, 251, 254
  Annakirche (Augsburg) 255
  Heilig-Geist-Spital (Augsburg) 255
  Perlachturm (Augsburg) 253
  Rathaus (Augsburg) 253
  Rotes Tor and City Walls
  (Augsburg) 255
  Stadtmetzg (Augsburg) 245, 254
  Town Hall (Augsburg) 254
  Westertor (Memmingen) 230
  Willibaldsburg (Eichstätt) 168
  Zeughaus (Augsburg) 252,
  255
Holl, Johannes 184, 256
Holnstein, Count von 84
Holy Home (Munich) 285
Holzer, Jenny 85
Holzer, Johann 221
Holzinger, Franz Josef 186
Hölzl, Felix 189
Hopfenstraße 163
Hospitals 301
Hotels 262–9
  Allgäu 269
  Lower Bavaria 268
  Munich 266–7
  Northern Swabia 269
  Upper Bavaria (East) 268
  Upper Bavaria (North) 267–8
  Upper Bavaria (South) 269
Huber, Professor Kurt 107
Huber, Wolfgang 204
Hugendubel (Munich) 287
Humboldt, Alexander 199
Hypo-Hochhaus (Munich) 139
HypoVereinsbank (Munich)
  302

I

Ignaz-Günther-Haus (Munich) 68–9
Iller River 236, 243
Ilm, River 169
Immenstadt 229, 236
  Alpenstraße tour 224

Impressionism 129
Indersdorf 163
Industry 23–24
Ingolstadt 39, 163, 170–1
　hotels 267
　map 171
　restaurants 279
Inn, River 192, 199, 208, 209
Insurance 300, 301, 314
Internationale Jazzwoche (Munich)
　34
(Munich) 143
Internet 304
Irish Embassy 299
Isar, River 91, 92, 140, 184
　rafting 309
Isartor (Munich) 67
Italia and Germania (Overbeck) 127,
　128

J

Jacob, St 189
Jadwiga, Princess 32, 35, 182, 183
Jan III Sobieski, King of Poland 44
Jank, Christoph 50, 234
Jawlensky, Alexej 119, 219
Jazz festivals 34
Jazzbar Vogler (Munich) 285
Jesuit College (Neuburg an der
　Donau) 173
Jesuitenkirche (Landshut) 184
Jesuits 107
Jochstraße
　Alpenstraße tour 224
Jodokkirche (Landshut) 184
Johann II, Duke of Bavaria
　46
Johanniskirche (Landsberg am
　Lech) 215
John Paul II, Pope 57, 197, 202
Jordaens, Jacob 124
Joseph II, Emperor of Austria 45
Jüdisches Zentrum Jakobsplatz
　(Munich) 69
Judith with the Head of Holofernes
　(Meit) 112
Junge Wilde movement 120
Justizpalast (Munich) 131

K

Käfer (Munich) 145, 287
Kaffee Giesing (Munich) 285
Kainer, Franz 222
Kaisergarten (Munich) 285
Kaisheim 249
Kaltenberger Ritterspiele 35
Kaltenthal, Jakob von 250
Kandinsky, Wassily 222
　Akademie der Bildenden Künst
　(Munich) 108
　Der Blaue Reiter 219
　Galerie im Lenbachhaus (Munich)
　119
　Münterhaus (Murnau) 219
　Schwabing (Munich) 109
Kaokao (Munich) 285

Kapuzinerkirche Hl. Kreuz
　und zur Heiligen Grabkirche
　(Eichstätt) 10, 167
Karl V, Emperor 43, 257
　Fürstbischöfliche Residenz
　(Augsburg) 257
　portrait of 123
Karl Albrecht, Elector
　(Emperor Karl VII) 45, 47
　Erzbischöfliches Palais (Munich) 84
　Palais Porcia (Munich) 84
　portrait of 136
Karl Theodor, Elector 45, 47
　Englischer Garten (Munich) 110
　Karlsplatz 130
　Karlstor (Munich) 62
　Lauingen 259
　Residenz (Munich) 81
Karlsplatz (Munich) 130–1
Karlsplatz (Neuburg an der Donau)
　172
Karlstor (Munich) 62, 130
　Street-by-Street map 60
Karmelitenkirche (Straubing) 188
Karoline Charlotte Auguste von
　Bayern, Princess 80
Karolinenplatz (Munich) 118
　Street-by-Street map 117
Karwendel 211
Kaufbeuren 233
Kaulbach, Friedrich von 95
Kaulbach, Wilhelm von 95, 128
Kehlstein, Mount 199
Kehlsteinhaus (Berchtesgaden) 52,
　204, 205
Kelheim 10, 39, 179
　Altmühl Valley tour 187
Kempten 39, 228, 240–1
　festivals 35
　hotels 269
　map 241
　restaurants 282–3
Kern family 208
Khnopff, Fernand
　I Lock My Door Upon Myself 126,
　129
Kinderreich (Munich) 147
Kirche St Jakob- und St Tiburtius
　(Straubing) 189
Kirche St Peter (Straubing)
　189
Kirchheim 233
Klauda, Manfred 68
Klee, Paul
　Akademie der Bildenden Künst
　(Munich) 108
　Der Blaue Reiter 219
　Galerie im Lenbachhaus (Munich)
　119
　Schwabing (Munich) 109
Klenze, Leo von 27, 119
　Alte Pinakothek (Munich) 122
　Glyptothek (Munich) 119
　Hofgarten (Munich) 89
　Independence Hall
　(Kelheim) 187

Klenze, Leo von (cont.)
　Ingolstadt 170
　Karolinenplatz (Munich) 118
　Ludwigstraße (Munich) 106
　Marstall (Munich) 89
　Max-Joseph-Platz (Munich)
　82
　Monopteros (Munich) 110
　Museums District (Munich) 115
　Odeonsplatz (Munich) 106
　Palais Porcia (Munich) 85
　Palais Töerring-Jettenbach
　(Munich) 87
　Propyläen (Munich) 119
　Residenz (Munich) 80
　Tegernsee 224
　Theresienwiese (Munich) 143
　Wittelsbacherplatz (Munich) 104,
　106
Klimt, Gustav 129
Klopfer, Heini 236
Kloster Indersdorf 10, 175
Kloster Niedernburg (Passau) 194
Kloster Notre Dame du Sacré Coeur
　(Eichstätt) 167
Kloster Seeon 208
Klosterkirche der Dominikanerinnen
　Hl. Dreifaltigkeit (Landsberg am
　Lech) 214
Klosterkirche St Anna (Munich) 94
　Street-by-Street map 92
Klosterkirche St Walburg (Eichstätt)
　168
Klösterle (Nördlingen) 246
Klotz, Matthäus 222
Kneipp, Sebastian 233
Kneipp-Verein München 293
Koch, Joseph Anton 128
Kochel am see 223
　hotels 269
Koehler, Bernhard 109
Kohl, Helmut 190
Kolomanskirche
　Neuschwanstein tour 235
König-Ludwig-Feier
　(Oberammergau) 35
Königssee 11, 199, 204
Königsplatz (Munich)
　Street-by-Street map 116–17
Königsquelle (Munich) 289
Korbinian, Bishop of Freising 40
Kornhaus (Kempten) 241
Kraillburg-Ortenburg, Joachim von
　196
Krebs, Thomas 256
Krenkl, Franz Xaver 179
Kreuther, Friedrich Jakob 130
Kreuzherrenkirche (Memmingen)
　231
Kreuztor and City Walls (Ingolstadt)
　170
Krieger, Joseph 202
Krumpper, Hans 30, 31
　Allerheiligenkirche am
　Kreuz (Munich) 73
　Heilig-Geist-Kirche (Munich) 67

...pper, Hans (cont.)
 ...ofgarten (Munich) 89
 ...aakobskirche (Dachau) 175
 Residenz (Munich) 78, 80, 81
Kruse, Käthe 250
Künstlerhaus (Munich) 86
Kurz, Michael 197

L

Lakes
 Ammersee 211, 213, 216
 Bavarian Alps 24–5
 boat trips 309
 Bodensee (Lake Constance) 237, 238
 Eibsee 221
 Hintersee 225
 Königssee 11, 204
 Schliersee 225
 Starnbergersee 217
 Tegernsee 224
 Walchensee 222
Lamberg Palace (Passau) 192
Lancret, Nicolas 125
Land of Cockaigne (Bruegel) 123, 124
Landesverband Bayern des DJH 265
Landsberg am Lech 211, 214–15
 hotels 269
 map 215
Landscape, Bavarian Alps 22, 24–5
Landschaftshaus (Landshut)
 Street-by-Street map 182
Landshut 180, 182–84
 architecture 26
 hotels 268
 restaurants 280
 Street-by-Street map 182–3
Landshuter Hochzeit
 (Landshut Wedding) 32, 35, 182
Ländtor (Landshut)
 Street-by-Street map 182
Lang, Lucas 195
Lange Nacht der Museen (Munich) 36
Lange Nacht der Musik (Munich) 34
Langwieder See 265
Lasso, Orlando di 84
Laufen 203
Lauingen 259
Le Bouchon (Munich) 285
Leb, Wolfgang 225
Lech, River 211, 214, 234, 243, 252
Lechwehr (Landsberg am Lech) 214
Lehmbruck, Wilhelm
 The Falling Man 120
Leibl, Wilhelm 209
 Akademie der Bildenden Künste (Munich) 108
 Galerie im Lenbachhaus (Munich) 119
 Neue Pinakothek (Munich) 129

Leibniz, Gottfried von 101
Leinberger, Hans 73, 174
Leitheim 249
Lenbach, Franz von
 Galerie im Lenbachhaus (Munich) 18, 116, 119
 Künstlerhaus (Munich) 86
 Museums District (Munich) 115
 Sammlung Schack (Munich) 111
Lenbachhaus (Munich) 18, 115, 119
Lenbachplatz (Munich) 130
Leonard, St 36
Leonardo da Vinci 125
Leonhardifahrten und
 Leonhardiritte 36
Leopold, Bishop of Passau 195
Leopold I, Emperor 195
Lespilliez, Karl Albrecht von 85
Leuchtenberg, Duke
 Maximilian 120
Libraries
 Bayerische Staatsbibliothek (Munich) 105, 107
 Internationale Jugendbibliothek (Munich) 143
Liebermann, Max
 Boys on the Beach 129
Liebfrauenmünster (Ingolstadt) 170
Lindau 21, 238–9
 hotels 269
 map 239
 restaurants 283
Linderhof 165, 213, 220–21
Lindmayr, Anna Maria 86
Lippi, Fra Filippo 125
Liss, Johann 124
Literaturhaus (Munich) 85
Littmann, Max 88, 111
Löbel, Friedrich 85
Lodenfrey (Munich) 145, 287
Löpsinger Tor and Town Walls (Nördlingen) 247
Lorenzkirche (Kempten) 241
Lost property 301
Loth, Ulrich
 The Pentecost 67
Lotsenstationen 315
Louis XIV, King of France 44, 51, 206, 220
Löwenbräukeller (Munich) 131, 285
Lower Bavaria 10, 179–97
 hotels 268
 map 180–1
 restaurants 280
Ludwig I, King of Bavaria 47, 48, 94, 98
 Alte Pinakothek (Munich) 125
 Ammerland 217
 Anger 203
 Bad Reichenhall 203
 Basilika St Bonifaz (Munich) 118
 Bayerische Staatsbibliothek (Munich) 107

Ludwig I, King of Bavaria (cont.)
 Feldherrnhalle (Munich) 86
 Glyptothek (Munich) 60, 123
 Hofbräuhaus (Munich) 92
 Ingolstadt 174
 Ludwig-Maximilians-Universität (Munich) 107
 Ludwigstraße (Munich) 106
 monument to 104, 106
 Museums District (Munich) 115
 Neo-Classical architecture 27
 Neue Pinakothek (Munich) 128
 Odeonsplatz (Munich) 106
 Oktoberfest 33
 Palais Töerring-Jettenbach (Munich) 87
 portrait of 39
 Propyläen (Munich) 119
 Residenz (Munich) 81
 Salvatorkirche (Munich) 84
 Schönheitengalerie (Nymphenburg) 136
 Siegestor (Munich) 108
 Staatliche Antikensammlungen (Munich) 118
 Theresienwiese (Munich) 143
 tomb of 116, 118
 Wittelsbacherplatz (Munich) 104
Ludwig I of Kelheim 46
Ludwig II, King of Bavaria 21, 22, 47, 48, 49
 castles 50–1
 death 217
 Feldafing 217
 Herrenchiemsee 11, 161, 199, 206, 207
 König-Ludwig-Feier (Oberammergau) 35
 Linderhof 161, 213, 220–21
 monument to 219
 Nationaltheater (Munich) 77
 Neuschwanstein 11, 160, 229, 234
 Schachen 221
 Schloss Nymphenburg 134, 136
Ludwig II's Night Sleigh Ride (Wenig) 50
Ludwig II the Severe, Duke of Bavaria 46, 72, 175
 tomb of 63
Ludwig III, King of Bavaria 47, 49
Ludwig IV, Duke of Bavaria (Emperor) 42-3, 46
 Alter Hof (Munich) 87
 Ettal 220
 Isartor (Munich) 67
 Maximilianeum (Munich) 93
 Sendlinger Tor (Munich) 72
 tomb of 64
Ludwig X, Duke of Bavaria 182, 184
Ludwig the Rich 32, 107, 170
Ludwig Beck (Munich) 145
Ludwig Ferdinand, Duke 106
Ludwig-Maximilians-Universität (Munich) 107
 Street-by-Street map 104

Ludwigsbrücke (Munich) 97
Ludwigskirche (Munich) 107
  Street-by-Street map 105
Ludwigsplatz (Straubing) 188
Ludwigstraße (Munich) 106
  Street-by-Street map 104–5
Lufthansa 307
Lüftlmalerei 11, 31, 216
Luidl, Johannes 215
Luitpold, Prince 47, 49
Luraghi, Giovanni Martin 194
Lurago, Carlo 192
Luther, Martin 43

M

Macke, August 119, 219
Magdalenenklause (Nymphenburg)
  135
Magzin, Domenic 196
Magritte, René 111
Maibaumaufstellen 34
Maibockausschank (Munich) 34
Mailboxes 304–305
Manet, Édouard 129
  Breakfast in the Studio
  127
Manlich, H. 80
Mann, Thomas 109
Mannerist architecture 26
Mannerist art 31
Maps
  Allgäu 228–9
  Alpenstraße 224–5
  Altmühl Valley tour 187
  Augsburg 252–3
  Bavarian Alps 160–1
  Castles of Ludwig II 51
  Central Munich 18–19
  Chiemsee tour 207
  Eichstätt 167
  Englischer Garten (Munich) 110
  Europe 17
  Germany 16–17
  Ingolstadt 171
  Kempten 241
  Landsberg am Lech 215
  Landshut 182–3
  Lindau 239
  Lower Bavaria 180–1
  Memmingen 231
  Munich 56–7
  Munich: Along
  Ludwigstraße 104–5
  Munich: Around the Isar 91
  Munich: Around Marienplatz 60–1
  Munich: Around the
  Residenz 76–7
  Munich: Further Afield
  133
  Munich: Königsplatz 116–17
  Munich: Maximilianstraße
  92–3
  Munich: Museums District
  115
  Munich: Old Town (North)
  75

Maps (cont.)
  Munich: Old Town (South)
  59
  Munich: Street Finder 148–57
  Munich: University District
  103
  Nationalpark Bayerischer Wald
  tour 191
  Neuburg an der Donau 173
  Neuschwanstein 235
  Nördlingen 247
  Northern Swabia 244–5
  Olympiapark (Munich)
  138–9
  Passau 193
  Starnbergersee tour 217
  Straubing 189
  train routes in Southern Bavaria
  309
  Upper Bavaria (East) 200–01
  Upper Bavaria (North) 164–5
  Upper Bavaria (South) 212–13
Marc, Franz 108, 109, 222
  Der Blaue Reiter 219
  Franz-Marc-Museum (Kochel am
  See) 11, 223
  Galerie im Lenbachhaus (Munich)
  119
  Heavenly Horses 222
  Kochel am see 223
Marc, Maria 109
Marcomanni 39, 40
Marées, Hans von 111
  Hesperides II 129
Maria Amalia, Empress 136
Maria of Brabant 175
Maria Gern 204
Mariä Himmelfahrt (Landsberg am
  Lech) 215
Maria Steinbach 237
Maria Teresa, Empress of Austria 45
Marie de Medici 124
Marienbrücke
  Neuschwanstein tour 235
Marienplatz (Munich) 10, 66
  Street-by-Street map 60–1
Markets
  Munich 145
  Viktualienmarkt (Munich) 68
Marktplatz (Eichstätt) 166
Marstall (Munich) 89
Marstallmuseum (Nymphenburg)
  134
Marstalltheater (Munich) 89
Martin, St 36
Martinskirche (Landshut) 184
  Street-by-Street map 183
Martinskirche (Memmingen) 230
Märzenbier 275
Master of St Veronica 124
Matisse, Henri 111
  Still Life with Geraniums 120
Matteo, Antonio 67
Mauth
  Nationalpark Bayerischer Wald
  tour 191

Mauz (Munich) 285
Max-Joseph-Platz (Munich) 82
  Street-by-Street map 76
Maximilian I, Elector 21, 44, 47
  Hofgarten (Munich) 89
  monument to 104, 106
  Residenz (Munich) 81
  Schleißheim Palace 176
  Tanzhaus (Nördlingen) 246
  tomb of 63
Maximilian I Joseph, King of Bavaria
  21, 46, 47, 48
  Blutenburg (Munich) 143
  crown 79
  Karolinenplatz (Munich) 118
  Ludwig-Maximilians-Universität
  (Munich) 107
  Maximilianstraße (Munich) 88
  monument to 192
  Museums District (Munich) 115
  Odeonsplatz (Munich) 106
  statue of 76, 82
  Tegernsee 224
Maximilian II, King of Bavaria 47
  Bayerisches
  Nationalmuseum (Munich) 112
  Maximilianeum (Munich) 95
  Maximilianstraße (Munich)
  92
  monument to 92, 95
  Regierung von Oberbayern
  (Munich) 94
  Schloss Hohenschwangau
  234
Maximilian II Emanuel, Elector 44–
  5, 47, 177
  Nymphenburg 134, 136
  Schleißheim Palace 176
  Schloss Lustheim 177
  tomb of 83
Maximilian III Joseph, Elector 45, 47,
  80
Maximilianeum (Munich) 57,
  95
  Street-by-Street map 93
Maximilianmuseum
  (Augsburg)
  Street-by-Street map 252
Maximiliansbrücke (Munich)
  Street-by-Street map 93
Maximilianstraße (Augsburg)
  Street-by-Street map 253
Maximilianstraße (Lindau)
  238
Maximilianstraße (Munich) 88
  Street-by-Street map 92–3
Maxlrain Palace 209
Mayer, Rupert 62
Maypoles 32
Medical assistance 301
Medientage München
  (Munich) 36
Meit, Conrad
  Judith with the Head of
  Holofernes 112
Memling, Hans 124

Memmingen 228, 230–1
  festivals 35
  map 231
  restaurants 283
Mendini, Alessandro 120
Menus 271
Menzel, Adolph von 129
Merani, Ignaz 214
Merkurbrunnen (Augsburg)
  Street-by-Street map 253
Merovingians 41
Métivier, Jean-Baptiste 86
Metsu, Gabriel 125
Metten 179, 186
Michaelskirche (Munich) 26, 62–3
  Street-by-Street map 60
Michaelskirche (Passau) 193
Michelangelo 107, 131
Mielich, Hans 30, 67, 84, 170
Millauer, Abraham 209
Miller, Ferdinand von 83, 92, 222
Miller, Oskar von 98, 223
Mindelburg Castle 233
Mindelheim 233
Mittenwald 222
  restaurants 282
Mobile phones 304
Modler, Johann Baptist 190
Modler family 192
Möhl, Jacob 96
Monasteries 28–9
  Aldersbach 196
  Andechs 216
  Benediktbeuern 40, 223
  Fürstenzell 190
  Kaisheim 249
  Klosterseeon 208
  Residence (Kempten) 240
  Tegernsee 224
  Weltenburg 40, 45, 186
  Wettenhausen 244, 258
  see also Abbeys
Mondrian, Piet 111
Monet, Claude 129
Moneygram 303
Montez, Lola 48
Montgelas, Count Maximilian 44, 48
Monuments
  Friedensengel (Munich) 57, 96
  Karolinenplatz (Munich) 117
  Ludwig I (Munich) 104, 106
  Max-Joseph-Platz (Munich) 76
  Maximilian I (Munich) 104, 106
  Maximilian II (Munich) 92, 95
  Propyläen (Munich) 119
  Rumford Memorial (Munich) 110
  Siegestor (Munich) 57, 108
Moritzkirche (Augsburg)
  Street-by-Street map 253
Moritzkirche (Ingolstadt) 171
Morrominiego, Francesco 86
Motorways 313, 314
Mountain sports 291, 293
  mountain shelters 264, 265
  safety 301

Mozart, Franz 257
Mozart, Wolfgang Amadeus
  81, 252, 257
Müller, Karl 97
Müller & Söhne (Munich) 285
Müllersches Volksbad
  (Munich) 91, 97
Multscher, Hans 215, 258
Munch, Edvard 129
München-Obermenzing 265
München-Tahlkirchen 265
Münchener Opernfestspiele
  (Munich) 35
Münchner Kammerspiele im
  Schauspielhaus (Munich) 88
Münchner Kindl 63
Münchner Stadtrundfahrten
  oHG 297
Munich 10
  airport 306–7
  Around the Isar 91–101
  banks 302
  entertainment 146–7
  festivals 34–7
  further afield 133–43
  history 39–53
  hotels 266–7
  Museums District 115–31
  Oktoberfest 21, 33, 36
  Old Town (North) 75–89
  Old Town (South) 59–73
  pubs, cafés and bars 284–5
  restaurants 276–9
  shopping 144–5, 286
  Street Finder 148–57
  travel in 310–13
  University District 103–113
Munich Agreement (1938) 52
Munich Film Festival 147
Munich Tourist Board 147
Münster "zur Lieben Frau" (Lindau)
  238
Münter, Gabriele
  Der Blaue Reiter 219
  Galerie im Lenbachhaus (Munich)
  119
  Münterhaus (Murnau) 219
Münzhof (Munich) 87
Murillo, Bartolomé Esteban 125
Murmann, Ferdinand 62
Murnau 215
  festivals 36
Museums District (Munich) 115–31
  area map 115
  hotels 267
  restaurants 278
  Street-by-Street map 116–17
Museums and galleries
  (general) 296
  admission charges 296
  opening hours 296
Museums and galleries (individual)
  Alpenländische Galerie
  (Kempten) 240–1
  Alpines Museum (Munich)
  93, 95

Museums and galleries (cont.)
  Alpinmuseum (Kempten) 240–1
  Alte Anatomie (Ingolstadt) 170
  Alte Pinakothek (Munich)
  56, 121, 122–25
  Archäologische Staatsammlung
  (Munich) 111
  Asamhaus (Munich) 72
  Bayerisches Nationalmuseum
  (Munich) 57, 112–13
  Bier-und Oktoberfest-museum
  (Munich) 68
  BMW Museum (Munich)
  138–9
  Deutsches Jagd- und
  Fischereimuseum (Munich) 61, 63
  Deutsches Medizinhistorisches
  Museum (Ingolstadt) 170
  Deutsches Museum
  (Munich) 98–101
  Deutsches Museum
  Verkehrszentrum (Munich) 142
  Freilichtmuseum an der
  Glentleiten 223
  Fuggereimuseum (Augsburg) 256
  Galerie im Lenbachhaus (Munich)
  18, 116, 119
  Gäubodenmuseum
  (Straubing) 188–9
  German Theatre Museum
  (Munich) 89
  Glyptothek (Munich) 27, 56, 119
  Haus der Kunst (Munich) 111
  Ignaz-Günther-Haus (Munich)
  68–9
  Jüdisches Museum (Munich) 68
  Literaturhaus (Munich) 85
  Marstallmuseum (Nymphenburg)
  134
  Moderner Kunst (Passau) 195
  Museum Brandhorst (Munich)
  130
  Museum Mobile (Ingolstadt) 170
  Museum "Reich der
  Kristalle" (Munich) 120
  Museumsdorf Bayerischer Wald
  190
  Mutterturm (Landsberg am Lech)
  215
  Neue Messe München (Munich)
  143
  Neue Pinakothek (Munich) 117,
  126–9
  Neues Stadtmuseum (Landsberg
  am Lech) 214–15
  Paläontologisches Museum
  (Munich) 116, 120
  Passauer Glasmuseum (Passau)
  195
  Pinakothek der Moderne
  (Munich) 120–21
  Residenz (Munich) 80–1
  Römermuseum Kastell
  Boiotro (Passau) 195
  Römisches Museum (Augsburg)
  255

Museums and galleries (cont.)
Sammlung Schack (Munich)
111
Schaezlerpalais (Augsburg) 254
SiemensForum (Munich) 85
Spielzeugmuseum (Munich) 67
Staatliche
Antikensammlungen
(Munich) 116, 118
Staatliches Museum Ägyptischer
Kunst (Munich) 78, 81
Stadtmuseum (Munich) 69
Stadtmuseum Weveldhaus
(Neuburg an der Donau)
172
Valentin-Karlstadt-Musäum
(Munich) 67
Villa Stuck (Munich) 19,
96
Völkerkundemuseum (Munich)
92, 94–5
Music
festivals 34, 35
Munich 146, 147
Mutterturm (Landsberg am Lech)
215

N

Napoleon I, Emperor 46, 48
Independence Hall
(Kelheim) 187
Karolinenplatz (Munich)
117, 118
Siegestor (Munich) 108
NASA 247, 248
National parks 291, 293
Nationalpark Bayerischer Wald
191, 293
Nationaltheater (Munich) 82, 147
Street-by-Street map 77
Nattier, Jean-Marc 125
Nazarenes 128
Nazis 49, 52
Dachau 175
"Eagle's Nest" 205
Hitler Putsch (1923) 83
Neidhart, Wolfgang 253
Neo-Classical architecture 27
Neu-Ulm
hotels 269
restaurants 283
Neubeuern 201, 209
Neuburg an der Donau 163, 165,
172-3
architecture 26
hotels 268
map 173
restaurants 280
Neue Künstlervereinigung
München 109
Neue Messe München
(Munich) 143
Neue Pinakothek (Munich) 126–9
Street-by-Street map 117
Neue Residenz (Passau) 192
Neue Sachlichkeit 120

Neues Rathaus (Lindau) 238
Neues Rathaus (Munich) 18, 63
Street-by-Street map 61
Neues Schloss (Ingolstadt) 171
Neues Stadtmuseum
(Landsberg am Lech) 210–11
Neuhauser Straße (Munich)
Street-by-Street map 60
Neuötting 202
Neureuther, Gottfried 108
Neuschwanstein 11, 50–1,
160, 229, 234
tour by car 235
New Zealand Embassy 299
Newspapers 305
Nibelungensäle (Schnorr von
Carolsfeld) 78
Niederbayern see Lower
Bavaria
Nikolaikirche (Munich) 96
Noemi & Friends (Munich)
145
Nordic Walking Association
293
Nördlingen 17, 246–7
hotels 269
map 247
restaurants 283
Nordsee (Munich) 285
Northern Swabia 11, 239–55
hotels 269
map 244–5
restaurants 283
Nymphenburg 45, 134–7

O

Oberammergau 160, 220
festivals 35
hotels 269
passion play 32
restaurants 282
Oberes Tor and Town Walls
(Neuburg an der Donau) 172
Oberjoch 236
Oberschleißheim 174
Oberstdorf 11, 37, 229, 236
hotels 269
restaurants 283
Odeonsplatz (Munich) 106
Street-by-Street map 104
Oettingen 248
Oettingen-Spielberg, Dukes of 244
Oettingen-Wallerstein family 249
Off & Co (Munich) 145
Oktoberfest 21, 33, 36, 143, 147
Old Town (North) (Munich)
75–89
area map 75
hotels 266
restaurants 276–7
Street-by-Street map 76–7
Old Town (South) (Munich) 59–73
area map 59
hotels 266
restaurants 276
Street-by-Street map 60–1

Olympia Einkaufszentrum (Munich)
145
Olympia-Eissportzentrum (Munich)
139
Olympiahalle (Munich) 147
Olympiapark (Munich) 133, 138–9
Olympiaturm (Munich) 133, 139
Opening hours
churches 297
museums 297
restaurants 271
shopping 286
Opera 146, 147
Orangery (Kempten) 240
Ortenburg 196
Osterhofen 197
Otto, Emperor 41
Otto I, Duke of Bavaria 42, 46
Propyläen (Munich) 27, 119
Residenz (Munich) 80
Otto II, Duke of Bavaria 46
Ottobeuren 28–9, 160, 232
Outdoor activities 290–3
Overbeck, Friedrich
Italia and Germania
126, 128

P

Pacelli Palais (Munich) 108
Pacher, Michael 124
Pacific Times (Munich) 285
Padovano 185
Palaces
Alter Hof (Munich) 87
Erzbischöfliches Palais (Munich)
76, 84
Fuggerhäuser (Augsburg)
255
Herrenchiemsee 11, 51, 161,
199, 206
Linderhof 220–21
Ortenburg 196
Pacelli Palais (Munich) 108
Palais Gise (Munich) 85
Palais Preysing (Munich) 85
Palais Pinakothek (Munich) 130
Palais Porcia (Munich) 84–5
\Palais Seinsheim (Munich) 85
Palais Töerring-Jettenbach
(Munich) **87**
Preysing-Palais (Munich) 77, **82**
Prinz Karl Palais (Munich)
27
Residenz (Munich) 57, 76–7, **78–81**
Schaezlerpalais (Augsburg) **254**
Schleißheim Palace 10, 27,
35, 163, 164, **176–7**
Schloss Nymphenburg 134,
136–7
Wittelsbacherplatz (Munich) 104,
106
see also Castles
Paläontologisches Museum
(Munich) **120**
Street-by-Street map 116

Palma, Jacopo the Younger 257
Parking 313, 315
Parks and gardens
  Alter Botanischer Garten (Munich) **131**
  Botanischer Garten (Munich) **138**
  Englischer Garten (Munich) 10, **110**
  Gärtnerplatz (Munich) **68**
  Hofgarten (Munich) **89**
  Lenbachhaus (Munich) 115
  Linderhof 161, 213, 220–21
  Max-Joseph-Platz (Munich) **82**
  Nymphenburg **134–5**
  Olympiapark (Munich) 133, **138–9**
  Promenadeplatz (Munich) **86**
  Schleißheim Palace **176–7**
  Tierpark Hellabrunn (Munich) 141
Partnach river gorge 221
Pascal, Blaise 101
Pasinger Fabrik (Munich) 147
Passau 10, 39, 179, **192–95**
  festivals 34
  hotels 268
  map 193
  restaurants 280
Passauer Glasmuseum (Passau) **195**
Passion plays 32, 220
Passports 298
Pater, Jean-Baptiste 125
Paulaner Bräuhaus (Munich) 285
Paulskirche (Passau) **195**
Peasants Playing Cards (Brouwer) 123, 124
Pedetti, Maurizio 166
The Pentecost (Loth) 67
Perlacher Einkaufspassage (Munich) 145
Perlachturm (Augsburg)
  Street-by-Street map 253
Perthaler, Anton 112
Perugino 125
Petel, Georg 31
Peterskirche (Lindau) **239**
Peterskirche (Munich) **66**
  Street-by-Street map 61
Peterskirche (Neuburg an der Donau) **172**
Petrol stations 315
Pezold, Georg 96
Pfaffenhofen **169**
Pfaffenwinkel 211
Pffarkirche St Annakirche (Munich) **94**
  Street-by-Street map 93
Pfarrkirche St Sebastian (Ramsau) 205
Pharmacies 301
Philip Ludwig, Duke 172, 259

Phonecards 304
Picasso, Pablo 111, 120
Pickpockets 300
Pietà (Botticelli) 122
Piloty, Karl Theodore von
  Seni before the Corpse of Wallenstein 127, 128–9
Pinakothek der Moderne (Munich) **120–21**
Pisano, Giovanni 220
Pissarro, Camille 129
Pittoni, Battista 216
Planetarium, Zeiss **101**
Play of the Waves (Böcklin) 127, 129
Pocci, Franz Graf von 217
Poison Help Line 301
Polack, Jan 30
  Bayerisches Nationalmuseum (Munich) 113
  Blutenburg 143
  Frauenkirche (Munich) 65
  Peterskirche (Munich) 66
  St Sixtus (Schliersee) 225
Police 300, 301, 315
Pompadour, Marquise de 123, 125
The Poor Poet (Spitzweg) 128
Porcia, Princess 84
Portrait of Karl V (Titian) 123
Portrait of Karl Albrecht as Emperor Karl VII (Desmarées) 136
Portrait of the Marquise de Pompadour (Boucher) 123, 125
Portrait of Willem van Heythuysen (Hals) 125
Porzellanmanufaktur Nymphenburg (Munich) 134, 287
Possenhofen
  Starnbergersee tour 217
Post-Impressionism 129
Postal services 304–305
Poussin, Nicolas 125
Preysing-Hohenaschau, Count Maximilian von 82
Preysing-Palais (Munich) **82**
  Street-by-Street map 77
Prinz Carl Palais (Munich) 27
Prinzregententheater (Munich) 147
Private houses, accommodation in 264, 265
Promenadeplatz (Munich) **86**
Propyläen (Munich) 27, **119**
  Street-by-Street map 116
Prunn Castle 161, 187
Public conveniences 297
Public holidays 37
Pubs **284**, 285
Die Puppenstube (Munich) 145
Puppets
  Augsburger Puppenkiste **255**
Pürkhel, Konrad 208
Pusser's (Munich) 285

Q
Qantas 307
Quaglio, Domenico 234
Quaglio, Lorenz J. 259

R
Radio 305
Radspieler (Munich) 287
Rafting 309
Railways see Trains
Rainfall 36
Raisting 211
Ramersdorf (Munich) **140**
Ramsau **205**
Randeck
  Altmühl Valley tour 187
Randeck, Erhard 225
Raphael 125
Rathaus (Augsburg) **254**
  Street-by-Street map 253
Rathaus (Kempten) **240**
Rathaus (Landsberg am Lech) **214**
Rathaus (Memmingen) **230**
Rathaus (Nördlingen) **246**
Rathausplatz (Kempten) **240**
Rauch, Christian Daniel 82
Rauch, Jakob 209
Realism 125, 129
Reformation 43
Regensburg 39
Regierung von Oberbayern (Munich) **94**
  Street-by-Street map 92
Regionalverkehr Oberbayern (RVO) 301
Reichle, Hans 30, 31, 255
Reifenstuel, Franz Michael 68
Reisebank AG (Munich) 302
Reit im Winkl **205**
  hotels 268
Religion 22–23
Rembrandt 125
  The Deposition 123
Renaissance architecture 26
Renaissance art 31
Renata of Lotharingia 63
Reni, Guido 123
Renoir, Auguste 129
Residence (Kempten) **240**
Residenz (Munich) 57, **78–9**
  Street-by-Street map 76–7
Residenzplatz (Passau) **193**
Responsible Tourism 298–9
Restaurants **270–83**
  Allgäu 282–3
  Lower Bavaria 280
  Munich 276–9
  Northern Swabia 283
  Upper Bavaria (East) 280–81
  Upper Bavaria (North) 279–80
  Upper Bavaria (South) 281–2
  see also Food and drink
Riedel, Eduard 94
Riedenburg
  Altmühl Valley tour 187

Riem Arcaden (Munich) 145
Riemenschneider, Tilman 113
Riemerschmid, Richard 88
Ries Basin 243, 246, **248**
Riva, Antonio 175, 197
Rivers, boat trips 309
Road signs 314
Roadside assistance 314, 315
Rococo art 31
Roggenburg **247**
Rohr **186**
Rohrdorf 209
Roman Empire **39–40**
  Archäologischer Park
  Cambodunum (Kempten)
  241
  Römermuseum Kastell
  Boiotro (Passau) **195**
  Römisches Museum (Augsburg)
  11, **255**
  Temple of Apollo Grannus
  (Lauingen) 259
Romanesque art 30
Romanticism 128
Romantische Strasse 11, 228, **250**
Romeis, Leonhard 120
Römermuseum Kastell Boiotro
  (Passau) **195**
Römisches Museum
  (Augsburg) 11, 255
Rosenburg
  Altmühl Valley tour 187
Rosenheim 200
Rosner, Johann 166
Rotes Tor and City Walls (Augsburg)
  255
Rott am Inn **209**
Rottaler, Lukas 64, 84
Rottenhammer, Hans 73
Rottmann, Carl 80
Roxy (Munich) 285
Rubens, Peter Paul 172, 233
  *The Abduction of the Daughters of
  Leukippos* 124
  Alte Pinakothek (Munich) 124
Ruhpolding **205**
Ruisdael, Jacob van 125
Rules of the road 315
Rumford, Count von 110
Rupert, Bishop of Salzburg 40

S
S-Bahn 307, 310–11
Safety, in the mountains 300–1
St John Nepomuk 70–1
St Luke Painting the Madonna
  (Weyden) 122
St-Mang-Kirche (Kempten)
  240
St Martin's Day 36
St Oswald
  Nationalpark Bayerischer Wald
  tour 191
St-Ulrich-und-St-Afra-Kirche
  (Augsburg) 26, **255**
Saldenburg 190

Salesian order 73
Salt works 199, 203, 204
Salvatorkirche (Munich) **84**
  Street-by-Street map 76
Salvatorkirche (Passau) **194**
Salzach, River 199, 202, 203
Samerberg 209
Sammarei **196**
Sammlung Schack (Munich) **111**
Sandtner, Jakob 112, 188
Sankt Hermann **190**
Sankt Wolfgang **174**
Scaligeri family 208
Scamozzi, Vincenzo 203
Scenic routes 292, 315
Schachen 51, 221
Schack, Friedrich von 111
Schaezlerpalais (Augsburg) **254**
Schäfflertanz (Munich) 37
Schaiblingsturm (Passau) **193**
Schanzer, Karl 138–9
Schäufelein, Hans 246, 247
Schaumberg, Martin von,
  Bishop of Eichstätt 168
Schauspielhaus (Munich) 88
Scheffler, Thomas 214–15
Scheyern 10, 163, **169**
Schieler, Egon 129
Schinkel, Karl Friedrich 119
Schleißheim Palace 10, 27, 35, 163,
  164, **176–7**
Schleißheimer Schloßkonzerte
  (Schleißheim) 35
Schlichting (Munich) 145
Schliersee **225**
  festivals 36
Schloss Hohenaschau 206
Schloss Hohenschwangau 229, **234**
  Neuschwanstein tour 235
Schloss Nymphenburg 134, **136–7**
Schloß Prunn
  Altmühl Valley tour 187
Schmidt, Albert 131
Schmidt, Heinrich von 194–5
Schmidt, Joseph 204
Schmuzer, Franz Xaver 220
Schmuzer, Johann 216
Schmuzer, Josef 221, 222, 250
Schmuzer, Matthias the
  Younger 248, 250
Schneitmann, Michael 194
Schnorr von Carolsfeld, Julius
  Nibelungensäle 78
Scholl, Hans 107
Scholl, Sophie 107
Schön, Heinrich 89, 176
Schönfeld, Johann Heinrich 31
Schongau **218**
Schuch, Karl 129
  Still Life with Asparagus 127
Schumann's (Munich) 285
Schutzengelkirche (Eichstätt) **166–7**
Schwabing **109**
Schwäbischwerder Kindertag
  (Donauwörth) 35

Schwanthaler, Ludwig 27
  Bayerische Staatsbibliothek
  (Munich) 105, 107
  Hofgarten (Munich) 89
  Ludwigskirche (Munich) 105
  Propyläen (Munich) 116
  Rumford Memorial (Munich)
  110
  Theresienwiese (Munich) 143
Schwarz, Christoph 63
Schwarzeck 161
Schwimmhalle (Munich) 139
Schwind, Moritz von 111, 128
Sckell, Ludwig von 110, 115, 131
Sea Life Olympiapark
  (Munich) 147
Security **300–1**
Seebruck
  Chiemsee tour 207
Seehaus (Munich) 285
Seeon
  restaurants 281
Seeshaupt
  Starnbergersee tour 217
Seewald, Richard 985
Seidl, Gabriel von 209
  Altes Rathaus (Ingolstadt) 171
  Bayerisches Nationalmuseum
  (Munich) 112
  Deutsches Museum
  (Munich) 98
  Pfarrkirche St Annakirche
  (Munich) **94**
  Galerie im Lenbachhaus
  (Munich) 119
  Karlsplatz 130
  Künstlerhaus (Munich) 86
Seitz, Rudolf von 93
Sendlinger Tor (Munich) **72–3**
Seni before the Corpse of Wallenstein
  (Piloty) 127, 128–9
Senior Travellers 298
Serro, Johann 172
Severinus, St 40, 195
Seybold, Matthias 166
Shopping **286–9**
  Munich **144–5**, 286
  tax refunds 298
  What to Buy in the Bavarian Alps
  288–9
Siebendächerhaus (Memmingen)
  231
Siegestor (Munich) 57, **108**
  Street-by-Street map 105
Sielenbach **250**
Siemens 23
Siemens, Werner von 85
SiemensForum (Munich) **85**
Signac, Paul 129
Sisley, Alfred 129
Sixt 315
Skifasching (Firstalm) 37
Skiing 37, **291**, 293
  Alpinmuseum (Kempten) **240–1**
  mountain safety 300–1
  Oberstdorf **236**

Slevogt, Max 129
Snow 36
Sobieska, Therese Kunigunde 83, 143
South African Embassy 299
Souvenir shops 287
Sozialverband Vdk 299
Spa resorts 265, 293
  Bad Aibling **209**
  Bad Reichenhall 203
Spannagl, Wilhelm 168
Spatenhaus an der Oper (Munich) 285
Specialist holidays 292
Specialist shops 287
Speed limits 315
Spielzeugmuseum (Munich) 67
Spielzone Ost Westpark Sendling 147
Spital (Nördlingen) **247**
Spitalkirche (Landshut) **184**
Spitzweg, Karl
  Galerie im Lenbachhaus (Munich) 119
  The Poor Poet 128
  Sammlung Schack (Munich) 111
Sport 147
Sporthaus Schuster (Munich) 291
SportScheck (Munich) 287, 293
Spring **34**
Spurwechsel (Munich) 313
Squares in Munich
  Karlsplatz **130–1**
  Karolinenplatz **118**
  Lenbachplatz **130**
  Wittelsbacherplatz 104, **106**
Staatliche Antikensammlungen (Munich) **118**
  Street-by-Street map 116
Staatliches Museum Ägyptischer Kunst (Munich) 78, **81**
Staatstheater am Gärtnerplatz (Munich) 147
Stadtcafé im Stadtmuseum (Munich) 285
Stadtgeburtstag (Munich) 35
Städtisches Fundbüro 301
Stadtmetzg (Augsburg) 245, **254**
Stadtmuseum (Munich) **69**
Stadtmuseum Weveldhaus (Neuburg an der Donau) **172**
Stadtresidenz (Landshut) **184**
  Street-by-Street map 182
Starkbierfest (Munich) 34
Starnbergersee
  Tour by car **217**
Steen, Jan 125
Stefan II, Duke of Bavaria 46
Stein an der Traun **206**
Steingaden 212, **218**

Stephan III, Duke of Bavaria 43
Stephanskirche (Lindau) **238**
Stephen, St 194
Steuerhaus (Memmingen) **230**
Stieler, Joseph 136
Still Life with Asparagus (Schuch) 127
Still Life with Geraniums (Matisse) 120
Stiller, Matthias 231
Stock
  Chiemsee tour 207
Stock Exchange (Munich) 130
Straub, Johann Baptist 31
  Cuvilliés-Theater (Munich) 81
  Dreifaltigkeitskirche (Munich) 86
  Erzbischöfliches Palais (Munich) 84
  Klosterkirche St Anna (Munich) 94
  Mariä Himmelfahrtskirche (Fürstenzell) 190
  Michaelskirche (Berg am Laim) 140
  Palais Töerring-Jettenbach (Munich) 87
Straubing 39, **188–9**
  festivals 35
  hotels 268
  map 189
  restaurants 280
Strauß, Franz Josef 21, 44, 53
  grave of 200, 209
Streiter, Michael von 170
Stuber, Nikolaus 67
Stuck, Franz von
  Die Sünde 96
  Villa Stuck (Munich) 19, 96
Student travel 297
Sturmannshöhle 236
Summer **35**
Die Sünde (Stuck) 96
Sunflowers (Van Gogh) 129
Sunshine 35
Susanna and the Elders (Altdorfer) 56
Sustris, Friedrich 30
  Michaelskirche (Munich) 62, 63
  Residenz (Munich) 80
Swabia *see* Northern Swabia
Swabian Sea *see* Bodensee
Sylvester 37
Symbolism 129
Synagogue (Augsburg) **255**
Systems (Munich) 36

T

Takeaway food, Munich **284**, 285
Tambosi (Munich) 285
Tanz der Marktfrauen (Munich) 37
Tanzhaus (Nördlingen) **246**
Tassilo III 41
Tassilogarten (Munich) 285
Tausch, Christoph 193
Tax refunds 297
Taxi-München 313

Taxis 307, **313**
Technology
  Deutsches Museum (Munich) **98–101**
Teck, Duke Ulrich von 237
Tegelbergbahn
  Neuschwanstein tour 239
Tegernsee **228**
  restaurants 282
Telephones **304**
Television 305
Temperatures 37
Tencalla, Carpoforo 192
Tennis **291**, 293
Terborch, Gerard 125
Thai Magic (Munich) 285
Thamasch, Andreas 249
Theater (Memmingen) **231**
Theatinerkirche (Munich) 56, 75, **83**
  Street-by-Street map 76
Theatre, Munich **146**, 147
Theatre Museum (Munich) 89
Theft 300
Theresa (Munich) 145
Therese von Sachsen-Hildburghausen 33, 118, 143
Theresienplatz (Straubing) **188**
Theresienwiese (Munich) **143**
Therme Erding 293
Thierchen Kindermode (Munich) 145
Thiersch, Friedrich von 93, 131, 238
Thorvaldsen, Bertel 44, 128
  Monument to Maximilian I 104, 106
Thumb, Michael **258**
Thurn und Taxis family 172
Tiberius 39
Tiburtius, St 188
Tiefenbrunner, Johann Georg 175
Tiepolo, Giovanni Battista 216, 254
  The Adoration of the Magi 117
  Alte Pinakothek (Munich) 123, 125
Tierpark Hellabrunn (Munich) **137**, 143
Tilly, Count Johann 83
  Feldherrnhalle (Munich) 77
  statue of 82
  tomb of 202
Time zones 298
Tintoretto 125
Tipping, in restaurants 271
Titian 125
  Portrait of Karl V 123
Tittmoning **203**
  restaurants 281
Toilets, public 297
Tollwood Festival (Munich) 35, 37, 147
Tourismusamt München 265, 299
Tourismusverband Allgäu/Bayerisch Schwaben 299
Tourismusverband München-Oberbayern 299

Tourismusverband Ostbayern 297
Tourist information bureaux **296**, 299
Tours by car
  Alpenstraße **224–5**
  Altmühl Valley **187**
  Chiemsee **207**
  Nationalpark Bayerischer Wald **191**
  Neuschwanstein **235**
  Starnbergersee **217**
Town Hall (Augsburg) **254**
  Street-by-Street map 253
Town Hall (Landshut)
  Street-by-Street map 183
Tracten Angermaier (Munich) 145, 287
Trachten-und Schützenumzug (Passau) 34
Traditions **32–3**
Trains 307, **308**, 309
Trams **310–11**
Travel **306–15**
  air travel **306–7**
  boat trips 309
  buses **308–9**, **310–11**
  cars **313**, **314–15**
  coach travel **308–9**
  cycling 312, 313
  S-Bahn **310**, 311
  taxis **313**
  trains 307, **308**, 309
  trams **310–11**
  U-Bahn **310–11**
Travel agents 309
Travellers' cheques 286, 302
Tresznjewski (Munich) 285
Troost, Paul Ludwig 111
Tropfsteinhöhle
  Altmühl Valley tour 187
Trübner, Wilhelm 129
Tschudi, Hugo von 126
Tucher von Simmeldorf family 249
Tutzing
  Starnbergersee tour 217

U

U-Bahn 310–**11**
Üblher, Johann Georg 220
Ulm 11
Ulrich II, Bishop of Passau 194
Underground rail network **310–11**
UNESCO 143, 218–19
United Airlines 307
United Kingdom Embassy 299
Universities
  Ludwig-Maximilians-Universität (Munich) 104, **107**
  Universität (Passau) **195**
University District (Munich) **103–113**
  area map 103
  Englischer Garten **110**
  hotels 267
  restaurants 278
  Schwabing **109**

Upper Bavaria (East) 11, **199–209**
  hotels 268
  map 200–01
  restaurants 280–81
Upper Bavaria (North) 10, **163–77**
  hotels 267–8
  map 164–5
  restaurants 279–80
Upper Bavaria (South) 11, **211–25**
  hotels 269
  map 212–13
  restaurants 281–2
Urfeld 219
"Urlaub auf dem Bauernhof" 265
Urschalling
  Chiemsee tour 207
Ursulinenkirche (Straubing) **188**
Useful bus routes and tram routes map 311

V

Valentin, Karl 67, 68
Valentin-Karlstadt-Musäum (Munich) 67
Van Dyck, Anthony 124, 254
Van Gogh, Vincent 129
  Sunflowers 129
Vegetarian food 271
Velázquez, Diego 125
Verband Deutscher Berg-und Skiführer (VDBS) 293
Verband Deutscher Gebirgs-und Wandervereine e.V. 293
Veste Oberhaus and Veste Niederhaus (Passau) **194**
Via Claudia 11, 250, 252
Viehscheid 36
Viktualienmarkt (Munich) **68**, 145
Villa Stuck (Munich) 19, **96**
Vilshofen 180, **197**
Vindelici tribe 39
Violins 222, 234
Visa regulations 296
Viscardi, Bartholomäus 197
Viscardi, Giovanni Antonio 62, 86, 169, 175
Vogt, Christoph 232
Völkerkundemuseum (Munich) **94–5**
  Street-by-Street map 92
Volt, August von 126
Von Rechberg family 232
Von Seutter family 238
Vries, Adriaen de 248, 253, 254
Vuillard, Édouard 129

W

Wackerle, Josef 131
Waging am See
  restaurants 281

Wagner, Ferdinand von 194, 195
Wagner, Johann Martin von 89, 105
Wagner, Richard 49, 50
  Linderhof 221
  Nationaltheater (Munich) 77, 82
  Neuschwanstein 234
Waisenhaus (Passau) **194**
Walburg, St 168
Walch, Joseph Anton 234
Walchensee **222**, 223
Waldberger, Wolfgang 246
Waldmüller, Ferdinand 128
Walking
  hiking safety 301
  in Munich 312
  walking holidays **290**, 293
Wallerstein **248**
Wallfahrtskirche Mariahilf (Passau) **195**
Wallgau **222**
Warhol, Andy 119
Wasserburg 228, **237**
Wasserburg am Inn **208**
  hotels 268
  restaurants 281
Water sports **290–1**, 293
Watteau, Antoine 125
Watzmann 199, 204
Weather **34–7**
Wedekind, Frank 88, 109
Weißenhorn **251**
Weizenbier 275
Welf dynasty 42
Welser, Felicitas 31
Weltenburg 10, 40, 45, 179, **186**
Wemding **248–9**
Wenig, Richard
  Ludwig II's Night Sleigh Ride 50
Werdenfelser Land 211
Werneck, Reinhold von 110
Werner (Munich) 287
Wessobrunn 31, **216**
Westend Café and Restaurant (Munich) 285
Western Union 303
Westertor and Town Walls (Memmingen) **230**
Westliche Wälder 243
Wettenhausen 244, **258**
Wetterstein 211
Weyden, Rogier van der
  The Adoration of the Magi 124
  St Luke Painting the Madonna 122
Wheelchair access see Disabled travellers
White Rose movement 107
Widmann, Joseph 238
Widmann, Max 106
Wiener's Kaffeebar (Munich) 285
Wienerwald (Munich) 285

Wieskirche 213, **218–19**
Wildlife **25**
Wilhelm II, Emperor 111
Wilhelm IV the Steadfast,
    Duke of Bavaria 46, 122
Wilhelm V the Pious, Duke of Bavaria
    44, 47, 63
    Bayerische Staatsbibliothek
        (Munich) 107
    Burg Traunitz 185
    Hofbräuhaus (Munich) 88
    Michaelskirche (Munich) 62
    Schleißheim Palace 176
Willibald, St 166, 168
Willibaldsburg (Eichstätt) **168**
Wimbachklamm 24
Winter **37**
Wintergarten (Munich) 285
Wiring Money 303
Wissreuter, Hans 175
Wittelsbach, Duke Otto 185
Wittelsbach family 42–3, 45,
    46–7, 48–9
    Alter Hof (Munich) **87**
    Bayerisches Nationalmuseum
        (Munich) 112
    Berchtesgaden 204
    Blutenburg (Munich) 143
    Burg Trausnitz 185
    Michaelskirche (Munich) 63
    Neuburg an der Donau 173
    Residenz (Munich) 78
    Schongau 218
Wittelsbacher Brunnen
    (Munich) 130
Wittelsbacherplatz (Munich)
    106
    Street-by-Street map 104
Wolff, Andreas 86
Wolff, Johann Andreas 140
Wolfgang, St 174
World War II 52, 53
Wrede, Karl Philipp von 77, 83

X

Xaver, Franz the Elder 251

Y

Youth hostels **264**, 265

Z

Zanetti, Domenico 62
Zauberflöte (Munich) 287
Zeckle, Johannes 170
Zeiller, Franz Anton 232
Zeiller, Johann Jakob
    Anastasiakapelle
        (Benediktbeuern) 223
    Ettal 220
    Mariä Himmelfahrtskirche
        (Fürstenzell) 190
    Ottobeuren 232
Zeiss Planetarium **101**
Zenith Flohmarkt (Munich)
    145
Zenith Kulturhalle (Munich) 147
Zentraler Kartenverkauf (Munich)
    147
Zeughaus (Augsburg) **255**
    Street-by-Street map 252
Ziebland, Georg Friedrich
    118
Zimmermann, Dominikus
    Bad Wörishofen 233
    Frauenkirche
        (Wettenhausen) **258**
    Historiches Rathaus (Landsberg
        am Lech) 214
    Johanniskirche (Landsberg
        am Lech) 215
    Klosterkirche der
        Dominikanerinnen Hl.
        Dreifaltigkeit (Landsberg am
        Lech) 214
    Mariä Himmelfahrt
        (Landsberg am Lech) 215
    Mariä Himmelfahrt
        (Schongau) 218
    Maria Steinbach 237
        Steingarden 218
    Zum Gegeißelten Heiland
        (Wieskirche) 219

Zimmermann, Johann Baptist 31,
    231
    Andechs 216
    Bad Wörishofen 233
    Cuvilliés-Theater (Munich)
        81
    Dominikanerkirche
        (Landshut) 184
    Erzbischöfliches Palais (Munich)
        76, 84
    Kernhaus (Wasserburg am
        Inn) 208
    Maria Brünnlein (Wemding)
        249
    Michaelskirche (Berg am
        Laim) 140
    Palais Porcia (Munich) 84
    Peters- und Paulskirche
        (Freising) 169
    Peterskirche (Munich) 66
    St Sixtus (Schliersee) 225
    Schleißheim Palace 176
    Zum Gegeißelten Heiland
        (Wieskirche) 219
Zoos
    Tierpark Hellabrunn
        (Munich) **141**
Zucalli, Enrico
    Dreifaltigkeitskirche
        (Munich) 86
    Ettal 220
    Nikolauskirche (Murnau)
        219
    Nymphenburg 134
    Palais Porcia (Munich) 84
    Schleißheim Palace 176
    Tegernsee 224
    Theatinerkirche (Munich) 83
Zuccalli, Giovanni 241
Zugspitze 25, 221
    Alpenstraße tour 224
Zumbusch, Kaspar von 95
Zurbarán, Francisco de 125
Zuse, Konrad 101
Zwergen 222–23
Zwinck, Franz Seraph 216
Zwitzel, Bernhard 87

Acknowledgments

Dorling Kindersley would like to thank the many people whose help and assistance contributed to the preparation of this book.

Additional Photography
Horst Höfler, Claire Jones, Katarzyna and Sergiusz Michalscy, Tomasz Myśluk, Werner Nikolai, Ian O'Leary, Gregor M. Schmid, Oda Sternberg, Paweł Wójcik

Additonal Contributor
Susi Cheshire, Jeremy Gray

Publishing Managers
Kate Poole, Helen Townsend

DTP Designers
Jason Little, Conrad Van Dyk

Production
Sarah Dodd

Consultant
Gerhard Bruschke

Fact Checker
Barbara Sobeck

Proofreader
Stewart Wild

Indexer
Hilary Bird

Director of Publishing
Gillian Allan

Revisions and Relaunch Team
Emma Anacootee, Sonal Bhatt, Arwen Burnett, Jo Cowen, Vidushi Duggal, Marcus Hardy, Rupanki Kaushik, Juliet Kenny, Sumita Khatwani, Shikha Kulkarni, Delphine Lawrance, Dieter Löffler, Carly Madden, Sam Merrell, Kate Molan, Casper Morris, Marianne Petrou, Dave Pugh, Sands Publishing Solutions, Azeem Siddiqui, Beverly Smart, Sadie Smith, Rachel Symons, Roseen Teare, Karen Villabona.

Picture Research Assistant
Rachel Barber

Special Assistance
The publisher would also like to thank the following for their assistance on the guide:

Anette Alwast, Ingrid Baudrexl-Czuraj, Prof. Dr Adrianowi von Buttlarowi, Tamarze and Jackowi Draberom, Daniel Fink (Pinakothek der Moderne), Erica Gingerich at Munich Airport, Iris and Wolfgangowi Hermannom, Barbarze Januszkiewicz, Irenie Hiemeyer, Aleksandrze Markiewicz German Book Information Centre, Goethe-Institut in Warsaw, Ulliemu Nerdingerowi, Wilhelminie and Wernerowi Nikolai, Dr Elisabeth Pfaud, Margarete Roeck, Dr Thomasowi Weidnerowi and Kartographie Huber (Gerhild Kemper-Wildtraut), Käthe-Kruse-Puppen-Museum in Donauwörth, Kultur- und Fremdenverkehrsamt der Stadt Landsberg am Lech (Ulla Kurz), Kur- und Ferienland Garmisch-Partenkirchen, Kurverwaltung Schwangau, Meteorologisches Institut der Universität München (Heinz Lösslein), Presse-und Öffentlichkeitsarbeit der Stadt Pfaffenhofen an der Ilm Sr. (Elisabeth Benen), Rieskrater-Museum in Nördlingen (Dr Michael Schieber, Monika Spörl), Stadt Donauwörth (Bernhard Kunz, Gudrun Reißer), Steigenberger Drei Mohren (Robert Strohe), Theresienthaler Krystallglasmanufaktur GmbH (Ralph A.W. Wenzel), Tourismus Straubing (Bettina Schauer), Tourist Info Kochel am See (Sabine Rauscher), Touristinformation Stadt Freising (Barabara Sibinger), Verkehrsverband Laufen, Verkehrsverein Lindau (Hans Stübner), Wittelsbacher Ausgleichsfonds, Inventarverwaltung (Andreas von Majewski, Sibille Herz)

Photography Permissions
The publisher would also like to thank all the people and institutions who allowed photographs belonging to them to be reproduced, as well as granting permission to use photographs from their archives: AB PhotoDesign in Kellberg (Dionys Asenkerschbaumer), Alois Dallmayr in Munich (Patricia Massmann), Alpines Museum in Munich (Ulrike Gehrig), Amt für Tourismus Straubing (Frau Baumhof), Archäologische Staatssammlung in Munich (Dr Dorothea van Endert) Artothek (Jürgen Hinrichs), Augsburger Puppenkiste, Bavaria Filmstadt in Munich, Bayerische Staatsgemäldesammlungen (Prof. Dr Christian Lenz, Christina Schwill, D. Cornelia Syre), Bayerische Verwaltung der Staatlichen Schlösser, Gärten und Seen (Eva Gerum, Michael Teichmann), Bayerisches Nationalmuseum in Munich (Dr Nina Gockerell, Dr Sgoff) Benediktinerabtei Ottobeuren, Bildvorlagen Römerschatz – Gäubodenmuseum in Straubing (Dr Prammer), Bischöfliches Ordinariat Augsburg (Monsignore Josef Heigl), Bischöfliches Ordinariat Passau (Franz Sr. Gabriel) BMW Group Mobile Tradition and.V. (Nikola von Ondarza), Britstock-Ifa in London, Café Luitpold in Munich (Carmen Brenner), Deutsche Bahn (Hans-Joachim Kirsche), Deutsche Press Agentur (Tanja Teichmann), Deutsches Museum in Munich (Marlene Schwarz), Diözesanbauamt Eichstätt (Dr Claudia Grund), Erzbischöfliches Ordinariat München (Dr Norbert Jocher, Dr Hans Ramisch, Hans Rohrmann, Gabriele Skornia), Flash Press Media (Sylwia Wilgocka), Flughafen München GmbH (Wilhelm Hennies, Fr. Kiener), Foto-Production in Gilching (Gregor M. Schmid), Fremdenverkehrsamt in Altötting, Fremdenverkehrsamt in Mühldorf (Peter-Alexander Berger), Galerie im Lenbachhaus in Munich (Daniela Müller), Haus der Bayerischen Geschichte-Bildarchiv in Augsburg (Dr Rudolf Wildmoser), Haus der Kunst in Munich (Claus Vogel), Heimatmuseum der Stadt Bad Tölz, Hilton München Park (Katharina Rösel), Hotel Königshof in Munich (Frieder Lempp), Hotel Residenz Passau (Dieter Austen), Hunsingers Pacific in Munich (M. Hunsinger), Institut für Kunst Geschichte TU in Brunswick (Dr 4c, 41b, 41bl, 43c, 48c, 49c, 53cl, Jura-Museum in Eichstätt (Jutta Streit), Alter Simpl Café in Munich, Kristall Museum Riedenburg, Kurdirektion des Berchtesgadener Landes (Vroni Aigner, Birgit Tica), Landeshaupt-stadt München, Referat für Arbeit und Wirtschaft Fremdenverkehrsamt (Stefan Böttcher), Leopold restaurant in Munich, Marionettenbühne in Munich, Mineralogische Staatssammlung in Munich (Dr G Simon), Münchner Stadtmuseum (Dr Götz), Museum "Reich der Kristalle" in Munich, Neue Messe München GmbH (Julia Spiegelhalder), Nürnberger Bratwurst Glöckl am Dom in Munich (Nadja Beck), Paläontologisches Museum in Munich (Dr H. Mayr), Parkhotel in Donauwörth (Eugen Schuler), Passauer Glasmuseum (Birgitte Holles), Ratskeller München (Renate Werner), SiemensForum in Munich (Dr Marie Schlund), Shop with devotional figures C. Huber in Augsburg, Staatliche Antikensammlungen und Glyptothek (Dr Martin Schulz, Vincent Brickmann), Staatliche Sammlung Ägyptischer Kunst in Munich, Stadt Kempten (Elli Cascio, Marlene Köhler), Stadtarchiv München (Dr Graf), Stadtbildstelle Augsburg, Stadtmuseum in Munich, Ursulinenkloster Straubing (Sr. Judith Reis, Oberin), Verkehrsamt der Stadt Nördlingen (Katja Jaumann), Villa Stuck in Munich, ZEFA (Ewa Kozłowska).

Picture Credits
a=above; b=below/bottom; c=centre; f=far; l=left; r=right; t=top.

The following works of art have been reproduced with the permission of the copyright holders:
Cover of *Der Blaue Reiter* (1912) © ADAGP, Paris and Dacs, London, 2011: 219cr
View of Munich Suburbia (1908) © ADAGP, Paris and Dacs, London, 2011: 109cl
Still Life with Geraniums (1910) Pinakothek der Moderne, © Succession H Matisse/DACS, 2011: 120ca

A1 Pix Herbke 291br; **Acquarello Restaurant:** 279tr.
Alamy Images Aflo Co. Ltd 204bl; Albaimages/Ronald Weir 15br; Arco Images 273tl; avatra images 301tl; BL Images Ltd 145cr; David R. Franzier Photolibrary, Inc. 298br; David Sanger Photography 272cl; Elvele Images Ltd 11tl; FAN travelstock/Jürgen Wackenhut 291tr; Foto28cla; Fotosonline/Klaus-Peter Wolf 291cla; imagebroker 14bc, 20, 34tl, 140tl, 224cl; imagebroker/Manfred Bail 145tl; imagebroker/Martin Siepmann 13tr; Imagestate Media Partners Limited-Impact Photos 114; Andre Jenny 144cr; Yadid Levy 144bl; LOOK Die Bildagentur der Fotografen GmbH 90; LOOK Die Bildagentur der

Fotografen GmbH/Jan Greune 290br; nagelestock.com 292tr; The Print Collector 8-9; Christoph Weiser 273c; travelstock44 132; Westend61/Franz Faltermaier 290cla; Craig Yates 210.

Allianz Arena Munchen Stadion GmbH 147tl

Alois Dallmayr (Munich) 286cl

Alpines Museum (Munich) 93bc, 95c

Amt für Kultur und Tourismus (Neuburg) Leander Hopf 172b

Amt für Tourismus Straubing 35cra

Archäologische Staatssammlung (Munich) 40b, 111c

Artothek 31tr, 56tr, 123tl, 129tr; W. Bahnmüller 47c, 47bl; Bayer & Mitko 123bl, 128b; Joachim Blauel 46tr, 47tc, 47tr, 47cl, 47bl, 117cr, 122ca, 122cb, 123cra, 123cla, 124br, 125cl, 125br, 126ca, 127crb, 127bl, 128tr, 128cla, 129cl, 129br; Blauel & Gnamm 47bl, 123cra, 120cb, 122tr, 122cl, 123br, 124tr, 124c, 125tc, 127ca, 127c, 127cr; Sophie-R. Gnamm 96tl; Toni Ott 46bl, 46br

Augsburger Puppenkiste 255tr

Bar Muenchen: 277tl.

Bayerische Staatsgemäldesammlungen (Munich) 119tc; Neue Pinakothek 126clb

Bayerische Staatsoper Wilfried Hosl 146bl

Bayerische Verwaltung der Staatlichen Schlösser, Gärten und Seen 42tl, 44cla, 50cl, 51tl, 51tr, 79tl, 136br, 137crb

Bayerisches Nationalmuseum (Munich) 57cra, 112tr, 112cla, 112clb, 112bl, 113tl, 113ca, 113crb, 113bc

Bier und Oktoberfestmuseum 68c

Bildvorlagen Römerschatz-Gäubodenmuseum (Straubing) 39br, 188tl

Bischöfliches Ordinariat Passau 27tc, 30tr, 45cl, 192cla, 192br, 197tr

BMW Group Mobile Tradition & V. (Munich) 23tr, 138tr

City of Munich – Fire Department 300crb

City Tour Card 296c

Corbis Walter Geiersperger 158-9; Zefa/Guenter Rossenbach 13br; Zefa/Herbert Spichtinger 146cr;

CSD München Michaela Handrek-Rehle 298ca

Dallmayr 270cla

DCC Europa-Preisträger 292bl

Deutsche Bahn (Berlin) Mann 308tl

Deutsche Presse Agentur (DPA) 23bl, 25tl, 32bl, 33tr, 33bl, 37cra, 37bc, 53bra, 274tr

Deutsches Historisches Museum (Berlin) 43b, 52c, 53bl

Deutsches Museum (Munich) 12, 98t, 98ca, 98cb, 98b, 99t, 99ca, 99cb, 99b,100tr, 100c, 100b, 101t, 101c, 101b, 174br

Dreamstime.com: Gary718 54-5; Manfredxy 12tr; Markus Gann 10bl; Mikhail Markovskiy 58; Superbo 74.

Erzbischöfliches Ordinariat München 64clb, 65tl, 65cr, 65bl, 65bc, 65br, 67tc

Flash Press Media 52bl

Flughafen München GmbH 306cr, 306bl, 307tr

Fremdenverkehrsamt (Altötting) 24tl, 34cra, 199b

Fremdenverkehrsamt (Mühldorf) 32c

Galerie im Lenbachhaus (Munich) 109cl, 109crb, 116cla, 219cr, 223cr

Gasteig München: 97tl;

Getty Images Peter von Felbert/LOOK 294-5; Michael Fellner 2-3; John MacDougall/AFP 300cr; Hans-Peter Merten/The Image Bank 198, 226.

Robert Harding Picture Library: 14tr.

Haus der Bayerischen Geschichte Bildarchiv 49tr, 52t

Haus der Kunst (Munich) 111t; Restaurant Herrenhaus: 281t.

Horst Höfler 264br

Hotel Hirsch Füssen: 263tl, 269bl.

Hotel Königshof (Munich) 263tl, 278t.

Hotel Residenz Passau 262br

Hotel Kriemhil: 267tr

Hunsingers Pacific (Munich) 270cra

The International Design Museum Munich George Meister 121br

Jura-Museum (Eichstätt) 168b

Kon-Ya Sushi: 283bl; Kristall Museum Riedenburg 187cr

Kurdirektion des Berchtesgadener Landes 52crb, 205bc

Landeshauptstadt München, Referat für Arbeit und Wirtschaft Fremdenverkehrsamt: Bjarne Geiges 275bl; Robert Hetz 53tl

Mandarin Oriental, Munich: 264tl, 266bc, 277bc.

Katarzyna and Sergiusz Michalscy 21t, 225clb, 248bl

Münchner Stadtmuseum 4tr, 5cl, 30cl, 30bl, 69br Dorothee Jordens-Meintker 38, 48b

Munich Police 300br

Munich Tourist Office Bernd Roemmelt 297cr

Museum Brandhorst Haydar Koyupinar 130tl

Neue Messe München GmbH Loske 143tr

Neuwirt: 268tl.

Paläontologisches Museum (Munich) 116tr

Passauer Glasmuseum 195c

Pinakothek der Moderne Proust's Armchair, 1978, Alessandro Mendini 120bc; 120ca, 121cra

Ratskeller München 271br; Residenz Heinz Winkler: 280bl.

Photo Scala, Florence 126tr

Sea Life München 147cr

Gregor M. Schmid half-title

SiemensForum (Munich): Bernd Müller 85cra

Staatliche Antikensammlungen und Glyptothek (Munich) 56cla, 118cr

Staatliche Sammlung Ägyptischer Kunst (Munich) 81cl

Stadt Kempten 241tc, 241bl

Stadtarchiv München 106b

Superstock: Manfred Bail/imagebro/imagebroker.net 162; imagebroker.net 242, 260-1; Martin Siepmann/image/imagebroker. net 102; Universal Images Group 178.

Oda Sternberg 88br

Tantris Restaurant: 279bl; Tomasz MyÊluk 230tr, 230cl, 231c

Restaurant Vaun: 282t; The Victorian House: 276bl; Villa Stuck (Munich) 19cr

Paweł Wójcik 24tl, 27b, 27bl, 33c, 35c, 49bl, 53br, 61clb, 66cr, 72tl, 72tr, 76br, 77tl, 82b, 84c, 84b, 86tl, 87c, 88tl, 89c, 104t, 105t, 107c, 108t, 116cb, 118tl, 142tl, 169bl, 186tr, 209cra, 209br, 230br, 237tr, 237c, 240tr, 240cla, 240br, 264c, 288tr, 288cla, 288clb, 288cra, 288crb, 288cb, 288bl, 288cb, 289tl, 289tc, 289tr, 289cl, 289c, 289cra, 289crb, 289cr, 289bl, 289bc, 289bca, 289bc, 297b, 310clb, 310b, 315cb, 315tl, 315b

Yum: 271tl.

ZEFA 66tl, 228cla; Rossenbach 161tl

Front Endpaper: Alamy Images: Imagestate Media Partners Limited - Impact Photos: Rbl; LOOK Die Bildagentur de Fotografen GmbH Rcr; Craig Yates Lbl; Dreamstime.com: Mikhail Markovskiy Rbc; Superbo Lbr; Getty Images: Hans-Peter Merten/The Image Bank Rtl, Lcl. Superstock: Manfred Bail/imagebro/imagebroker.net Ltr; imagebroker.net Ltl; Martin Siepmann/image/imagebroker.net Rc; Universal Images Group Rtr.

Jacket: Front and spine – 4corners: Davide Ernetta/SIME

Map Cover: 4corners: Davide Ernetta/SIME .

All other images © Dorling Kindersley.

For further information see: www.dkimages.com

Phrase Book

In an Emergency

Where is the telephone?	**Wo ist das Telefon?**	voh ist duss tel-e-fone?
Help!	**Hilfe!**	hilf-uh
Please call a doctor	**Bitte rufen Sie einen Arzt**	bitt-uh roof'n zee ine-en artst
Please call the police	**Bitte rufen Sie die Polizei**	bitt-uh roof'n zee dee poli-tsy
Please call the fire brigade	**Bitte rufen Sie die Feuerwehr**	bitt-uh roof'n zee dee foyer-vayr
Stop!	**Halt!**	hult

Communication Essentials

Yes	**Ja**	yah
No	**Nein**	nine
Please	**Bitte**	bitt-uh
Thank you	**Danke**	dunk-uh
Excuse me	**Verzeihung**	fair-tsy-hoong
Hello (good day)	**Guten Tag**	goot-en tahk
Hello	**Grüß Gott**	grooss got
Goodbye	**Auf Wiedersehen**	owf-veed-er-zay-ern
Good evening	**Guten Abend**	goot'n ahb'nt
Good night	**Gute Nacht**	goot-uh nukht
Until tomorrow	**Bis morgen**	biss morg'n
See you	**Tschüss**	chooss
See you	**Servus**	sayr voos
What is that?	**Was ist das?**	voss ist duss
Why?	**Warum?**	var-room
Where?	**Wo?**	voh
When?	**Wann?**	vunn
today	**heute**	hoyt-uh
tomorrow	**morgen**	morg'n
month	**Monat**	mohn-aht
night	**Nacht**	nukht
afternoon	**Nachmittag**	nahkh-mit-tahk
morning	**Morgen**	morg'n
year	**Jahr**	yar
there	**dort**	dort
here	**hier**	hear
week	**Woche**	vokh-uh
yesterday	**gestern**	gest'n
evening	**Abend**	ahb'nt

Useful Phrases

How are you? (informal)	**Wie geht's?**	vee gayts
Fine, thanks	**Danke, es geht mir gut**	dunk-uh, es gayt meer goot
Until later	**Bis später**	biss shpay-ter
Where is/are?	**Wo ist/sind...?**	voh ist/sind
How far is it to...?	**Wie weit ist es...?**	vee vite ist ess
Do you speak English?	**Sprechen Sie Englisch?**	shpresh'n zee eng-glish
I don't understand	**Ich verstehe nicht**	ish fair-shtay-uh nisht
Could you speak more slowly?	**Könnten Sie langsamer sprechen?**	kurnt-en zee lung-zam-er shpresh'n

Useful Words

large	**groß**	grohss
small	**klein**	kline
hot	**heiß**	hyce
cold	**kalt**	kult
good	**gut**	goot
bad	**böse/schlecht**	burss-uh/shlesht
open	**geöffnet**	g'urff-nett
closed	**geschlossen**	g'shloss'n
left	**links**	links
right	**rechts**	reshts
straight ahead	**geradeaus**	g'rah-der-owss

Making a Telephone Call

I would like to make a phone call	**Ich möchte telefonieren**	ish mer-shtuh tel-e-fon-eer'n
I'll try again later	**Ich versuche es später noch einmal**	ish fair-zookh-uh es shpay-ter nokh ine-mull
Can I leave a message?	**Kann ich eine Nachricht hinterlassen?**	kan ish ine-uh nakh-risht hint-er-lahss-en
answer phone	**Anrufbeantworter**	an-roof-be-ahnt-vort-er
telephone card	**Telefonkarte**	tel-e-fohn-kart-uh
receiver	**Hörer**	hur-er
mobile	**Handy**	han-dee
engaged (busy)	**besetzt**	b'zetst
wrong number	**Falsche Verbindung**	falsh-uh fair-bin-doong

Sightseeing

entrance ticket	**Eintrittskarte**	ine-tritz-kart-uh
cemetery	**Friedhof**	freed-hofe
train station	**Bahnhof**	barn-hofe
gallery	**Galerie**	gall-er-ree
information	**Auskunft**	owss-koonft
church	**Kirche**	keersh-uh
garden	**Garten**	gart'n
palace/castle	**Palast/Schloss**	pallast/shloss
place (square)	**Platz**	plats
bus stop	**Haltestelle**	hal-te-shtel-uh
free admission	**Eintritt frei**	ine-tritt fry

Shopping

Do you have/ Is there...?	**Gibt es...?**	geept ess
How much does it cost?	**Was kostet das?**	voss kost't duss?
When do you open/ close?	**Wann öffnen Sie? schließen Sie?**	vunn off'n zee shlees'n zee
this	**das**	duss
expensive	**teuer**	toy-er
cheap	**preiswert**	price-vurt
size	**Größe**	gruhs-uh
number	**Nummer**	noom-er
colour	**Farbe**	farb-uh
brown	**braun**	brown
black	**schwarz**	shvarts
red	**rot**	roht
blue	**blau**	blau
green	**grün**	groon
yellow	**gelb**	gelp

Types of Shop

chemist (pharmacy)	**Apotheke**	appo-tay-kuh
bank	**Bank**	bunk
market	**Markt**	markt
travel agency	**Reisebüro**	rye-zer-boo-roe
department store	**Warenhaus**	vahr'n-hows
chemist's, drugstore	**Drogerie**	droog-er-ree
hairdresser	**Friseur**	freezz-er
newspaper kiosk	**Zeitungskiosk**	tsytoongs-kee-osk
bookshop	**Buchhandlung**	bookh-hant-loong
bakery	**Bäckerei**	beck-er-eye
butcher	**Metzgerei**	mets-ger-eye
post office	**Post**	posst
shop/store	**Geschäft/Laden**	gush-eft/lard'n
film processing shop	**Photogeschäft**	fo-to-gush-eft
clothes shop	**Kleiderladen, Boutique**	klyder-lard'n boo-teek-uh

Staying in a Hotel

Do you have any vacancies?	**Haben Sie noch Zimmer frei?**	harb'n zee nokh tsimm-er-fry
with twin beds?	**mit zwei Betten?**	mitt tsvy bett'n
with a double bed?	**mit einem Doppelbett?**	mitt ine'm dopp'l-bet
with a bath?	**mit Bad?**	mitt bart
with a shower?	**mit Dusche?**	mitt doosh-uh